HISTORY
of
PARADISE

HISTORY
of
PARADISE

The Garden of Eden in
Myth and Tradition

JEAN DELUMEAU

Translated from the French by Matthew O'Connell

University of Illinois Press
Urbana and Chicago

First Illinois paperback edition, 2000
Un Histoire du Paradis: Le Jardin des Délices © 1992
by Libraire Arthème Fayard
English translation © 1995 by The Continuum Publishing Company
Published by arrangement with The Continuum Publishing Company,
New York

Library of Congress Cataloging-in-Publication Data
Delumeau, Jean.
[Histoire du paradis. English]
History of paradise : the Garden of Eden in myth and tradition /
Jean Delumeau ; translated from the French by Matthew O'Connell.
p.   cm.
Originally published: New York: Continuum, 1995.
Includes bibliographical references and index.
ISBN 0-252-06880-7 (pbk. : alk. paper)/ISBN 978-0-252-06880-5
1. Paradise—History of doctrines. I. Title.
BT846.2.D4513   2000
236—dc21   99-049451

P 6 5 4 3 2

Contents

List of Maps and Illustrations

Introduction

"The dreams of human beings are part of their history and explain many of their actions." This penetrating observation of Marjorie Reeves,[1] who is speaking of Joachim of Fiore and his posterity, is the best introduction to the new project in historiography that I am presenting in this book.

The book has its place in the long and solitary journey that I undertook twenty years ago. The journey began with *La Peur en Occident* and continued with *Le Péché et la peur, Rassurer et protéger,* and *L'Aveu et le pardon.* The very list of titles shows an internal logic at work that is independent of fashions. To begin with, I wanted to find out what it was that our Western ancestors feared. I then studied the remedies they applied to perils that they perceived as threatening them, whether from nature or from human beings or from the other world. But I still had to bring to life for myself their dreams of happiness, and this I have attempted to do in this history of paradise.

Henri Michaux has written that "we do not live in a paradisal century."[2] Does not our age, more than any other, need to know the paradises of which our predecessors dreamed? It was this question that suggested taking the dream of happiness as the subject of a historical inquiry. But the subject is almost infinite in its extent, and reasonable boundaries had to be set. To begin with, I shall, as in my earlier works, restrict myself to the West and shall pay special attention to the fourteenth to eighteenth centuries, which constitute the period to which I have preferred to devote myself. I shall then go on to study three major themes, to the exclusion of other possible ones: (1) nostalgia for an earthly paradise; (2) the expectation of a kingdom of happiness that is to be established on our earth and to last for a millennium; and (3) the hope of perfect and unfailing joy in the divine light of the Christian other world. A volume will be devoted to each of these three major collective meditations on happiness. The present volume, the first of the three, will deal with the fortunes and misfortunes of the "garden of delights."

In the course of this long and exacting work, and in order to bring as much possible new light to the subjects discussed, I have set a golden rule for myself and will continue to follow it here, as I have in my earlier works: to remain in permanent contact with firsthand documents, for nothing can replace their savor and truthfulness. Their voices, with their original freshness, will accompany the reader and myself on our journey from century to century.

We doubtless shall not bring back from this new journey through time one of those crystal balls with which two cherubs play in the humorous paradise of Théodore Zeldin and which the author's ambassadress brings back to this world and places in a shop window with the label, "Fragment of happiness found in paradise."[3] My purpose is quite different.

Historians attempt as best they can to reconstruct the universes of former times. But this reconstruction remains seriously incomplete if they do not include what our ancestors had to say about happiness, as well as the images on which they drew.

I would liken the journey on which we are embarking here to the journey through the winding "labyrinth" of the cathedral of Chartres, though I am working at a level that is both more psychological and more metaphysical. The journey at Chartres is known as "the league" because it takes as long to travel it on one's knees as to travel a league on foot; the distance from perimeter to center is 261.50 meters (286 yd.). But at Chartres, as in many other churches, the "labyrinth" leads the watchful and persevering pilgrim toward the heavenly Jerusalem.

It is likely that in the course of the journey through time that we are now beginning, we shall have to let many illusions fall by the wayside, just as the people contemporary with the Renaissance were forced to remove from their vision of the world the Happy Isles and the kingdom of Prester John, in both of which their predecessors had believed. But I trust that this abandonment will help to a clearer understanding of the hope still left to us and of the meaning of our lot.

Like my earlier works, this one owes a great deal to two collaborators, Angela Armstrong and Sabine Melchior-Bonnet; I express my gratitude to them once again.

The illustrations in the book were secured for me by Danièle Alexandre-Bidon, who had already provided me with the cover of L'Aveu et le pardon. I am grateful to her as well.

Chapter 1

The Mingling of Traditions:
From Moses and Homer
to St. Thomas Aquinas

"The Lord God Planted a Garden in Eden"

Initially, and for a long time thereafter, "paradise" meant the earthly paradise. In most writers of the patristic period, that is, until the sixth and even the eighth century of our era, the word "paradise" without any limiting adjective meant almost always the garden of delights in which Adam and Eve lived for a short time.

For many centuries (almost three millennia) first the Jews and then Christians, with only a few exceptions, did not doubt the historical character of the story in Genesis about the wonderful garden that God caused to appear in Eden:

> The Lord God planted a garden in Eden, in the east; and there he put the man whom he had formed. Out of the ground the Lord God made to grow every tree that is pleasant to the sight and good for food, the tree of life also in the midst of the garden, and the tree of the knowledge of good and evil.
>
> A river flows out of Eden to water the garden, and from there it divides and becomes four branches. The name of the first is Pishon; it is the one that flows around the whole land of Havilah, where there is gold; and the gold of that land is good; bdellium and onyx stone are there. The name of the second river is Gihon; it is the one that flows around the whole land of Cush. The name of the third river is Tigris, which flows east of Assyria. And the fourth river is the Euphrates.
>
> The Lord God took the man and put him in the garden of Eden to till it and keep it. (Gen 2:8–17)*

---

*The translation of the Bible that will be used throughout, unless otherwise noted, is the New Revised Standard Version. The only Gihon known to us is the spring that provided Jerusalem with water. There was a locality known as Havilah in Arabia, where bdellium (a gum extracted from the palm tree) and precious stones were to be found. Another Havilah is

3

We shall see as we go that, especially in the sixteenth and seventeenth centuries, the geographical details given by Genesis gave rise to a vast literature and brought treasures of learning into play. But even during the time of the old covenant the picture of paradise that had been given in Genesis was confirmed and enriched with more details by many other texts. In Isaiah we read that God "will make her [Zion's] wilderness like Eden, her desert like the garden of the Lord; joy and gladness will be found in her, thanksgiving and the voice of song" (Isa 51:3). Ezekiel's prophecy against the king of Tyre, a hero punished for his pride, likewise recalls the garden of God but fills it with precious stones:

> You were the signet of perfection,
>   full of wisdom
>   and perfect in beauty.
> You were in Eden, the garden of God;
>   every precious stone was your covering,
> carnelian, chrysolite, and moonstone,
>   beryl, onyx, and jasper,
> sapphire, turquoise, and emerald. . . .
> You were on the holy mountain of God.
>   (Ezek 28:12–14)

Another prophecy of Ezekiel gives the exiled Jews in Babylon a vision of the restored temple, from which a new river will flow. This river will manifest the life-giving power of God: "On the banks, on both sides of the river, there will grow all kinds of trees for food. Their leaves will not wither nor their fruit fail, but they will bear fresh fruit every month, because the water for them flows from the sanctuary. Their fruit will be for food, and their leaves for healing" (Ezek 47:12). Ezekiel is here taking over the image of the wonderfully watered garden of Eden, in which the "tree of life" bears its fruit in the midst of luxuriant vegetation.

Thus the constitutive elements of the earthly paradise are already in place by the time of the Babylonian captivity (sixth century B.C.). Paradise is first and foremost a garden. The Old Persian word *apiri-daeza* meant an orchard surrounded by a wall. Ancient Hebrew took this word over in the form *pardès*. Then the Septuagint used *paradeisos* to translate both *pardès* and the more classic Hebrew word for garden, *gan*. In this garden, which was set in the midst of a prosperous countryside (*eden*), everything was pleasant, savorous, and fragrant. The man and the woman lived there in harmony with nature, and water flowed abundantly (such a flow of water represented

---

mentioned as located in southern Palestine, close to Egypt. Cush most often refers to Nubia, but there was also a Cush in Palestine, near the Gulf of Aqaba.

supreme happiness to people who were constantly threatened by aridity and desertification). Their lives were meant to be unending and were lived in joy and, as Isaiah tells us, amid "the voice of song."

The images of the cosmic mountain on which Ezekiel locates the garden of Eden and of the precious stones with which he fills it will be applied in the Johannine Apocalypse to the messianic Jerusalem. This new Jerusalem will shine "like jasper, clear as crystal," and the foundations of its wall will be adorned with sapphires, emeralds, topazes, and nine other precious stones (Rev 21:11–22). From the heavenly throne of the Lamb who was slain "the river of the water of life" will flow (22:1–2). The poetic imagination will embellish these central themes in countless ways. Initial golden age, bountiful nature, abundant water, soft light, perpetual springtime, sweet fragrances, and heavenly music: all these will ordinarily be associated with the idea of the paradisal enclosure, and this enclosure itself will often be located on a high mountain or somewhere distant.

Scholars have not failed to show parallels and even connections between the sacred garden of the Bible and the sacred gardens of the other religions and civilizations of the ancient East.[1] The Sumerian myth of Enki begins with a description of the paradisal peace that reigns at Dilmun: here the beasts do not fight among themselves, and human beings are untouched by illness. There is, however, no fresh water. Enki, the great Sumerian god of water, obtains the water needed for the garden from Utu, the sun god. Now a normal life can develop.[2] The epic of Gilgamesh likewise contains "stage settings" found in the Bible: the mountain covered with cedars, the wonderful garden of the gods, the source of rivers, and the plant that gives life. Mesopotamian temples also had atop their ziggurats a sanctuary consisting of a grove of trees. Analogies with the biblical orchard have also been sought in Iran, which provides sagas connected with the garden (located on a high mountain) of Jima, king of the golden age. In that garden magical trees grew, most notably a tree of life, and from the garden flowed an abundant stream that brought fertility to the entire earth.

There is, however, a basic element that distinguishes the paradise of Eden from the gardens of Mesopotamia and Persia: the presence of "the tree of the knowledge of good and evil." Obedience to God's command regarding it was necessary for immortality, while disobedience led to death. There are other differences that should be noted: Dilmun (which, it is agreed, is to be identified with the island of Bahrain) becomes a "paradise" only when the sun god has made up for Enki's "distraction." The coming of water is what in fact allows civilization to develop.[3] Gilgamesh, for his part, is a hero in pursuit of immortality, but he is not successful in preserving the plant that gives life. In the end, he settles for seeking to win by noble deeds a glory that will enable him to live on in the memory of humanity. Finally, Jima, who likewise attempts to wrest immortality from the gods, is closer to Prometheus than to Adam.

On the other hand, it remains true that until a recent period, that is, until the emergence of the fact of evolution and of the slow and difficult rise of the "human phenomenon," many civilizations believed in a primordial paradise that was characterized by perfection, freedom, peace, happiness, abundance, and the absence of duress, tensions, and conflicts. In that paradise human beings got on well together and lived in harmony with the animals. They also communicated effortlessly with the divine world. This belief gave rise in the collective consciousness to a profound nostalgia for the lost but not forgotten paradise and to a strong desire to recover it.

The happiness that marked the beginnings had its place both in religions that conceived of time as cyclical and in those that saw time as a stream leading from one paradise to another. In the former (the religions of India that on this point agreed with the ideas of Hesiod and Plato) the golden age must return periodically. In the latter, and especially in Judeo-Christianity, human beings must regain familiarity with God and the elimination of death. Humanity's journey to the "promised land" will enable it, provided it submits to God's law, to gain definitive possession, in the eschatological paradise, of the blessings that it possessed only in a precarious way in the garden of Eden.

Golden Age, Elysian Fields, and Happy Isles

In the mentalities of earlier times a quasi-structural link existed between happiness and garden; this link was the result of an at least partial fusion, beginning in the Christian era, of Greco-Roman traditions with biblical memories of the orchard in Eden. Inside a favored area, the generosity of nature was joined to water, pleasant fragrances, an unvarying springtime climate, an absence of suffering, and peace between human beings and animals. Three major themes kept alive this memory of a happy portion of earth: the golden age, the Elysian Fields, and the Happy Isles, the three being sometimes combined, sometimes kept separate.[4]

Hesiod tells us in his *Works and Days* that in the golden age, human beings

lived like gods without sorrow of heart, remote and free from toil and grief: miserable age rested not on them, but with legs and arms never failing they made merry with feasting beyond the reach of all evils. When they died, it was as though they were overcome with sleep, and they had all good things; for the fruitful earth unforced bare them fruit abundantly and without stint.

They dwelt in ease and peace upon their lands, with many good things, rich in flocks and loved by the blessed gods.[5]

Further on in this poem Hesiod connects the golden age with a specific location: these fortunate people "lived untouched by sorrow in the islands of the blessed along the shore of deep swirling Ocean, happy heroes for whom the grain-giving earth bears honey and sweet fruit thrice a year."[6]

Plato, in *The Statesman*, recalls the happy time when Chronos reigned:

Under his care there were no states.... They had fruits in plenty from the trees and other plants, which the earth furnished them of its own accord, without help from agriculture. And they lived for the most part in the open air, without clothing or bedding; for the climate was tempered for their comfort, and the abundant grass that grew up out of the earth furnished them soft couches.[7]

The golden age theme is also very much a part of Latin literature as represented by Virgil and Ovid. Virgil, writing about 40 B.C., proclaims in his fourth eclogue that the period of primordial happiness will return in the near future: the soil will bear only good fruit, the animals will live in peace with one another, and human beings will work without fatigue.[8] Ovid, for his part, refuses to prophesy, but in his *Metamorphoses*, like Hesiod before him, he does take pleasure in recalling the first age of human history:

Golden was that first age, which, with no one to compel, without a law, of its own will kept faith and did the right. There was no fear of punishment, no threatening words were to be read on brazen tablets; no suppliant throng gazed fearfully on its judge's face, but without judges lived secure.... There was no need at all of armed men, for nations, secure from war's alarms, passed the years in gentle ease.

The earth herself, without compulsion, untouched by hoe or plowshare, of herself gave all things needful. And men, content with food which came with no one's seeking, gathered the arbute fruit, strawberries from the mountain-sides, cornel-cherries, berries hanging thick upon the prickly bramble, and acorns falling from the spreading tree of Jove.

Then spring was everlasting, and gentle zephyrs with warm breath played with the flowers that sprang unplanted. Anon the earth, untilled, brought forth her stores of grain, and the fields, though unfallowed, grew white with the heavy bearded wheat. Streams of milk and streams of sweet nectar flowed, and yellow honey was distilled from the verdant oak.[9]

The Elysian Fields, too, became a place of enchantment. In the fourth book of the *Odyssey*, Proteus tells Menelaus: "To the Elysian plain and the bounds of the earth will the immortals convey thee, where dwells the fair-haired Rhadamanthus, and where life is easiest for men. No snow is there, nor heavy storm, nor ever rain, but ever does Ocean send up blasts of the shrill-blowing West Wind that they may give cooling to men."[10]

In his second Olympian ode, written in 476 B.C., Pindar gives the Happy Isles as the place of happiness for the just who have passed through three earthly incarnations and have victoriously met the test of judgment. They are rewarded with an everlasting happiness on these islands that are refreshed by the sea breeze and where suffering and fear have been banished: there "flowers of gold are blazing, some on the shore from radiant trees, while others the water fostereth; and with chaplets thereof they entwine their hands, and with crowns, according to the righteous councils of Rhadamanthus."[11]

The sixth book of the *Aeneid* likewise gives a fine picture of the Elysian Fields, which are inhabited both by those who, like Anchises, have achieved a permanent blessedness and by others, the majority, who have drunk the water of Lethe before being reincarnated. The Elysian Fields are an earthly paradise, located in the lower world. Aeneas makes his way

> to the happy place, the green pleasances and blissful seats of the Fortunate Woodlands. Here an ampler air clothes the meadows in lustrous sheen, and they know their own sunlight and a starlight of their own. Some exercise their limbs in tournament on the greensward, contend in games, and wrestle on the yellow sands. Some dance with beating footfall and lips that sing...within a scented laurel-grove whence Eridanus river surges upward full-volumed through the wood.[12]

The same enchanting natural world, but located this time on our side of death, is described by Homer in book 7 of the *Odyssey*. Homer is speaking of the garden of Alcinous on the island of the Phaeacians, "a great orchard...and a hedge runs about it on either side":

> Therein grow trees, tall and luxuriant, pears and pomegranates and apple-trees with their bright fruit, and sweet figs, and luxuriant olives. Of these the fruit perishes not nor fails in winter or in summer, but lasts throughout the year; and ever does the west wind, as it blows, quicken to life some plants and ripen others; pear upon pear waxes and ripens, apple upon apple, cluster upon cluster, and fig upon fig.... There again, by the last row of vines, grow trim garden beds of every sort, blooming the year through, and therein are two springs, one of which sends its water throughout all the garden, while the other, over against it, flows beneath the threshold of the court toward the high house; from this the townfolk drew their water.[13]

What a splendid evocation of the "other place" (here an island, as so often in future writers) where all forms of happiness are combined! Hesiod follows Homer when, in his *Theogony*, he locates "beyond the glorious Ocean" the garden in which the Hesperides, virgin daughters of Night, "guard the rich, golden apples and the trees that bear them."[14]

Horace in his sixteenth epode likewise sees the Happy Isles rising out of the sea,

> where every year the land, unploughed, yields corn, and ever blooms the vine unpruned, and buds the shoot of the never-failing olive; the dark fig graces its native tree; honey flows from the hollow oak; from the lofty hill, with plashing foot, lightly leaps the fountain. There the goats come unbidden to the milking-pail, and the willing flock brings swelling udders home; nor does the bear at eventide growl 'round the sheepfold, nor the ground swell high with vipers.... Rainy Eurus does not deluge the cornland with his showers; and... the fertile seeds are not burnt up in the hard-baked clods.... No murrain blights the flock; no planet's blazing fury scorches the herd.[15]

At the end of this description the poet says that "Jove reserved these shores for a pious race at the time when he alloyed the purity of the golden age with bronze."

In the Middle Ages and even during the Reformation we shall still find the belief that a place close to paradise, and sharing to some extent in its privileges, still exists in some far off part of our planet and might be accessible to the boldest of our race.

At the time when Horace was describing the Happy Isles, Diodorus the Sicilian, in *The Library of History*, was telling the story of how a certain Iambulus voyaged from Ethiopia to an island far to the south, in the region of the equator. Its inhabitants (Diodorus says) are tall, well proportioned, and very like one another, and they have bodies at once strong and supple. They have hair on their heads, and eyelashes and eyebrows, but no other hair on their bodies. Their ears are larger than ours. They seem to have two tongues, so that they can carry on conversations with two people at once. The climate of the island is temperate despite its latitude, and the inhabitants suffer neither heat nor cold. Water is abundant, in the form of both warm springs and refreshing streams. Nature produces in abundance all the necessities of life. It gives birth to extraordinary but harmless and useful animals.

The islanders (Diodorus continues) usually experience no illness and can reach the age of 150 years. At that point, they are urged to leave this life by lying down on a special plant that lulls them into a permanent sleep. They do not marry; all children are shared by all, and things are so arranged that mothers do not know which children are their own; as a result there are no rivalries among the mothers. The islanders live in kinship groups of no more than four hundred members. Rules require that everyone eat the same food: one day, fish; another, meat; and so on. Harmony reigns among them, and civil discords are unknown.[16] "Utopian" islands like these will have a long history in the West.

In the course of Greco-Roman antiquity the garden theme was thus quite naturally combined with the themes of the golden age and the Happy Isles. The themes enriched each other and thereby strengthened the imagined picture of paradise and the description of the earthly paradise as an "ideal landscape" and a *locus amoenus* (place of charm and beauty). As a result, there were three types of description of the earthly paradise: a landscape arranged as a garden; nature in a wild state but wonderfully blessed by the gods; and a pastoral setting for love.[17]

A. B. Giamatti, who proposes this division, sees the realm of Alcinous as an example of the first type of garden. The Homeric *Hymn to Demeter* provides an illustration of the second type when it describes Persephone "playing with the deep-bosomed daughters of Oceanus and gathering flowers over a soft meadow, roses and crocuses and beautiful violets, irises also and hyacinths and the narcissus, which Earth made to grow . . . for the bloom-like girl — a marvellous, radiant flower."[18]

As for the connection between landscape and love that, beginning with Theocritus, will form the basis of pastoral poetry, it too will facilitate a mingling of pagan and Christian paradise themes and will enable many authors, Milton for one example, to speak of the chaste and tender kisses exchanged by Adam and Eve in the garden of Eden. The seventh idyll of Theocritus (315–250 B.C.) supplied the model for a genre that was to have a long history. The poem gives expression to the nostalgia of all those who down the ages have looked back with regret to the "state of nature":

> A wealth of elm and poplar shook o'erhead;
> Hard by, a sacred spring flowed gurgling on
> From the Nymphs' grot, and in the sombre boughs
> The sweet cicadas chirped laboriously.
> Hid in the thick thorn-bushes far away
> The treefrog's note was heard; the crested lark
> Sang with the goldfinch; turtles made their moan,
> And o'er the fountain hung the gilded bee.
> All of rich summer smacked, of autumn all:
> Pears at our feet and apples at our side
> Rolled in luxuriance; branches on the ground
> Sprawled, overweighed with damsons.[19]

The Christianization of the Greco-Roman Myths

The first Christian writers rejected the myths of the golden age and the Happy Isles. But beginning in the second century these myths were gradually Christianized.

Important in this respect is the *Exhortation to the Greeks* that is attributed to St. Justin Martyr (d. 165). The writer claims that Homer became acquainted with the Pentateuch in Egypt. There Homer translated the passages in Moses that dealt with the first phases of the creation of the world. Moses had said, in effect: "In the beginning God created heaven and earth; then the sun, the moon, and the stars." Homer imitated this account and transposed it into a different key by making use of a fiction: the idea of Vulcan depicting the creation of the world on Achilles' shield. "He later used the garden of Alcinous to give a picture of [the earthly] paradise, for he describes an orchard that is always in bloom and filled with fruits." In support of this claim the writer cites verses 110–33 of book 7 of the *Odyssey* and asks: "Are not these verses a clear and obvious imitation of what Moses, the prince of prophets, had written about paradise?"[20]

Tertullian (d. 222), like Justin, was convinced that the teaching of the Bible is older than pagan culture and therefore has a superior claim to acceptance. In fact (he says) the pagans honored the God of Moses without realizing that they were doing so. What their poets had to say about the Elysian Fields was in reality derived from the description of the earthly paradise in Genesis.[21]

St. Clement of Alexandria (d. 215) uses a great many comparative chronologies in endeavoring to prove that "Hebrew philosophy is the oldest of all the forms of wisdom."[22] "Truth is one, whereas falsehood takes a thousand forms. Philosophical sects, be they Greek or barbarian, each received a fragment of it."[23] This view of history led logically to the position that the pagan myths were derived from the Hebrew narratives.

Lactantius (d. 330), an African who was deeply imbued with classical culture and whose influence in the age of Christendom was deep and lasting, insists that when ancient pagans described the reign of Saturn they were in fact unconsciously honoring the true God; moreover, when they created the myth of a golden age they were speaking of the happy state of humanity before the fall. At that time, "Human beings were so open-handed that they did not enclose the crops which the earth produced for them, but allowed the poor to share the fruits of their labors. Here flowed streams of milk, and yonder streams of honey" (citing Ovid, *Metamorphoses* 1.11).[24] Lactantius cites, in addition to Ovid, Cicero's *The Nature of the Gods* and Virgil's *Georgics* and *Aeneid;* then, after giving Virgil's description of the reign of Saturn, "He [Lactantius] turns like any classical poet to the depravity of the world under Jupiter,"[25] that is, after original sin.

This paradise that earth was before the fall of Adam and Eve is also described and explained at length in the nine homilies on the six days of creation that St. Basil the Great (d. 379) preached at Caesarea. These became very famous in their day and gave rise to a new genre, the hexaemeron; they were translated into Latin, were used by Augustine in *The Literal Meaning of Genesis*, and left their traces in the citations that Isidore of Seville, the Venerable Bede, and St. Thomas Aquinas made from them. Then, after a period of forgetfulness, the Renaissance rediscovered them. They inspired Tasso's *Sette Giornate*, Du Bartas's *Semaines*, Passero's *Essamerone*, and others. While not giving a detailed description of paradise, Basil's sermons did explain, in a high style and according to the science of the time, the marvels of creation as this came from the hands of God and before it was marred by sin.[26]

This (unfinished) course of sermons of St. Basil was completed by a homily that was for a long time attributed to the great Cappadocian and that gave a lavish and enticing description of the earthly paradise. This work by Pseudo-Basil was as important as the *Hexaemeron* itself and exerted a major historical influence on the combining of the garden of Eden in Genesis with pagan descriptions of the golden age and the Happy Isles. At this point the topos, or motif, was fully established.

According to Pseudo-Basil, the earthly paradise was an "ideal spot," a "place of safety," "admirable and splendid" in its beauty, dominating the rest of the world, provided with all the riches of creation, bathed in utterly pellucid air, and favored all year long with a pleasant and unvarying temperature. No storms here, no thunder or hail, no winter's ice, no autumnal drought. Summer did not wither the flowers, and the fruits all reached maturity. This was a fertile land that flowed with milk and honey and had abundant water; it produced all kinds of utterly delicious edible fruits. The meadows always had flowers, and the roses had no thorns. In this blessed spot there was no sadness, no anxieties, whereas today "every time I look at a flower, I am reminded of my sins, in punishment for which the earth yields thorns and tribulations." Before the fall, in the garden of Eden, there was nothing but happiness, immortality, color, and fragrance.[27]

We shall see, further on, that St. Ephraem the Syrian (d. 373), a deacon of Edessa, would have us understand this garden in a spiritual sense. And yet, precisely because of the power of his poetical descriptions, his celebrated *Hymns on Paradise* helped to spread the myth of the garden in which there was no winter. He wrote of "the silent fig trees in the enclosure..., the light-filled dwellings, the fragrant springs." He maintained that there "shadowy February smiles like May, December is...like August with its fruits, June like April." Flowers spring up everywhere, the air is "virginal" and "transparent," and "pleasant springs" water a fruitful soil that yields an abundance "of wine and milk, honey and butter." The trees display a "limitless fertility," and

> when two neighboring flowers,
> each with its own color,

> combine together
> and become a single flower,
> they bring a new color into the world,
> and when fruits combine,
> they yield a new beauty
> and their leaves take on a new appearance.[28]

Within this enclosure, which is a veritable "granary of perfumes," "lambs feed, free of fear."[29]

The fusion of the Greco-Roman golden age with the garden of Eden was effected through a number of other poetic works that strongly influenced subsequent generations. There is, for example, the poem *De Ave Phoenice,* which for a long time was attributed to Lactantius; although it does not expressly describe the orchard of Genesis, it was generally regarded as being a description of it. The immortal bird, the phoenix, provides the occasion for recalling the existence of a place somewhere that had now become unreal. This place of happiness is said to be a distant locale, situated "at the beginning of the East" and "wide open to the eternal pole," a grove crowning a mountain that rises out of a broad plain. It is a country of unending springtime, ignorant of cloud and rain yet having an abundance of running water. No one there experiences "draining sickness" or "bitter fear."[30]

Just as Lactantius was thought to be the author of this poem, so Tertullian was regarded as the author of another poem, the *De Judicio Domini,* which was clearly inspired by the first but was doubtless composed only in the sixth century. It dwells with pleasure on the trees, the abundant water, and the even, agreeable climate of the orchard in Eden, but also emphasizes three motifs that will henceforth be considered essential elements of the Christian earthly paradise: the perfumed odors (here, the fragrance of cinnamon and cardamom), the fountain at the garden's center whence arise four great rivers, and finally the precious stones (emeralds, rubies, and so on) with which the paradisal meadow is strewn.[31]

In the fourth, fifth, and sixth centuries a whole group of Christian Latin poets described the earthly paradise in Virgilian accents and successfully combined the description in Genesis with the Greco-Roman tradition. The poet who was to have the greatest influence was the Spaniard Prudentius (d. 410), whose *Cathemerinon* finds in the garden of Eden elements that were to become classical: welcoming foliage, multicolored meadows, perpetual springtime, wonderful fragrances, and abundant water that divides into four rivers.[32] There were also poets in Gaul who were in agreement with this picture: Claudius Marius Victor, a rhetor of Marseilles (beginning of fifth century); Alcimus Ecdicius Avitus, bishop of Vienne around 490; and Sidonius Apollinaris, bishop of Clermont (d. 487–89).

Victor, in particular, speaks twice of the theme of the earthly paradise: in his *Genesis,* where Adam and Eve enjoy both health and wisdom and have the advantage of an enchanting natural world that is strewn with precious stones, and in his *Alethia,* in which the garden of Alcinous and the Elysian Fields of Virgil make their appearance and enable the poet to describe the orchard of Eden as a golden age land, with special emphasis on the variety and quality of the perfumes, which surpass those of Media, Assyria, and Palestine. In this place of happiness Adam and Eve had no need of food. They lived like the angels, and the fruits of the orchard were there simply for their pleasure.[33]

A year before becoming a bishop, Sidonius Apollinaris, a well-read aristocrat, wrote his *Panegyric on Anthemius,* which is not, strictly speaking, a Christian poem. But the combined influences of Virgil, Ovid, Pseudo-Lactantius, and Claudius Marius Victor make possible a description of a garden in which it is always springtime and which is richly endowed with perfumes and precious stones; it is a place that pagans could identify with the landscape of the golden age or the Elysian Fields and that Christians could identify with the earthly paradise of the Bible.[34]

Avitus, whose poem on "the Mosaic history" was written around 507, makes his Christian intentions explicit and tells his readers that before the fall Adam and Eve were united in chaste love against a background of angelic music. The orchard of Eden as he describes it is the happy place by now familiar to us: beauty, perfumes, and colors are all combined there. There is neither mist nor excessive heat nor frost nor raging storms. The vegetation is always green; the trees retain their leaves; the lilies do not wither, "nor does the violet that is touched shrink back."[35]

The same themes are found once again in the *Carmen de Deo,* composed in the fifth century by a Carthaginian lawyer, Aemilius Dracontius, who was imprisoned by the Vandals: a wonderful natural beauty, turf sprinkled with jewels, fragrant plants, leaves that promote health, and so on.[36] A more original aspect of this poem is the emphasis on the tender love of Adam and Eve (a description that Milton will remember). Eve was like a nymph, naked but modest, with a body white as snow, blushing cheeks, and hair that was abundant and beautiful. Adam and his companion did not possess the vast fund of knowledge with which they would later be endowed by the many writers and poets who comment on or paraphrase Genesis in the sixteenth and seventeenth centuries. Dracontius shows them, rather, as frightened by the first sunset and overjoyed when they feel the warmth of its rays once again.[37]

The fusion that I have been emphasizing of the biblical earthly paradise with the Greco-Roman traditions about the golden age, the Elysian Fields, and the Happy Isles explains the caution that Isidore of Seville (d. 636) thought it necessary to give in his *Etymologies*. In this encyclopedia, which was to enjoy a lasting renown, Isidore mentions the Happy Isles and tells his readers that these islands abound in vines, valuable trees, and fruits of every kind. But he also urges them not to confuse the Happy Isles with the garden of Eden.[38]

In fact, however, the fusion had already taken place in the collective imagination. It would persist through a lengthy series of medieval writings among which we find these important works: in the twelfth century, the *De mundi universitate* of Bernard Sylvestris and the *Pantheon* of Godfrey of Viterbo, and, in the thirteenth, the *De laudibus divinae sapientiae* of Alexander Neckham, who claimed that the earthly paradise had escaped the flood because it was on the top of a mountain that reached to the moon.[39] Dante would later locate the earthly paradise on the highest point of our planet.

Other works of the thirteenth century are the *Imago mundi* of Gautier of Metz, the unfinished *Weltkronik* of Rudolf of Ems, and the *Spieghel Historiael* (ca. 1282–90) of the Hollander, Jacob van Maerlant, which was followed in 1325–30 by the *Der Liken Spieghel* of one his continuators, Jan van Boendale. Generation after generation, these writers renewed the longing for the lost paradise and in doing so brought about an inseparable fusion of the Bible and pagan culture.

In his *History of the World*, of which I shall have occasion to speak again, Walter Raleigh (d. 1618), a pioneer in Elizabeth I's effort to colonize America, wrote as follows:

> Where did Homer get his description of the garden of Alcinous if not, as Justin Martyr noted, from Moses' description of paradise? And where do the beautiful descriptions of the Elysian Fields originate if not in the story of paradise?...It is evident that Orpheus, Linos [lyre-player and teacher of Orpheus], Pindar, Hesiod, Homer, and, after them, Ovid, along with Pythagoras, Plato, and their disciples, all successively enriched their descriptions by drawing on the treasures hidden in the sacred writings and changing these by means of secular additions veiled by poetic adornments.[40]

Raleigh thus made his own the argument of Justin, Tertullian, and Clement of Alexandria, and justified the fusion of the pagan and Christian traditions.

The Earthly Paradise as "Historical" Reality

Some sharp minds, especially in the eastern part of the Roman empire, had thought that the description of the garden of Eden in Genesis was to be taken figuratively. This was true especially of Philo (d. A.D. 50), a Jew of the Diaspora whose writings influenced both the Letter to the Hebrews (attributed to Paul) and the Christian school of Alexandria, which counted Origen among its most famous representatives.

Speaking of the garden that had been given to Adam and Eve, Philo advises interpreting it with reliance on allegory, which is "a favourite with men capable of seeing through it."[41] He says categorically: "To think that it here meant that God planted vines, or olive trees, or apple trees, or pomegranates, and any trees of such kinds, is mere incurable folly."[42]

Origen (d. 252 or 254), while not denying the past or present existence of a place somewhere between earth and the kingdom of heaven (we shall return to this in a later chapter), does urge in his turn that the biblical text be interpreted allegorically. "What is so silly as to believe that God, after the manner of a farmer, 'planted a paradise eastward in Eden,' and set in it a visible and palpable 'tree of life,' of such a sort that anyone who tasted its fruit with his bodily teeth would gain life; and again that one could partake of 'good and evil' by masticating the fruit taken from the tree of that name?"[43]

In the fourth century St. Ephraem gives a wonderful description of the garden in his well-known *Hymns on Paradise*.[44] He warns, however, that the colorful descriptions which he lavishes upon us must be transposed to the spiritual order. It is "with the eye of the mind that I saw paradise. . . . A spiritual eye and spiritual food befit spiritual persons."[45] "Although the words make Eden seem earthly, it is in its essence pure and spiritual."[46]

The Cappadocian teacher St. Gregory of Nyssa (d. 394) comes close to thinking of the whole business of the earthly paradise as an eschatological proclamation written in the past tense. In his view the garden of Eden represents "the land of the living" to which the elect will some day come, "the land which death has not entered, and the way to which has not been found by sinners."[47] "Relying on scripture, I do not believe at all that the passage was referring to bodily food or fleshly pleasure."[48]

But even in the East, the theologians who preferred a symbolical reading of the sacred text about the paradisal garden were a minority. St. Theophilus of Antioch (d. ca. 181) disagrees with them and says: "By the expressions 'out of the ground' and 'eastwards,' the holy writing clearly teaches us that Paradise is under this heaven, under which the east and the earth are."[49] St. Irenaeus (d. 202) asks: "Where, then, was the first man placed?" and he answers: "In paradise, certainly, as the Scripture declares: 'And God planted a garden [*paradisum*] eastward in Eden'. . . and then afterwards. . . he was cast out thence."[50] St. Hippolytus (d. 235) speaks even more clearly: "Some persons claim that paradise is in heaven and is not a created thing. But when one sees with one's own eyes the rivers that flow from it and that can still be seen today, one must conclude that paradise is not heavenly but part of creation. It is a place in the east and a favored region."[51]

Bishop Epiphanius (d. 403), a fierce adversary of the Origenists, expounds the same argument: "The paradise from which we were expelled...is the place whence the Tigris, the Euphrates, and other rivers flow and make their appearance here....Adam could not have been expelled from heaven, but only from this garden located in the east."[52] In like manner, Theodore of Mopsuestia, a very down-to-earth mind and a representative of the Antiochene school that was very hostile to the allegorism of Origen, says without reservation: "[God] chose as a dwelling [for human beings] a special region that he adorned with trees and called 'paradise.' This most estimable part of the world is the one which the rising sun illumines first."[53]

St. John Damascene (d. 749) would later express the same conviction and emphasize the concrete reality of the "divine garden":

> Since God intended to fashion man after His own image and likeness from the visible and invisible creation to be a sort of king and ruler over the whole earth and all things in it, He prepared a sort of kingdom for him in which he might dwell and lead a blessed and blissful life. And this divine paradise prepared in Eden by the hands of God was a treasure house of every joy and pleasure. For "Eden" is interpreted as meaning "delight." It was situated in the east and was higher than all the rest of the earth. It was temperate in climate and bright with the softest and purest of air. It was luxuriant with ever-blooming plants, filled with fragrance, flooded with light, and surpassing all conception of sensible fairness and beauty. In truth, it was a divine place and a worthy habitation for God in His image. And in it no brute beasts dwelt, but only man, the handiwork of God.[54]

Later on, Moses Bar Cephas, bishop of Bethraman near Baghdad (ca. 900), explains in his *Commentary on Paradise* that the garden of Genesis can be looked at from two points of view: the physical and the mystical. The second part of the bishop's work adopts this second viewpoint. Accordingly, paradise stands for the perfect spiritual life, and its four rivers are the four cardinal virtues or the four evangelists. But insofar as paradise belongs to our universe, it was indeed planted not outside the earth but on it: in the East, beyond the ocean, and on a site higher than any other on the planet. Paradise was distinct from Eden in that it was even more beautiful than the pleasant countryside that surrounded it. As Milton would say later on, water defied gravity and climbed from Eden to the high plateau allotted by God for the wonderful orchard of Adam and Eve; then it cascaded down and disappeared under the sea, to reappear at our level and produce the four largest rivers on our earth. In this garden Adam and Eve lived naked and innocent.[55]

With a few exceptions — among them St. Ambrose,[56] who interweaves the ancient myth of a golden age with the spiritual interpretation of the divine orchard that Philo had proposed — the vast majority of westerners chose realism when it came to the paradise of Adam and Eve. Lactantius, for example, is one who understood the text of Genesis in a material sense (*corporaliter*) and saw it as describing a real place: "God placed man there...in the most fruitful and pleasant garden that has ever existed: in the regions of the East. He had planted in it every kind of tree and shrub, so that man might feed on its varied fruits and, free of all need to labor, might serve God his Father with the greatest devotion."[57]

St. Augustine (d. 430) tackled head-on the question of the historical reality of the earthly paradise. Given the enormous influence that the bishop of Hippo exercised on Latin Christendom, his answer evidently weighed heavily on his successors. At the beginning of book 8 of *The Literal Meaning of Genesis*, he states that there are three main opinions on the paradise in which Adam and Eve were placed. Some interpret it "in an exclusively corporeal sense," others give it "an exclusively spiritual meaning," and still others take it in both senses, "sometimes corporeally and at other times spiritually." He states his own position at the outset: "I admit that the third interpretation appeals to me."[58]

However, despite this complex and nuanced statement, he finally leans more to realism than to allegorism. He even explains how his thinking evolved. When he had been engaged in debate with the Manicheans, he had left open the possibility of believing that the account was "set forth in figures and enigmas" (he is citing his *On Genesis against the Manicheans* 2.2.3). But "now the Lord has wished that I should look and consider the same matter more thoroughly, and I believe that according to His will I can reasonably hope that I shall be able to show how the Book of Genesis has been written with a proper rather than an allegorical meaning in view."[59] We may therefore see in the account of creation all the figurative meanings we desire, provided we accept the truth that the events narrated "really happened."[60] The "unfamiliar character of the deeds" is due to the fact that what is being described is "the creation of things for the first time." The tree of life in the garden of Eden was "a real material tree." And of the spring in the garden, and then of the four rivers that flowed from it, Augustine says: "Need I make any further effort to establish the fact that they are true rivers, not just figurative expressions?"

These facts should persuade us to take the first meaning of the other details of this narrative in the literal sense and not to assume that the account is allegorical, but that the facts narrated really exist and that they also have some figurative meaning....A river, therefore, went out from Eden, that is, from the delightful place, and it watered paradise, that is, all the beautiful and fruit-bearing trees which shaded all the land of that region.[61]

Generation after generation of Western Christians took these statements of St. Augustine as infallible. His words had a decisive impact on the minds that would play a part, down the centuries, in shaping collective convictions. I shall mention here only the most important, beginning with Isidore of Seville, whose *Etymologies* was intended as an encyclopedia of the religious and secular knowledge of his time. It is for that reason that he has been called "the great educator of the Middle Ages."

From the Carolingian period we have dozens of manuscripts of the *Etymologies*, which were recopied at an early date in Ireland, England, Germany, and Gaul.[62] On the question that concerns us here Isidore, after some wavering, adopts the Augustinian point of view. He says that according to the bishop of Hippo the description of the garden in Genesis can be taken in three ways: in a literal sense, in a figurative sense, and, finally, in a way that safeguards the historicity of the story but adds a "mystical" interpretation. In like manner, Noah's ark, the ark of the covenant, and the Jerusalem temple were all "historical realities," but at the same time we can take them as pointing to the mystery of the church. "What is there to keep us from thinking that our first parents were put in a place where no creature could harm them, no fire burn them, no water drown them, where the wild beasts did not kill or the thorns prick or the lack of air cause asphyxiation?" Their bodies were protected against pain, old age, and death.[63]

In subsequent centuries other major authorities adopted the same view. One of them was Bede (673–736), the learned Anglo-Saxon who was one of the "founders" of the Middle Ages and one of the authors most read and most frequently cited during the next five hundred years, to the point that he was respected as the equal of the fathers of the church; it was for this reason that he became known as "the Venerable."[64] Bede expressly says: "Let us have no doubt that the paradise in which the first human being was placed is to be understood as a real place, even if we also regard it as a figure of the present Church or of our future fatherland. The text speaks of a place of delights, shaded by fruit trees, and of a broad dwelling place, from which sprang a great river."

Rabanus Maurus (d. 856), abbot of Fulda and then archbishop of Mainz, represented Germany in the Carolingian Renaissance and has been called the "teacher of Germany" (*praeceptor Germaniae*). He emphasizes, more than Bede does, the mystical meaning of the "garden of delights" as being an image both of the church and of the future land of the living. He nonetheless maintains unambiguously that the earthly paradise was rich in all kinds of perfumes and fruit trees, that it experienced neither frost nor scorching heat, and that from its midst sprang a stream that watered the entire garden and then opened out into four rivers.[65]

In the twelfth century Honorius of Autun (who was in fact a German) wrote his *Elucidarium*, which is both a catechism and a summary of the beliefs and science of the time; in it he asks: "What was [the earthly] paradise?" He answers:

It was a place...in which trees of different kinds had been planted that met all possible needs; for example, if a person ate the fruit [of one of them] at the right time his hunger would be satisfied, if of another, his thirst would be slaked, if of still another, his weariness would disappear; finally, if he turned to the tree of life, he would escape old age, sickness, and death.[66]

It is revealing that this passage is repeated in the *Hortus deliciarum* that Abbess Herrad of Landsberg (d. 1195) composed for her novices.[67]

Peter Lombard (d. 1160) could not avoid dealing with the important question of the earthly paradise in his *Sentences*. Here, as in other matters, he was heir to the Augustinian tradition; he adopts it in its entirety, repeats St. Augustine's thoughts almost word for word, and expresses himself on this subject with a perfect clarity (a point that needs to be emphasized, given the lasting role played by his work):

The Lord God had planted a paradise of pleasure in the beginning, and in it he placed man whom he had formed (Gen 2:8). By these words Moses implies that man was first created outside of paradise and then placed in it.... This paradise in which man was placed should be taken in a local and corporeal sense. By and large there are three views regarding this paradise. One view sees in it only a corporeal reality; another, only a spiritual reality; a third, finally, takes paradise to be both. I prefer this third view, namely, that man was placed in an earthly paradise which began its existence at the moment when the waters had receded from the land and the land was ordered to produce grass and trees. Even though this paradise provided an image of the present or future Church, it must be understood in a literal sense, as a very pleasant place filled with fruit trees, a broad expanse from which sprang a great river.[68]

St. Thomas Aquinas takes the *Sentences* of Peter Lombard as his starting point (the continuity between the two men becomes obvious) and in his turn asks the question: Is paradise a corporeal place? As is his custom, the great doctor gives the arguments for and against a positive answer and then adopts the position of St. Augustine, who had written: "Nothing prevents us from holding, within proper limits, a spiritual paradise; so long as we believe in the truth of the events narrated as having there occurred."[69] St. Thomas concludes with the bishop of Hippo: "Whatever Scripture tells us about paradise is set down as matter of history; and wherever Scripture makes use of this method, we must hold to the historical truth of the narrative as a foundation of whatever spiritual explanations we may offer."[70] The tree of life was "a material tree and [was] so called because its fruit was endowed with a life-preserving power.... Yet it had a spiritual signification; as the rock in the desert was of a material nature, and yet signified Christ."[71] A little further on the *Summa* says: "Paradise did not become useless through being unoccupied by man after sin."[72]

The historical character of the earthly paradise, and of a creation account that was regarded as completely literal, was taken for granted by that age. This acceptance helps us understand how Vincent of Beauvais (d. 1264), one of the great popularizers of the thirteenth century, could make such precise chronological statements in his *Speculum historiale:* "We believe that on the very day of their creation, which was the sixth of the world's existence, Adam and Eve committed their sin in paradise around midday. Shortly after, around the ninth hour, they were expelled."[73] In parallel fashion, Jesus was crucified at noon and died at the ninth hour after having reopened paradise to the thief. According to Vincent of Beauvais, then, our first parents enjoyed the garden of delights for only a few hours.

We should not attribute this naïveté simply to medieval mentalities. We shall learn better when we come to the Renaissance and the seventeenth century. But we must first turn to a relatively unknown manifestation of the earthly paradise idea, namely, its transformation into a dwelling place of the just who have died and are waiting there for their resurrection. We shall then come back to the land of the living.

Chapter 2

Paradise as a Place of Waiting

Jews and Christians were for a long time convinced that the earthly paradise had really existed. For many centuries many of them believed, in addition, that paradise still existed as a place where the just awaited the resurrection and final judgment, which was thought to be close at hand.

Within this general view there were divergent opinions. Some thought of paradise as existing in a remote part of the earth, where it was preserved in its original state but had become inaccessible except to travelers possessing an unusual passport and an angelic guide. Others thought that paradise had been removed from our earth and transported to heaven or, more exactly, to the "third heaven" to which St. Paul was caught up and that was not to be confused with the "seventh heaven" of eternal happiness and beatific vision. In this place of waiting, wherever it might be located, two persons in particular were dwelling: Enoch (Gen 5:24) and Elijah (2 Kgs 2:1–18), both of whom had been removed from the sight of the living without passing through death.

Jewish and Christian Apocalypses

The *First (Ethiopic) Apocalypse of Enoch* is a good witness to this tradition, which was first of all a Jewish tradition. The work has been preserved in its entirety only in an Ethiopic version of the fourth or fifth century A.D. The original, however, was written in Aramaic (fragments of it have been discovered at Qumran), and the work is today regarded "as one of the great classics of the Essene congregation, perhaps even as the most fundamental of all their works."[1]

It seems that the various elements making up this *First (Ethiopic) Apocalypse of Enoch* were combined at Qumran in the first century B.C.; some parts of it may go back as far as the third century B.C.[2] In this apocalypse Enoch tells what he saw on his unparalleled journeys. In particular, he sees in the West (chaps. 17–25) "a great and high mountain of hard rock" and in it four caverns, three of them dark and one filled with light. Raphael explains to the traveler that these caverns were formed to hold the souls of the dead "until the day of their judgment and the appointed time of the great judgment upon them" (22).

The three dark caverns are reserved for sinners, while the well-lit one is for the souls of the just (22). To this first localization in the West, another in the East (chaps. 28–33) is added during a second journey of Enoch to the "garden of righteousness" (32), a land of perfumes wherein grows the tree of knowledge, the fruit of which resembles clusters of grapes.[3]

It is important to note that, independently of these differences in localization, the texts show a belief in retribution after death, a belief that begins to appear in Jewish literature in the third century B.C. The ancient Hebrews had thought that the dead were all penned up without differentiation in Sheol. The *First (Ethiopic) Apocalypse of Enoch* exercised a great influence; it is cited in the Letter of Jude (vv. 14–16).

Another "intertestamental writing" is the *Third (Greek) Apocalypse of Baruch,* which is a Jewish work with Christian interpolations and was composed not later than the time of the severe persecution suffered by the Jewish community in Egypt in A.D. 115–17. When Baruch reaches "the third heaven," he asks the angel who is guiding him: "Show me which is the tree which caused Adam to stray." But this third heaven also contains Hades, a plain whose "appearance was gloomy and unclean" (chap. 4) and on which lives the demonic serpent. Thus the garden of the just and the place of punishment of souls are once again located close to one another but on one of the heavenly spheres.[4]

The *Fourth Book of Ezra* is of greater importance as far as influence is concerned, since in its Latin translation this book was included in some manuscripts of the Vulgate. The existence of a Greek translation is generally admitted. Also known are translations into Syriac, Arabic, Georgian, and Armenian. Before the discoveries at Qumran the book was often attributed to Pharisaic circles; it now seems that "many themes have Essene overtones, but of an Essenism that precedes the dispersion of 70."[5] The presence of this book in manuscripts of the Vulgate ensured its wide diffusion, and the Renaissance brought a renewal of interest in it.

In the course of one of his visions (chap. 7) Ezra asks his angelic guide: "If I have found favor in your sight, my lord, show this also to your servant: whether after death, as soon as every one of us yields up his soul, we shall be kept in rest until those times come when you will renew the creation, or whether we shall be tormented at once?"

The angel answers that the wicked will not enter into "habitations" but will "wander about in torments, ever grieving and sad in seven ways." One of these ways consists in this, that "they shall see how the habitations of the others are guarded by angels in profound quiet." As for the souls of those who have followed the ways of the Most High, they first see, to their great joy, the glory of the One who receives them; they also have rest "in seven orders." Here are the last four of these:

> The fourth order, they understand the rest which they now enjoy, being gathered into their chambers and guarded by angels in profound quiet, and the glory which awaits them in the last days. The fifth order, they rejoice that they have now escaped what is mortal, and shall inherit what is to come; and besides they see the straits and toil from which they have been delivered, and the spacious liberty which they are to receive and enjoy in immortality. The sixth order, when it is shown to them how their face is to shine like the sun, and how they are to be made like the light of the stars, being incorruptible from then on. The seventh order, which is greater than all that have been mentioned, because they shall rejoice with boldness, and shall be confident without confusion, and shall be glad without fear, for they hasten to behold the face of him whom they served in life and from whom they are to receive their reward when glorified.

Ezra asks further: "Will time therefore be given to the souls after they have been separated from their bodies, to see what you have described to me?" The angel answers: "They shall have freedom for seven days, so that during these seven days they may see the things of which you have been told, and afterward they shall be gathered in their habitations."[6]

This book thus speaks of a place intermediate between the present life and eternity. For the elect these provisional "habitations," which are guarded by angels as the earthly paradise was, are places of rest and peaceful silence, in which they have knowledge of their future happiness.

Jacques Le Goff has with good reason noted the lasting influence of the visions of the other world in the *Fourth Book of Ezra*.[7] Clement of Alexandria refers to them in his *Stromata* (3.16). More importantly, Ambrose refers explicitly to them in his *De bono mortis*, where he says that the "habitations" of Ezra are the same as the "dwelling places" (*mansiones*) of which Jesus speaks when he says, "In my Father's house there are many dwelling places" (John 14.2). Ambrose's eschatology thus has place for a "storehouse of souls" (*promptuarium animarum*), which is a pleasant and agreeable place of waiting, an earthly paradise regained, prior to definitive entrance into the kingdom of heaven.[8]

The Jewish tradition long maintained the belief in an intermediate paradise in which the souls of the elect await resurrection and entry into the kingdom of heaven. According to Bishop Eusebius of Caesarea (d. 340), the Jews of his day taught that one must endeavor by the practice of virtue after death to merit a return to the paradise of God.[9] Much later on, the *Zohar*, an esoteric treatise that was composed between 1270 and 1300 and had considerable influence, would say that "when the souls of the just leave this world, they enter into a palace located in the lower Eden and they remain there for as long as is necessary to prepare them for the ascent to the higher Eden."[10]

This distinction between the two Edens passed from the Jewish tradition into Christian eschatology. It can be seen especially in the apocryphal literature, including the *Apocalypse of Peter* and the *Apocalypse of Paul*. The second is much more important for our subject than the first, but the first is older and influenced the second.

The *Apocalypse of Peter* dates probably from the middle of the second century A.D. and perhaps even earlier. It takes the form of a revelation of Christ to Peter, who in turn passes it on to his disciple, St. Clement of Rome. A recall of the Transfiguration scene enables the writer to make a distinction between (earthly) paradise and heaven. On the holy mountain on which Moses, Elijah, and numerous just persons of the Old Testament make their appearance beside Jesus, Peter discovers "a great open garden. It was full of fair trees and blessed fruits. Its fragrance was beautiful." The place is described as the "rest" of the just. Peter wants to set up three tents there, but a cloud opens up and in it Jesus, Elijah, and Moses "went into the second heaven."[11]

The *Apocalypse of Paul* calls for our full attention here because it became such a widely known document. The first versions were most likely written in Greek, toward the middle of the third century. One hundred and fifty or two hundred years later, an introduction was added that connects the *Apocalypse of Paul* with the ecstatic experience of which the apostle of the Gentiles tells his readers: "I know a person in Christ who fourteen years ago was caught up to the third heaven — whether in the body or out of the body I do not know, God knows" (2 Cor 13:1–5). The Latin translation of the work dates from no later than the beginning of the sixth century. This was then copied quickly and frequently — there are at least fifty-two manuscripts of it. Also known are ancient translations into Syriac, Coptic, Slavonic, Armenian, Arabic, and Ethiopic. In the Middle Ages there were also translations into French, Provençal, Romanian, English, Welsh, German, Danish, Bulgarian, Serbian, and other languages. The success of this apocalypse was especially notable in the eighth and eleventh centuries, during which Latin "editions" were made, that is, abridgments or revisions of the ancient "long texts."[12]

The *Apocalypse of Paul* has links with the *Apocalypse of Peter* but also with the *First (Ethiopic) Apocalypse of Enoch* and the revelations of Ezra as well as with other apocalypses. The identification of the earthly paradise as a staging point before the definitive heaven is especially clear.[13] As Paul looks up to the heights, he is allowed to see angels "with faces shining like the sun; their loins were girt with golden girdles and they had palms in their hands...and they were clothed in raiment on which was written the name of the Son of God." He asks the guiding angel who these heavenly beings are. The angel replies: "These are the angels of righteousness; they are sent to lead in the hour of their need the souls of the righteous who believed God was their helper." The vision goes on to bring the apostle into the presence of God himself as he prepares to judge the soul of one of these faithful who has just died. The Lord decides: "As it [this soul] has had compassion, so I will have compassion on it. Let it therefore be handed over to Michael, the angel of the covenant, and let him lead it into the paradise of jubilation, that it may be there until the day of resurrection and become also a fellow-heir with all the saints."

Paul then visits a "land...seven times brighter than silver." He asks the angel who accompanies him: "Sir, what is this place?" The answer: "This is the land of promise. Have you not yet heard what is written: '*Blessed are the meek, for they will inherit the earth*'? The souls of the righteous, however, when they have come out of the body are sent for a while to this place."[14] A river of milk and honey flows in this place. Each tree bears fruit twelve times a year, yielding different fruits each time. The vines have ten thousand branches and a million buds. When the first earth — ours — is destroyed, this other will descend from the firmament to replace it, and the saints will dwell there with Jesus for a thousand years.

I shall come back to this millennialist eschatology in another volume of the present series. For the moment, let me emphasize the point that the earthly paradise, which has apparently been removed from our planet, receives the souls of the just "for a time." Further evidence of this localization is the fact that Paul is then taken from this place and led (chap. 23) into the "city of Christ," made "entirely of gold" and surrounded by twelve walls. This final stage in salvation is described in imagery taken both from the Apocalypse of St. John and from the picture of the glorious Jerusalem in Ezekiel.

From the point of view that I am adopting here, the visions narrated in the *Apocalypse of Paul* can be compared with those in an older and likewise famous document: the *Passion of Perpetua and Felicity*. This account is contemporary with the persecution of Christians in Africa under Sulpicius Severus in 203.[15] Two women, Perpetua and Felicity, and three men, Saturus, Saturninus, and Revocatus, were put to death at Carthage in that year. During the days preceding their martyrdom Perpetua and Saturus were able to write down or communicate orally to others their memoirs and visions, to which was later added an epilogue describing the death of the victims.

The document tells us that Saturus, a deacon, had a vision in which he learned what would become of himself and Perpetua after their torments.

> We had died... and had put off our flesh, and we began to be carried towards the east by four angels who did not touch us with their hands.... While we were being carried by these four angels, a great open space appeared, which seemed to be a garden, with rose bushes and all manner of flowers.... The trees were as tall as cypresses, and their leaves were constantly falling.... And there we began to recognize many of our brethren, martyrs among them. All of us were sustained by a most delicious odour that seemed to satisfy us.[16]

This text has sometimes been attributed to Tertullian, but this seems incorrect. Tertullian does, however, shed light on its meaning when in his work *De anima* he distinguishes three dwelling places for the souls of the dead: Sheol for the faithful generally; the earthly paradise even now accessible to martyrs (this is the place Perpetua and her companions have reached); and finally "the heavenly realms that shall be opened at the end of the world."[17]

Other ecclesiastical writers adopt the same view as Tertullian in this matter and seem to have maintained that only the martyrs, the good thief, Enoch, and Elijah already enjoy the paradise of Adam, which is distinct from the kingdom of heaven. Among these authors mention may be made of St. Hippolytus of Rome (d. 235), St. Hilary of Poitiers (d. 367), St. Ambrose (d. 397), and St. Jerome (d. 420).[18]

The only three occurrences of the word *paradeisos* in the New Testament were understood in the light of this belief in an intermediate place of happiness, a place that served as an antechamber for souls before the general resurrection and that was often viewed by the early Christians as receiving others besides the martyrs. The dying Jesus tells the good thief: "This day you will be with me in paradise" (Luke 23:43). Paul tells his readers that he "was caught up into paradise and heard things that are not to be told" (2 Cor 12:4). (He has just referred to the "third heaven," at a time when the current cosmology taught the existence of seven heavens.) Finally, in the Apocalypse of John: "The Spirit is saying to the churches: To everyone who conquers I will give permission to eat from the tree of life that is in the paradise of God" (Rev 2:7).

A connection was quickly made between this intermediate paradise and the "bosom of Abraham" to which Lazarus the beggar "was carried away by the angels" after his death; the rich man saw him there, on the other side of the "great chasm" that separated them (Luke 16:19–31).

With regard to the promise of Jesus to the good thief the *Dictionnaire de la Bible* has this to say: "The word 'paradise' in Jewish writings as in early Christian literature is usually not a synonym for heaven.... The background of Jesus' statement can be seen in Jewish speculations on the original garden. Jesus speaks as do the apocrypha and is thinking only of the place where the just await God's final intervention in their favor."[19]

Jesus Reopened "Paradise"

It was rather widely held in the church of the first centuries that when Jesus made his promise to the good thief, he was reopening the earthly paradise that had been shut since the sin of Adam and Eve.

This is the conviction of St. Athanasius the Great (d. 373), who says: "[Jesus] opened for us the gates of the paradise from which Adam had been expelled and into which he entered once again in the person of the good thief to whom Jesus said: 'This day you shall be with me in paradise.' It was to this paradise, too, that St. Paul was caught up."[20] St. Gregory of Nyssa (d. 394) speaks as follows to God: "You expelled us from paradise and you called us back to it."[21] One Friday St. John Chrysostom (d. 407) assured his congregation: "On this day God opened for us the paradise that had been closed for over five thousand years. God brought the thief into it on the same day and at the same hour [as the expulsion]."[22]

Proclus of Constantinople (d. 485) later says: "Today the good thief made his way into the paradise that had for fifty-five hundred years been barred by the fiery sword."[23] And St. John Damascene (d. 749) has Christ speak as follows to the good thief: "It is I who drove them [the first parents] out [of Eden]; I myself will lead you into it, I who shut the gates of paradise and barred the approach to it with a fiery sword. If I do not lead you in, the gates will remain shut."[24]

This "paradise" is not the heavenly kingdom of everlasting blessedness. Commenting on Luke 23:43 the Bulgarian bishop Theophylact (d. 1085) states: "Let no one tell me that paradise and the kingdom are one and the same. No ear has heard tell of the blessings of the kingdom, nor has any eye seen them."[25]

Two sermons of Pope Leo the Great (d. 461) explain this important distinction. Preaching on the Lord's passion Leo says: "The good thief's faith opened the gates of paradise so that the Christian people is now able to return to the lost fatherland, far from which humanity was exiled long ago."[26] But on Ascension Day he is more specific: "Today we are not only confirmed in our possession of paradise, but Christ has also made us ascend with him to the heavenly heights."[27] I could readily add to this anthology of citations from ecclesiastical writers who profess the same conviction.

But the overall picture calls for nuances. I have been calling attention

simply to a prevailing view and am quite conscious of the inevitable ambiguity of some texts as well as the indecisiveness that was sometimes to
be seen in the thinking of the faithful (as Christian epigraphy shows)[28] and
in the minds of many writers as they described the geography of the other
world. Thus St. Gregory of Nyssa sometimes seems to identify the paradise of the first Adam with eternal blessedness.[29] St. Basil (d. 379) does
not distinguish between "heaven" and "paradise" and uses the two terms as
synonyms.[30] St. Augustine wavers at times between several different views.
In fact, he changed his opinion over the years. He does indeed teach that
the saints are not yet where they will be after the parousia; that their enjoyment of God is incomplete until the resurrection; that heaven is divided into
different dwellings; and that the place of happiness distinct from the heaven
of the angels is paradise or the bosom of Abraham.[31] But elsewhere he says
that he cannot decide what the "bosom of Abraham" is, and he asks at times
whether paradise is not the same as heaven.[32]

Not all the Christian writers of the early centuries completely identify the
intermediate place of happiness with the paradise in which Adam and Eve
lived. But a good number of them do agree with St. Jerome that Enoch and
Elijah were received into the paradise from which Adam and Eve had been
expelled.[33] They even anticipate that the final judgment will take place in
the garden of Eden. In addition, Christian life was generally presented as a
return to the lost paradise, a return made possible especially by baptism.[34]

Whereas some rigorists allowed only the martyrs and a few privileged
others (Adam, the good thief, Enoch, and Elijah) into the intermediate place
of happiness (whether or not this was identical with the earthly paradise
regained), there were many others who relied on the promise of Jesus to the
thief and on his liberating descent into "hell" in order to give all the just a
place in paradise.[35] Seven bishops who had gathered in council at Pergamum
in 152 asserted their belief that "the soul [of a deceased just person] dwells
in paradise and is happy there until it receives its immortal body . . . thanks to
which human beings become sharers in the kingdom of heaven."[36]

St. Irenaeus (d. 202) teaches that "those who were translated were transferred to that place (for paradise has been prepared for righteous men) . . . and
there they . . . remain until the consummation [of all things], as a prelude to
immortality." Here is the reason for the delay:

> For as the Lord "went away in the midst of the shadow of death," where
> the souls of the dead were, yet afterwards rose in the body, and after the
> resurrection was taken up [into heaven], it is manifest that the souls of His
> disciples also, upon whose account the Lord underwent these things, shall go
> away into the invisible place allotted to them by God, and there remain until
> the resurrection, awaiting that event; then, receiving their bodies and rising in

their entirety, that is, bodily, just as the Lord arose, they shall come thus into the presence of God. "For no disciple is above the Master, but every one that is perfect shall be as his Master."[37]

St. Clement of Alexandria (d. ca. 211–16) states that "at the end of the ages the angels will carry those truly repentant to the supercelestial taberna-cles... in the kingdom of heaven." For the time being, however, the just are in the "septenary of repose" in which paradise is located.[38]

Origen gives a somewhat more complex explanation:

> I think that the saints as they depart from this life will remain in some place situated on earth, which the divine scripture calls "paradise." This will be a place of instruction and, so to speak, a lecture room (*auditorium*) or school for souls, in which they may be taught about all that they had seen on earth.... If anyone is "pure in heart" and of unpolluted mind and well-trained under-standing he will make quicker progress and quickly ascend to the region of the air [and to the various spheres and new stages of instruction] until he reaches the kingdom of the heavens... whose names alone we have heard.[39]

Although, as we saw earlier, Origen urges an allegorical interpretation of Genesis,[40] this "lecture room" of souls, which represents the lowest degree of happiness after death, is seen by him as concrete and material. "Far be it from me," he writes, "to say that this world is incorporeal and to regard it as simply a phantasm of the mind and an idea without any reality."[41]

In the patristic period, then, there is a cloud of convergent witnesses to the conviction that an intermediate place of happiness or at least of rest, namely, "paradise," receives the souls of the just until these recover their bodies and make the final ascent to the kingdom of heaven. In a Roman inscription of 382 that can be seen at St. Agnes Outside the Walls and that has to do with a young woman, Theodosia, who died at twenty-one, we read: "She has journeyed to the stars and now she rejoices in the court of Christ.... She has entrusted her noble soul to the saints for ages to come. Amid the exquisite perfumes of paradise she reigns where a perpetual springtime keeps the lawns alive on the river banks; there she waits for God who will raise her to higher regions."[42]

At a more official level, SS. Athanasius, Didymus (d. 398), Epiphanius (d. 403), Gregory of Nyssa, and John Chrysostom all agree that heaven will become accessible only on the last day, but also that the "saints" who have gone before us, the "meek" and the "just," are already "at rest" in "the unique and supremely pleasant place" that is paradise.[43]

Aphraates, a Syrian (d. after 345), likewise sees the entrance of the elect into glory as delayed until the day of the resurrection and universal judgment, when the good will be definitively separated from the wicked.[44] St. Ephraem, who was also a Syrian, urges indeed that we understand in a spiritual sense everything that is said of paradise and all the charming descriptions that he himself gives of it (exquisite fragrances, multicolored flowers, fruits, music, fresh water), but he also says that the mountain where Eden is located still exists, that it was spared from the flood, and that at its foot there is an entrance hall, a "refuge," where the souls of the just wait for resurrection in a condition of relative happiness or at least in a kind of sleep or, to change the image, in a state of limited life comparable to that of the embryo in the maternal womb.[45]

Theodoret of Cyr (d. 466) teaches that the saints, although not yet risen and not yet in heaven, already engage in their dances and make the melodious sounds of their hymns heard in paradise.[46] Cassiodorus (d. 580), praetorian prefect turned monk, says that the elect are gathered in the "bosom of Abraham" while awaiting the enjoyment of the promised heavenly rewards.[47] Isidore of Seville, in his *De ordine creaturarum,* expounds the view of those who distinguish between the heavenly paradise (located above our atmosphere but below the firmament) and the paradise of Adam, which has remained in our world (though barred to us). The souls of the just are at rest in "this pellucid dwelling place in the subcelestial spaces," before they ascend at the last judgment to the final heaven, the heaven of God and the angels which is located above the firmament.[48]

The geography of the other world as described by the Venerable Bede contains the same basic distinction. He writes: "In the Church there are many just persons who immediately after the dissolution of the flesh enjoy the rest and happiness of paradise. There, amid the mighty retinue of the blessed, they wait in gladness for the moment when they will regain their bodies and come into the presence of the Lord."[49]

These few extracts from Greek, Syrian, and Latin writers (the list could easily be extended) justify the statement of the *Dictionnaire d'archéologie chrétienne et de liturgie* that in the church of the early centuries "paradise does not yet mean ... the 'kingdom of heaven,'" as it will later on. "As yet it is simply a temporary dwelling place in which the souls of the just await the hour of the resurrection. That same hour will bring the general judgment, which will be followed by their entrance into the kingdom in which the heavenly Father will manifest himself to the elect who have been admitted to the beatific vision."[50] Jean Daniélou confirms this interpretation: "[The idea of paradise] that was most fully developed in the early centuries ... was the one that sees it as the place where the souls of the just await the eschatological resurrection."[51]

Belief in this place of waiting was evidently connected with the conviction that the parousia, or return of Jesus, would not be long delayed. Furthermore, we must not confuse the limbo of the fathers (*limbus patrum*), that is, the "bosom of Abraham," so often referred to by the fathers of the church, with the limbo of children (*limbus puerorum*), which made a late appearance in the Christian vocabulary to designate the place in which infants who have died without baptism are for ever deprived of the beatific vision, even though they do not suffer. It is St. Thomas Aquinas who suggests this distinction.[52] The question of a limbo of children did not worry the fathers of the church or the Christians of the early centuries; it became a concern only beginning in the twelfth and thirteenth centuries.[53]

Harking back again to the beginnings of Christianity, I wish to emphasize once more the point that a certain vagueness persisted in the minds of the faithful and even of the teaching church regarding the journey of the elect in the after-death world. The words "paradise" and "heaven" are rather rare in Christian epigraphy, and iconographic representations of paradise are not numerous. But the statement, relatively frequent in inscriptions, that a dead person is now *in bono* (literally: in good) or *in bonis* (in good things/places) is explained by Cassiodorus in a commentary on Psalm 24:

> Since the just, on leaving this life, do not immediately receive the complete blessedness promised to the saints at the resurrection, their souls are said to repose "in good things" (*in bonis*) because, while they do not yet receive the reward which "eye, ear, and mind cannot comprehend" [see 1 Cor 2:9], they do enjoy delight, since they have a firm hope of the reward that is to come.[54]

In the light of all that has been said thus far we can more readily understand the early liturgical texts that speak of the deceased. Mentions of (the final) heaven are not many. The Christians of the early centuries prayed that the dead might reach the place of "rest," which was regarded as the normal stage preceding resurrection. Some of these prayers are given in the following paragraphs.

"[Lord,] we pray you for the sleep and repose of this man (or: woman), your servant. Refresh his soul and his spirit in the places of pasture, in the dwellings of rest.... As for his body, raise it up on the day you have appointed" (from the *Euchology* of Serapion, fourth century).[55] "Be mindful of them [the deceased], grant them rest, and place them in the dwellings of light, in the place of the blessed spirits, in the heavenly Jerusalem, in the Church of the firstborn who are written in the heavens" (*Liturgy of St. Ignatius of Antioch*, used by the Syrian Jacobites).[56]

The *Liturgy of St. Clement of Rome*, used, again, by the Syrian Jacobites, contains this prayer:

> [Place them, Lord,] in the habitations of light and joy, in the tents of shade and rest, in the midst of the treasures of delight... where souls wait without

suffering for the first-fruits of life and where all the spirits of the just are turned toward the reward that has been promised to them. [Place them] in that realm where the wearied laborers contemplate paradise and where the wedding guests await the coming of the heavenly spouse.[57]

The *Coptic Liturgy of St. Basil,* attested from the fifth century on, says: "Welcome them into the bosom of Abraham, Isaac, and Jacob; receive them into the verdant place with its refreshing waters, into the paradise of delights."[58]

The funeral liturgy attributed to St. John Chrysostom (d. 407) prays that the deceased may be admitted into "the heavenly habitations, the paradise of delights, the tents of light, the place of rest."[59]

The Western liturgies agree with those of the East in this area. The Sacramentary of Pope Gelasius (d. 496) pleads with God that the deceased person

> may possess joy amid the sparkling jewels of paradise...and find the gates of the heavenly Jerusalem opened to him.... [Lord,] grant him rest and the kingdom, that is, the heavenly Jerusalem; deign to place him in the bosom of our patriarchs Abraham, Isaac, and Jacob; let him share in the first resurrection and journey with the elect on their way to the right hand of the Father.... Deign, Lord, to grant him the place of light, refreshment, and peace.[60]

The Sacramentary of Pope Gregory the Great (d. 604) has a similar prayer: "We beseech you, Lord, that in your mercy you would grant [to these deceased] the place of refreshment, light, and peace."[61]

The Gallican liturgy, the origin of which goes back to the seventh and eighth centuries, addresses God as follows: "Ordain that [these deceased] be placed in the bosom of Abraham and escape the pains of hell and that when the time of the resurrection comes, they may be united with the hosts of angels."[62]

To close this list of citations, which the reader may find to be already rather lengthy, here is a petition from the Mozarabic liturgy (which can be dated back to the sixth and seventh centuries): "[Lord,] preserve these souls from the fiery furnace; ordain that they reach the joys of paradise and that, gathered in the bosom of Abraham, they awaken to the first resurrection with your saints."[63]

Philippe Ariès has called attention to the ambiguity of the word *refrigerium,* which meant both a "place of refreshment" and the commemorative meal that early Christians ate at the tombs of the martyrs (as well as the offerings that they placed on the tombs).[64] I mention this double sense here only as a point of information. For when *refrigerium* is connected, as in the passages cited, with *lux* and *pax* in the traditional formula, *locum re-*

frigerii, lucis, et pacis, there can be no doubt as to how the formula is to be understood.

On the other hand, there was in fact some confusion in the minds of the early Christians on the meaning of *requies* (rest, repose). Did the word refer to a sleep preceding the resurrection or to a relaxed and pleasant stay in the green pastures where the just sang and danced as they waited for the gates of heaven to be opened? The Acts of the Apostles say that when St. Stephen died by stoning "he fell asleep" (Acts 7:60). And St. Paul tells us in his First Letter to the Corinthians that after his resurrection Jesus "appeared to more than five hundred brothers and sisters at one time, most of whom are still alive, though some have fallen asleep" (1 Cor 15:6).

With good reason Ariès has connected this belief in the sleep of the dead with the legend of the Seven Sleepers of Ephesus that was handed down in the West by Gregory of Tours, Paul the Deacon,[65] and Jacob of Voragine (*The Golden Legend*). In the fourth century there was a heresy abroad that denied the resurrection of the dead. It was to combat this heresy that God raised to life seven martyrs of Ephesus who had been "asleep" for several centuries. Crowds gathered around the returnees, who explained: "It is for your sake that God has raised us up before the day of the great resurrection. . . . For even as the child lives in his mother's belly without feeling any needs, so we have been living, resting and sleeping, without experiencing any sensations."[66] After this statement the seven martyrs "fell asleep" once again.

How can we, whose outlook has been shaped by the discoveries of Freud, fail to take note of the identification by the early Christians of death with sleep, untroubled rest, and a secure sojourn in the maternal womb? In the view of those Christians, paradise before the resurrection meant the silent peace of the cozy nest provided by a pregnant woman. The ancient idea of the place of rest was long kept alive by tombs, which often had such inscriptions as: "Hic pausat, hic requiescit, hic dormit" (Here he ceases from activity, here he rests, here he sleeps). In the same spirit, the rite of Last Anointing (reserved to clerics in the Middle Ages) was called *dormientium exitium* (the departure of the sleepers).[67]

Confirmatory evidence can be found in ecclesiastical literature. At Autun, St. Germain questions St. Cassian, who is buried there, and receives this answer: "I am in full enjoyment of my pleasant rest, and I am waiting for the coming of the Lord."[68] As St. Martin lay dying, he said to the devil, who had come to him: "You will find nothing mortal in me; I am going to the bosom of Abraham."[69] This was another, likewise very current, way of referring to the restful shelter in which the souls of the deceased fear no danger.

Throughout one whole period of the Middle Ages, the idea of a place where souls are waiting was very much alive in monastic writings that follow the model of the "apocalypses" of Peter and Paul and report the visions given to some privileged individuals who were able to journey into the next world. One of these stories comes from Alberic dei Settefrati, a monk of the monastery of Montecassino at the beginning of the twelfth century.[70] With St. Peter as his guide, Alberic lingers especially in places of punishment, whether definitive or "purgatorial." But from the latter he then moves on to the *refrigerium*, a field of joy and peace, made fragrant by lilies and roses. It is inside this meadow that the definitive paradise is located, into which most souls will enter only after the last judgment. The only persons already in it are the angels and the saints.

More famous than the preceding is the vision of Tnugdal, which was written down in 1149 by Mark, a native of southern Ireland and probably a monk. It is offered to the reader as the Latin translation of an account given by a nobleman named Tnugdal.[71] This vision, too, takes us on a lengthy journey through the infernal regions. Then it guides us to the place of happiness. The latter, however, is preceded by an intermediate area, which in turn is divided in half by a wall.[72] On the hither side of the wall dwell the souls of "those who are not entirely bad"; they have light and have escaped the stench of hell, but they remain exposed to rain and wind. On the far side of the wall dwell the souls of "those who are not entirely good"; they are set in the meadow of joy where the fountain of life flows. They do not yet experience complete happiness and do not yet merit the companionship of the saints; theirs is the classical place in which the just are waiting.

St. Patrick's Purgatory is another story of an imaginary journey into the beyond and was widely known in the Middle Ages. The work was likewise composed by a monk, in this case an English Cistercian of the monastery of Saltrey, and dates from after 1189.[73] The story has to do with Owein, a knight, who accompanies a monk of the Abbey of Saltrey to Ireland and goes down into the pit of St. Patrick. This was a round, dark hole that Jesus had shown to the apostle of Ireland. Anyone who in a spirit of faith and repentance spent a day and a night therein would be cleansed of his sins and would see the torments of the wicked and the rewards of the good. Owein tries it. He sees the punishments of the former, which this time are described at even greater length, as well as the purgatorial punishments inflicted on souls that are indeed saved but must first make expiation for their sins. The knight then emerges from the pit, crosses a bridge, and reaches the earthly paradise. Gathered there are those who after their purgatorial punishments have attained to rest and joy but are not yet worthy of ascending to heaven. Each day some souls "pass from the earthly paradise to the heavenly paradise."

It has been said that *St. Patrick's Purgatory* was one of the best-sellers of the Middle Ages. It was translated into French by the celebrated (English) poetess Marie de France at the very end of the twelfth century.[74] There would subsequently be many versions of the story in Latin and in the vernacular languages. Caesarius of Heisterbach, Vincent of Beauvais, Jacob of Voragine, Bonaventure, Froissart, and later Rabelais, Ariosto, Shakespeare, and Calderon (the list is not complete) will refer to *St. Patrick's Purgatory*. Jacques Le Goff notes that the account gives a detailed description of the "new place" in the other world that was known as "purgatory." The point that calls for attention here is that this "new place" continues the ancient belief in an antechamber of heaven in which souls experience "rest" and even joy before attaining definitive blessedness.

Finally, Gervase of Tilbury, an Englishman who wrote around 1210 and dedicated his work *Otia imperialia* to Emperor Otto IV, presents the same geography of the other world, although with some nuances and intricacies. He distinguishes two paradises and two hells: the highest heavens and the earthly paradise, on the one hand, and the "earthly hell" and the place of suffering, on the other. The symmetry is only apparent, since the "earthly hell" is not a gehenna but an antechamber in which there is no suffering. "It is said to be located in a pit in the earth, and in this hell there is a place far removed from the place of chastisement; because of its tranquillity and its remoteness it is called a 'bosom,' as one speaks of a bosom [= gulf] of the sea; it is also called the 'bosom of Abraham' because of the parable of the rich man and Lazarus."[75] Commenting on this text, Jacques Le Goff notes that purgatory, which was coming to birth (as both a noun and a place) at this period, undergoes the attraction of two opposite poles: paradise and hell.[76] In Gervase of Tilbury it is still drawn more to the first and consequently is closer to the peaceful setting in which the souls of the just waited for the resurrection.

In 1240 the University of Paris had condemned as heretical the teaching about a place in which the just waited. Not until the fourteenth century, however, did the Catholic Church officially and categorically reject the idea of the *refrigerium*; the condemnation was the result of views proposed by John XXII, which were now regarded as "intolerable novelties," when in fact they were simply a return to the past. On All Saints Day, 1331, the pope had said that the just will not enjoy the beatific vision prior to the resurrection of their bodies and the last judgment. He repeated his statement on the eve of Epiphany, asserting once again that prior to the resurrection separated souls do not have access to the intuitive vision of God. In 1332 he added that the demons will enter hell only after the end of the world. But at this point in history his statements caused a scandal, at least at higher levels in the church. In the following year, King Philip VI of France had this view condemned by a council in Vincennes. The rejection was repeated by Benedict XII in 1336 and then by the Council of Florence in 1439.[77]

The place of waiting had contracted to a purgatory in which the just suffer while also hoping. The verdant meadow around the heavenly Jerusalem had disappeared.

Chapter 3

The Earthly Paradise and Medieval Geography

During the High Middle Ages the intermediate dwelling in which the just awaited the resurrection gradually disappeared from the Christian imagination. Longer lived, however, was the conviction that the garden of Eden had not vanished from the earth although it had indeed become inaccessible. To this belief was added another that was a spur to the great voyages of exploration: while the earthly paradise was now barred, there existed happy, wonder-filled lands, more or less close to paradise or at least somewhere far off, which daring men could reach and which would provide them with fabulous wealth. It is this twofold geography that I must here attempt to reconstruct.

The Earthly Paradise Still Exists on Earth

From the Book of Jubilees *to St. Thomas Aquinas*

The belief that the earthly paradise had not disappeared from our planet is older than Christianity. The *Book of Jubilees,* which was composed between 167 and 140 B.C., at the time when the Maccabees were resisting the Seleucids, tells of how Noah divided the earth by lot among his three sons, Shem, Ham, and Japheth. Shem received the best part, bounded in the north by the River Tina (the Don) and in the south by the River Gihon (the Nile). It included the garden of Eden in the east, Mount Zion at the center of the inhabited world, and Mount Sinai in the south; Shem's part was, therefore, pretty much Asia. "Noah rejoiced because this portion was assigned to Shem and for his sons. . . . He knew that the garden of Eden was the holy of holies and the dwelling of the Lord. And Mount Sinai (was) in the midst of the desert and Mount Zion (was) in the midst of the navel of the earth. The three of these were created as holy places, one facing the other."[1]

At the beginning of our own era, Flavius Josephus, himself a Jew (d. A.D. 100), states it as certain that the principal rivers of the world flow out of the earthly paradise: "Phison... denotes a multitude... and is by the Greeks called Ganges.... The name Euphrates, or Phrath, denotes either a dispersion, or a flower; by Tigris, or Diglath, is signified what is swift, with narrowness; and Geon runs through Egypt, and denotes what arises from the east, which the Greeks call Nile."[2]

This line of thought was followed by an entire Christian literature (we have already met representatives of it in the persons of SS. Theophilus, Irenaeus, Hippolytus, and Epiphanius). Although, as we saw earlier,[3] St. Ephraem the Syrian (d. 373) moved beyond this naturalistic vision of paradise and conceived of the place as a cosmic temple of which the Jerusalem temple is the visible image, he nonetheless contributed a great deal to the inclusion of the earthly paradise in a sacred geography. His influence in this matter was lasting.

In line with a tradition that goes back to Ezekiel (28:14), Ephraem describes paradise as a mountain: "With the eyes of the spirit I saw paradise, and beneath it were the tops of all the mountains. The flood rose only to its feet, though it covered the tops of the mountains."[4] Further on in his *Hymns*, he compares paradise to the ring of light that circles the moon and to the golden crown that Moses put around the altar; he says: "Thus paradise surrounds the world, and earth and sea are included within it." Elsewhere, in his *Commentary on Genesis*, he mentions the questions raised about "the four rivers that flow from the fountain in paradise," and he gives his answer:

> The four are the Nile, the Danube, the Tigris, and the Euphrates. Although we know the places where they arise, these are not their original source. The reason is that paradise is situated on a great height; the rivers sink into the ground around paradise and drop into the midst of the sea as through an aqueduct; then the land allows them to rise to the surface each in its own place.[5]

In Ephraem's overall picture (remember that he assigns the souls of the just to a place of waiting), paradise is both the place where history begins and the place where it terminates. But the point that posterity especially retained, and this in a very concrete way, was the emphasis on paradise as a high place and as a girdle around the world. The statement, already to be found in Philo of Alexandria and Hippolytus, that the waters flowing from paradise travel underground and rise up at the four corners of the world, will likewise have a long life, to the point even that writers will speak more often of the Ganges or the Indus than of the Danube. A final point to be kept in mind from Ephraem's sacred geography is the way in which our earth is related to paradise.

Not long after Ephraem, Philostorgius (d. 425), a Cappadocian who was sympathetic to the Arians, likewise asks about the location of paradise and about the course of the rivers that have their source in it. He is convinced that paradise is located in the East, at the equator. To his mind, the river Hyphase, which he doubtless confuses with the Indus or the Ganges, is the Pishon of Genesis and has its headwaters in paradise. On its banks are to be found carnations that, the inhabitants believe, come from paradise, because the entire region upstream is deserted and barren. If then the river provides this flower, it is a sign that it does not flow underground, since an underground river could not yield such a thing. There is another sign of the link between the Hyphase and paradise: people with high fevers who bathe in its waters are immediately cured.

The Tigris and the Euphrates, on the other hand, do flow underground and then come to the surface again. The same is true of the Nile, which Moses calls the Gihon. It too, "as best we can conjecture," flows out of paradise, crosses the Indian Ocean in a kind of circular course ("But who can have accurate knowledge?"), goes underground and makes its way to the Red Sea, and surfaces again in Africa under Moon Mountain. There it divides into two mighty streams, close by one another, which cascade their waters down from a great height. The river thus formed hurtles down steep cliffs and reaches Egypt via Ethiopia.[6]

In the sixth century, Cosmas Indicopleustes, a former merchant and traveler turned monk and now living in Alexandria, likewise developed an interest in the present location of the earthly paradise. His *Topographia christiana*[7] rejects the pagan geography of "fabulists" such as Ptolemy, as well as every notion of an earthly sphere surrounded by a heavenly sphere. In his view, the tabernacle that God revealed to Moses on Sinai was an image of the world. As shown by the symbolism of the table in the tabernacle, the inhabited world of Cosmas is "oblong" or "rectangular" in form. But this earthly plane is not horizontal; rather it slopes up from southeast to northwest, so that the northern and western regions rise up like a wall (see Map 1). This configuration has two results: (1) during its daily passage through the east and south the sun illumines the inhabited world; but when it is in the west and north it passes behind the screening mountains, and darkness results; and (2) the Tigris and the Euphrates run rapidly because they descend to the south; the Nile, on the other hand, runs slowly because it is climbing northward.

According to Cosmas, the inhabitable earth is surrounded on all sides by an ocean; beyond this there is a further land, which includes in particular the

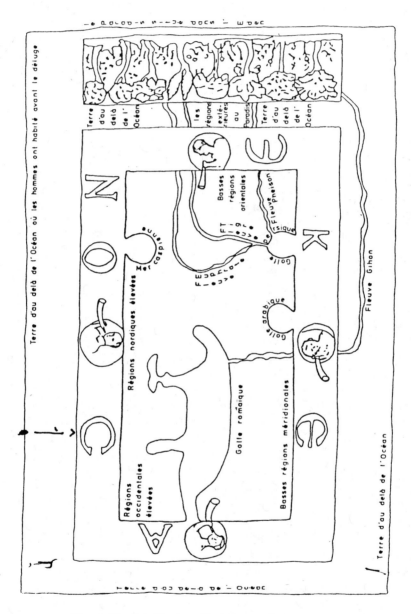

Map 1. The inhabited world of Cosmas Indicopleustes'
Topographia christiana (9th century)

paradise in which God placed Adam. After the original sin Adam and his first descendants lived in another place on this same strip of land, but it was hard to till and was infested by wild beasts. These human beings lived there until the flood, the time when God saved Noah and his family by means of the ark, which took 150 days to cross the ocean and reach our earth. Ever since, "It has been impossible to cross the ocean, just as it is impossible for us to ascend to heaven as long as we are mortal." Although the earth that human beings now inhabit and the land where they once lived and where paradise is located are separated by an impassable ocean, the two remain linked by the four rivers "which the divine writings say emerge from paradise and then, having crossed the ocean, spring up again on our earth."

The earthly paradise has become inaccessible, but it has not disappeared, and it continues to supply the great rivers of the world: such are the ideas that Christian geography would keep alive for a long time in both the Greek and the Latin traditions. In the eighth century, St. John Damascene, who would be cited frequently during the Renaissance, thought of paradise as something mystical but also as a corporeal reality; speaking of the latter he says that the divine paradise was "situated in the east and was higher than all the rest of the earth."[8] If, unlike Cosmas, he is not convinced that the four rivers flow out of paradise, he does think that the ocean is formed of water coming from that original wellspring:

> The ocean is like a river surrounding the earth; in my opinion, the divine scripture speaks of it when it says that "a river flowed out of Paradise." Its water is sweet and potable; from the seas it collects the water that stagnates there and becomes bitter, since the sun evaporates its volatile part, sucking it up as through siphons. The ocean also produces the clouds and rains, whose water is sweet because it has been distilled. This river has four heads, that is, it divides into four streams.[9]

Moses Bar Cephas, ninth-century bishop of Bethraman and later of Mossoul, will likewise be often cited by commentators on Genesis in the sixteenth and seventeenth centuries. Like St. John Damascene, he considers paradise first as symbolic and then as something concrete, but teaches that the two are one and the same reality. In his view no doubt is possible: paradise is located in the East, beyond the ocean. It sits at a height far greater than that of any place inhabited by human beings. It does not indeed belong to the lunar sphere, for how could the four rivers fall to the earth from such a height? These four rivers flow from it to water the rest of the world.[10]

The works of Ephraem, Philostorgius, Cosmas, John Damascene, and Moses Bar Cephas thus show a common geography, even if they are not always consistent with one another. The picture may be simplified: the earthly paradise is now beyond human reach, either because it sits on an inaccessible height or because it is located beyond an impassable ocean. But it is not therefore unconnected with our earth. It supplies the earth with water (some authors regarding it as the source of the ocean, others as the real though mysterious origin of the great rivers that make life possible in our inhabited world).

In the West, where St. Augustine was the dominant influence, Isidore of Seville, one of the shapers of the medieval mind, played an essential role in regard to the location both of the earthly paradise and of other wonderful lands that might to be thought to resemble paradise. I noted earlier that Isidore distinguishes two paradises: one is "earthly," and our first parents were placed in it; the other is "heavenly" and is the place where the souls of the just await the resurrection.[11] When writing of the geography of Asia, Isidore has this to say of the earthly paradise:

> [Asia] includes many provinces and regions whose names and locations I shall list briefly, beginning with paradise. Paradise is a place in the east, a Greek name which means *hortus* ["garden"] in Latin. In Hebrew it is called *Eden,* a word which in Latin means *deliciae* ["delights"]. The two words together give *hortus deliciarum.* This garden has all sorts of trees, especially fruit trees, and also contains the tree of life. Cold and scorching heat are unknown there; the air is always mild [a theme of the ancients when describing the golden age or the Happy Isles]. In its midst is a spring that irrigates the entire garden and gives rise to four rivers. Ever since man's sin, access to this place has been barred to humanity. It is surrounded on all sides by a flame that resembles a two-edged sword, that is, by a wall of fire whose flames rise as high as heaven. One of the cherubim...has been ordered to bar the entrance to paradise against every spirit and all flesh.[12]

The Augustinian message, which can be traced from Isidore of Seville to St. Thomas Aquinas, was of the utmost importance in the West in lending credibility to paradise as a "corporeal" reality in which Adam and Eve were placed. Quite logically, then, these same writers agree that the lost paradise still exists but is barred to humanity.

The Venerable Bede is no less a "realist" than Isidore. He also wants the reader to see the earthly paradise as a symbol both of the church and of our future fatherland, but one may by no means reject a "literal" understanding of Genesis. The ancient translations of the Bible take the words *a principio* (in the beginning) to mean *ad orientem* (in the East),

> so that many people think of paradise as located in the eastern part of the earthly round, but separated by a very large expanse of ocean or land from all the regions in which the human race now dwells outside of paradise. The waters of the flood, which covered the entire surface of our earth to a great

depth, could not reach the heights on which paradise was. But, whether God created it there or somewhere else, there can be no doubt that so important a place was and is earthly (*tantum locum fuisse et esse terrenum*).[13]

Note the shift from "was" to "is:" there can no doubt that the earthly paradise still exists on our planet.

The influence of Isidore of Seville can be seen in the fact that Rabanus Maurus in his *De universo* cites verbatim the passage from Isidore that I cited above (at n. 12). He goes on indeed to speak of the symbolic meaning that the word "paradise" has as an image of the church, but, faithful to the Augustinian tradition, he retains as part of his geography this blessed place that has become inaccessible but has not disappeared.[14]

The same outlook is shared by the great twelfth-century popularizer, Honorius of Autun. Speaking of Asia, he tells us first of all that at its eastern extremity is "paradise, a place rendered extraordinary by all kinds of amenity, but now inaccessible to human beings and surrounded by a wall of fire that reaches to heaven." It still contains the tree of life that would confer immortality on anyone who succeeded in eating its fruit. "Furthermore there is a spring there that divides into four rivers. These disappear into the soil of paradise but surface again far away." They become the Ganges (= the Pishon), the Nile (= the Gihon), the Tigris, and the Euphrates. According to Honorius, the earthly paradise is surrounded by a no man's land, "an immense space, deserted and unworkable because of the serpents and wild beasts that live there."[15]

Among the medieval writers who exerted the greatest influence a very important one is obviously Peter Lombard, who died in 1160 as bishop of Paris. His major work, the *Summa Sententiarum*, became the obligatory manual in schools of theology, and the greatest masters wrote commentaries on it. Peter Lombard says:

> The phrase *a principio* was translated in antiquity as *ad orientem.* Thus people thought that paradise is located in the eastern region of the world, separated by a wide expanse of land or water from the regions in which human beings live; also that it is located at a height which touches the sphere of the moon so that the waters of the flood were unable to reach it.[16]

In this authoritative passage Peter Lombard represents the entire Greek tradition that I described earlier and brings together several tenets of medieval geography: the earthly paradise still exists in the East; it was spared by the flood; but it is unreachable because of its height and because of the lands or seas that separate it from us.

In this same twelfth century many authors share and give expression to similar convictions.[17] Repeating what had been said in a *de imagine mundi* written around 1100, Gervase of Tilbury follows Isidore of Seville closely in describing paradise as a place "possessing every amenity," but surrounded by a wall of fire that reaches to heaven. In the midst of paradise is the tree of life and the spring that divides into four rivers that then disappear underground. Outside this blessed enclosure is a stretch of deserted land filled with serpents and wild beasts.[18]

A work entitled *De situ terrarum*, which has been attributed without any proof to Hugh of St. Victor, likewise locates paradise in Asia and repeats the classic description, which is put in the present tense, not the past: "Non est ibi frigus, non aestus; sed perpetua aeris temperies" (There is no cold there nor scorching heat, but the air is always mild).[19]

Abelard cites Bede and Isidore and makes his own the claim that the spring in paradise gave birth to the four principal rivers of the world.[20] Also from the twelfth century is the *Account of Elysaeus*, which is partially based on a letter supposedly written by the legendary Prester John: it locates the earthly paradise on the top of four mountains in India. Access to it is made impossible by a barrier of darkness. The four rivers that flow from it carry precious stones and fragrant apples. Those who breathe the fragrance of these apples no longer hunger or thirst, and have the power to heal.[21] In a poetic mode Bernard Silvestris likewise emphasizes the flowers and fragrances of paradise.[22]

The earthly paradise also makes its appearance in a well-known work of the twelfth century, *Alexandri Magni iter ad paradisum*, which was composed by a Jewish writer between 1100 and 1175. The story is as follows: when Alexander and the best of his companions have reached the banks of the Ganges, they go off to look for the earthly paradise. They finally make their way along a high city wall beside the river, but it is unbroken and offers no way of entering. Finally, at the end of three days sailing upstream, Alexander and his companions see a little window in the wall. An old man appears at it, and the visitors demand that the city agree to pay tribute henceforth to Alexander, the king of kings. The old man answers that this is the city of the blessed and that it is dangerous for the travelers to stay there any longer, because the current is strong enough to pull them down. He does, however, give Alexander a mysterious stone that the latter carries back to Babylon. A wise man there tells him its meaning: when put into the tray of a balance it is heavier than any amount of gold, but when sprinkled with dust, it becomes lighter than a feather; it is a symbol of what happens to ambition, glory, and power when death supervenes. Alexander understands the lesson and ends his life peacefully in Babylon.[23]

Alexander's *Iter in paradisum* was translated into German and became the *Strasbourg Alexander*. The French translation was entitled *Voyage au paradis terrestre* and was incorporated into the *Roman d'Alexandre* as well as into the *Faits des Romains.* The *Fatti di Cesare* and the *Manchester Epitome* likewise incorporate this story of Alexander's journey. The point of interest to us here is that this adventure story about the great conqueror assumes the present existence of a paradisal place.

In the Latin text Alexander and his companions see "a city extraordinary for its height and length."[24] The *Faits des Romains,* on the other hand, describes "a small manor beautifully decorated and enclosed by a high wall and possessing a beautiful orchard" at the foot of a high mountain. In the "rich" orchard, which no one could enter, there is a tree so extraordinary that "anyone who ate of its fruit could not die."[25] In the *Iter in paradisum* Alexander says in effect that he had heard of the earthly paradise but had not known where it was located; now he does know the place where the beautiful tree of immortality spreads its branches, but no human being can force a way into this blessed place.[26]

From the point of view that is ours here, the *Journey of Alexander the Great to Paradise* can be compared to *Huon de Bordeaux* (end of the twelfth century or beginning of the thirteenth), which is one part of the "epic of Charlemagne." Huon has killed one of the emperor's sons. In order to make amends, he must go to Babylon and there cut off the emir's beard and pull out four of his teeth, and then bring them all back to Charlemagne. In the emir's garden there flows "a stream that originates in the river of paradise" and gives health to the sick and youth to the aged.[27]

From St. Thomas Aquinas to Christopher Columbus

In the same twelfth and thirteenth centuries that saw the translation or broadcasting of the *Journey of Alexander* and *Huon de Bordeaux* there were numerous writers of great authority who agreed not only that the earthly paradise was a historical reality but also that it still existed and that Elijah and Enoch were living in it. That is the conviction of St. Thomas Aquinas, who devotes question 102 of part 1 of his *Summa theologica* to paradise and its location. The authorities to which he appeals on this subject are St. Augustine, Isidore of Seville, the Venerable Bede, and St. John Damascene.

Like Isidore, St. Thomas locates paradise in the East. He cites St. Augustine (*The Literal Meaning of Genesis* 8.7): "It is probable that man has no idea where paradise was, and that the rivers, whose sources are said to be known, flowed for some distance underground, and then sprang up elsewhere. For who is not aware that such is the case with some other streams?" (a. 1, ad 2). He then goes on to say: "The situation of paradise is shut off from the habitable world by mountains, or seas, or some torrid region, which cannot be crossed; and so people who have written about topography make no mention of it" (a. 1, ad 4).

St. Thomas therefore does not think that paradise abuts on the sphere of the moon. But is it to be found in the area of the equator? Here is his answer:

> Those who say that paradise was on the equinoctial line are of [the] opinion that such a situation is most temperate, on account of the unvarying equality of day and night; and that it is never too cold there, because the sun is never too far off; and never too hot, because, although the sun passes over the heads of the inhabitants, it does not remain long in that position. However, Aristotle distinctly says (*Meteor.* II, 5) that such a region is uninhabitable on account of the heat. This seems to be more probable; because even those regions where the sun does not pass vertically overhead, are extremely hot on account of the mere proximity of the sun. But whatever be the truth of the matter, we must hold that paradise was situated in a most temperate situation, whether on the equator or elsewhere. (a. 2, ad 4)[28]

St. Bonaventure, a Franciscan, agrees with St. Thomas, a Dominican, on this subject, while drawing on both St. Augustine and Bede. He does not locate the earthly paradise close to the sphere of the moon, but he is convinced that it is situated at a high altitude where the air is pure. While agreeing that "paradise" does have a symbolic meaning as an image of the church triumphant, he retains the literal meaning as well, declaring: "It is a bodily [= material] place of delights and beauty."[29]

The best minds of the Middle Ages saw no geographical impossibility in such a location of the earthly paradise. Therefore Vincent of Beauvais did not surprise anyone when in his great work of popularization, *Speculum majus,* he reproduced verbatim the passage from Isidore of Seville about the *hortus deliciarum* that was lost to humanity but had not disappeared.[30]

There would be no end to a list of passages of the same tenor in the writers of the "great thirteenth century." Authors have often cited a passage from Jean of Joinville's account of the seventh crusade in which he explains the source of the Nile; I cannot do better than to cite it once again:

> Before I go any further I must tell you about the river that flows through Egypt, and also about the earthly paradise.... Before this river enters Egypt, the people who usually do such work cast their nets of an evening into the water and let them lie outspread. When morning comes they find in their nets such things as are sold by weight and imported into Egypt, as for instance ginger, rhubarb, aloes, and cinnamon. It is said that these things come from the earthly paradise; for in that heavenly place the wind blows down trees just as it does the dry wood in the forests of our own land.[31]

Joinville's belief regarding the earthly paradise can be compared, to some extent, with the legend of Seth that came into existence in the *Gospel of*

Nicodemus, a work that was still read throughout the Middle Ages and was given pictorial form in the famous fresco of Piero della Francesca in the church in St. Francis in Arezzo. The legend has it that Adam, now elderly and ill, sent his third son, Seth, to the earthly paradise to obtain some oil with curative powers. But the angel stationed at the gate of the forbidden garden gave him not a bodily remedy but "the oil of mercy" in the form of a prediction of redemption; thanks to this Adam was able to fall peacefully asleep in death.

The *De laudibus divinae sapientiae* of grammarian and poet Alexander Neckham, the *De proprietatibus rerum* of Franciscan Bartholomew the Englishman, and the *Weltkronik* of Rudolf of Ems all agree on the essential point, even while differing in details: the earthly paradise was unaffected by the flood; all forms of beauty, happiness, and riches are to be found there; Enoch and Elijah still live there; but the paradise is irretrievably lost to humanity.[32] Significant in this respect is the poem *Le Miroir du monde,* which Gautier of Metz composed around 1247 and which was published at the beginning of the fourteenth century. Note the following lines in particular:

> The earthly paradise is located
> and set at the point where
> Asia begins, and is so filled with contentments
> that no one can grow weary
> of being there or tire of it,
> so full of pleasure is the place.
> Within is the tree of life
> which Adam wanted to eat.
> Whoever would eat of this fruit
> would never die,
> but no human being can reach it,
> for the angel of God will not allow it.
> It is barred by hot fire
> whose flames reach the clouds.
> A spring too is there that produces
> four great rivers as has been said.[33]

These four rivers are, of course the "Phison," identified with the Ganges, the "Geôn," identified with the Nile, the Tigris, and the Euphrates.

We find a similar geography in the *Li Livres dou trésor* of Brunetto Latini, written around 1265. Latini was a former teacher of Dante and an unyielding Guelph who had to go into exile in France (which explains why his book was written in the langue d'oïl). He writes:

> The earthly Paradise is in India; it contains all the kinds of trees and apples and other fruits to be found on earth; there too is the tree of life which God

gave to the first human being. There is neither cold nor great heat there but a moderate and temperate climate. In the center is the spring that sends water everywhere, and from it flow the four rivers of which you know: the Phison, the Gihon, the Tigris, and the Euphrates. Know that after the first human being sinned, the place was barred to all others.[34]

Dante does not have much to say about the earthly paradise in his *Divine Comedy*. He deals at much greater length with hell, purgatory, and the supreme heaven. At the same time, the elements that make up his picture of the earthly paradise were so many reminders to his readers of ideas familiar to them. He locates the earthly paradise atop the mountain of purgation. This siting of the place was shared by Ephraem, Lactantius, Pseudo-Basil, John Damascene, Bede, and Peter Lombard, all of whom located the garden of Eden on a mountain so high that the waters of the flood did not reach to it. Dante does, however, name two rivers as flowing in the meadow of paradise: the Lethe and the Eunoe. But behind these names taken from Greek antiquity (recall the mingling of traditions of which I spoke in chap. 1) we find at least the essentials of the description in Genesis: "A river flows out of Eden to water the garden, and from there it divides and becomes four branches" (Gen 2:10). Dante has reduced the four to two.

In other respects, he follows the surest traditions in his description of the earthly paradise. The place was endowed with a "forest — dense, alive with green, divine — which tempered the new day before my eyes." There blew there "a gentle breeze, which did not seem to vary within itself,...with no greater force than a kind wind's." "To the leaves, with song, birds welcomed." There was "an abundant variety of newly-flowered boughs." This was the place, the poet says, that God "gave man...as pledge of endless peace." "The holy plain on which you find yourself is full of every seed." The description ends with the well-known verses:

> Those ancients who in poetry presented
> the golden age, who sang its happy state,
> perhaps in their Parnassus dreamt this place.
> Here, mankind's root was innocent; and here
> were every fruit and never-ending spring;
> these streams — the nectar of which poets sing.[35]

It would be a mistake to regard this description as simply a poetic fiction. Dante's contemporaries certainly understood it as referring to a concrete geographical place. With Dante they believed that the earthly paradise had not disappeared, even if it was located on an inaccessible height.

As a result, during this period the earthly paradise plays an almost mandatory role in allegorical journeys. One example is the *Dittamondo* of Fazio degli Uberti (d. 1368), an unfinished story of the author's imaginary journey around the world. We should not be surprised to find him describing the earthly paradise that "most people locate in the East." It is on a mountain that rises to the first heaven; there is neither frost nor heat there, neither rain nor clouds. There is a perpetual springtime; all kinds of flowers, especially lilies and roses, grow there. Streams, perfumes, and melodies combine to enchant the soul. "Those fortunate enough to enter it know neither old age nor illness, as Enoch and Elijah prove."[36]

The same kind of thing is to be seen in the *Quadriregio* of Federico Frezzi (d. 1416), an imitator of Dante. He narrates a journey through the four kingdoms of Love, Satan, the Vices, and the Virtues, a journey that starts with original sin and ends in eternal happiness. The earthly paradise is located in the kingdom of Love. It is in the East and filled, as we would expect, with fragrant flowers and varied fruits. From outside of it the poet glimpses the tree of life and the tree of knowledge, as well as the spring that supplies the four rivers, and the venerable figures of Enoch and Elijah.[37]

In this matter the fourteenth century continued along the line followed by its predecessors. John of Hesse says that he saw the earthly paradise from a distance on a voyage to the Far East.[38] Giovanni Marignolli was told by inhabitants of Ceylon that "Adam's mountain" was only forty miles distant from the earthly paradise and that on some days it was possible to hear the noise of the water falling from the river "that flows out of Eden to water the garden."[39]

Also very important are Mandeville's *Travels* and Higden's *Polychronicon.* "Sir John Mandeville," born around 1300, was the author of a fanciful (to our minds!) account, written in French, of a journey to the Levant, India, and China. In all likelihood, "Mandeville" was in fact a French physician of Liège, whom a tradition dating back to the end of the fifteenth century transformed into an Englishman. His compilation, written in the first person, is much less the story of a journey than it is a description of the world in the light of fourteenth-century knowledge of it. It brings together the geographical ideas current in his time and takes over for its own use data found especially in the *Liber de quibusdam ultramarinis partibus* of William of Boldensele and the *Descriptio orientalium partium* of Odoricus of Pordenone, both of whom wrote around 1300.[40]

Mandeville mentions the journey of Seth to the earthly paradise and his return with the oil of mercy.[41] On the other hand, he asserts that between the kingdom of Prester John (of which I shall be speaking in the next chapter) and the earthly paradise, "there is ... only wastes and wilderness and great crags and mountains and a dark land, where no man can see by night or day, as we were told."[42] Regarding the earthly paradise itself Mandeville says that

"I cannot speak properly, for I have not been there," being unworthy to enter it. But he has heard people speak of it, and it is this hearsay that he reports:

> The Earthly Paradise, so men say, is the highest land on earth; it is so high it touches the sphere of the moon. For it is so high that Noah's flood could not reach it, though it covered all the rest of the earth. Paradise is encircled by a wall.... There is no way into it open because of ever burning fire, which is the flaming sword that God set up before the entrance so that no man should enter.
>
> In the middle of Paradise is a spring from which come four rivers, which run through different lands.... And men say that all the fresh rivers of the world have their beginning in the spring that wells up in Paradise.
>
> You should realize that no living man can go to Paradise.... Many great lords have tried at different times to travel by those rivers to Paradise, but they could not prosper in their journeys; some of them died through exhaustion from rowing and excessive labour, some went blind and deaf through the noise of the waters, and some were drowned through the violence of the waves. And so no man, as I said, can get there except through the special grace of God.[43]

There is, of course, nothing about original sin in this paradisal description of the farthest region of Asia, but on the contrary a repetition (important for our understanding of a collective mentality) of themes trotted out over and over again: from the highest place in the world, now barred by a wall of fire and raging waters, flow all the fresh waters of our planet. But Mandeville's *Travels* became enormously popular. Two hundred and fifty manuscripts have come down, fifty-two of them in French. The invention of printing led to one hundred and eighty editions in a dozen languages. Martin Behaim cited it at length. Martin Frobisher took it with him when he sailed in 1576 to discover the Northwest Passage. Hartman Schedel, Abraham Ortelius, John Bale, John Seland, Richard Hakluyt, and Samuel Purchas, or, in other words, the best geographers of the Renaissance, turned Mandeville into the Ulysses of the modern age.[44] Christopher Columbus seems to have had in his library the *Travels* of both Mandeville and Marco Polo, two men linked together.[45]

The *Polychronicon* or universal history written in Latin by Ranulf Higden, an English Benedictine (d. 1364), was translated into English as early as 1385 and partially printed in 1482; it was regarded in England as a masterpiece of the genre. Speaking of the earthly paradise, Higden first proves that it exists, using four arguments: (1) "Historical narratives" compare paradise with the region of Sodom before the latter was destroyed. (2) Competent witnesses claim to have seen it. (3) Another important piece of evidence is the four rivers that flow from paradise and whose sources have not been found either in habitable lands or in the sea, despite the efforts of the kings of Egypt and others. (4) Finally, "The tradition about paradise has continued unbroken for over six thousand years, that is, from the beginning of the world to our own time. But a tradition based on an error ordinarily fades away, either because it is forgotten or because it is ousted by a contrary view."[46]

Higden, who cites the *Etymologies* of Isidore of Seville and the *Hexae-meron* of St. Basil, does not believe that paradise is situated at the height of the moon, because it would eclipse the moon, nor that it is separated from our habitable world by a wide expanse of sea. We ought not follow here the opinion of people "of limited intelligence and little experience....The learned conclude that the earthly paradise is located in the farthest east and makes up a sizable part of the earth's mass, being no smaller than India or Egypt, for the place had been intended for the whole of the human race, if man had not sinned."[47]

Having laid down these basic premises, Higden joins so many others before him in asserting that paradise is a place of perfect health; that it enjoys a constant temperate climate; that there is no death there; that Enoch and Elijah are still living there; that its trees do not lose their leaves nor do its flowers fade; that the waters of the flood did not reach it because of its altitude; and that it is surrounded by a wall of fire that reaches to heaven.[48]

Nor is the continued existence of the earthly paradise questioned in a Portuguese compilation, *Orto do esposo*, which was written at the end of the fourteenth or beginning of the fifteenth century but was not published until 1956.[49] The author depends especially on Isidore of Seville, John Damascene, Bede, Bartholomew the Englishman, and others. He does not take literally the statement that the earthly paradise abuts on the sphere of the moon. When people talk this way, what they are trying to do (in his opinion) is to bring out its high position in relation to the earth and things here below. But once this nuance has been introduced, the *Orto do esposo* follows all the other authorities whom we have seen in describing the constancy of the pleasant climate, the abundance of all material blessings, the generosity of the sun, and the absence of corruption, all of which characterize the earthly paradise.[50]

From Ranulf Higden and the author of the *Orto do esposo* it is a logical step to Cardinal Pierre d'Ailly (d. 1420). His *Ymago mundi* was one of Christopher Columbus's favorite books, if we may judge by the hundreds of marginal notes in the copy that Columbus owned and that had been printed at Louvain in 1483. Pierre d'Ailly wrote:

> There is in the earthly paradise a spring that waters the garden of delights and spreads out in the form of four rivers. According to Isidore, John Damascene, Bede, Strabo, and the *Magister historiarum* [= Peter Comestor], the earthly paradise is a pleasant spot, located in certain regions of the east that are separated by land and sea from our inhabited world. It is so high up that it abuts on the sphere of the moon, and the water of the flood did not reach

it. This need not be understood to mean that the earthly paradise literally touched the circle of the moon; the expression is a hyperbole signifying only that its altitude is immeasurable in comparison with our lowlying earth and that it reaches into the level of serene air above the turbulent atmosphere which is the high point for those emanations and vapors that, as Alexander [of Aphrodisias] says, flow back and forth in the direction of the lunar sphere. The waters that descend from this very high mountain form a vast lake; it is said that these falling waters are so noisy that they make the inhabitants of the region deaf, the din being so great as to destroy the sense of hearing in the little children. Such at least is the testimony of Basil and Ambrose.

From this lake as from their main source flow (it is believed) the four rivers of paradise: the Pishon, that is, the Ganges; the Gihon, which is no other than the Nile; and the Tigris and the Euphrates; although their sources seem to be in different places.[51]

Like Ranulf Higden and the author of the *Orto do esposo,* Pierre d'Ailly is cautious when it comes to the height of the earthly paradise, but he does not doubt its existence or its elevated location or its role as source of the four greatest rivers of the inhabited earth.

Christopher Columbus disputes the localizations of the earthly paradise that his predecessors had proposed, but he does not depart in any fundamental way from traditional beliefs about paradise. It is worth transcribing here the famous passage in his report of his third voyage (1498), during which he reached South America in the area of the Gulf of Paria and the mouth of the Orinoco:

Holy Scripture testifies that Our Lord made the earthly Paradise in which he placed the Tree of Life. From it there flowed four main rivers: the Ganges in India, the Tigris and the Euphrates in Asia... and the Nile, which rises in Ethiopia and flows into the sea at Alexandria.

I do not find and have never found any Greek or Latin writings which definitely state the worldly situation of the earthly Paradise, nor have I seen any world map which establishes its position except by deduction....

I believe that, if I pass below the Equator, on reaching these higher regions I shall find a much cooler climate and a greater difference in the stars and waters. Not that I believe it possible to sail to the extreme summit or that it is covered by water, or that it is even possible to go there. For I believe that the earthly Paradise lies here, which no one can enter except by God's leave....

I do not hold that the earthly Paradise has the form of a rugged mountain, as it is shown in pictures, but that it lies at the summit of what I have described as the stalk of a pear, and that by gradually approaching it one begins, while still at a great distance, to climb towards it. As I have said, I do not believe that anyone can ascend to the top. I do believe, however, that, distant though it is, these waters may flow from there to this place which I have reached, and form this lake [the Gulf of Paria].

All this provides great evidence of the earthly Paradise, because the situation agrees with the beliefs of those holy and wise theologians and all the signs concord strongly with this idea. For I have never read or heard of such a quantity of fresh water flowing so close to the salt and flowing into it, and the very temperate climate provides a further confirmation. If this river [the Orinoco] does not flow out of the earthly Paradise, the marvel is still greater. For I do not believe that there is so great and deep a river anywhere in the world.[52]

Commenting on the works of the great discoverer and in particular on the passage just cited, Alexandre Cioranescu justly observes:

Columbus...believes in the manner of a typical medieval person, that is, he believes everything, without exercising any discernment or making any distinction between opinions and articles of faith. His belief is not only a religious sentiment but also a method which he applies indiscriminately to all areas of thought: he believes in the earthly paradise just as he believes in the authority of the ancients, the making of gold by bringing to bear the rays of the sun, the mountain of water that forms the navel of the earth, and the stories of Marco Polo.[53]

The important point for us in the present context is that Christopher Columbus believed firmly in the continued existence of the earthly paradise; that he located it at a great height and in a region with a pleasant climate; and that he regarded it as the source of an enormous amount of fresh water.

When Bartolomé de Las Casas reproduces the above passage from the great "admiral," he disagrees respectfully with the localization of the earthly paradise in the Americas, but otherwise he tries in his turn to justify Columbus's belief that the earthly paradise had not disappeared. Columbus's view is not "unreasonable" but on the contrary rests on "probable and serious" arguments. At the end of a lengthy discussion he can say: "Finally, we must conclude that the earthly paradise is located in the highest place in all the world, one that is higher than all other mountains, however high these may be. The waters of the flood could not reach it."[54]

As late as the eighteenth century, a certain Pedro de Rates Hanequim, who had lived in Brazil for twenty-six years, claimed that the earthly paradise still existed — in Brazil; that the tree of good and evil still grew in it; and that the Amazon and San Francisco Rivers are two of the four rivers of paradise. It was in America, therefore, that God created Adam, who then traveled dryshod to Jerusalem, the sea opening before him as it did for the Jews fleeing Egypt. The flood did not reach Brazil. Hanequim, a Hollander and probably a Jew, mixed these claims with heretical doctrines and was implicated in a plot; he was condemned to death and perished at the stake.[55] Had the earthly paradise gone up in smoke?

Earthly Paradise and Medieval Cartography

As we would expect, for many centuries medieval cartographers made room for the earthly paradise in their pictures of the world. For a long time such maps were the product of monastic workrooms, where no one questioned the geographical erudition of St. Augustine, St. Ambrose, or Isidore of Seville. On the broader scene, the various *cosmographiae* and *mappae mundi* reflected the generally held conviction that the earthly paradise still existed somewhere far off. Its continued existence seemed as certain as that of the elephants of India.[56] A ninth-century manuscript (with Latin and Greek captions) that forms part of the priceless cartographic encyclopedia of the Vicomte de Santarem (d. 1856) reproduces the map of the world drawn by Cosmas Indicopleustes (Map 1). Here the rectangular inhabited world is entirely surrounded by the ocean. Beyond this, to the east, another rectangle represents the land in which the earthly paradise exists and from which flow the four rivers that pass beneath the sea and reappear in our inhabited world.[57]

The world-map of Cosmas Indicopleustes does have one distinguishing mark by comparison with many later medieval maps: it is oriented to the North. The reason is that Cosmas adopted the Arab model, which placed either the North or the South at the top of maps, whereas the planispheres, world-maps, and other maps produced in medieval workshops from the ninth to the twelfth centuries usually put the East at the top. Sacred history here determined geographical conceptions: the earthly paradise was situated at the beginning of the human enterprise and at the top of graphic representations. The same logic led mapmakers to place Jerusalem or at least Judea in the central part of the map, the point being that the gaze of the faithful ought to focus on the place of their redemption.

It is understandable, in light of this mentality, that world-maps accompanied commentaries on the Apocalypse. One such commentary was composed around 787 in Spain and was dedicated to Eutherus, bishop of Osma. The British Museum possesses a copy that dates from 1109 and was probably made at the monastery of Silos in the diocese of Burgos. It contains a world-map that nicely exemplifies the sacred geography I have just been describing. The East is at the top of the map, and the (rectangular) inhabited earth is surrounded by the ocean (Map 2). But contrary to Cosmas's conception of things, the earthly paradise is on this side, and not the far side, of the ocean. At the top of the picture a large square vignette catches the eye: it shows Adam and Eve, the tree of knowledge, and the serpent. The earthly paradise is situated between the names of the Caucasus, Assyria, Persia, Chaldea, and India. Judea and Palestine are in the central area, but are less accentuated than Alexandria.[58] Spain, at bottom left, is given special importance.

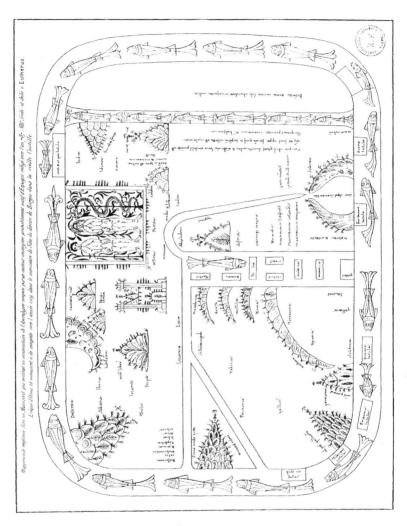

Map 2. World-map accompanying a commentary on the Apocalypse, dated 1109 and dedicated to Eutherus, bishop of Osma (diocese of Burgos)

Another copy of the commentary dedicated to Eutherus is preserved at Turin in a twelfth-century manuscript (some scholars date it to the tenth century) and is likewise accompanied by a world-map (Map 3). Like the previous map, this one shows the inhabited world surrounded by the ocean, and it locates the earthly paradise at the top, that is, in the East. At the bottom is the name of Santiago de Compostella (the document is of Spanish provenance), while Jerusalem is in the center.[59]

Many other world-maps of the twelfth and thirteenth centuries deserve our attention. One is the work of "Lambert, son of Onulf, of Saint-Omer" and was drawn around 1120 as an illustration for his *Liber Floridus*. Manuscripts of this work are to be found in Ghent, The Hague, and Paris. They show a world not only entirely surrounded by the ocean but also divided into two great sections: inhabited land to the north, uninhabitable land to the south. The earthly paradise is located on an island just above "farthest India" (Map 4).[60] On the other hand, the earthly paradise is not explicitly mentioned on a map in a *Liber Guidonis* preserved at Brussels (twelfth century); but in the East, and therefore at the top of the map, appear the names of the Pishon, Gihon, Tigris, and Euphrates. Samaria, Judea, and Jerusalem occupy the central part of the picture (Map 5).[61]

The same remark about the earthly paradise holds for the *Descriptio mappe mundi* of Hugh of St. Victor (1128–29).[62] We also find the earthly paradise and its four rivers on an island opposite the mouth of the Ganges, at the top of the map drawn in about 1130 by a canon of Mainz and dedicated to Emperor Henry V of Germany (Corpus Christi College, Cambridge). Galilee and Jerusalem, as we would expect, are placed at the heart of the inhabited world (Map 6).[63]

Also belonging to the same cartographic system are the world-map of the Abbey of Ebstorf (it dated from about 1235 and was destroyed during the Second World War) and the one in the Cathedral of Hereford (from about 1300) (Map 7). In the first of these, the world is shaped like the body of Christ, with the head dominating the picture. The head is therefore in the East, just beside the representation of the earthly paradise, while the Savior's arms extend north and south.[64]

The map drawn by Richard of Haldingham with pen and ink on vellum and preserved in the Cathedral of Hereford is quite large (2 m by 1.60 m [2.2 yd. by 1.7 yd.]). It was inside a cupboard with two doors and reflects the same theological vision as the maps we have already seen. The earthly paradise is on a round island in the East, beneath the Christ of the last judgment and above the inhabited world. The traditional four rivers flow from the foot of the tree of knowledge, around which the serpent is coiled. Adam and Eve are in the act of eating the forbidden fruit. The garden of

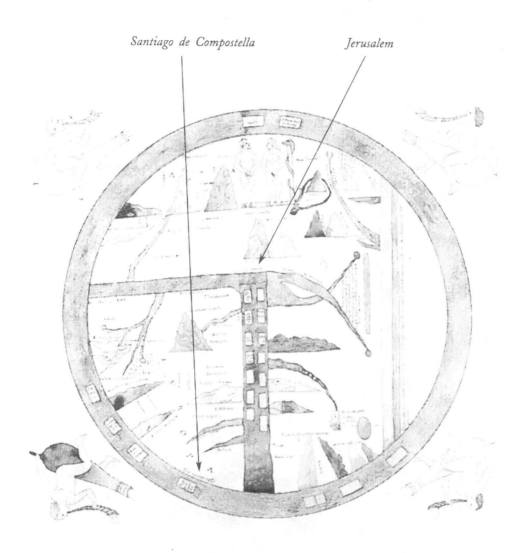

Map 3. World-map in the Turin Bible, from the 10th century(?)

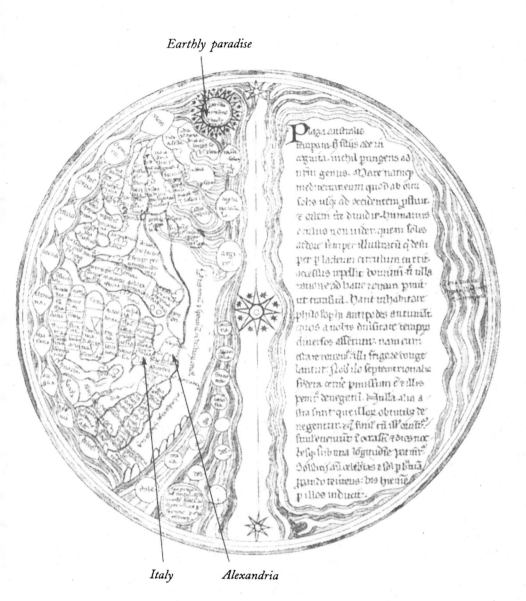

Map 4. World-map in the Paris MS of the *Liber Floridus*
of Lambert of Saint-Omer

The four rivers flowing from the earthly paradise

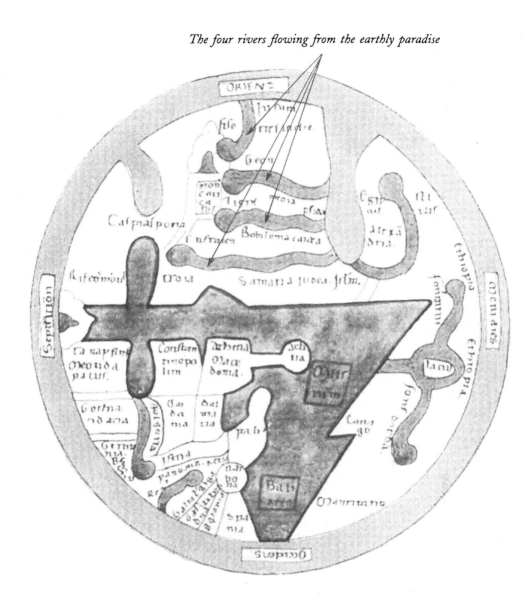

Map 5. Twelfth-century world-map from the *Liber Guidonis*

Babel   *Earthly paradise*   *Jerusalem*

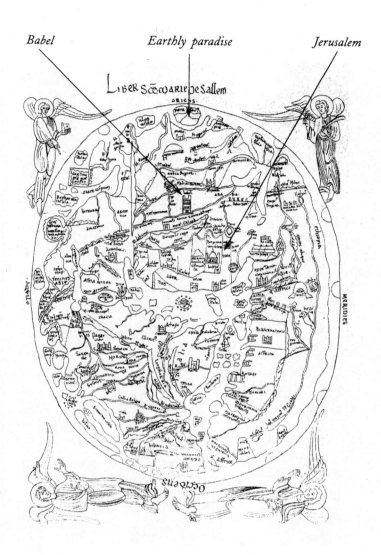

Map 6. Map of 1130, dedicated to Henri V

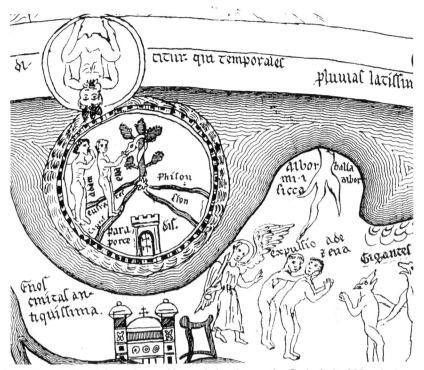

Map 7. Detail from the world-map belonging to the Cathedral of Hereford

Eden is surrounded by a circular wall that has a single fortified gate, and this gate is closed. Thus access to the blessed island is barred, but the island still exists (Map 7).[65]

Fourteenth- and fifteenth-century maps of the world continue to reflect this tenacious tradition, despite the advances in marine cartography that had more limited ambitions but that endeavored to give as exact as possible a description of coastlines; despite, too, the accounts of the journeys of Marco Polo and Odoricus of Pordenone, who had not seen the garden of Eden on their Eastern travels. The maps that accompanied Higden's *Polychronicon* and constituted a whole family of world-maps at the end of the Middle Ages are evidently adapted to the text of the English Benedictine. They depict the inhabited world as an oval inside a surrounding ocean. As Higden says in his text, the earthly paradise, located at the top of the map, is not separated from our earth by a wide expanse of sea but is simply its high point. Jerusalem is, logically, at the center of the inhabited world.[66]

A variant of Higden's map (in the British Library) has an empty space at the point usually reserved for the earthly paradise. The lacuna is not, in my

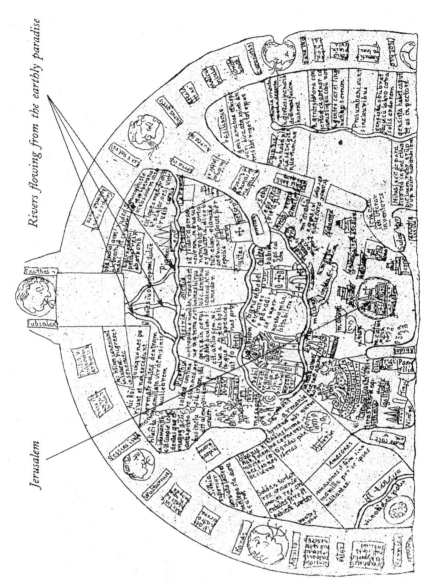

Map 8. World-map accompanying the *Polychronicon* of Ranulf Higden

opinion, meant to call the author's sacred geography into question, all the less so since rivers emerge from this rectangle at the top. May it not be simply that the map was not finished (Map 8)?[67]

In any case, we see that the traditional model is followed in a stylized world-map of the fourteenth century belonging to the Library of Arras and in another (in the Library of Saint-Geneviève) that was part of the *Grandes Chroniques de saint Denis au temps de Charles V* (1364–72): the East and the earthly paradise are at the top, and Jerusalem is in the center. The map in the *Grandes Chroniques* has the earthly paradise within the inhabited world, on this side of the ocean that surrounds the earth; the garden is enclosed by a ring of fire (Map 9).[68]

It is surprising to see that in the fifteenth century the story in Genesis still had a strong influence on geographical representations despite the many voyages to distant parts of the world, the expansion of sea trade, and a growing desire for accurate maps. A world-map from the beginning of the fifteenth century, published by Santarem and to be found in the Vatican Library, puts the South at the top of the map (after the manner of the Arabs) and the East to the left. But it does not forget to include the *hortus deliciarum* at the eastern end of India, where it is separated from the rest of the earth by a wall of fire. An angel stands between Adam and Eve, and a single river, the Ganges, flows out of the garden.[69]

A little later, the well-known map of Andrea Bianco (1436) shows the cartographer to be well informed about the Mediterranean, but it contains many things we would think odd when dealing with Africa and Asia. It continues to place the East at the top of the map; here in this upper section are located both the earthly paradise, with the four rivers flowing from it, and the "Hospice of St. Macarius," on the spot where St. Macarius was halted by the angel's sword when he tried to enter the earthly paradise (Map 10).[70]

Among the mapmakers of the fifteenth century, Fra Mauro, a Camaldulese monk of the Convent of Murano, became quite famous. It was at the request of the Venetian authorities that he drew the great map of the world that he completed in 1459. Fra Mauro was a scholar with a good knowledge of the ancients, and he kept himself informed about Portuguese voyages along the coasts of Africa. In addition, he devoted a great deal of care to depicting Europe and a whole section of Africa. He too breaks with most other cartographers by placing the South at the top of his world-map. But "he gets lost in the immensity of the East." When it comes to locating the earthly paradise, he takes over unquestioned the views of St. Augustine and Bede and excludes the garden of Eden from his representation of the inhabited world.[71]

Fra Mauro's world-map does nonetheless reflect the current questioning of traditional geographical models. The atlas that Marino Sanudo of Venice had compiled at the beginning of the fourteenth century for his great work *Liber secretorum fidelium crucis* still had the East at the top of the map and Jerusalem at the center of the inhabited world, which in turn was surrounded by the ocean. But he no longer included the earthly paradise, except to the

Map 9. World-map in the *Grandes Chroniques de saint Denis du temps de Charles V*

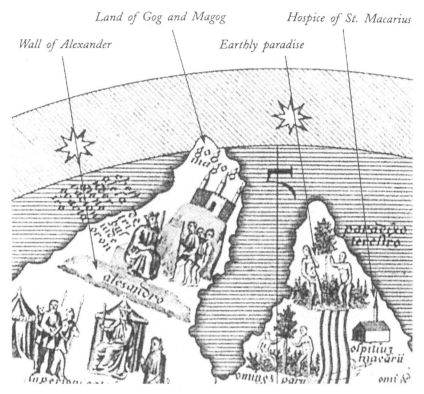

Map 10. Detail from the world-map of Andrea Bianco (1436)

extent of giving the name Gihon to a river that then becomes the Indus.[72] So too, the great Catalan map of 1375–78 no longer included the earthly paradise; it had the North at the top. The coasts of the Mediterranean and of western Europe were drawn with an accuracy remarkable at that time.

At what was by now a rather late date, the *Rudimentum novitiorum*, printed at Lübeck in 1475, still had the East at the top of its picture of the world, and Jerusalem at the center. At the top, the island of the earthly paradise, with the four rivers flowing from it, is represented as an enclosed garden in which Enoch and Elijah are still living.[73] This same map of the world appears in successive editions of the anonymous *Mer des hystoires*, a variant of the work just described; it went through numerous printings at Lyons and Paris between 1491 and 1555 (Map 11).[74]

Three main factors led mapmakers gradually to alter their pictures of the world. One factor was the rediscovery of the *Cosmographia* of Ptolemy, which was translated into Latin at the beginning of the fifteenth century and

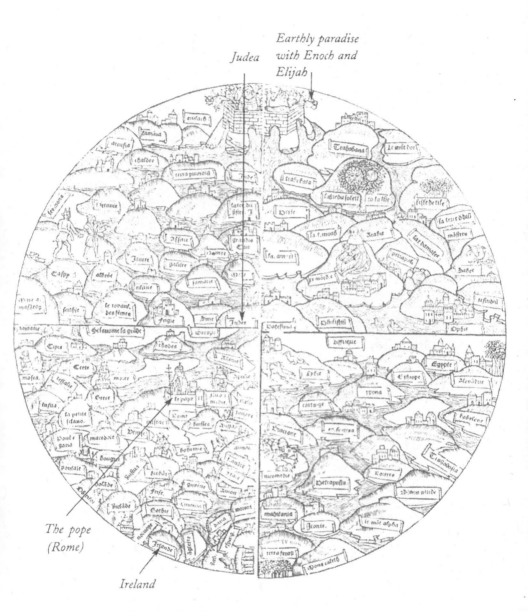

Map 11. Map from the anonymous *Mer des hystoires*

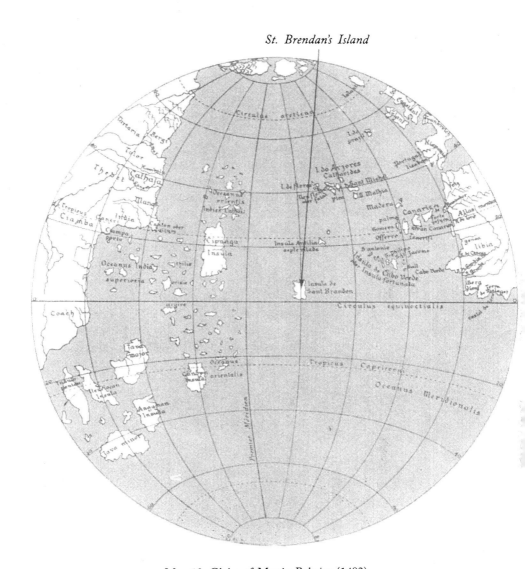

Map 12. Globe of Martin Behaim (1492)

printed as early as the 1470s, with the inclusion of maps that became more and more numerous as further printings followed. These maps no longer have the East at the top and no longer make any reference to sacred history. The earth, crossed now by a network of lines of latitude and longitude, has ceased in principle to be the hierarchized construct of places that was to be seen on medieval world-maps, which made Jerusalem or the Mediterranean Basin their center.[75]

In addition to the secularizing influence of Ptolemy *redivivus*, there were two other factors: the increasing accuracy of portolanos and the information gained on voyages of discovery earlier even than those of Christopher Columbus and Magellan. Thus a map whose maker claims to have taken into account the Portuguese voyages along the African coasts up to the year 1489 has the North at the top; in addition it no longer places Jerusalem at the center of the world and neglects to mention the earthly paradise.[76]

The famous globe of Martin Behaim (1492) still has "St. Brendan's Island" somewhere between Europe and Cipangu (a legendary island east of Asia), but omits any mention of the earthly paradise (Map 12), although Behaim claims in his commentary that when it came to Asia he had supplemented the *Cosmographia* of Ptolemy with information given by Marco Polo and that "honorable doctor and knight, John of Mandeville." Now, as we saw earlier, Mandeville has a paragraph on the earthly paradise in his description of the East. Martin Behaim's omission of this reference revealed a change of outlook in circles interested in the discoveries. Behaim had himself traveled down the coast of Africa on Portuguese ships.

From the sixteenth century on, the vast majority of world-maps have the North at the top and no longer suggest that the earthly paradise might still exist on our earth, somewhere in the East.[77]

Chapter 4

The Kingdom of Prester John

The Success of a Forgery

To the tenacious conviction that the earthly paradise still existed on our planet in a place rendered inaccessible by original sin there was added, in the course of the centuries, an enduring certainty that the approaches to this earthly paradise were not beyond human reach and that blessed lands still existed that, because of their closeness to the earthly paradise or their isolation or both, retained many of the attractions and privileges of the garden of Eden. The most famous of these dreamlands was the kingdom of Prester John. The legend of Prester John seems to go back to the beginning of the twelfth century, and it survived down to the seventeenth.

Beginning in the early decades of the twelfth century, as a result of contacts made possible by the crusades, the Latin peoples came to know of a Christian ruler who reigned not far from the country of the Blacks and whom the West tended to identify with the emperor of Ethiopia. Was the name "John" a distortion of "Zan," a name at one time given to the sovereign ruler of Ethiopia? And was the attribution of priesthood to this John due to the fact that the emperor of Ethiopia was ordained a deacon at the time of his accession? Some scholars have thought so. But today a different hypothesis, which I shall explain in a moment, is gaining favor, the reason being that the name "Zan" is attested only beginning in the sixteenth century.[1]

From the second half of the twelfth century on, the location of Prester John's kingdom gradually shifted to Asia, a process facilitated by geographic confusions about the name "India." A distinction was often made between *India inferior* (lower India, i.e., the west side of the Ganges), *India superior* (upper India, i.e., beyond the river), and *India ultima* or *India Egypti* (farthest India or Egyptian India). Two traditions seemed to confirm the belief in an Asiatic Christian kingdom. One was that St. Thomas, after evangelizing the Medes, Persians, and Parthians, had reached the Malabar and Coromandel coasts and Christianized these regions, in which his tomb was supposed to be located (at Madras). The other tradition had the three Magi-Kings coming from an East fabled for its wealth, inhabitants, flora, and fauna. In the Western imagination Prester John then became a Christian king reigning somewhere in "Asia," near the earthly paradise.

Some (Nestorian)[2] Christian communities did in fact exist out there: some on the slopes of the Deccan, others scattered about central Asia as far as China. This explains how the West heard about a "Patriarch John," who was guardian of the tomb of St. Thomas and who eventually lent substance to the legend of a king named "Prester John." For there was in circulation an anonymous account of a visit that the "patriarch of the Indies" supposedly paid to the pope in 1122.

The patriarch supposedly filled the court of Callistus II with wonder by his description of the city in which he resided. In its midst flowed the river Pishon, "one of the rivers of paradise, with crystal-clear waters that carry along very precious gold and also very precious stones, thanks to which the lands of India are extremely rich." Only faithful Christians live there. For as soon as a heretic or an unbeliever there hears authentic Christian doctrine, either he is immediately converted or he falls to the ground stone dead. A short distance from the city walls, on a mountain that is surrounded by a lake, is the church dedicated to St. Thomas. Because of the expanse of water the mountain is inaccessible except during the eight days before and after the saint's feast. During this period the lake dries up and allows pilgrims to go and come. In the holy of holies there is a ciborium of gold and silver, magnificently wrought and adorned with some of the precious stones brought down by the Pishon.[3]

This anonymous letter, with its descriptions that bring a smile to our faces, does at least hark back to a real event. For another letter, written by Odo, abbot of Saint-Remy in Rheims, confirms the fact that in 1122 an "archbishop from India" came to Rome with a Byzantine delegation. He spoke there (exaggeration now takes over again) of the wealth and treasures of the country in which the body of St. Thomas rests. The letter mentions the mountain with its sanctuary and the surrounding great river that dries up once a year to permit the archbishop and faithful to visit the shrine. On this occasion, the body of the apostle is brought from its tomb and displayed in the cathedral. The saint raises his arm and opens his hand to receive the gifts brought by the visitors. But if a heretic slips in among them, the hand closes and refuses the offering.[4]

The Latins, who had established themselves in the East since the first crusade, knew on what shaky ground they stood amid a Muslim world and especially in relation to the king of Persia. They rejoiced therefore at every bit of news or evidence offering hope that Christian princes — from Georgia or

Armenia or a more distant "Asia" — might neutralize the aggressive Muslim powers or even attack them from the rear. This hope and this expectation, combined with the twelfth-century stories about the "patriarch of India," led to the forging of the legend of Prester John.

In 1141 Sanjar, king of Persia, who was regarded in the Holy Land as overlord of the Muslims of Syria and Mesopotamia, was conquered by the leader of the Mongol tribe of the Kara Kitay, who had been driven from China and were at this time carving out an empire in Asia. A bishop of Frankish Syria, Hugh of Gabala (Byblos), offered an interpretation of this event that deserves our attention here; his testimony was recorded at Viterbo in 1145 by historian Otto of Freising, half brother of Emperor Conrad III. According to Hugh, a "certain John," a Christian of the Nestorian rite and a descendant of the Magi, who was both king and priest and who lived "in the Far East beyond Persia and Armenia (*ultra Persidam et Armeniam in Extremo Oriente*)," had decided to come to the aid of the church of Jerusalem. He had conquered the Medes and the Persians and had captured Ecbatana, but had been unable to cross the Tigris.[5] Here we meet the title "Prester John" for the first time.

But while an Asian location for Prester John was given preference, it never entirely eclipsed the Ethiopian location in the Middle Ages. The two localizations are a difficulty that the recent and fundamental work of Jacqueline Pirenne has tried to resolve by showing that the legend of Prester John had a double origin, one Nestorian, the other Ethiopian.[6] I shall summarize her demonstration.

The first point in her argument: the personage known as Prester John was conjured up in a Nestorian setting before being then located in Ethiopia.[7] He emerged from the *Acts of St. Thomas*, which was composed at Edessa, a Nestorian center, between the middle of the third century and the end of the fourth.[8] This work relates that Thomas, apostle of India, became a carpenter for King Gudnafor, one of the Magi-Kings, and then was executed by order of Mazdai, another king of India. But the latter had a son, Vizan, whom Thomas had converted and who interred the apostle's body in a royal tomb. Thomas had also converted Sifur, a companion of Vizan. Vizan was subsequently transformed into John, and a reversal of roles took place, so that Vizan-John, son of the king, became the priest and Sifur the deacon.

Among the Nestorians of Edessa, central Asia, and the Coromandel Coast, "Prester John" was not simply an honorary title. The phrase refers to a function: that of successor to Vizan-John as spiritual and temporal leader of the "St. Thomas Christians." This means that, as far as the Nestorian Christians were concerned, many persons could have a right to the title.[9]

Still to be explained is how an Ethiopian Prester John could have existed so far from the Nestorian part of the world. We must bear in mind here the geographical unity of the three Indias, as conceived by the Middle Ages. Furthermore, maritime relations gave rise to links between India and Ethiopia, so that the Indians may well have been aware that there were emperors in Ethiopia. We may then suppose that the Nestorians of India thought of one of these emperors as deserving to be called a "Prester John." According to Jacqueline Pirenne, this was the case with King Yimrha Christos, who ruled around 1170–73 and who, according to tradition, had been ordained a priest before his accession. He had a reputation for holiness. Furthermore, the occupation of Jerusalem by the crusaders made it easier for Ethiopians to visit the Holy City. Here, too, is a significant detail: the capital of the dynasty to which Yimrha Christos belonged is known to us by the name of Roha, which is the Syriac name for Edessa. Relations between Ethiopia and Palestine continued even after Saladin occupied Jerusalem in 1198. It was he who gave the Ethiopians a place on Mount Olivet. These convergent bits of evidence explain why in the years 1217–21 Jacques de Vitry, bishop of Saint-Jean-d'Acre, located the kingdom of Prester John both in Asia and in East Africa,[10] the latter being regarded, at that time, as a section of the former.

But the most novel part of Jacqueline Pirenne's posthumous book (she was killed by a reckless driver before its publication) has to do with the letter or, rather, letters of Prester John. In a monumental study published from 1879 to 1893, German scholar Friedrich Zarncke published the oldest version known at that time of a letter that Prester John supposedly sent to Byzantine Emperor Manuel I, Comnenus. It was supposedly written around 1165. Archbishop Christian of Mainz, an envoy to Constantinople in 1170, is said to have translated it into Latin so that it might be read to Frederick Barbarossa. Zarncke attributed the composition of this "forgery" to a Latin cleric living in the East. He also thought that this letter, in its Latin form, served as model for others supposedly derived from it and sent to the king of France, the pope, and the emperor respectively. In addition, Zarncke endeavored to reconstruct the first version of the letter by collating almost a hundred manuscripts of the Latin "translation."

Later studies, however, have made it impossible to accept Zarncke's historical reconstruction. To begin with, a Latin manuscript from a different line has been discovered.[11] It was then seen that it depended on the French version and that the latter could not derive from the Latin version supposedly translated by Archbishop Christian.[12]

Finally, and most importantly, as early as 1888 attention was called to some Hebrew versions of the letter, three specimens of which were published by two scholars in 1982.[13] These Hebrew versions are indeed fairly close to the Romance versions (French, Italian, and Provençal) of the letter, but they also display a real autonomy in relation to these. Hence the hypothesis of Jacqueline Pirenne, who goes beyond her predecessors and thinks (1) that there was not a single original letter, supposedly translated from Greek into Latin and the source of the other versions, but four original letters: to the emperor of Byzantium, the king of France, the emperor, and the pope; and (2) that the four letters, whose content when analyzed shows that each has its specific character, were nonetheless written by a single author. This author was probably "a well-read Jew who had travelled in the East to gather information about Jewish communities there but had at the same time acquired information about the Nestorians and about trade with India."[14] The Hebrew versions show that the author was familiar with the *Book of Eldad the Danite* and was acquainted with the bishop of Samarkand, a city that possessed a large Jewish community. He would seem to have been a native of Provence, because Provençal terms have crept into the Hebrew text. Though a Jew by culture, he seems to have had an open mind toward Christianity.[15]

The relevant point as regards this complex question is this: the four letters would seem to have had a single author, who composed a Hebrew original and then (alone or with the help of friends) produced the translations that Prester John was thought to have had made into French for the king of France and the emperor, into Latin for Manuel Comnenus (with "showy Hellenisms"), and into Italian for the pope. To some extent, these versions differed from each other in content; the difference is to be explained by the fact that the versions were adapted to their respective addressees. The Latin version in particular differs from the other three.

The latter, which are richer and more serious in their content, give the impression of being "implicitly a political and social critique because of the way they call attention to what ought to be."[16]

> The letters of Prester John to the principal men of the Europe of his time constituted a campaign inspired by the desire to move away from a Christianity marked by rivalries, ambitions, betrayals, fratricidal struggles, wars, massacres, and misery among the people; they were implicitly subversive, for they sketched a picture of a truly Christian empire. The archbishop of Mainz substituted for them a piece of popular writing about the "wonders of India," in the country of an unpleasant and pretentious king of the East....Thus it was the archbishop who produced a forgery.[17]

Given these clarifications, the point that is important to us here is that the Latin version produced by the Archbishop of Mainz was immensely successful, unlike the other three. No one in the Middle Ages doubted its

authenticity. Zarncke identified ninety-three manuscripts of it. It was translated into most of the European languages. Its influence on the medieval
mind was therefore deep and lasting, and this is what is significant for us in
dealing with the subject of the present book.

In the oldest Latin text as reconstructed by Zarncke[18] we read the
following:

> I, Prester John, am the lord of lords (*dominus dominantium*), and I surpass
> all the kings of the entire world in wealth, virtue, and power. Seventy-two
> kings pay tribute to me. I am a devout Christian, and we everywhere defend
> and help with our alms those poor Christians who are subject to our indul-
> gent authority.... Our splendor rules over the three Indies, and our territory
> extends from farther India, where the body of St. Thomas rests, to the desert
> of Babylon near the tower of Babel.

There follows a list of the living things in this extraordinary country;
mention is made, in particular, of elephants, dromedaries, camels, hippopota-
muses, crocodiles, panthers, tigers, white lions and red lions, white bears,
silent cicadas, gryphons, wild human beings, human beings with horns,
fauns, pygmies, dog-faced baboons, giants, cyclopes, and "the bird known
as the phoenix."

This land, in which milk and honey flow, is crossed by a river that flows
out of the earthly paradise; it carries emeralds, sapphires, topazes, beryls,
amethysts, and other precious stones. The land contains, among other things,
a forest that produces an abundance of pepper. The forest is located at the
foot of Mount Olympus, from which flows a spring whose waters then run
close to the earthly paradise and whose fragrance combines the fragrances
of all the spices. If persons drink three times from this water while fasting,
they will never fall sick and will remain throughout their lives as they were
at thirty-two. "One of the wonders of our land," Prester John continues, "is
a waterless sea of sand. The sand is always moving and swells into waves
like the sea." This strange sea is never in repose. It cannot be crossed, and
therefore no one knows what lies beyond it. But on its banks there are various
fish that make very good eating.

Further on, Prester John says: "In our indulgence we welcome all guests
and pilgrims from other lands. There are no poor among us. There is no
theft nor sycophancy nor greed nor divisions." Lying is also unknown. "No
vice reigns among us." In war the troops are preceded by thirteen large crosses
made of gold and precious stones. Each is followed by ten thousand soldiers and one hundred thousand footmen. The palace of the priest–ruler
has ceilings and joists made of wood that cannot rot. Atop the building are
two golden apples, each surmounted by a crystal. The gold shines during

the day and the crystals during the night. Some of the tables used for the court's meals are made of gold, others of amethyst. The legs of the tables are of ivory.

Thirty thousand men, among them seven kings, sixty-two dukes, three hundred and sixty-five counts, twelve archbishops, twenty bishops, and "the patriarch of St. Thomas," lunch in the palace every day. The royal chamber there is adorned with gold and precious stones, and fragrant resins burn there constantly. The bed is made of sapphire, a stone that favors chastity. "We have very beautiful women, but they join us only four times a year and then only in order to beget children. Then, once they have been sanctified by us, as Bathsheba was by David, they return each to her own apartment." The ceiling of the palace looks like the sky, being strewn with very luminous sapphires and topazes that resemble stars. The floor is of crystal. To the interior walls are attached fifty columns that narrow at the top; each carries a carbuncle as large as an amphora. Thus the palace has no windows, for it is illumined by these precious stones no less than it would be by the sun.

In front of the royal edifice is a public square where judicial duels are fought; on it is a mirror set on a high place that is reached by twenty-five steps made of precious stones. The mirror is perched atop an unusual structure: at the bottom is a column that is capped by a base that in turn supports two columns with a new supporting base atop each of them. As one climbs the stairs one passes four, eight, sixteen, thirty-two, and sixty-four columns successively; then the number of columns begins to decrease. The mirror shows all that is going on "for and against us" throughout the kingdom and the adjacent provinces. It is guarded day and night by twelve thousand soldiers.

The letter ends with this proud claim: "Our country extends on one side a march of almost four months, and on the other a distance no one can know. If you can count the stars in the heavens and the sands of the sea, you can also measure our empire and power."

This letter makes it easy to reconstruct the imaginative picture of the East that well-read westerners had in the twelfth century. In this distant area of which they knew little they jumbled together a Christian military power that was to attack Islam from the rear, a vast kingdom near the earthly paradise, the fountain of youth, pepper and precious stones galore, a proliferation of strange animals, and a "sea of sand" that was nonetheless rich in fish. Prester John resembles both a Croesus and a saint in an empire in which there is no place for anything but virtue. I said earlier that Jacques de Vitry was confused about the location of the kingdom of Prester John. In 1217 he wrote: "A trader has just informed me that the inhabitants of the country of Prester John have just abandoned Nestorianism and have become Jacobites."[19]

The reference was obviously to the Monophysites of Ethiopia. But in a letter of 1220 the same Jacques de Vitry spoke of "Christians who occupy the greater part of India, are Nestorians, and are subjects of a very powerful prince whom the people call Prester John."[20] This time, the reference could only be to Asia. In this first quarter of the thirteenth century the Asiatic localization of the kingdom of Prester John was given new impetus by the circulation of a *Relatio de Davide*, which reached Damietta in 1221. It told of victories that a King David, a Nestorian and descendant of a King John, had won over the Muslims. Abridged versions of the report make this David the son of Prester John or, more simply, replace the name of David with the name of John.

The successes attributed to David were in fact an echo of the conquests that Genghis Khan (d. 1227), after invading China, went on to achieve in Persia and Turkistan. The invasion of 1240–41 soon led the Mongols into the very heart of Europe: to Krakow and Hungary. The pope and Western rulers were initially frightened but then tried to establish relations with the Mongols and even to convert them, always with the hope of using them to take the Muslims from the rear. The embassies sent to the Mongols also had as one of their purposes to make inquiry about the kingdom of Prester John, regarding which, however, less exhilarating information was beginning to circulate.

In his account of the seventh crusade (1248–54), Joinville tells how the "Tartars" rebelled against Prester John and killed him.[21] In 1253 Vincent of Beauvais tells us in his *Speculum historiale* that Prester John was at one time emperor of India and lord over the "Tartars," who paid him tribute; in the time of Genghis Khan, however, the Tartars rebelled and attacked David, John's son, and killed him and his family, except for a single daughter, who became the wife of Genghis Khan and had children by him.[22] Finally, Thomas of Cantimpré, a Dominican (d. 1263), says that when Louis IX learned that the "king of the Tartars" had a Christian mother, he sent messengers to him.[23]

In fact, the Council of Lyons in 1245 sent a Franciscan, John of Piano Carpini, to Mongolia (where he stayed in 1246–47), and St. Louis entrusted another Franciscan, Willem of Rubruck, with a mission to the Great Khan, which took place in 1253–54.

Many of these Western travelers who made their way along the roads of the Far East in the thirteenth century and the beginning of the fourteenth and visited the Mongol empire (especially Willem of Rubruck, the members of the Polo family from 1255 to 1295, and Odoricus of Pordenone from 1290 to 1330) tried to deflate the myth about the country of Prester John, even though they did not question its existence. Willem of Rubruck got as far as Karakorum (250 km [155 mi.] west of Ulan Bator). When he reached the country of the Naïman (the upper basin of the Irtysh and Ob Rivers), he noted:

> On a plain between these mountains there was a Nestorian, a shepherd who enjoyed great authority and governed a people known as the Naïman, who were Nestorian Christians. At the death of Coir Khan, this Nestorian proclaimed himself king. The Nestorians called him King John and went far beyond the truth in speaking of him. The Nestorians who come from those lands do the same: they make great stories out of nothing. I travelled through his grazing areas, and no one but these Nestorians knew anything about him.[24]

No one could be more circumspect or mistrustful regarding rumors "that go far beyond the truth."

Marco Polo has two sets of statements about Prester John. In a first account, he gives substance to the story of the conflict between Prester John and his vassal Genghis Khan, which ends with the defeat of the Christian ruler and the marriage between the conqueror and the daughter of the conquered John.[25] Later, in the chapter on the province of Tenduc, that is, the region north of the loop in the Yellow River, a passage on the kingdom of Prester John lays the emphasis chiefly on its past greatness:

> Let us now proceed to another province farther east, called Tenduc, where we shall enter the dominion of Prester John.
> Tenduc is a province containing many towns and villages. The chief city is named Tenduc. The people are subject to the Great Khan, for so also are the descendants of Prester John. The province is ruled by a king of the lineage of Prester John, who is a Christian and a priest and also bears the title "Prester John." His personal name is George. He holds the land as a vassal of the Great Khan — not all the land that was held by Prester John, but a part of it.
> This province produces lapis lazuli in plenty and of good quality, besides excellent camlets of camel hair. The inhabitants live by stock-rearing and agriculture. There is also a certain amount of commerce and industry. The rulers, as I have said, are Christians.[26]

To sum up: according to Marco Polo there exists a Christian, that is, Nestorian, realm in the Far East, but its king is a vassal of the Mongol ruler. It is certainly quite prosperous, but there is nothing paradisal about it.

Odoricus of Pordenone, a Franciscan from the Friuli region, is no less reserved in his language when he writes: "We came to the land of Prester John, which they call the Island of Penthexoire; but not even a hundredth part of what they say about its rich soil and noble countryside is true."[27] He locates this land, which he also calls "Presticane," about fifty days' journey west of Peking.

Prester John comes up again in a letter written in 1305 by John of Monte Corvino, who was sent to China in 1289 and became bishop of Peking. When he converted King George, head of the Turkish tribe of the Ongüt, from Nestorianism to Catholicism, he was convinced that he had converted the descendant of "the great king known as Prester John of India."[28]

Over against the relative circumspection of the few westerners who visited the Far East stood the amalgam of traditional legends that were widespread in the West. An example is the compilation by John of Hildesheim, a Carmelite, entitled *De gestis trium regum;* it dates from the end of the fourteenth century and enjoyed considerable popularity even a century later. In this work Prester John is presented as the heir of the Magi-Kings. His son David sided with the Nestorians against the "Tartars" and was conquered and slain by them. But the leader of the "Tartars" was warned by the Magi in a dream to make an alliance with Prester John; as a result, the son of one of the two rulers always marries the daughter of the other.[29]

Also in circulation in fourteenth-century France was a work entitled *Nouvelles de la terre de Prestre Jehan,* in which is to be found the substance of the apocryphal Latin letter of 1165. Here Prester John claims "the most exalted and noblest crown in all the world, as well as gold, silver, and precious stones" and says that he is overlord of "forty-two mighty kings and good Christians." In his realm is "a city called Orronde the Great, which is the most beautiful and strongest city in all the world." "Know, too, that no Christian king has as much wealth as We do.... And in our land is the tree of life from which chrism comes,... and this tree is close to the earthly paradise, only a day's journey away, and We bring this chrism to the St. Thomas patriarch, and he consecrates it; with it we are all baptized."

The king's palace is described as follows: "The walls are of crystal, and the ceiling above is made of precious stones and adorned with stars like those of the heavens. The floor is of crystal, and this palace contains neither windows nor door. In the palace are forty-two hundred pillars made of gold and silver and precious stones of all kinds." The king goes on to say that in his kingdom all the poor are supported by alms and that in his land live "red, green, black, and blue lions," "birds known as gryphons, which can carry a head of cattle and a horse to their nests," other birds "the color of fire," with wings "sharp as razors," and, finally, "the phoenix, the most beautiful bird in the world," which dies at the age of a hundred and is reborn from its own ashes.

"In our land," Prester John continues, "there is an abundance of bread, wine, flesh, and all the things useful in sustaining human life,... and no beast can enter it which is by nature poisonous." Pepper grows without being sown, and there is a fountain so extraordinary that anyone able to drink its water three times while fasting will not fall ill for thirty years; as long as he is well, he will feel as though he had been eating the best foods and spices in the world, for the fountain is filled with the grace of God and the Holy Spirit. And anyone able to bathe in this fountain, even though he be two hundred or a thousand years old, will return, in appearance, to the age of thirty.

Thus the realm of Prester John is once again described as a fabulous world, a land of plenty, but one in which the greatest virtue reigns. "Thieves" are unknown there. "No one dares commit the sin of lust there, for he will straightway be burned at the stake.... Nor does anyone dare to lie, for a liar will be slain or hanged."[30] The ruler and his realm thus represent the heights of power and virtue.

But it is in the fourteenth century, in Mandeville's *Travels* (chaps. 30–32), that we find the most incredible description of the Christian kingdom in India, with its "many noble cities and fair towns, and many isles great and broad."[31] "This land of India is divided into isles on account of the great rivers which flow out of Paradise and run through and divide up [Prester John's] land." The sovereign is lord over many kings, islands, and peoples. His country is very rich, although less so than that of the Great Khan. This limitation, the only one in the entire description, is explained by the very insularity of the island of Prester John. It is difficult to reach because the surrounding sea is strewn with magnetic rocks that attract any bit of iron in ships and cause them to be pulled apart. "King Prester John and the Great Khan of Tartary are always allied through marriage; for each of them marries the other's daughter or sister." As a result, the two men are the most powerful rulers under heaven.

Prester John "has under his rule seventy-two provinces, each one ruled by a king. These kings have other kings under them, and all are tributary to Prester John. In the land of Prester John there are many marvels." One of these is "a vast sea of gravel and sand, and no drop of water is in it," yet "there are great waves on it" and there is "great plenty of good fish caught on its shores." But no ship can cross it. Near this sea are "great mountains, from which flows a large river that comes from Paradise. It is full of precious stones."

Beyond the river, toward the deserts, is a plain on which trees spring up in the morning and grow until midday. Then they bear fruit, but no one dares eat of it because it is enchanted. The trees then decrease in size during the afternoon and disappear into the earth again at sunset. In the deserts live horned wild men of horrible appearance, and wild dogs and many parrots that speak to people crossing the area.

When Prester John sets his army in array for battle, he has his troops follow not a banner but thirteen crosses made of fine gold and precious stones. Each cross is placed in a richly decorated chariot that is guarded by ten thousand armed men and a hundred thousand foot soldiers, independently of the regular army.

The ruler lives most of the time at Susa, and his palace is so richly made that it surpasses all anticipation. The great gates are made of sardonyx with ivory trim. The windows of the halls and chambers are of crystal. The dining tables. are adorned, some with emeralds, others with amethysts, and still others with gold and precious stones. The seven steps to his throne are made respectively of onyx, crystal, green jasper, amethyst, sardonyx, carnelian, and chrysolite, with borders of fine gold, precious stones, and pearls from the East. In his bedchamber the pillars are likewise of fine gold and have many carbuncles set in them that shine at night; a crystal vase filled with balm spreads its fragrance and keeps any polluted air away from the emperor. The royal bed is made of gold and sapphires, which assures the sovereign of a sound sleep while at the same time keeping any lust away. For he sleeps with his wife only four times a year, and then only to beget children.

Prester John always has twelve kings at hand to serve him; these in turn are assisted by seventy-two dukes and three hundred and seventy counts. Twelve archbishops and twenty bishops are always in residence at his court, and "the Patriarch of Saint Thomas is there rather like a Pope. All the archbishops and bishops and abbots there are kings and lords of great fiefs." The kingdom of Prester John is a four months' march in breadth, and immeasurable in length. It is impossible to list all its riches and the enormous quantity of precious stones that it contains. Most of its inhabitants are believers and moral people. The priests sing Mass and consecrate the bread in the Greek manner, and their liturgies are simpler than those of the Latins, because they hold fast to the teaching of St. Thomas and the apostles. "They know nothing of the ordinals and additions of the court of Rome that our priests use."[32]

Such are the characteristics of this Asiatic Christian state, in which are gathered all the wonders of creation, the riches of the universe, the Christian faith, and a mighty sovereign who is supported by the power of his relative and ally, the Great Khan. There can be no better proof than Mandeville both of the lasting survival of the great themes developed in the apocryphal letter of 1165 and of the way in which these were expanded during the two centuries that followed.

Asia Around the Kingdom of Prester John

Mandeville's chapters on the country of Prester John and its surroundings mention numerous islands that to some extent anticipate the utopian lands (usually islands) of the Renaissance. On the island of Bragman (or Brahmin) live a "good" and "honest" people among whom there are no murderers or prostitutes. They fast daily and are as chaste as religious. In return, they experience neither tempests nor storms, neither plagues nor famines. They hold everything in common and do not esteem wealth. The inhabitants usually die not of sickness but of old age. They believe in a God who created all things, and they worship him.[33]

Two other islands are named Oxidrace and Gynoscripha and are likewise inhabited by people of sound faith but who live naked. They do not know the articles of the Christian creed, but they do practice a natural religion, and for this God loves them and heaps blessings on them. Four thousand years before the Savior's birth they knew of prophecies foretelling the incarnation, but they do not know that the incarnate God suffered and died for us.[34]

In thus gathering up legends current in his day about Prester John and the wonder-filled countries of Asia, Mandeville gave new life to the entire range of paradisal situations that could be imagined at that time. In one setting are to be found power, wealth, music, fragrances, and the fountain of youth; in another, sobriety, the sharing of possessions, but also the absence of sicknesses and disasters. In one setting, lavishness; in another, nudity; but everywhere moral decency and a religion that is fully lived even if it has no dogmas.

But the paradises of Asia are sometimes more agitated, when they are no longer associated with that devout ruler, Prester John. The story of the "rich man," better known as "the old man of the mountain," is to be found not only in Mandeville.[35] Odoricus and Marco Polo also tell it. This old man (they tell us) enclosed a mountain and, says Odoricus, "he put there the most beautiful maidens he could find, as well as everything that could bring pleasure to the human body; this place they call paradise."[36] Vigorous young men are obvious applicants to such a paradise. The old man welcomes them, allows them to taste all the delights of the place, then casts them into a sleep and has them carried out of the place. When they wake, he has them summoned and tells them that they may return "to paradise" only on condition that they kill this or that person. In this way, the fearsome old man always has killers, "assassins," at his service.

Marco Polo tells the same story about the leader of the "assassins" (a romanticized allusion to a sect that was wiped out by a Mongol khan in 1256). To a greater extent than Odoricus, he revels in describing the old man's gar-

den, its four rivers (of wine, milk, honey, and water), and its gilded palaces.[37]
"There were fair ladies there and damsels, the loveliest in the world, unri-
valled at playing every sort of instrument and at singing and dancing. . . . And
the ladies and damsels stayed with [the young men] all the time, singing and
making music for their delight and ministering to all their desires."[38]

This false paradise of "the old man of the mountain" anticipates Hieronymus Bosch's booby-trapped *Garden of Earthly Delights.*

Let me repeat: the theme of the garden has been at the very heart of
dreams of paradise, first in the Middle East and then in the West. The
reason is that paradise was first imagined in lands in which water was rare
and the countryside easily turned into desert. The Arabs and Persians had a
real passion for gardens; this shows in *The Thousand and One Nights,* which
sometimes describes real gardens filled with fruit-laden trees and traversed
by streams of sweet, clear water,[39] and sometimes gardens out of fable. Thus
when Aladdin on one occasion descends a terrace, he finds trees he had never
seen before: some white like crystal, others red like rubies or green like emeralds or blue like turquoises or violet like amethysts.[40] To those who fear God
the Qur'an promises, in the next world, "gardens and vineyards" with "clusters of fruits within reach," "pleasant mansions" in Edenic "gardens watered
by running streams." "They shall recline on couches raised high in the shade
of thornless sidrahs and clusters of talh; amidst gushing waters and abundant
fruits."[41]

The liking for the marvelous and the attraction to dream gardens made
Western travelers and chroniclers believe that there existed, far away, places
where nature retained some of its original luxuriance. Jordan of Séverac, who
wrote around 1323, gives an almost Edenic description of Ceylon.[42] Mandeville delights in describing the gardens of Egypt that bear fruit "eight
times a year" and produce delicious "(long) apples" that people call "apples
of paradise."[43]

In distant lands — an "elsewhere" for westerners — everything is possible, and the wonder felt by travelers causes them to embellish even further
the astonishing realities they encounter or of which they hear tell. According
to Marco Polo, Madagascar is incredibly rich: ivory, sandalwood, ambergris,
gold, and silken fabrics are abundant there, and the fauna is extremely varied.[44] Marco Polo did not visit Madagascar, but he was received in the palace
of the Great Khan, which seemed to him to be something out of fairyland:

> Inside, the walls of the halls and chambers are all covered with gold and silver
> and decorated with pictures of dragons and birds and horsemen and various
> breeds of beasts and scenes of battle. . . . The number of chambers is quite
> bewildering. . . . The roof is all ablaze with scarlet and green and blue and

yellow and all the colours that are, so brilliantly varnished that it glitters like crystal and the sparkle of it can be seen from far away.[45]

Claude Kappler, who cites this passage,[46] rightly compares it with the description of the wonderful place in which Badoure, princess of China, lives according to *The Thousand and One Nights*: "The first palace is made of rock crystal, . . . the sixth of silver, and the seventh of massy gold; all are furnished with unparalleled magnificence."[47]

But the distant place may also be a realm containing much that is disturbing and even monstrous, with the best and the worst rubbing elbows in these regions where everything is carried to excess. According to Mandeville, "Beyond these isles I have told you of, beyond the deserts in the empire of Prester John, going still east, there is . . . a dark land, where no man can see by night or day, as we were told. That dark land and those deserts last right to the Earthly Paradise."[48]

In addition to the fairy islands that, as we have seen, are more or less under the control of Prester John, there is an extraordinary land in which is located the "Vale Perilous," four miles long and "full of devils, . . . and men of those parts say it is an entrance to Hell." There is indeed an abundance of gold and silver in this "Vale of Enchantment," but there is also and before all else the living "head and face of a devil, very hideous and dreadful to see. . . . He looks at each man so keenly and so cruelly, and his eyes are rolling so fast and sparkling like fire, and he changes his expression so often, and out of his nose and mouth come so much fire of different colours with such an awful stench, that no man can bear it."

Before Mandeville and his companions enter this gorge (we know, of course, that this is an imaginary journey), they make their confessions to some Friars Minor among them and receive communion — a viaticum very necessary amid this darkness in which they are "often struck to the earth."

> And there was a great a multitude of beasts . . . which ran between our legs and caused us to fall. . . . And we were knocked down by thunderbolts, by lightning and strong winds, to the point that it was like being struck in the back by an iron rod. . . . And we found so many dead persons beneath our feet, who complained that we were walking on them; it was a very terrible thing to hear. And I am certain that if we had not received *Corpus Domini*, we would all have remained and been destroyed in this valley.

As a result of beatings and falls, Mandeville and his companions "swoon as though dead, and in this swoon we saw many wonders of which I dare not speak."[49]

Mandeville likes to fantasize, but Odoricus, too, crossed a valley that was like hell, although he does not use this word. It was a music-filled wilderness in which the sound of instruments soon turned into a racket produced by "invisible enemies." He was warned that, according to the people of the country, "a person may enter there but can never come out."[50] He goes in despite the warning and, like Mandeville, finds a multitude of corpses and "a very horrible and hideous human face on a rock in a fissure of the mountain. It was so terrible that I almost died of fear, and I spoke these words: 'The Word was made flesh.'"[51] Finally, Odoricus finds in this wilderness "a great deal of silver," but he avoids yielding to the temptation that it represents: "I took some of it on my lap but I removed none of it, and I left the place."

A story with elements of initiation in it (at that time an almost obligatory passage in accounts of distant voyages) is here combined with real experiences. Thus when Marco Polo crosses the Desert of Lop, although otherwise quite realistic in the details he gives about the area, he nonetheless witnesses a wonder: voices call individuals by their names and draw them into places in which they perish. Even during the day one may hear "the strains of many instruments, especially drums."[52] Other travelers likewise mention a desert full of sound in central Asia. But the experience is coupled with interpretations that reflect the surprises westerners met in these countries that were so different from the landscapes familiar to them.

In an Asia that is partly mythical and located close to the earthly paradise and the kingdom of Prester John, everything is possible: the extraordinary becomes real, and the best rubs elbows with the worst. For westerners, India is the land of the unusual. Pygmies do battle there with cranes, and giants with gryphons. There are dog-headed men who growl and bark; others have no heads but do have eyes in their bellies; still others protect themselves against the sun by lying on their backs and holding up their single large foot as a cover.[53] According to Mandeville, in Taprobane (which here refers to Ceylon) there are "great hills of gold, which ants busily look after, purifying the gold and separating the fine from the unfine."[54] Under the pen of Pierre d'Ailly the ants become gryphons and dragons.[55] A fifteenth-century work entitled *Secret de l'histoire naturelle* tells us that in Traponée (Taprobane) "grow the largest snails in the world. . . . And the people of the country live on the flesh of these snails. The men and women of the country lodge in the snails' shells, so large are these, and have no other dwellings."[56]

We will, therefore, not be surprised to find the accursed peoples of Gog and Magog living in a remote corner of Asia, this always fascinating and disturbing continent. Even before cartographers introduced the kingdom of Prester John, these peoples had a place in the *Descriptio mappe mundi* of Hugh of St. Victor (first half of the twelfth century), a work that has been called "the first geographical treatise of the Middle Ages."[57] The island of these peoples is located in northern Asia, opposite "the region of the Amazons."[58] Later on, these peoples become almost inseparable from the kingdom of Prester John, and their country — whether on an island or on the mainland — is a kind of photographic negative of Prester John's. Generally speaking, the geography of Asia as habitually understood by westerners from the twelfth to the fourteenth centuries located the Islamic world beyond Christendom, and beyond Islam in turn, but in a highly confused jumble, the country of the Amazons, the land of God and Magog, the kingdom of Prester John, and, finally, very far away and on a high mountain, the earthly paradise.

The "wicked" peoples of Gog and Magog, whose spread at the end of time is predicted in the Apocalypse (20:7), were thought of as having been imprisoned by God, at the request or by the action of Alexander, behind a mountain barrier. They were often identified with the ten tribes of Israel, which were punished in this way for having worshiped the golden calf.[59] The idea was rather widespread in the Middle Ages that Prester John now acted as a warder who prevented the peoples of Gog and Magog from leaving the land in which they were imprisoned. On Sanudo's map (ca. 1320) the peninsula on which the "Tartars" are imprisoned is located behind a high wall, on which sits "the castle of Gog and Magog," and in the immediate neighborhood of *India inferior presbiteri Johannis* (lower India of Prester John) (Map 12).[60] Andrea Bianco's world-map mentions Gog and Magog and Mount Alexander (Maps 10 and Map 13). A Genoese world-map of 1447 adorns the mountain chain from which the Ganges flows with a number of towers and says that Prester John built them so as to close the natural barrier behind which these accursed peoples are penned.[61]

The oldest known localization of the peoples of Gog and Magog places them beyond the Caspian Gates or Gates of Alexander. Thus Jacques de Vitry locates in Georgia the *Montes Caspii* "where the ten imprisoned tribes await the coming of the Antichrist."[62] But the Muslims, who likewise believed in the existence of the peoples of Gog and Magog, tended to locate these unclean peoples far off in the East. It was perhaps due to Muslim influence that westerners did the same. Vincent of Beauvais, who reflects the panic that came over the West at the time of the Mongol invasion of 1241, explains as follows the various names of the "Cham" (the Khan) (he is citing Simon of Saint-Quentin):

> His names *Kyne* and *Gog* mean the same thing in their language; *Gog* is his own name and *Magog* that of his brother. For the Lord through his prophet Ezekiel [chaps. 38–39] predicts the coming of Gog and Magog [in Ezekiel = the king of the Scythians] and threatens us with ruin and destruction at their hands. The Tartars also have a name of their own for themselves: *Mongles* or *Mongols*. The mind of this *Gog Cham* is wholly on fire with de-

sire for the destruction of human beings; he is like a fiery furnace, ready to consume.[63]

Here we see "Tatar" becoming "Tartar" (association with Tartarus or hell) and "Mongol" becoming "Magog." The people who await the Antichrist do indeed live in the Far East.

From Asia to Africa

Many world-maps at the end of the Middle Ages still place the kingdom of Prester John in Asia: in particular, the map of Sanudo (Map 12), the Genoese map of 1447, and the famous globe that Martin Behaim constructed in 1492. Works of popularization such as the *Rudimentum novitiorum*, published at Lübeck in 1475, and the *Mer des hystoires*, published at Lyons in 1491, show the same placement. The same legendary tradition is followed in a Castilian narrative that Gómez de Santisteban composed at the beginning of the sixteenth century and that describes the journeys of Prince Dom Pedro of Portugal, brother of Henry the Navigator, "to the seven parts of the world."[64]

Dom Pedro and his companions have crossed "the river Pishon which comes out of the earthly paradise"; they have paid their respects to "Mourad the Great in the city of Cappadocia," visited the lands where the giants live, made their way into the Indies, and finally reached Alves, the capital city of Prester John. This is "the best and noblest city in the world." It has nine hundred thousand inhabitants. Not only is it girded by ramparts but it also has, within this fortified circle, some six hundred inner ramparts and as many streets, so that one cannot pass in open air from one street to another. On the other hand, there are numerous underground passages. The system was conceived as a way of rendering ineffective any siege by the "Moors."

One enters the presence of Prester John only after having paid one's respects to thirteen guardians; twelve of these are like bishops and the thirteenth like an archbishop. At table the king is accompanied by fourteen kings and served by seven others. The royal dining room is richly appointed. The walls are blue, and the ceiling is made of gold tiles. The floor is made entirely of precious stones, and the table top wholly of diamonds. Four urns are always placed before the king while he eats: one contains a skull, the second some earth ("Remember that you are dust"), the third some glowing embers (Watch out for hell!), and the fourth some fruits, brought from the region between the Tigris and the Euphrates, which, no matter how they are cut open, display within them the image of the crucifix.

In the kingdom of Prester John priests have wives and children, but when they are widowed they may not marry again, and the same rule holds for widows of priests. These priests begin the Mass with the Ite Missa Est and end it with the Confiteor. They oblige the faithful to make confession every two weeks. The clergy here are closely dependent on the sovereign, since their only benefice consists of occasional offerings. In addition, they cannot have any animal for riding or pasturing, nor can they wear anything of gold, silver, copper, or iron.

The body of St. Thomas rests in the city of Alves, which is also named Edicia. The arm and hand that the apostle thrust into the Lord's side remain as incorrupt as if they were still alive. On the eve of the saint's feast, a vine shoot cut long before is placed in this hand; there it produces tendrils and grapes from which is pressed the wine for the king's Mass; Prester John celebrates the holy sacrifice only three times a year: the feasts of St. Thomas, Corpus Christi, and August 15.

The account of Dom Pedro's journeys also tells us that before reaching the capital of Prester John the prince and his companions had discovered in the mountains of India "an unnatural race" of people, the "Ponces." These are "the most Catholic Christians in the world." They have only one leg, which they never bend, and only one foot, and their genitals are in the middle of their body. Their foot, which is like a horse's, is two hands wide and two hands long.

Before returning to the West, Dom Pedro and his companions wanted to travel in the direction of the earthly paradise. The king therefore provided them with guides and dromedaries. For seventeen days they crossed a desert in which there was no road to show them the way. Finally they came within sight of mountains. Prester John's people advised them to go no farther. They then made their way

> toward the Tigris, the Euphrates, the Gihon, and the Pishon, which are the
> four rivers that flow out of the earthly paradise. Branches of olive and cypress
> float on the Euphrates, branches of palms and myrrh on the Euphrates, a tree
> known as the aloe on the Gihon, and parrots in their nests on the Pishon.
> The whole world receives water from these rivers, since from them all others
> are formed.

After this expedition Dom Pedro and his companions returned to Prester John and stayed with him another thirty days; they then asked permission to depart. The ruler gave them nine thousand gold pieces and a letter "for the peoples of the West."[65]

Here, then, is an Asiatic version of the Prester John legend from the beginning of the sixteenth century, in this case one spiced with some mistrust of the Latin clergy, since the clergy of the Christian kingdom in India were not bound to celibacy and were not wealthy. The usual elements of the legend are to be seen in this account of an imaginary journey: the strangeness of the human beings and things, fabulous wealth accompanied by austere morals, the tomb of St. Thomas in the capital city of the priest–king, unusual neighboring races, closeness and inaccessibility of the garden of Eden, whose reality, however, is shown by the rivers that flow out of it, one of these carrying the nests of parrots, that is, those paradisal birds that are capable of speech and have fascinating colors. If I have emphasized this document, it is because the work composed by Gómez de Santisteban went through no less than 111 printings from the time of its publication at the beginning of the sixteenth century; 55 of these were in Spanish.

At the end of the Middle Ages, however, and in the sixteenth century, the land of the legendary Christian king was most often placed in Africa; this was the original localization that had never been completely rejected and that came back into favor under the influence of several factors. On the one hand, we may recall that the geography of the day often assigned to Africa a "third India," comprising Abyssinia and Ethiopia, these two being sometimes separated, sometimes identified. On the other, since the impulse behind the crusades had exhausted itself beginning in the fourteenth century, the Muslim rulers of Egypt were no longer as fearful of an alliance between the Christians of the West and those of Africa; they therefore allowed Catholic embassies to travel to Abyssinia and Nubia.[66]

The *Mirabilia* of Jordan of Séverac, which was composed around 1323, says that the inhabitants of the "third India" speak of "the emperor of Ethiopia, whom you call Prester John."[67] An Irish Franciscan who visited Egypt in 1328 states that after having sailed up the Nile for seventy days he reached "Upper India, where Prester John resides."[68] In the following year, Pope John XXII wrote to the ruler of Abyssinia, while a bishop was installed — briefly — in Dongola, the capital of Nubia. Giovanni Marignolli, a papal envoy to the East (from 1338 to 1353), maintained, after his return, that the "Guyon" surrounds the territory of Ethiopia, "in which the people are black and which is called the land of Prester John."[69] Around 1350, the *Libro del conoscimiento de todos los regnos*, written by an anonymous Spanish Franciscan, makes Prester John "the patriarch of Nubia and Ethiopia." In the fifteenth century, a number of Abyssinian embassies came to the West and especially to Venice, Rome, and the court of the kings of Aragon.

Logically enough, cartography reflected this African placement of the kingdom of Prester John, but the mapmakers displayed varying degrees of imagination. The famous atlas that Charles V of France commissioned in 1375–78 from Catalan cosmographers, who were the most renowned of the time, indicates on one of its six parchment maps "the Christians of Nubia, who are under the rule of the emperor of Ethiopia, the country of Prester John."[70] The world-map of the Venetian Andrea Bianco (1430) locates "the empire of Prester John" at the eastern end of an Africa that is dispropor- tionately extended in that direction so that it is parallel there with "Middle Asia" and "Upper Asia," but separated from them by a lengthy gulf that is strewn with islands (Map 13). The world-map of another Venetian, Fra Mauro (1459), allots a large area of Africa to the kingdom of Prester John, which it locates in Abyssinia (Map 14).[71] Captions on this map inform us that this ruler "has over one hundred and twenty kingdoms" and that "his power is very great." The proof of this power is that when he sets out for war, "He has with him a million men who go naked into battle, except that many of them wear crocodile skins."[72]

On an *orbis terrarum* of 1452, which is engraved on enamelled metal and is in the Vatican Museum, the South is at the top of the map and the North at the bottom, after the Arabic manner; this map places, "south of the deserts of Egypt, a Christian Nubia which is the domain of Prester John," whose empire extends as far as "the Straits of Cadiz [= Gibraltar] and the river of gold [= the Senegal or the Niger]" (Map 15).[73]

Finally (in a list that is not exhaustive), the world-map drawn in 1500 by Juan de la Cosa, a Biscayan pilot who had accompanied Christopher Colum- bus on his second voyage (1493–96), likewise places the realm of Prester John in Africa, bordering it with Egypt on the north, Ethiopia on the west and south, and the Nile on the east.[74] Noteworthy about this map is the con- trast between the remarkably accurate depiction of the African coasts in the north and the west (mapmakers were now taking into account the reports from Portuguese voyages down the west coast) and the inevitably fantastic character of the names assigned to the interior of the continent. Ethiopia, for example, extends westward far out of proportion, while "Babylonia" is lo- cated between the Nile and the Red Sea. Thus Prester John, who appears on this map wearing a miter, still reigns over a semimythical country (Map 16).

Gradually, however, relations were established between the Latins and the Christian kingdom in Africa. A number of Italian missions went there dur- ing the fifteenth century; in 1482 a Franciscan delegation was received by the Negus. In the opposite direction, Ethiopians belonging to a monastery in Jerusalem took part in the Council of Florence in 1441 and provided infor- mation about their country that Fra Mauro used in his world-map of 1459. The Portuguese in particular made many attempts to contact Prester John, whose realm was increasingly located in Africa by Iberian political circles and those on whom they relied for information.[75]

A recent hypothesis seeks to establish a connection between, on the one

Kingdom of Prester John

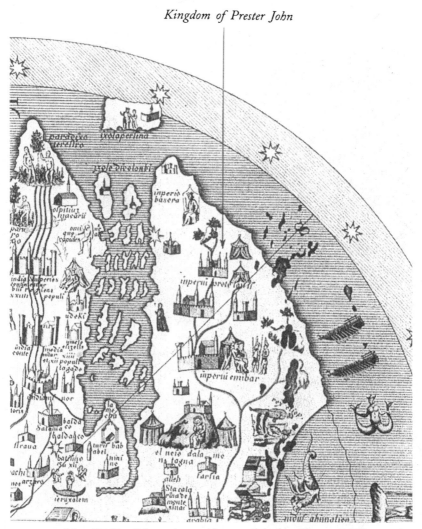

Map 13. Detail from the world-map of Andrea Bianco (1436)

hand, the interest that Henry the Navigator, prince of Portugal, took in Ethiopia and, on the other, the occasional conflation of the legend of Prester John with the Grail theme from the poem by Chrétien de Troyes. In some adaptations of this novel Prester John becomes the nephew of Parsifal and is entrusted, together with the Templars, with the protection of the Grail. After the trial of the Templars (1285–1314) the order survived in Portugal under the name of "the Order of Christ," of which Henry the Navigator was

Kingdom of Prester John

Map 14. Detail from the world-map of Fra Mauro

the commanding officer. The discovery of the realm of Prester John would have enabled the prince to reestablish contact with the eternal temple. I felt obliged to mention here, without taking sides, this hypothesis that Jacqueline Pirenne accepts in her recent book on Prester John.

In 1487 Lisbon sent two travelers to Africa on a mission to establish contact, at any cost, with Prester John. One of these travelers, Covilhan, actually reached the kingdom of the Negus in 1493, but was not permitted to leave. In the years 1520–27 a Portuguese embassy came to Abyssinia; the story of their mission was told by Francisco Álvarez, the priest who accompanied the group. His book, *Ho Preste Joan das Indias* (1540), gives a good description of the land of the Negus (despite the word *Indias,* which may cause confusion).[76] In 1535 some Muslims from Harar invaded Abyssinia, and the ruler of the latter asked Portugal for help. Because communications between the two countries were so slow, Portuguese military aid (in the form of 450 soldiers) did not become operational until 1542; these soldiers did, however, though not without effort, manage to save Prester John, but the latter's kingdom was henceforth in large measure demythologized.

Not entirely, however. The work of a Dominican, Luis de Urreta, *Historia . . . de la Etiopia, monarchia del emperador llamado Preste Juan de la Indias* (Valencia, 1610), still describes Mount Amara as a paradisal place that had

Kingdom of Prester John

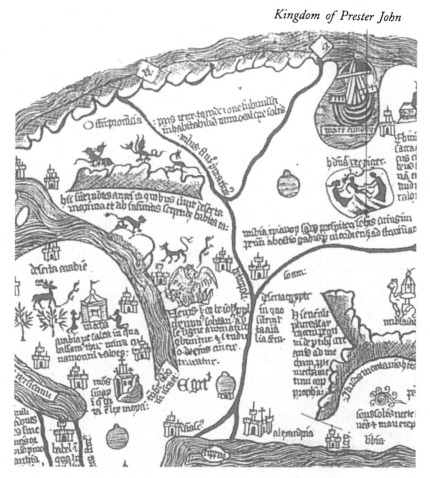

Map 15. The kingdom of Prester John on a world-map of 1452

become the impregnable fortress of Prester John.[77] In fact, he tells his readers, in Ethiopic "Amara" means "paradise."

Despite the long survival of a cloud of dreams around the person of Prester John, at the beginning of the modern age the latter's kingdom gradually lost its fairy character and its fantastic localizations. Indicative in this regard is the very sober Latin commentary on it in one section of Gerard Mercator's *Atlas* (first edition, 1569). We are told there that a Nestorian priest had carved out an empire for himself in the East, beginning at the end of the eleventh century; the priest was known as Prester John. At his death, his brother succeeded him and took the same title, but he was soon

Map 16. The kingdom of Prester John on the world-map of Juan de la Cosa

overthrown in a revolt of his Mongol or Tartar subjects, in 1187. From that time on the reigning Prester John paid tribute to the Mongols. "Such are the facts about Prester John who is believed, down to the present time, to be reigning in Asia. He is a completely different person from the one in Africa who even today is called Prester Giam."[78]

Chapter 5

Other Dreamlands

Paradisal Islands

The scientific caution of Mercator is characteristic of an age (the sixteenth century) that as a result of the voyages of exploration was forced to set aside a geography that revolved around a belief in the continued existence of the earthly paradise. But the abandonment was not easy, since it ran contrary to a profound tendency of the human soul, which tries and will always try to set its heart on the impossible.

In this context, the lengthy medieval period gives us an exemplary instance of a dialectic that maintains, on the one hand, the existence of the garden of Eden on our earth, even though this garden has become inaccessible, and, on the other, the existence of blessed lands, accessible to the bold, that preserve desirable remnants of the lost paradise. Thus Giovanni Marignolli, a Florentine religious who traveled the East from 1338 to 1353, passed through Ceylon, where he discovered an "Adam's Peak": this, he said, was so close to the earthly paradise that from its top one could see paradise were it not for the cloud cover that hides it from view. One morning, however, just before sunrise, he was granted a momentary glimpse of it. It was as bright as a flame of fire. The natives told him, moreover, that it was possible at times to hear the noise made by the waters of Eden before they divided into the four rivers.[1]

The earthly paradise is thus beyond reach, although in Ceylon one is close to it. Ceylon itself is described as an Edenic country by the first Western travelers who visited it. Jordan of Séverac, who wrote his *Mirabilia* around 1323, found there birds of every color. Some "are entirely as white as snow, others as red as scarlet cloth, others as green as grass; still others have colors so variegated and beautiful that they are beyond description. There are parrots of every color except black.... In truth, these birds seem to be creatures out of paradise." In Jordan's eyes Ceylon is an extraordinary world of its own. It contains, for example, a pond with miraculous properties: any metal dipped into it is transformed into gold. In the midst of the pond stands a tree: when a leaf from this tree is rubbed on a wound, the wound heals quickly. In Ceylon the flora and fauna are larger than elsewhere: there are winged cats and leaves large enough to shelter five men.[2]

Dante too gave the earthly paradise the characteristics of an island, and in many medieval travel stories, especially Mandeville's, the kingdom of Prester John is located on an island. According to Mandeville, mysterious India is "divided into isles on account of the great rivers which flow out of Paradise."[3]

Claude Kappler offers this well-founded comment: "If there are any places that have a special appeal for the imagination, it is islands." Unlike a continent, which represents a closed universe, an island "is by its nature a place where marvels exist for their own sake outside the laws that generally prevail. . . . Ever since Greek antiquity, islands have been favorite places for the most astounding human and divine adventures." It is not surprising, then, that "medieval travelers were led to make use of this mythology once again when they came upon the many islands of the Indian ocean."[4] Celtic legends likewise had a great attachment to strange islands.

Mandeville is an outstanding example of this tendency to connect island and mystery. "It is very likely," says Kappler, "that if Mandeville had to draw a world-map, the continents would have occupied a small place in the midst of seas strewn with islands. Once Mandeville reaches the East, each chapter describes an island and contains episodes which in turn describe still other islands."[5] Distance lends enchantment, and isolation preserves things in existence. Later on, many "utopias," among them that of Thomas More, would be located on islands.

In this respect the earliest medieval cartography reflects the travel stories: the sea that encircles the inhabited world is full of islands, which are synonymous with the unknown and mysterious. In later atlases and world-maps islands are still plentiful. Relying on a legend, the Catalan map that was drawn for Charles V in 1375–78 says that "in the sea of the Indies there are 7548 islands, the marvelous riches of which, including gold and silver as well as spices and precious stones, we cannot list in detail here." In fact, the map indicates only four of these islands: Ceylon, the *insula nudorum*, Caynam, and Trapabona (which in this case is Sumatra). Regarding this last, the map says: "There are two summers and two winters annually. The trees and grass have two growth cycles each year. . . . The island has an abundance of gold, silver, and precious stones."[6] Martin Behaim's globe, which was made just before the voyages of Christopher Columbus, makes the Atlantic and Pacific one ocean, as was usual at the time. The globe populates this ocean with numerous islands along the edge of Asia; the largest of these is the Cipangu of Marco Polo, later known as Japan.

Among the fairy islands of the medieval imagination the Happy Isles and Saint Brendan's Island call for special mention. As we saw earlier, the Happy Isles stand in a Greco-Roman poetic tradition that is based on passages in Homer, Hesiod, and Plutarch.[7] According to this tradition, beyond the towering Atlas there lie islands with enchanted gardens, a constant temperate climate, and fragrant breezes, where human beings have no need to work. In the Christian era Isidore of Seville gave this belief a new popularity by assigning it a place in his geography, which then exerted a lasting influence on Western culture. Isidore certainly did not want these blessed islands to be confused with the earthly paradise, which he claimed still existed in the East. But once he had made this distinction, he plainly asserted the reality of the islands:

> The name "Happy Isles" means that they produce all sorts of good things; that they enjoy a quasi-blessedness and have the advantage of happy abundance. By their very nature they give birth to precious trees and fruits. The slopes of the hills are naturally covered with vines. Instead of grass the soil for the most part yields crops and vegetables. This explains the error of pagans and the songs of secular poets who, because the land is so fruitful, believed that these islands were paradise. In fact, they are located in the ocean, left of Mauretania, close to the setting sun, and separated from each other by the sea.[8]

Isidore's description was repeated from century to century, by, among others, Gervase of Tilbury (thirteenth century) in his *Otia imperialia*,[9] Bartholomew the Englishman (fourteenth century) in his *De proprietatibus rerum*,[10] and Pierre d'Ailly in his *Ymago mundi*, in which we read:

> The name "Happy Isles" means that these islands contain all good things. It is the fruitfulness of the soil that makes people believe that paradise was located in these islands....
> All these islands are full of birds and wooded with palmtrees, walnut trees, and pines. There is honey in abundance there. The forests are full of animals, and the waters abound in fish.
> These islands are located in the ocean to the left of Mauretania, between midday and sunset, close to the West. They are separated from each other by the sea.[11]

A further success: the Happy Isles of Isidore of Seville were identified with the island of Avalon of Celtic literature. In his *Historia regum Britanniae*, which is the source of the Arthurian legends, Welsh bishop Geoffrey of Monmouth (d. 1154) tells his readers that at the end of his life Arthur was taken to the island of Avalon so that his wounds might be healed.[12] Then, in his *Vita Merlini*, Geoffrey describes the *insula pomorum que fortunata vocatur* (the island of apples that is called the happy island), while borrowing from Isidore and his continuators the details that describe the

Happy Isles.[13] *Insula pomorum* became another name for Avalon, the "island of apples" of Celtic literature, which Geoffrey thus assimilated to the Happy Isles of Christianized Greco-Roman tradition.[14]

Maps in turn made room for the Happy Isles. A world-map of the twelfth century that accompanies a copy of the commentary on the Apocalypse dedicated to Eutherus[15] mentions "Happy Isles" that are located in the West, in the ocean that surrounds the earth (Map 17). The *Descriptio mappe mundi* of Hugh of St. Victor (first half of twelfth century), which in the classical manner has the earth surrounded by an ocean, locates six "Happy Isles" in the open sea off Mount "Atlas," that is, west of North Africa.[16] The Heresford world-map (ca. 1230)[17] and the family of maps based on Higden's *Polychronicon* (ca. 1360) likewise have Happy Isles. A note by Higden says: "The Happy Isles are like a paradise; the trees are 140 feet high," and he refers to chapter 14 of Isidore's *Etymologies* (Map 18).[18] The large map that two Venetians, Francesco and Domenico Pizzigani, drew around 1362–67 mentions *Ysole dicte Fortunate*, located, wide apart, west of Morocco and above the *Isola Canaria*.[19]

It is, however, in the Catalan atlas commissioned by Charles V that the annotation on the Happy Isles is most extensive (it cites Isidore's *Etymologies* at length and expands upon them). A caption written west of a string of islands, among them the *Insula de Canaria* and the *Insula de Lanserano* (= Tenerife), has this to say:

> The Happy Isles are located on the broad sea to the left that abuts the edge of the West, but the islands are not far out at sea. Isidore has this to say in his Book XV [= this should be Book XIV]: the islands are called "Happy" because they abound in all good things: grain, fruits, and trees. Pagans think that paradise is located there because of the sun's pleasant warmth and the fertility of the soil. Isidore also says that the trees grow to a height of at least 140 feet and yield many fruits. On these islands are milk and honey, especially on the Island of Capria, so named because of the many goats that live there. The Island of Canaria takes its name from the many large, strong dogs that live on it. Pliny, an expert in geography, says that among the Happy Isles there is one that produces all crops and all fruits without any need to sow or plant. On the mountain tops are trees that emit a strong fragrance and are always covered with leaves and fruits. The inhabitants of the Isles eat of these fruits for part of the year; they then reap the harvest. The pagans of India likewise think that after death their souls will dwell on these islands and will continue to live forever on the fragrance of these fruits. They believe that their paradise is located there. In truth, however, this is but a fable.[20]

Thus one of the most detailed maps from the end of the Middle Ages still teaches, on the authority of Isidore of Seville, that there exist in the West paradisal islands "that abound in all good things." These islands combine

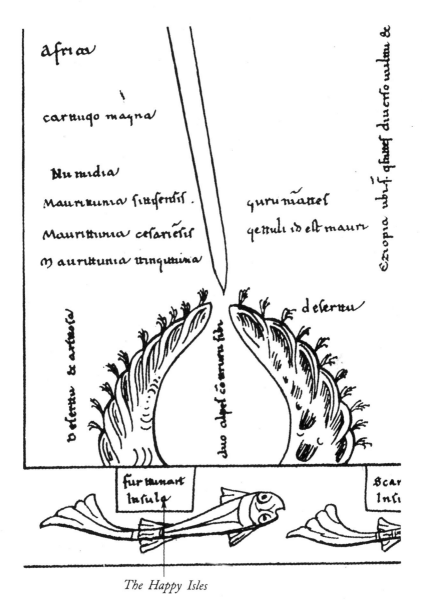

The Happy Isles

Map 17. The Happy Isles on the world-map accompanying the commentary
on the Apocalypse dedicated to Eutherus, bishop of Osma

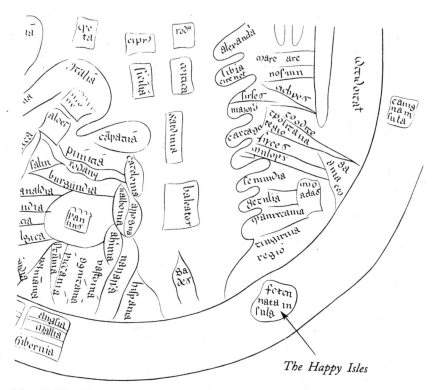

The Happy Isles

Map 18. The Happy Isles, detail from a map in the *Polychronicon* of Ranulf Higden

most of the elements that make for an earthly paradise: pleasant warmth, perpetual spring, delicious and fragrant fruits.

Starting in the next century Europeans became familiar with the Atlantic archipelagoes off the coasts of Spain and Morocco. The Portuguese settled on Madeira between 1418 and 1430, on the Azores (previously explored by the Italians in the fourteenth century) between 1432 and 1457. As for the Canaries, which had perhaps been known to the Carthaginians but which for centuries were legendary islands and were confused (as we saw a moment ago) with the Happy Isles, they were visited in 1402 by John of Béthencourt; colonists settled there three years later as lieges of Castile. The real world was gradually taking clearer shape.

But the dream of a paradisal island or archipelago died hard. It found expression in the Middle Ages and even later either in other localizations or under other names. The Catalan map, which as we saw has a great deal to say about the Happy Isles, has another section in which the following is said of Ireland:

The Happy Isles

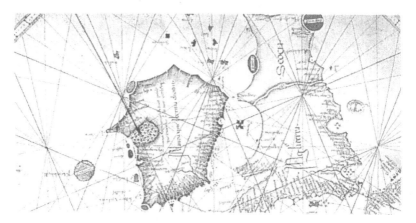

Map 19. The 367 "Blessed Islands" on the map of Grazioso Benincasa

In Ireland there are many islands which we may well think places of wonder. Among them there is a small one on which human beings never die; when they are old enough to die, they are carried away from the island. On this island there is no snake or frog or poisonous spider; the soil there will not suffer any poisonous animal. On this island is a lake with its own island. In addition, there are trees that yield birds as other trees yield fruits. In Ireland there is also another island on which women never give birth; when their time comes, custom requires that they be carried off the island.[21]

Almost a hundred years later, Grazioso Benincasa of Ancona, on his map of 1467, shows a gulf on the western side of Ireland and fills it with 367 islands; a caption reads: "Lacus fortunatus, ubi sunt insule que dicuntur insule sancte beate CCCLXVII" (The Happy Waters on which are 367 islands known as "The Holy, Blessed Islands"). Here the location of the Happy Isles has been shifted to northern Europe (Map 19).[22]

This localization is certainly to be linked to the success of the story of St. Brendan's voyage. This bishop, who was abbot of Clonfert, Ireland, and died at the end of the sixth century, established monasteries in England and undertook a journey into Scotland that became the stuff of legend. The legend found expression in the *Navigatio sancti Brendani*, one of the most famous medieval novels of adventure. St. Brendan's voyage thus became as well known as the vision of Tnugdal or the legendary travels of Mandeville. The story has to do with the voyage of the saint and his companions among islands known respectively as "Plain of Pleasure," "Land of Happiness," and "Land of the Blessed." In an Anglo-Norman version of the poem that can be dated to around 1200, this last-named island is described according to the model created by Isidore: it is a blessed land whose inhabitants enjoy all kinds of bliss and experience neither hunger nor thirst, neither cold nor heat, neither sickness nor suffering.[23] There are at least eighty different versions of the *Navigatio sancti Brendani;* the story was evidently widely known and read.[24]

Cartographers of course made room for the islands of St. Brendan, but in most instances they transfer this paradise of northern origin to a more southerly location. Thus the Hereford world-map, which links the Happy Isles and the islands of St. Brendan, has an archipelago off Africa, with the notation *Fortunatae Insulae sex sunt, insule Brendani* (The Happy Isles are six in number, the islands of Brendan).[25] The beautiful map of the Pizzigani brothers adopts the same outlook when it inserts a black, diamond-shaped island north of the *Insula Canaria* and adds the somewhat mysterious caption: *Ysole dicte Fortunate* (the islands called happy) and, just beneath it, another: *Sey isole ponzelle (= ?) Brandani* (the six [*ponzelle* = ?] islands of Brendan). A representation of St. Brendan provides confirmation that these six islands are close to the Happy Isles or, rather, are confused with them (Map 20). Martin Behaim's globe, which is kept at Nuremberg and measures 50.7 cm (19.8 in.) in diameter (it has been described as "a major monument in the history of the discovery of the world"), likewise does not fail to make a place for St. Brendan's islands, which are here placed near the equator and halfway between the Cape Verde Islands and Cipangu (the future Japan). In the sixteenth century St. Brendan's islands will have a place in a number of atlases, and the name may still be seen in 1587 on a map of the great Dutch traveler Jan van Linschoten.[26] Between 1526 and 1721 four naval expeditions left the Canaries in search of the "Promised Land" that St. Brendan and his companions supposedly reached.[27]

In addition, a connection was sometimes made between St. Brendan's island and another mythical place, the island of Brasil (Brazil) or Bracile or Bracir. Contrary to what was long thought, the word "Brazil" does not come from a plant that yielded a glowing red dye, but from a Dutch term, *Hy Bressail* or *O Brazil,* meaning "Happy Isle."[28] This accounts for the connection established on many maps, notably that of Grazioso Benincasa, between the island of Brasil and that of St. Brendan. Both had their roots in Celtic mythology. A nineteenth-century Irish poet, Gerald Griffin, would later speak of the island of O Brazil as the island of the blessed. In *Finnegan's Wake* (chap. 3) James Joyce would in his turn link the mythical island of Brazil with the islands of St. Brendan.

The island of Brazil appears for the first time on a Catalan map of 1325 or 1330.[29] Subsequently it is to be seen on, among others, the map of the

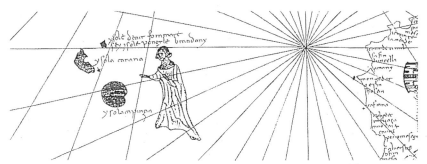

Map 20. St. Brendan in the Canary Islands, detail from the world-map
of the Pizzigani brothers (1362)

Pizzigani brothers, the great Catalan map of 1375–78, and the 1436 map of
Andrea Bianco, all of which locate the island west of Spain.

Beginning in the second half of the sixteenth century, O Brazil refers
increasingly to the land discovered by Pedro Álvars Cabral. But an atlas compiled before 1568 by Fernão Vaz Dourado, a Portuguese, shows "Hobrasili"
as the name of present-day Brazil and "Obrasill" as the name of a mysterious island located southwest of Ireland.[30] In the summer of 1486 two ships
had left Bristol "in order to find an island known as the 'Isle of Brasile.'"
They sailed with one of the best pilots of England to guide them. After two
months of fruitless searching they were drawn by currents toward the coasts
of Ireland.[31] Nonetheless, an island named "High Brazil Rocks" is still to be
seen on an English map drawn by Findlay in 1853.[32]

A connection was also made between the island of St. Brendan and the
legend of the "seven cities." This is the story of seven bishops who fled
Moor-dominated Spain and sailed boldly out into the Atlantic. They finally
came upon an island on which they built seven cities. Among the people in
Henry the Navigator's entourage so much credence was placed in this story
that one sea captain told the prince he had in fact discovered the island,[33]
which, like St. Brendan's islands and the island of Brazil, became a magnet
for curious explorers. In the sixteenth century the fabled island of the bishops was transformed into the land containing "the seven cities of Cibola," for
which Spanish military leaders and adventurers searched in vain from 1530
to 1540 in the interior of what would eventually become the United States.
They did at least discover the Grand Canyon (1540) and reached both the
prairies of Kansas by river and the coasts of Oregon by sea.[34]

The conquistadors believed that the land of the "seven cities of Cibola"
abounded in gold and other riches. Others who dreamed of an accessible
"Eldorado" sought confirmation in the Bible. The Bible did in fact tell them

Ophir   The Nile   Nubia of Prester
                                            John

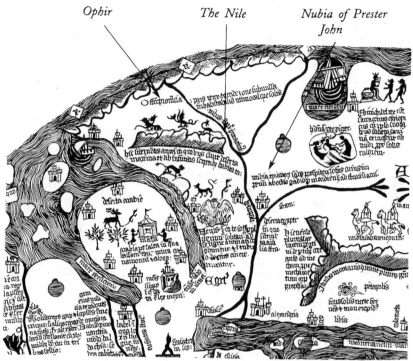

Map 21. "The Province of Ophir" on a world-map of 1452

that Solomon and the king of Tyre had gold, ivory, precious stones, and valuable woods brought from Ophir by way of the Red Sea. We should therefore not be surprised to find "Ophir" on medieval maps. One of these, which accompanies a twelfth-century manuscript of the works of St. Jerome, locates Ophir on the left bank of the Indus, just above the mouth of this river.[35] On the world-map that was etched in 1452 (formerly in the Borgia de Velletri Museum, now in the Vatican) and that has the South at the top, Ophir is placed in Africa, east of the Nile and the Nubia of Prester John (Map 21).[36] In the anonymous book sometimes known as the *Rudimentum novitiorum* (Lübeck, 1475), sometimes as the *Mer des hystoires* (Lyons, 1491), Ophir is represented as a fortified city in Arabia on the shores of the Red Sea (Map 22).[37] But when Christopher Columbus returned from his second voyage (to Cuba and Jamaica) and brought with him an Indian wearing a heavy gold chain, he told the pope that he had discovered Solomon's Ophir: "This island is the same as Tarshish or Cethioa or Ophir or Phaz or Cipangu, and we have named it Hispaniola."[38]

The belief in the existence of Ophir also explains the voyage of the Vene-

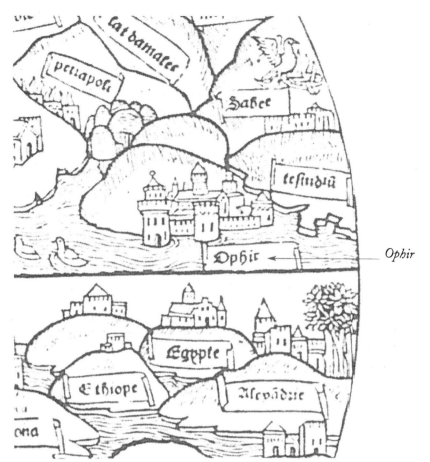

Map 22. "Ophir," detail from a map in the anonymous *Mer des hystoires*

tian Sebastian Cabot (Sebastiano Caboto) to the Americas in 1526. Cabot,
a pilot who transferred from the service of England to the service of Spain,
received from Charles V the mission of sailing westward and "discovering
the Moluccas, Tarshish, Ophir, Cipangu, and Cathay and, when he did, filling his ships with gold, silver, precious stones, pearls, medicines, spices, silks,
brocades, and other valuable items."[39] As chance would have it, the flagship
of the expedition ran on a rock off the coast of Brazil. Cabot then changed
plans and sailed up the Rio de la Plata, then the Parana, and finally the
Paraguay. There he heard of a land filled with silver, which turned out, some
years later, to be the Peru of the Incas.

But sixteenth-century Europeans tended to locate the American Eldorado more in the northern and eastern part of South America, in a kind of transposition to the new world of the kingdom of Prester John or, if you will, of a new Ophir that had not been attested in the Bible. The Spaniards, who began to travel up and down South America in the years from 1520 to 1530, heard of an Indian ritual that had long been practiced on the sacred lake of Guatavita, near Bogotá. On a particular day of the year a local king coated his body with turpentine and then rolled around in gold dust. Thus gilded and gleaming, he boarded a small boat and from it threw offerings of gold, emeralds, and precious materials into the center of the lake; he then bathed in the lake. On the shore the crowds cheered, sang, and danced.[40] Between 1531 and 1617 Europeans, beginning with Germans sent by the Welser bankers of Augsburg, searched most energetically for the country of "El Dorado," the gilded king, a country that, like that of Prester John, shifted with the passing years from one region to another, and specifically from present-day Colombia to as far as the Orinoco and Guyana.

The search for this land of gold is an interesting instance of the combination of two pipe dreams. In about 1539–49 a group of Tupi-Nambas emigrated from the Pernambuco region to the "Land of the Great Ancestor," the "Beloved Country," the "Land of Immortality and Everlasting Rest."[41] This trek to the earthly paradise led them to Peru, where they met Spaniards to whom they told wonderful tales of cities filled with gold. The result was the tragic 1560 expedition of Pedro de Ursúa and Lope de Aguirre (the former soon murdered by the latter), which deserves credit at least for providing better information about the routes to the mouth of the Orinoco.

After the failures of the Germans and then the Spaniards, which nonetheless did make it possible, at the cost of terrible ordeals, to discover and cross territories most difficult to reach, the Englishman Walter Raleigh tried in his turn to reach the land of "El Dorado" on three expeditions (1595, 1596, 1617) that ascended the Orinoco. Raleigh did not find his dreamland and was later executed in the Tower of London.

But the wealth of Ophir had reached Solomon through the ports of the Red Sea. Therefore, after making their way around Africa the Portuguese quite logically looked beyond the Red Sea for the country that had long ago sent its precious products to the king of Jerusalem. When they had established themselves in Sofala, they learned of a native ruler, the Monomotapa ("Lord of the Mines"), who reigned over a mysterious empire south of the Zambezi. The power and wealth of this Bantu monarch seemed to them comparable to those of Prester John and "El Dorado."[42] As in the latter two cases, there was an element of truth in the rumors that circulated about the Monomotapa. Arab traders had traveled to his country, although well after the time of Solomon, and had brought back ivory and gold via Sofala.

Furthermore, excavations carried out since 1871 have uncovered, between the Zambezi and Limpopo Rivers in what used to be Rhodesia, the imposing ruins of the "Great Zimbabwe," ruins that go back chiefly to the thirteenth and fourteenth centuries. But, like the kingdoms of Prester John and "El Dorado," once the kingdom of the Monomotapa was identified with the biblical Ophir, it too became a new land of legend.

In the years 1530–40 the Portuguese ascended the Zambezi and managed to establish a degree of trade, chiefly in ivory but also in gold, pearls, and spices, with the country of the Monomotapa. Then in 1560 a group of Jesuits went to the capital of the country. This was located on a hill named Faro, and the religious regarded Faro as a corruption of Ophir. The ruler initially welcomed the missionaries and received baptism. Later, however, he had the leader of the missionary band strangled, and he returned to the religion of his ancestors.

King Sebastian, ruler of Portugal from 1557 to 1578 and an ascetic and mystic who dreamed of crusades and died in Morocco in the terrible battle of Alcazarquivir, wanted to avenge the failure of the Jesuit mission. At the same time, he wanted to establish, south of the Zambezi, a vast Portuguese territory that would rival in size and wealth the Spanish possessions in Mexico and Peru. He too believed that the Monomotapa's country was the biblical Ophir. A contingent of over a thousand soldiers left Lisbon for East Africa in 1569. In the following years and in the course of two expeditions this force was decimated both by fever and by struggles with the natives. Not only that, but the Portuguese did not discover the gold mines that they had hoped to find.

Despite all this, the kingdom of the Monomotapa continued to haunt the Western imagination for a long time still. When German geologist Carl Mauch reached Great Zimbabwe in 1871, he enthusiastically adopted the belief in "King Solomon's mines," as did Cecil Rhodes some years later. In 1896 a company with the title Rhodesia Ancient Ruins Ltd. was set up, officially in order to conduct excavations but in fact to look for gold. It did find gold but in insignificant amounts. The company ceased its activity in 1902.[43] There was certainly a great deal of gold in southern Rhodesia, but it was located farther west.

America and Paradise

Scholars have long pointed out how the search for paradisal islands was an important stimulus to voyages of discovery from the fourteenth to the seventeenth centuries. Nostalgia for the garden of Eden; the conviction of

Christopher Columbus and missionaries that the end time was at hand; the will to bring religion to new lands; and the desire to find gold, precious stones, and other rare commodities: all these combined to spur travelers, religious, sailors, and conquerors on to new horizons. Their culture and the dreams it brought with it led them, at least in the beginning, to see in the strange lands opening up before them the characteristics of those blessed countries that had haunted the Western imagination since antiquity.

Christopher Columbus was obsessed by the idea that the New Indies were located close to the earthly paradise. Deeply impressed by the beauty of Haiti, he declared this island to be unmatched in all the world because it was covered with all sorts of trees that seemed to touch the sky and never lost their leaves.[44] Of another insular landscape, that of Cape Hermoso, he wrote: "When I reached this cape, the scent of flowers and trees blew offshore and this was the most delightful thing in the world."[45]

Columbus was not the only one to be thus dazzled. It has rightly been noted that in describing the New World many chroniclers of Iberian discoveries during the Renaissance used the words in which Ovid described the golden age: words that had been copied, cited, and read countless times in the preceding fifteen centuries.[46] Amerigo Vespucci spent the years 1499–1502 in reconnoitering the coasts of Surinam and Brazil. In a letter to Lorenzo de Medici in which he describes nature in South America, he uses all the motifs of paradisal literature, writing of

> the friendly land, covered with countless very tall trees that do not lose their leaves and that emit sweet and fragrant odors and are loaded with tasty fruits that promote the body's health; the fields of thick grass that are filled with flowers which have a wonderfully delightful perfume; the great throng of birds of various species, whose feathers, colors, and songs defy description. Vespucci adds: "For myself, I thought I was near the earthly paradise."[47]

This letter of Vespucci underwent an apocryphal revision that was printed many times at the beginning of the sixteenth century under the title *Mundus novus*. Here the Florentine explorer's descriptions are all recast in the superlative mode. In particular, Vespucci is represented as saying: "If the earthly paradise exists anywhere on earth, I think it must not be very far from this area."[48]

The first historian of the Americas, Petrus Martyr of Anghiera, an Italian humanist who later lived in Spain, likewise speaks of "the Elysian land" in which the people of Caramaira (present-day Venezuela) live: "It has fine vegetation and is fertile; it endures neither the rigors of winter nor the burning heat of summer." With regard to the Caribbean the author claims: "Our fellow countrymen have discovered countless islands that might be paradise, countless Elysian regions."[49] These praises are matched by Francesco Hernández, at the end of the sixteenth century, who says that in New Spain "the soil produces everything of its own accord" (a repetition of Ovid's formula, *Per se dabat omnia tellus* [The earth herself gave all things],[50] with reference, of course, to the golden age). It would be easy to extend this dossier of expressions of wonder. I shall cite only this further judgment of Brazil by an anonymous English writer in 1554:

> All who have gone there agree that the best and greenest fields and countrysides in the entire world are to be found there, the most pleasant mountains, covered with trees and fruits of every kind, the most beautiful valleys, the most delicious rivers of fresh water, filled with an endless variety of fishes, the thickest forests, always green and laden with fruits. As for gold, silver, and other kinds of metal, spices of all kinds, and fruits desirable both for their taste and touch and for the salutary effects they have: so abundant are they that until now it has not been possible even to imagine that they could be as many elsewhere as here. In conclusion, it is now thought that the earthly paradise can only be located on the equinoctial line or close to it, for the only perfect spot on earth has its place there.[51]

The voyages of discovery not only dethroned the ancient idea that the sea ends at the equator, the area south of the equator being thought to be uninhabitable; they also led to high praise of the equator and the region between the tropics. Walter Raleigh, who attempted to establish English colonies in the Americas, tells us in his *History of the World* that the regions beneath or close to the equator are refreshed during the day by a wind from the east that lessens the impact of the sun's rays, so that people there do not experience excessive heat. Moreover, the nights are of equal length all year round and always cool. As a result, he says, "I know of no other place in the world that has a better and more unvarying climate."[52]

Aristotle had claimed that the sun's heat is too intense in these regions; Portuguese missionaries, like Raleigh, observed that, on the contrary (it is a seventeenth-century religious who writes here), "the intensity of the sun's heat is moderated by cool winds from the sea and by the humidity of the land; these, combined with the coolness of the forests that cover the entire land, make the life of the inhabitants a pleasant one."[53] It was of Brazil, once again, that another religious, Rui Pereira, wrote in a letter to Portugal in 1560: "If there is a paradise on earth, I would say it exists presently in Brazil. . . . Anyone who wants to live in the earthly paradise has no choice but to live in Brazil."[54] This was the land without excessive heat or severe cold that had been the dream of the ancient poets . . . and of Isidore of Seville.

The fruits that Europeans discovered in South America likewise seemed to them fruits of paradise. In the view of Antonio de León Pinelo, coun-

cillor of the king of Spain in the seventeenth century and historian of the
New Indies, the fruit of the tree of good and evil could only be the *maracuja*,
whose fragrance and taste could well have stirred Eve's appetite and whose
mysterious flower clearly shows the instruments of the passion, thus earning
its Christian name of "passion fruit."[55] Others praised the exceptional virtues
of the *ananas* (pineapple), which Jean de Léry discovered in Brazil in 1555.
In a book on the fruits of Brazil that Antonio do Rosario, a Capuchin, published later on, in 1702, he ranked the *ananas* above the passion fruit and
gave it its own mystical meaning. According to this pious Franciscan, *ananas*,
a Guarani word, was to be interpreted as *Anna nascitur* (Anna is born), referring to Anna, mother of the Mother of God.[56] A Florentine writer at the
end of the sixteenth century had already made the claim that the *ananas* was
"the best of all the world's fruits."[57]

South America also seemed to possess a wealth of emeralds, and this too,
at least initially, helped linked the continent with the myths of paradise. For
the medieval allegories and visions of Eden had assigned great importance
to the emerald, which was regarded as a symbol of everlasting life.[58] Another factor that contributed to connect South America with paradise was
the discovery of the many kinds of parrots in the New World. For the parrot
occupied a special place in the traditional imagery of paradise. All the other
animals had lost the power of speech as a result of original sin; the parrot
alone had retained this faculty that linked it with human beings. In addition,
parrots live to a great age; they may therefore have experienced the earthly
paradise.[59] In the sixteenth and seventeenth centuries the parrot was always a
"bird of paradise." When Rubens made a copy (now in the Prado) of Titian's
Original Sin, he introduced a parrot perched on the trunk of a tree. Another
painting of the earthly paradise that has been attributed either to Rubens or
to Jan Brueghel (now in the Royal Museum of The Hague) shows an Edenic
landscape inhabited by parrots and ducks.[60]

Favored as it was in many ways (climate; abundant water; exceptional
fruits; precious stones; birds from the earthly paradise), America between the
tropics seemed to Europeans a blessed land that had preserved some characteristics that earth had had before original sin. The result was the rather
widespread belief that the Indians of the Americas, and especially those of
Brazil, lived longer lives than the inhabitants of Europe.[61] Here ancient paradisal motifs were surfacing, for it seemed to many that the longevity of the
early patriarchs as attested by the Bible was a substitute for the immortality
that our first parents enjoyed before original sin. Then, too, was not Prester
John said to live five hundred years? The Happy Isles of the Arthurian cycle likewise had the privilege of bestowing longevity on their inhabitants.[62]
Pierre d'Ailly, who in his *Ymago mundi* describes Taprobane as an island on

which the earthly paradise might well have been located, says of its inhabitants that "they live longer than the average span allotted to human weakness, so that the death of those who die at a hundred is regarded as premature."[63] We know that this work, which Christopher Columbus had in his library, was one of those that inspired the great voyages of exploration; opposite the sentence that I have just cited, Columbus has this marginal note: "Etas istorum est prolixa" (These people live to an advanced age).

Amerigo Vespucci's letter of 1502 did a great deal to accredit the legend of Brazil as full of vigorous old men and women who live to the age of 130 (1700 lunar months divided by 13 per year).[64] The *Mundus novus*, which both plagiarized and embroidered Vespucci's letter, upped the number from 130 to 150 and added, speaking of the Indians, that "they are rarely sick; and if they suffer an illness of any kind, they cure themselves with the roots of certain plants. . . . The air here is temperate and healthy and does not transmit any contagion. Unless they die by violence, the natives live long lives. I think this is because of the unceasing southeast winds, especially those to which we give the name Eurus."[65] The author thus asserts a connection between warm winds and health. Let us remember that the apocryphal letter that went under the name of *Mundus novus* reached a wide readership; there were at least ten printings in Germany before 1515.[66]

Antonio Pigafetta, who accompanied Magellan on his voyage around the world that began in 1519 and who wrote a report on it, claimed for the Indians of Brazil a long life of from 125 to 150 years.[67] His work, which appeared in Italian in 1536, reached a vast audience when it was reprinted in the *Navigationi e viaggi* of G. B. Ramusio (3 vols.; Venice, 1554–65). His claim was confirmed by Jean de Léry, who spent twelve months in Brazil in 1557–58 and stated, with a bit more moderation than his predecessors, that the Indians of this region usually reached the age of 100 or 120. He also maintained that the "Toüopinanbaoults" are stronger, sturdier, and less subject to sickness than Europeans and that among them there are no misshapen or deformed individuals; he explains this fact by the quality of the air and the climate, since severe cold is unknown there, and the forests, grass, and fields are always green.[68]

A number of people appealed to this longevity, regarding which the first Europeans seem to have been mistaken, as part of a defense of primitive man; this defense became in turn the source of the myth of the "noble savage." These apologists said that the Indians of America lived to an old age because they had retained something of the "state of innocence" of Adam and Eve. In fact, the majority of settlers and missionaries did not agree with this optimistic picture of *homo americanus*. On the other hand, the picture was defended by several eminent persons, led by Bartolomé de Las Casas (whose *Historia de las Indias* circulated in manuscript but was not published until 1875):

> God created these simple people without evil and without guile. They are most obedient and faithful to their natural lords and to the Christians whom they serve. They are most submissive, patient, peaceful and virtuous. Nor are they quarrelsome, rancorous, querulous or vengeful. Moreover, they are more delicate than princes and die easily from work or illness. They neither possess nor desire to possess worldly wealth. Surely these people would be the most blessed in the world if only they worshipped the true God.[69]

The baton was then taken over by Jean de Léry, a Reformed Christian, in his *Histoire d'un voyage faict en la terre antarctique* (published in 1578):

> So too they do not draw in any way on the muddied or, more accurately, pestilential sources from which flow so many of the streams that eat away our bones, suck out our marrow, weaken our bodies, and consume our spirits, or, in short, that poison us and cause us to die before our time. I am referring to our distrust of one another, the avarice that distrust breeds, our lawsuits and quarrels, our envy and ambition. Nothing of all this torments them, much less dominates them and becomes a passion with them.[70]

Jean de Léry in turn inspired Montaigne's chapter "Of Cannibals" in his *Essais* (chap. 31). Here Montaigne makes a very clear connection between a benevolent climate and the longevity and natural goodness of the people of Brazil, who wage only defensive wars. Here are the relevant passages from this well-known chapter:

> These nations . . . seem to me . . . still very close to their original naturalness. . . . This is a nation . . . in which there is no sort of traffic, no knowledge of letters, no science of numbers, no name for a magistrate or for political superiority, no custom of servitude, no riches or poverty, no contracts, no successions, no partitions, no occupations but leisure ones, no care for any but common kinship, no clothes, no agriculture, no metal, no use of wine or wheat. The very words that signify lying, treachery, dissimulation, avarice, envy, belittling, pardon — unheard of. . . .
>
> For the rest, they live in a country with a very pleasant and temperate climate, so that according to my witnesses it is rare to see a sick man there; and they have assured me that they never saw one palsied, bleary-eyed, toothless, or bent with age.

Montaigne could therefore only admire the "purity" of these peoples, to the point, he said, that "I am sometimes vexed that they were unknown earlier, in the days when there were men able to judge them better than we."[71] In his view, the discovery of the Americas came too late. It could no longer be of moral profit to a European civilization that was already too far gone in corruption and that would inevitably destroy the last paradisal land still existing on our planet.

But the more northern part of America, where the English began to settle at the end of the sixteenth century and the beginning of the seventeenth, seemed to give the lie to this pessimistic prognosis. To the religious dissidents who abandoned a hostile England, North America seemed a blessed land without evil, and even a land of plenty where they could begin human history anew on new foundations. New England was sometimes described as "like the garden of Eden," a place where the partridges were so fat that they could not fly and turkeys were as big as lambs.[72] George Alsop described Maryland as a new "earthly paradise"; its trees, plants, fruits, and flowers seemed to him to be "hieroglyphs of our original, adamic situation."[73] Another writer thought he had discovered the "future eden" in Georgia, a region located on the same latitude as Palestine.[74] North America, a new Eden; this persuasion and identification played no little part in the history of the United States and in the pushing back of its "frontier" to the West.[75]

Chapter 6

Nostalgia

A Sorrowful Look Back at the Golden Age and the "Happy Isles"

As we shall see in the next chapter, the sixteenth and seventeenth centuries gradually abandoned the belief in the enduring existence of the earthly paradise as an oasis of happiness that is barred to us now but is preserved somewhere at the end of the world. But this turn to realism was not accomplished without pain. Never did people dream so much of the golden age, the Happy Isles, the fountain of youth, idyllic pastoral scenes, and a land of plenty, as they did during these two centuries. And never before in the West had gardens had so prominent a place and been so highly regarded. The geography of the planet was now better known, or at least less poorly known, and was therefore less fanciful than the geography of the past; but if minds were to accept it, there was need of some compensation for past fantasies. The theme of the earthly paradise and its variants thus led to the rediscovery of both the "dreams" and the "melancholy" of the Renaissance, on which I have laid so much stress in my earlier works.[1]

Beginning in the fifteenth century, first the Italians and then other westerners put a great deal of skill and imagination into the evocation of mythological paradises whose eternally young inhabitants thought only of love. According to Politian, the dwelling place of Venus above Cyprus is an "everlasting garden," in which "cheerful Spring, always present, lets the breeze toss her blond locks and weaves a garland of countless flowers" (*Stanze per la Giostra,* 1475). To a great extent, the return to mythology was a way of dreaming about the golden age. It offered an opportunity to re-create an imaginary land in which the eye was delighted by charming young nudes who never grew old.

Even in the fantastic epics that kept alive a "Christian sense of the marvelous," poets introduced artificial paradises that were destined indeed to crumble because they were the work of agents of the devil, but that were nonetheless the most successful parts of the stories and accounted for their popularity. Thus in Ariosto's *Orlando Furioso,* the palace of Alcine "surpasses all others in wealth," while the shapes taken by the blond magician are "more perfect than any painter could ever have imagined." As for Armida's gardens of delight that are described in *Gerusalemme liberata,* they are located, as one might suspect, on the Happy Isles. There the wily woman causes crystalline waters to spring up as well as trees that everlastingly bear flowers and fruits at the same time. In such a setting, Rinaldo, now drawn outside of time, never wearies of Armida's kisses.

Arcadia, too, was one of the Renaissance's escapes, for the pastoral genre experienced a new and lasting success, beginning with Boccaccio's *Ameto* and reaching a high point once the humanists discovered the *Idylls* of Theocritus and the *Bucolics* of Virgil. Thenceforth for many centuries the educated public was fascinated by the rural loves and games of shepherdesses who lived amid a nature that was friendly and harmonious. It is to Arcadia — not the austere region of the Peloponnesus but a verdant countryside in which the trees possess "an incomparable beauty" — that Sannazzaro sends his shepherd Sincero to console himself for his disappointments in love. His *Arcadia* (1502), a novel combining prose and verse, and the most remarkable of the Italian pastorals, had an extraordinary posterity that can be traced in the *Diana enamorada* of Jorge de Montemayor (1559), the *Aminta* of Tasso (1573), the *Galatea* of Cervantes, the *Pastor fido* of Giovanni Guarini, and the *Astrée* of Honoré d'Urfé (1607–27). These fictions about rural life with its benevolent nature that knows no winter and its eternal youth in an Arcadia outside of space and time are expressions of a stubborn longing for the golden age, in which people pretended to believe for the space of a reading or a dramatic presentation. And yet Politian in his *Stanze per la Giostra* had warned that "no mortal can enter" the dwelling of Venus that is located on "a charming mountain" overlooking Cyprus.

The Renaissance claimed indeed to have rediscovered the golden age, and one might cite as evidence the famous, though isolated, enthusiastic exclamations of Giovanni Rucellai, Marsilio Ficino, Ulrich von Hutten, and Rabelais. In addition, political propaganda played its part, and the festivals in honor of sovereigns, as well as the victors' chariots built for these occasions, would have the spectators believe (though the very repetitions made the whole business suspect) that the golden age would return under Lorenzo the Magnificent or Leo X or Henry II, Henry IV, or Elizabeth.[2] Was the public persuaded?

In any case, regretful longing for the *aetas aurea* was a characteristic of the Renaissance. The vision had come from antiquity and was never absent throughout the Middle Ages; it had reached the educated public through the many versions of Ovid in which the poet was "moralized" by means of allegorical interpretation. The second part of the *Roman de la rose* contains near the beginning an eloquent and beguiling description of that now vanished time of happiness:

> No plowing then was needed by the soil,
> But by God's care it foisoned by itself,
> Providing all the comforts that men wished. . . .
> Whene'er as if 'twere everlasting spring
> The wind had been appeased, and soft and sweet
> The weather had become, with pleasant breeze . . .
> Free from all thoughts of harlotry or rape
> Those who were pleased to play the game of love
> With kisses and embraces would unite.
> In groves the verdant trees stretched out their limbs,
> Protecting thus the lovers from the sun
> With curtains and pavillions made of leaves.[3]

But during the Renaissance, a period that we too readily think of as a time of hope and joy, regret for the lost golden age and the fairy lands took on a new dimension that is a historically verifiable fact. In 1377, Coluccio Salutati, chancellor of Florence, in a letter to Leonardo Bruni, sang the praises of that mythical age in which people knew how to be satisfied with the gifts of nature: "O happy age, O truly golden century, that nourished humanity with fruits produced spontaneously, without effort or care, and, even better, without superfluity!" Then minds not rendered torpid by wine and food could rise easily from consideration of inferior beings to contemplation of the heavenly sphere.[4]

Sebastian Brant's *Ship of Fools* (1494) gloomily described the distant "bygone days" when "peace spread abroad and reigned in the world."[5] Erasmus, in *The Praise of Folly*, tells us that "the simple folk of the golden age flourished without any armament of sciences, being guided only by nature and instinct." But then "the pristine simplicity of the golden age little by little slipped away."[6] In 1525 Clément Marot devotes a rondeau to "love of ancient times" and seeks to persuade his readers that "in the good old days love set the pace. . . . But now what love ordained has been lost."[7] Franciscan scholar and humorist Antonio de Guevara in his *Reloj de príncipes* (1529) describes "the first age and golden world" in which "all lived together in peace." "Each person took care of his own bit of land. Each planted his trees and sowed his grain. Each harvested his crops and pruned his vines. . . . All lived without harming or jostling others."[8]

Another sorrowful lament for the vanished age is that of Don Quixote, who mourns for the time when "thine" and "mine" did not exist and when nature gave generously to all:

> In that blessed age all things were in common; to win the daily food, no labor was required of any save to stretch forth his hand and gather it from the sturdy oaks that stood generously inviting him with their sweet ripe fruit.... Then all was peace, all friendship, all concord.... [Nature] without compulsion yielded from every portion of her broad fertile bosom all that could satisfy, sustain, and delight the children who then possessed her.[9]

On the eve of his death, Lope de Vega (d. 1635), a representative of what we call Spain's "golden age," wrote a poem in the same vein, entitled *El Siglo de oro;* its pervading tone is sadness. In that bygone time Nature was like a beautiful young woman whose beauty was not spoiled by cosmetics and prostitution. Today that golden age makes us aware of the treachery, the lies, and the deceptions that our own age heaps upon us.[10]

The escape into the other world of utopia, a genre that began to flourish once again in the sixteenth century after an interval of fifteen centuries, seems closely allied to this regretful longing for the golden age. We may wonder what the real intentions of Thomas More were when he revived the genre with his *Utopia* (1516). According to French poet Barthélemy Aneau, author of a foreword to the French translation of More's work, "The wise Chancellor of England ... [intended] to present, in the guise of a story about the new island named Utopia, ... a moral republic and most perfect polity: so perfect indeed that it never existed, does not exist now, and will not by any chance ever exist in the future."[11] And such indeed seems to have been the intention of Erasmus's friend.

In any case, in its day *Utopia* had its place in a vast international literature that cast a sad eye upon the age and contrasted it with "bygone days" and an "idyllic elsewhere," thus helping to intensify the nostalgia. The island that More imagines as existing at the other end of the world is a dreamland whose fifty-four cities are "all spacious and magnificent," whose farmers "breed a vast quantity of poultry," and whose gardens "are so well-kept and flourishing that I never saw anything more fruitful and more tasteful anywhere"; the island produced in abundance all the things needed to sustain life and even to make it pleasant.[12] More broadly, the many "utopias" (More's proper name became a common noun) that flourished in the Renaissance bore witness to the painful gap that an elite saw as existing between their aspirations and everyday reality. The utopias served as a kind of refuge.[13]

This same spirit can be seen in Ronsard, who saw religious conflicts reaching a dangerous level under Henri II and who urged his friend Marc-Antoine Muret to emigrate with him to the Happy Isles. A purely scholastic exercise,

of course! Neither of the two fled their Old World. They were simply in-
dulging in a melancholic dream that would help them forget for a moment
"poor Europe" and "horrid Mars" who "was shedding Christian blood on all
sides." In those "blessed isles,"

> I lie not when I say that the trees turn yellow
> with fruits as many as their buds;
> and at all times without fail the fields are daubed
> with countless varied flowers,
> free as they are of the dry chilling wind,
> and from the high rocke the springs
> are always bubbling forth milk.[14]

In this happy land, "Avarice has not enclosed the fields," nor does the wolf
frighten the cattle. There are no "rumbling lightning bolts" nor comets "with
long trailing hair." "Husbands are not saddened / to see their wives dying in
their arms."

> There no justice corrupted by gold
> nor saddening laws engraved on bronze
> nor senates, nor wicked folk
> disturb the repose of those fields.[15]

In this insular "elsewhere," then, this earthly paradise that had been preserved, everything needed for a happy human life was to be found: the beauty
and fruitfulness of nature, the absence of storms and comets, peace, justice,
equality, or, in short, the opposite of what we experience and what Ronsard
saw in his day.

This melancholy and this nostalgia for the *locus amoenus* that was Eden
help us to understand the attempts made to re-create the conditions of
paradise in gardens.

The Enclosed Garden

The ideal garden in the medieval West was initially a *hortus conclusus*, an enclosure, whereas the earthly paradise of the Bible was seemingly open to the
land of Eden. The idea of enclosure came from the traditional translation of
the Song of Song 4:12: "My sister, my spouse, is a garden enclosed, a garden enclosed, a fountain sealed up" (the Ecumenical Translation of the Bible
reads: "You are a bolted garden, my sister, my spouse: a well that is bolted,
a fountain sealed up"). The story of the expulsion of Adam and Eve from
"the paradise" (Gen 3:24) pointed the imagination in the same direction. "At

the east of the garden of Eden he [God] placed the cherubim, and a sword flaming and turning to guard the way to the tree of life." Henceforth, if a place of peace and happiness could still be found on earth, it could only be a place cut off from the rest of an unhappy and sinful world. Rabanus Maurus teaches that "the Church is paradise, for the Song of Songs speaks of the Church as 'my sister, a garden enclosed.'"[16] Herrad of Landsberg, abbess of Sainte-Odile in Alsace (d. 1195), in the well-known spiritual anthology *Hortus deliciarum,* which she composed for her sisters, explains to them the many meanings of "the earthly paradise." The term signifies, separately or in combination, the Christian soul, a pure conscience, virginity, monastic life, the cloister, the church watered by the four streams of the Gospels, and, finally, the heavenly Jerusalem.[17]

Let me call attention here to the connection Herrad makes between the earthly paradise and the cloister. Monasteries needed gardens, especially in order to cultivate medicinal plants. But these gardens soon became places for meditation and were bounded by arcades known as cloisters. The Cistercians liked square cloisters, whose four sides recalled the four rivers of paradise, the four Gospels, and the four cardinal virtues. St. Bernard wrote: "Truly, the cloister is a paradise, a realm protected by the rampart of a discipline that contains a rich abundance of priceless treasures."[18] St. Bernard thus combined cloister and cloister garden in a single monastic image and hymn of praise. Many monastic gardens had a well in the center: a utilitarian structure, indeed, but also symbolic, since it evidently reminded the religious of the "river [that] flows out of Eden to water the garden; and from there it divides and becomes four branches" (Gen 2:10).[19]

This journey back up the river of history also showed the goal to be reached: "The cloister garden with its four square sections and the fountain in the middle already offered a model of the cosmos, and commentators were often ready to read it as a diagram of the paradise which the monks would reach through contemplation."[20] In his *Rationale divinorum officiorum* Bishop William Durandus (d. 1296) wrote: 'The [monastic] garden with its trees and grass represents the large number of the virtues; the well with its living water represents the abundant gifts that quench thirst here below and that extinguish the fire of thirst in the future life."[21]

It was doubtless as a result of the mediating role played by the cloister garden that the *hortus conclusus* acquired so important a role in the literature and iconography of the second half of the Middle Ages, where it operated on the two levels of the sacred and the profane. An unknown author of the mid–fifteenth century gave the following instructions for stage managers of the mystery play, *The Resurrection of the Lord:*

Then there must be shown a beautiful earthly paradise, the best and most glorious you can provide, well stocked with all sorts of trees, flowers, fruits, and other rural things, and in the middle the tree of life, finer than all the others....

This paradise is to be made of paper; within it there should be branches of trees, some with flowers on them, others loaded with fruits of many kinds, such as cherries, pears, apples, figs, grapes, and other such, all artificial, and other branches of May-green, and rose bushes whose roses and flowers rise above the crenellated walls; these ought to be freshly cut and placed in vessels of water so as to keep them fresh.

Another manuscript of the same mystery play adds "plums, German pears, oranges, pomegranates, rosemary, and marjoram" to the paradise, and specifies that the stage managers must not forget "the fountain whose water divides into four streams."[22]

The mention of walls leads to the logical conclusion that the garden was a *hortus conclusus,* a garden enclosed by a wall. Quite revealing in this respect is the *Little Garden of Paradise* (now in Frankfort), which was painted around 1430 by a nameless artist known now as the Master of the Upper Rhine. Here a crenellated wall surrounds a garden spangled with lush flowers. The figures within this enclosure seem at first sight to be ladies and lords. But a second examination of the picture enables us to identify them: the Virgin is reading a book, the Child Jesus is playing St. Cecilia's lyre, and St. Michael is conversing with St. George and another sainted knight. This earthly paradise symbolizes Mary's virginity.[23]

Even more revealing is the illustration that Jean Fouquet painted for *The Antiquities of the Jews* of Flavius Josephus (MS fr. 247, B.N., Paris).[24] It depicts the marriage of Adam and Eve in the garden of Eden. The garden is surrounded by a fortified wall, which in turn is surrounded by water, but it has openings in four places to allow passage of the four rivers that flow from the fountain of life. In this *hortus conclusus* grow trees that bear leaves and fruit together. The most diverse animals — lion, lamb, stag, rabbit — feed side by side. The protective mantle of the Almighty, which is red on the outside and blue on the inside, like that of a Virgin of Mercy, protects our first parents, who are naked but wholly innocent. Eve has magnificent long blond hair. The angels, birds, and rays of the sun join in this festival of creation and love. The vivid colors — blue, red, gold, and green — create an atmosphere full of light and happiness. This paradisal enclosure was meant to be as it were a wonderful parenthesis within time and space, an island of happiness of which we always have the right to dream.

The Antiquities of the Jews of Flavius Josephus starts with the beginning of the world and the six days of creation. As a result, at the end of the Middle

Ages manuscripts of this work were often decorated with illuminations depicting the story of Adam and Eve. The enclosed garden can be seen in, for example, a fifteenth-century French manuscript, now in the Bibliothèque de l'Arsenal (no. 5082, fol. 3): the earthly paradise, containing the fountain of life and the tree of the knowledge of good and evil, is surrounded by structures with pepper-box towers and tiers of gables. The controlling image is still the enclosed garden.[25]

As the *Little Garden of Paradise* suggests, the *hortus conclusus* of the earthly paradise gradually came to have a Marian symbolism and to remind the viewer of the virginity of Mary. Mary, said the monastic poets, was "an enclosed garden, into which Christ descended like dew."[26] The authority for this idea was St. Jerome, who had written that "the *hortus conclusus* . . . is an image suggesting Mary, Mother and Virgin."[27] The result was numerous depictions of Mary in the middle of an enclosed garden, carrying the divine child or adoring him. In her catalogue of illustrations for the symbolism of gardens and flowers in Italian Renaissance art, Mirella Levi d'Ancona lists eleven paintings from the Iberian Peninsula in the fifteenth and sixteenth centuries that have the Marian *hortus conclusus* as their subject. The fifteenth-century *Livre des chants royaux*, now in the National Library in Paris (MS fr. no. 145), shows a standing Virgin who holds the Child Jesus and whose tall figure towers over a rectangular garden that surrounds her. Outside the enclosure, a kneeling figure with joined hands (the donor) addresses these words of praise to Mary: "O garden enclosed, in which the true Laurel grew!"[28] This kind of iconography was in practice a way of reciting the Virgin's praises with the aid of images.

The *hortus conclusus* also served as the setting for numerous representations of the Annunciation. I cite as an especially convincing example a fresco painted in 1514 by G. M. Falconetto in the church of San Pietro Martire in Verona. Mary is seated in the middle of an area closed off by a crenellated wall. A unicorn, symbol of virginity, rests one paw on her knees. Outside the wall, we see, on one side, the angel who brings the message and, on the other, a kneeling warrior beside whom is the inscription: "He descended like dew on the fleece." This fresco, which is rather overcrowded with animals, towers, and mock-antique buildings that form the setting, marks, for us at least, the end result, a very sophisticated end result, of the theme of the Marian enclosure. On the wall is written *Ortus conclusus*, and right beside this inscription is a large Renaissance-style door with the inscription *Porta aurea*. At Mary's left in the garden the artist has inevitably placed a fountain of life (very mannered in its construction).[29]

Since the earthly paradise could not but be a place of flowers — flowers that never fade — Marian symbolism takes the form of flowers that enable the viewer to pass in a moment from the time of sin to the time of grace. In a song in honor of the Virgin, Abbot Adam of Perseigne had exclaimed: "Mary, you are the garden enclosed, in which the white lily of virginity grows without fading, the inviolable violet of humility spreads its perfume, and the rose of tireless love glows red."[30]

Starting in the fourteenth century, nature began to play a real part in Western painting; one result was that the plants of paradise multiplied in artistic works, but in accordance with a code that the spectators, or at least the more educated among them, understood. Everyone knew, for example, that the apple and the cucumber, plants signifying evil, were contrasted with the vine and the cherry, symbols of the passion of Christ. When Christianized, the orange tree in the Garden of the Hesperides became a tree in the earthly paradise, because it did not lose its leaves and produced fruit in winter.[31] Similarly, the strawberry, which Ovid associates with the golden age (*Metamorphoses* 1.4), signified, in its new setting, the happiness of the garden of Eden.[32] Flowers associated with the gods, as for example the carnation, which was an image of profane love, joined the company of Marian flowers. In religious painting the daisy, synonymous with springtime, signified the innocence of Christ.

The rose — along with the lily and the violet, as we have just seen — was especially associated with Mary. Consequently it was also placed among the flowers in paradise. St. Ambrose had claimed that in the earthly paradise the roses had no thorns.[33] In the same spirit, a twelfth-century song addresses Mary, who was exempted from original sin, and says: "Rose without thorns, you have become a mother."[34] This idea accounts for iconographic representations of Mary in the midst of roses. I am thinking here especially of *Madonna of the Rose Garden* (Castelvecchio, Verona), in which Stefano of Verona (d. after 1438) shows Mary sitting in a paradise of roses, birds, and mannered angels; of *Madonna of the Rose Bush,* by Stephan Lochner, 1450 (Wallraf-Richartz Museum, Cologne); and, above all, of Schongauer's masterpiece, *Virgin with the Rose Bush* (1473; church of St. Martin in Colmar). In this last-named work, Mary, crowned by two angels, holds the Child Jesus in her arms; her face is recollected; she wears a red robe and mantle. Behind her, a latticework supports rosetrees with large red flowers. Birds sit on the branches. Viewers who were believers could derive a twofold lesson from this moving image: Mary, the woman without sin, would have deserved to live in the earthly paradise; her red garments and the color of the roses signify the cruel death to be suffered one day by the child whom she clasps so tenderly to herself.

From a Christian perspective the enclosed garden, a place of happiness that was protected from the ugliness of the sinful world, appeared to be also a place of refuge. In this respect it is akin to the humanists' desire to cultivate *otium,* far from the agitated life of the cities. Petrarch may be said to have been the first of the "humanist gardeners." On his "transalpine Helicon" at Fontaine-de-Vaucluse he desired to duplicate the island-garden described by Cicero in his *De legibus.* Beside a "murmuring brook" he found the inspiration of the Muses. His Provençal estate, on which he erected altars "at the spot where tumultuous waters erupt from hidden springs," made it possible for him to "rise to great thoughts."[35]

An exemplary *hortus conclusus* that links echoes of antiquity with Christian inspiration is imagined by Erasmus in his colloquium *The Godly Feast* (1522). The garden's owner, Eusebius, "marvel[s] at people who take pleasure in smoky cities." One of his guests, Timothy, objects that Socrates "preferred cities to fields, because...cities afforded him means of learning. In the fields, to be sure, were trees and gardens, fountains and streams, to please the eye; but they had nothing to say and therefore taught nothing." Eusebius replies that "Nature is not silent but speaks to us everywhere and teaches the observant man many things if she finds him attentive and receptive. What else does the charming countenance of blooming nature proclaim than that God the Creator's wisdom is equal to his goodness?" The countryside is thus seen as a refuge for the spirit, "a retreat" in which the spirit can find itself once again.

But, to be more concrete, the place where Eusebius receives his guests is "near town," where he has "a modest but well-cultivated place." The garden is divided into halves. One, adorned with flowers and foliage, contains numerous engraved texts from the Bible, in Latin, Greek, and Hebrew: "If thou wilt enter into life, keep the Commandments"; "Repent ye, therefore, and be converted"; and so on. The guests are led past a statue of Jesus and by a "little fountain bubbling merry with excellent water. It symbolizes in a manner that unique fountain which refreshes with its heavenly stream all those who labor and are heavy laden." Eusebius then urges them to enter the second, "more cultivated" garden, which is enclosed by the walls of the house. Here we find the *hortus conclusus* of the monasteries. "Here nothing grows but fragrant herbs," and in it flows a "little fountain whose stream seems to smile on all the herbs and promises to keep them cool in the heat." Its stream divides the garden into two equal parts, and in it "all its herbs are reflected as though in a mirror."[36] The humanist from Rotterdam dreamed of an enclosed garden that would foster *otium,* that is, recollection and the contemplative life and that would revive for the use of men of letters the setting and functions of the green space that was surrounded by the cloisters of medieval monasteries.

This Christian version of a garden of "refuge," far removed from the agitation, misfortunes, and sins of the world, was also imagined by Bernard

Palissy in his *Recepte veritable* (1563), a work that contains, among other things, "the plan for as delightful and useful a garden as has ever been seen."[37]

The author tells his readers that this will be "as beautiful a garden as ever existed under heaven, apart from the garden in the earthly paradise."[38] Its purpose is "to provide people with the opportunity... to abandon all occupations and vicious pleasures and evil dealings and to play at tilling the soil."[39] Again: "I want to construct my garden as a place of withdrawal in dangerous and evil days, so that I may flee the wickedness and malice of men and serve God in all freedom."[40] At the time when Palissy, a Protestant, was writing his book, he saw the beginnings of the wars of religion, and he tells the readers of the *Recepte:* "If you had seen the terrible human excesses that I saw during these disturbances, not a hair of your head but would have trembled, for fear of falling into the hands of such vicious people."[41]

It was quite natural, then, that this designer of "rustic vases" should organize his garden of "refuge" as a *hortus conclusus.* The square area will be "shut off" by mountains and boulders on the sides where the north and west winds blow,[42] and by low walls on the other two sides. It will be divided into "four equal sections" with a booth in each corner and another in the middle, on "a little island around which poplars will be planted."[43] Palissy thus rediscovered the shape of monastic gardens; in addition, he adopted suggestions from Erasmus by carving, in this place of "wisdom," texts from the Psalms and the Book of Wisdom.[44]

From Enclosed Garden to Open Garden

Contrary to what the plan of the artist from Saintonge might suggest, the Renaissance garden also had non-Christian and, in particular, Eastern origins, and the favor it enjoyed was helped by a convergence of influences. The gardens and palaces of Islam reflected the traditions of Persian "paradises" as seen in the mirror of Greco-Roman civilization. In their enclosures, which served as protection against the desert winds, these gardens contained all the perfumes offered by trees and plants, as well as all the species of animals that flourished in the realm. "There, sheltered by the high walls of the park, the king has at his disposal the flora and fauna of the entire kingdom, and this large piece of nature that has been domesticated and taken captive symbolizes his prominent role as guardian of the forces of fertility and life."[45]

In addition there was the great dream of Muslim dwellers in the desert: following the Qur'an, they imagined the next world as an orchard. Thus the *Book of the Ladder of Muhammad,* which tells the story of the nocturnal journey during which the prophet, guided by the angel Gabriel, traversed the heavens and hells, teaches that Muhammad saw seven successive "paradises" that were so many "orchards." The dwelling place of God himself, the seventh heaven, is also described as an orchard, enclosed by walls and containing fountains and trees loaded with fruit; in it is to be heard the music of instruments and the sweet singing of the young girls whom the orchard shelters.[46]

From Baghdad and Damascus to Grenada, Muslim rulers planted magnificent orchards such as are described in *The Thousand and One Nights*. Writers have left enthusiastic and no doubt exaggerated descriptions of the garden of Harun al-Rashid in Baghdad, in the period when Charlemagne was ruling in the West. In particular, there was, in the middle of a circular basin, a tree made of silver in whose branches sat mechanical birds that chirped and moved. Some of the birds were gilded, others silvered, and the twigs and branches were accented with gold.[47] The design of this garden was taken to Constantinople. Furthermore, the Muslims took their penchant for gardens to Sicily and Andalusia. The clever use of water in the gardens of the East and Sicily impressed the crusaders. One of these, Robert of Artois, passed through Palermo in 1270 and admired the orchards around the city; on his return to Hesdin in Picardy he built a park that was later kept up by the dukes of Burgundy and remained the only one of its kind in the West for many centuries. It contained mechanical toys and various aquatic "illusions" hitherto unknown in that part of the world.[48]

Helped by the example of the East, the theme of the garden of love that is enclosed on all sides was already present in the literature of the twelfth century. The *Roman de Thèbes* mentions a "garden" "enclosed by a thick wall on all sides."[49] In *Floire et Blanchefleur* we read:

> The orchards are both low and high,
> The world has not seen better.
> On all sides this wall encloses it....
> On the other side there runs, I think,
> A river of paradise....
> It was surrounded by it,
> So that nothing can enter
> Unless it can fly over it.[50]

In Chrétien de Troyes's novel *Cligès*, the two lovers spend long months of happiness in an orchard "enclosed by a high wall."[51] Another work that dates from the end of the twelfth century is the *De amore* of André Chapelain, who describes the circular garden of the "King of love": it is an enchanted place ringed with many varieties of pleasant-smelling fruit trees and having at the center a spring of pure water and a magnificent tree, taller than any

of the others, that gives shade to the entire circle and covers it with its pro-
tecting branches. The weather there is always mild. The earthly paradise is
thus restored but laicized. Its name is *Amoenitas* (Pleasant Spot), and it is
surrounded by two forbidding areas named *Humiditas* (Wetness) and *Siccitas*
(Dryness).[52]

The most famous medieval garden of love — and how difficult it is
to reach! — is doubtless the one that Guillaume de Loris (ca. 1225–30)
describes in the first part of the *Roman de la rose:*

> High was the wall, and neatly built and squared.
> Its bulk, in place of hedge, a garden fenced,
> To which no low-born man had ever come,
> For it was quite too fine a place for such.
> Willingly would I have found a guide
> Who, by means of ladder or of stile,
> Might bring me therewithin; for so great joy
> And such delight as in that place might be
> Were seldom known to man, as I believe.
> A generous and safe retreat for fowl
> That garden was; ne'er was a place so rich
> In trees bedight with songsters of all kinds.[53]

The author makes an interesting point: "Idleness," who opens the door of
the orchard to the young man of the story, tells him that Diversion "owns
this garden full of trees / That he had brought especially for him / From that
fair land where live the Saracens."[54] There can be no doubt, therefore, about
Eastern influences on the work.

At the end of the Middle Ages, the garden of love that is cut off from the
rest of the world has become a classic theme of iconography and literature.
A fourteenth-century fresco at Sorgues, near Avignon, shows a court of love
in this kind of garden setting. Jean Froissart's "bush of love" is "as round as
an apple, like a pavillion."[55] According to an addition to the *Livre du Cueur
d'amours espris,* the island of love contains "a beautiful park enclosed by a high
fence made entirely of cedar wood and aloe wood."[56] In the *Hypnerotomachia
Poliphili* of Francesco Colonna (completed in 1467), the island of Cythera, a
happy place of dreams, is described as an enclosed space in which the nymphs
pay "honor to Cupid their lord." In the French translation of 1546 we read
the following:

> This place was beautiful and so pleasant and delightful that the most eloquent
> would find themselves at a loss for words and figures of speech and nuances,
> were they to try describing it.... For it was a real refuge of happy consolations
> and delights, made up of gardens, orchards, and little copses, organized for
> the end and ultimate purpose of every kind of pleasure....

The climate was not subject to inconstant and changing weather nor to the danger of harmful winds, heats, frosts or fogs; it was always lushly productive and healthy, intended to be everlasting, and yielding all the good things nature can provide....

The place is located in the midst of the sea, which surrounds it with clear water that contains no rocks, mire, or stones.... All about the island beautiful cypresses are planted three paces apart, and beneath these is a dense, bushy hedge of myrrh that forms a wall one and half paces high; within this wall are enclosed the trunks of the cypresses, which rise above the hedge a pace and a half before their lowest branches begin. This hedge serves as an enclosure for the entire island; in it at suitable points are entrances and exits; but the hedge is so thickly leaved that one cannot see through it, and it is as straight as a wall, as though someone were carefully pruning it every day.[57]

As one reads this passage, one cannot but note the emphasis on the words "surrounds," "wall," "enclosed," "enclosure," and, once again, "wall." The paradisal island is as it were outside of time and space. There, as in the golden age, the climate is constant and pleasant. Flowers and fruits grow in abundance, and the author tells us, further on, that all the "fruit trees ... bear fruit of equal size, weight, and breadth; moreover, the trees are always green and loaded with fruit that does not drop with the seasons; for as soon as one piece is plucked, another is ready to be plucked."[58]

The earthly paradise becomes a solid place once again in this erotic dream of a Venetian religious, but it is completely paganized and, like the utopias of the sixteenth century, completely isolated in the midst of the sea. The journey of the young hero subsequently takes him through a whole series of gardens, each enclosed inside the previous, and ends in the garden of Venus, where Polifilo finally embraces Polia. The "hiddenness" of this ultimate refuge is emphasized by a trellis fence. The courtly laicization of the *hortus conclusus* ends, in the imagination of Francesco Colonna, in this mannered elaboration of a pseudoantique world.

The Renaissance does not break completely with the enclosed garden; one proof of this is the very place that Polifilo reaches at the end of his initiatory journey. Material embodiments are to be seen in the gardens of the palace of Té at Mantua, the garden of Montalto at Pavia, where it clings to the slopes of the Apennines, and, above all, the garden laid out for Cosimo I dei Medici in 1540 at Castello near Florence. The main feature of this last was a square garden surrounded by low walls, with a circular fountain dedicated to Venus in the center. This central garden was flanked on each side by two other smaller gardens, likewise enclosed, while at the far end there was an entrance into an orchard of lemon trees.

Other examples could be added. Furthermore, many gardens laid out after the Middle Ages included within the much larger whole a *hortus conclusus* that might be used by lovers... or philosophers. An extreme case, but it is only an extreme case: the great courtyard of the Belvedere that Donato Bramante designed for Julius II still gives the impression of an enclosed space, since two long galleries connect the Belvedere villa to the Vatican. But the charms of a retreat and a garden were here counterbalanced by papal pomp and the placement of ancient statues. In addition, Bramante adapted the terrain itself and the structures on the slope of the hill so as to make the buildings appear to rise out of the site, and he furnished the courtyard with terraces and steps and a stage for plays. Finally, this enclosed garden was of an unusual size.

The great innovation of the Renaissance in this area was the open garden, the theory of which was set forth by Leone Battista Alberti in his *De re edificatoria* (1452). His idea, which was novel at the time, was that house and garden should be treated as a single whole and that the green space, when remodeled by the architect, should harmonize with the surrounding countryside and open out into it.[59] Bramante's work was an at least partial implementation of this program. The discovery of the *Domus aurea* in Rome, a new interest in Hadrian's villa at Tivoli, and the imitation of antiquity soon led to the building of real palaces in the countryside, palaces that blended as it were into a natural world tamed by architects and experts in the control and management of water.

Did people continue to dream of the *aetas aurea* and the earthly paradise when they were in these gardens, enclosed or open, of the Renaissance? To some extent yes! "The myth of the golden age dictated the arrangement both of the villa which Poggio built at Caiano for Lorenzo [the Magnificent] and the villa built at Castello for Cosimo."[60] On a visit to the Lake Garda region, Andrea Mantegna found "wooded gardens which were so like paradise that they seemed to have sprung into being as an utterly delightful proof of the Muses' presence."[61] When the term "delights" is applied at this period to a garden or part of a garden, we must remember that a lengthy semantic tradition has made earthly paradise and *hortus deliciarum* synonymous. People spoke of the "delights" of Belriguardo and of Belfiore near Florence,[62] Poggioreale at Naples, the Villa d'Este at Tivoli,[63] and others. Someone said of Hampton Court in 1525 that it was "more like unto a paradise than any earthly habitation," and in fact there was in the garden "a parterre which they call Paradise."[64] And from a different viewpoint it is possible to speak of the "impossible restoration of Eden"[65] that was the aim of the imposing gardens of Europe during the Renaissance and the following centuries.

These gardens are said to have had three main distinguishing marks: the *bosco* or woods, that is, arrangements of trees that effected a transition to the surrounding landscape; the bringing of water into play by means of waterfalls, canals, and fountains; and, finally, the displaying of space by means of lengthy prospects. The famous villas of Tivoli and Bagnaia and, later, of the Borromean Islands, to cite only a few examples that set a pattern, show us the spirit in which they were conceived. The aim was showiness and illusion. Artifacts (various automata) and pseudonatural elements (grottoes) were multiplied in order to rouse astonishment and wonder. The countryside was subordinated to art. Technology won the day over nature. A garden became a stage and even a setting for sumptuous ceremonials.

In the account of his journey to Italy, Montaigne has given a description of the great villa at Pratolino that was designed for Francesco I dei Medici in the sixteenth century.[66] The central avenue leading to the house was fifteen meters (forty-nine feet) wide. It was filled with remarkable fountains and automata. Luigi Zangheri, the greatest present-day expert on this now vanished garden,[67] tells us that Pratolino seemed

> like an entirely new kind of organism, made up of a large villa that was a veritable jewel box of curios, and a garden-park, half of which was given over to the glories of the past and half to the wonders of the present. The originality of Pratolino was due to the fact that it was at once an extraordinary museum of *mirabilia*, a veritable *studiolo* or cabinet in the open air, and a large irregular labyrinth throbbing with the life emanating from grottoes and fountains.

Against the backdrop of an Olympus portrayed by images of Jupiter, Venus, Apollo, and Aesculapius, dramatic works were performed by automata that played out scenes from everyday life (the knife-grinder, the miller, and so on) and stories of human beings that had become demigods (Narcissus). In the grottoes of Pratolino there were depictions of all the kinds of actual metal and silver mines and of the way in which these were worked. These same grottoes were filled with "coral and other very highly esteemed stones," while the fields were "dotted with a countless variety of flowers"; the great aviary contained "a throng of birds," the fishponds were occupied by "large and varied fishes," and the copses were the home of a "large number of hares, goats, and partridges." The waters were piped in from springs several kilometers away, and "amid the burning heat of summer" people enjoyed here "the sweet pleasures of springtime."[68]

The garden of the sixteenth and seventeenth centuries can be described as a "complicated" and coded "conceptual system"[69] in which nature was "denied" and even "subjected to force and shattered."[70] Such a garden exalted the *virtù* of its owner, whereas the garden of a medieval monastery directed the soul to God. In addition, by reason of its many subtle arrangements it represented a break with the supposed simplicity of Eden. In the middle of the seventeenth century, dramatist James Shirley (d. 1666) thinks tulips too costly and says of a garden that is too carefully arranged:

> This garden does not take my eyes,
> Though here you shew how art of men
> Can purchase nature at a price,
> Would stock old Paradise again.[71]

Thus people created artificial paradises for themselves because they knew that the real one had disappeared. This is the interpretation that has been given of elements chosen for the Villa Lante in Bagnaia, near Viterbo, in the sixteenth century. The great green oaks from which according to Ovid honey flowed in the golden age, and the fountain of Bacchus, which according to the *Georgics* was the source of rivulets of wine during that same golden age, were meant (it is said) to recall that *aetas felicior*. In the future, in contrast to the golden age, the age of Jupiter would be represented; this was symbolized by the Italian type of garden in which human art triumphs over nature. In fact, the arrangement chosen at Bagnaia placed at the end of the prospect a fountain of the flood, which brought the golden age to a tragic end.[72] Labyrinths or mazes, so often found in European gardens beginning in the Renaissance, and the initiation routes, sometimes lined with monstrous figures as in the "sacred wood" of Bomarzo (1552), reminded visitors that ever since the original sin the human journey has been a difficult one and that a great deal of effort is needed to discipline a natural world that has turned rebellious.

The transition from the *hortus conclusus* to the open garden that is characteristic of the Renaissance can also be seen, at the same period, in depictions of the story of Adam and Eve. Hugo van der Goes (*The Original Sin*, at Vienna), Hieronymus Bosch (*The Garden of Delights*, in the Prado), and Henri Met de Bles (*The Earthly Paradise*, in the Rijksmuseum, Amsterdam) had already introduced trees of paradise into the broad landscape. This trend became more marked as time went on. Lukas Cranach, who painted his *Earthly Paradise* (Vienna) about 1530, has broad openings into the countryside of Eden.

The dismantling of the *hortus conclusus* is completed around 1550 in the magnificent Brussels tapestries devoted to the opening chapters of Genesis (the tapestries are now in the Galleria dell'Academia in Florence). The naming of the animals, the several phases in the original sin, and the expulsion of our first parents all take place amid broad spaces in which can be seen trees, hills, many flowers, much foliage, and numerous birds as well as representatives of many other species of animals.[73] Rubens and Jan Brueghel, who in the next century collaborated on a picture entitled *Adam and Eve*

in the Earthly Paradise (in the Mauritshaus, The Hague), followed the same
course, which henceforth became the most common, if we may judge from
the treatment of the same subject by Isaak von Oosten (d. 1661; in the
Musée des Beaux Arts, Rennes) or the eighteenth-century artist who depicted the earthly paradise with a tasteful choice of themes and colors on the
pavement of the church of San Michele in Anacapri.[74]

Flowers and Fountains

While the garden of Eden was losing its enclosing wall, flowers acquired an
increasingly large place in the sensibility and art of the West. Many influences combined to bring about this emphasis on flowers: the cultivation of
flowers in medieval cloisters, the influence of Eastern gardens, the return to
antiquity that revived the pagan symbolism of such flowers as the rose and
the carnation. Add to these the concern for detail that has been so typical
of our civilization since the end of the Middle Ages; the introduction of real
landscapes into artistic compositions, for example, in *The Miraculous Catch* of
K. Witz (1444) in the Geneva Museum; the attention to plants that can be
seen in, among others, many watercolors of Dürer and Höfnagel; the studies of Leonardo da Vinci; and the scenes of Giovanni da Udine, which are
inspired by ancient grotesques.

With all these factors combining, interest in botany and horticulture developed rapidly in the West, especially from the fifteenth century on, and
affected the two areas of the sacred and the secular. Some examples: the approximately fifteen plants that have been identified in the paradisal meadow
of Hubert Van Eyck's *Mystical Lamb* (Saint-Bavon in Ghent); the "thousand
flower" tapestries so popular in France at the end of the fifteenth century and
the beginning of the sixteenth; or the flower-filled garden that the author of
the *Hypnerotomachia Poliphili* imagines planted in a ruined Roman amphitheater. According to Francesco Colonna, on the steps of this amphitheater
grow cyclamens, cornflowers, carnations, and narcissuses. The center is occupied by covered galleries and avenues that are shaded by rosebushes, myrtles,
and clipped cypresses, side by side with columbines, lilies, stock, lilies of the
valley, carnations, violets, periwinkles, marigolds, and gladioli.[75]

Ronsard wrote poems on the marigold, the pine, and the holly. In England, the first commercial tree nurseries appeared in the Tudor period.[76] In
1546, the keeper of the garden of the king of England bought no less than
three thousand rosebushes with red flowers.[77] The sixteenth century saw the
arrival in France of the tulip, hyacinth, anemone, and crocus.[78] The centers
from which the use of flowers in gardens spread were initially Italy, Spain,

and southern France, but from 1580 on the Spanish Netherlands and the United Provinces took the lead in this area. This accounts for the place of the tulip in the cultural life of these regions.[79]

The same period saw the emergence of botanical gardens. The oldest of these was established at Venice in 1533. Then came those of Padua (1545), Pisa (1546), Bologna (1568), Paris (1576), Leiden (1577), Leipzig (1580), and Montpellier (1598). Did people hope to recover the lost paradise with the help of botanical gardens? They pretended to believe this was possible. Keith Thomas cites seventeenth- and eighteenth-century English works on gardening with such titles as *Paradise Retrieved, Paradise Regained,* and *Paradisus in Sole.* In 1783 a French naturalist, Pierre-Joseph Buchoz, gave this title to a treatise on botany: *Le Jardin d'Eden, le paradis terrestre renouvelé dans le jardin de la Reine à Trianon, ou Collection des plantes les plus rares qui se trouvent dans les deux hémisphères* (The garden of Eden, the earthly paradise renewed in the queen's garden at Trianon, or: collection of the rarest plants to be found in the two hemispheres).[80]

Let me repeat, however, that as far as the main subject of this book is concerned, the beginnings of European modernity were marked by a keen sense of the impossibility of returning to the golden age or the earthly paradise (these two unreal places of the past were often identified in people's minds). It is revealing that the sixteenth and seventeenth centuries saw a proliferation of several combined themes: the Land of Cocagne (Land of Plenty), the fountain of youth, more or less comical *impossibilia,* "the world turned upside down"[81] (for example, on the Feast of Fools), and others. These inverted worlds certainly made people laugh or smile or at least dream, but the stress placed on them cannot leave historians indifferent. They were the expression of a powerful collective fantasy. Let me point out an uncertainty among experts that is very significant: a painting by Lucas of Leiden that is now in the Rijksmuseum of Amsterdam is sometimes identified as a depiction of the Land of Cocagne, sometimes as a depiction of the golden age.[82]

The importance of the legend of the fountain of youth during this period deserves special attention here. The Middle Ages had already dreamed of it, locating it within the kingdom of Prester John or having knights errant search for it throughout the world. In the fourteenth century it can be seen in a miniature in the *Roman de Fauvel* (Bibliothèque Nationale, Paris) and on ivory plates used to make boxes or caskets. But in the fourteenth century the theme becomes more widely used. A manuscript of the *Histoire du roi Alexandre* from the library of the dukes of Burgundy (and now in the Petit-Palais, Paris) shows a fountain in the middle of a paradisal garden. The fountain is guarded by lions and griffins, and in a basin fed by water from the fountain people recover youth and health. A caption explains the scene: "How Alexander discovered the fountain of youth."

The fountain could be given an allegorical, Christian explanation in which the water symbolizes spiritual regeneration. But under the influence of the Renaissance, erotic themes came to play a major part in representations of this fountain of happiness and youth, as in a fresco to be found in the Piedmontese chateau at Manta and attributed to Giacomo Jaquerio (first half of the fifteenth century). In two basins, one above the other, young men and girls embrace while watching Love shoot his arrows.

From among the many works that subsequently displayed the theme of the fountain of youth — panels on chests, etchings, tapestries from Colmar, engravings on wood from Beham, various paintings — I single out as an exemplary witness the painting of this subject that was done in 1546 by Lukas Cranach the Younger (Staatliche Museum, Berlin), whose father had painted *The Golden Age* in 1530 (now in the Oslo Museum). Here we see the sick, the elderly, and the crippled being carried to the edge of the miraculous water in carts, in wheelbarrows, on stretchers, and even on the backs of men. There they are stripped of their garments; they go down into the basin and emerge from it healed, young, happy, ready for dancing, banquets, and love. On the left, the side representing old age, the landscape is hilly and disquieting; on the right, the side of youth, nature is gentle and welcoming.[83]

In the sixteenth century, Ponce de León, who in 1513 had discovered Florida on the day of *Pascua florida* (feast of flowers = Easter Sunday), was said to have set out with the intention of seeking a mysterious fountain of youth; according to the Indians, he found it. Petrus Martyr d'Anghiera tells us that in Spain "everyone" regarded this report as "true," as did "not a small number of those who are set apart from the common folk by virtue and fortune." This Jordan of the Americas restored youth to old people. But Petrus Martyr adds that he himself could not allow nature such power. "I maintain that God has reserved to himself this prerogative which is no less extraordinary than the power to read the hearts of human beings or to create things out of nothing." In his view, the report was comparable to the fable of Medea restoring the youth of her father-in-law, Aeson, or of the Sibyl of Erythrea being transformed into a plant. Fernández de Oviedo, another chronicler of the conquest of the Americas, thinks it absurd to attribute to a Christian a plan for discovering a fountain of youth.[84]

The fountain of youth appears twice in a triptych by Hieronymus Bosch that is now in the Prado and has been given the title *Garden of Earthly Delights*. In the left-hand panel, which depicts the earthly paradise, that is, the "garden of delights" in the original sense, the Creator is calling Adam and Eve to life. Behind them can be seen a strangely formed rose-colored fountain that shoots up from a pool of calm blue water. While this section of the work contains comical strokes and unusual details (as in all of Bosch's work), the overall impression is of peace amid a tranquil countryside. A giraffe and an elephant, both white, stand on either side of the fountain. Other animals are drinking without fear from a sea.

But ever since original sin the garden of Eden has either disappeared or is barred to humanity. Let us therefore distrust the false delights of this world! The center panel of the triptych, which depicts false earthly pleasures, has, once again, a fountain of youth. Pretty women, white and black, frolic in it. Tasty fruits, flowers, and colors so mannered and delicate that they remind us of Persian miniatures, create an atmosphere of enchantment. The intrusion of disturbing and even obscene elements show that this is a false paradise. An odd face looks through a glass tube at a rat inside a crystal sphere in which two lovers are caressing each other. On the left is a giant owl, which is Satan's bird; on the right, a man is already falling headlong into the abyss.[85] The right-hand panel, where the reading of the work terminates, shows, quite logically, the triumph of evil in a hell of inexhaustible torments.

For a long time, clear-sighted people had been warning against the snare of tempting gardens. In *Le Paradis de la reine Sibylle* of Antoine de La Salle (d. 1460), the young hero, Guarino, known as Meschino, after many adventures reaches the palace of the fairy Alcine. "After he had eaten, they led him into a garden which seemed a paradise to him; in it were all the fruits the human tongue could name. But he realized then that all this was but an illusion, since there were many fruits there which were not in season."[86] This was an example of what that age spoke of as diabolic "deceptions."

Octavien de Saint-Gelais, a *rhétoriqueur* or poet of refined and sophisticated style who became bishop of Angoulême and died in 1502, teaches the same lesson in his *Séjour d'Honneur*. The Actor, who is the principal personage of the story, arrives at an island "most abundant and fruitful in all pleasures and every kind of joy"; in particular, it contains a "place of delights" and an "agreeable orchard" in which the trees and plants flower all year long and in which ladies and young girls dance to music. The hero of the story initially abandons himself "to every lustful act." Fortunately, however, divine grace exerts its power over him once again, and a revelation bids him leave this "island of empty hope." For this present world is but a "vale of wretchedness."[87]

Spenser gave expression to the melancholy felt by an entire age when he wrote as follows in a poem entitled "The Ruins of Time":

> Then did I see a pleasant Paradize,
> Full of sweete flowres and daintiest delights,

Such as on earth man could not more devize....
But O short pleasure bought with lasting paine,
Why will hereafter anie flesh delight
In earthly blis, and joy in pleasures vaine,
Since that I sawe this gardine wasted quite,
That where it was scarce seemed anie sight?
That I, which once that beautie did beholde,
Could not from teares my melting eyes withholde.[88]

The exegetes confirmed this view: the "garden of delights" has indeed disappeared. But humanity still had the right and even the duty to find out where God had planted it.

Chapter 7

The New Learning and
the Earthly Paradise

The Earthly Paradise at the Center of a Culture

Do we perhaps think that the "naive" belief in the earthly paradise was peculiar to the Middle Ages and was challenged by the intellectual advances
of the Renaissance? When Dürer, Henri Met de Bles, Michelangelo, and
later on Rubens[1] represented Adam and Eve in their innocent nakedness,
amid a nature subject to them, and when the makers of the great window
at Beauvais[2] and of the stained-glass windows, now replaced, in the church
of the Vieux-Marché in Rouen did the same, did they all think they were
merely conjuring up a beautiful legend, a wonderful subject for artistic representation? Surely not! On the contrary, these artists, each according to his
imagination and talent, gave new life to a golden age that everyone was
convinced had really existed before the disastrous disobedience of our first
parents. In addition, claims and speculations regarding the earthly paradise
were more alive than ever at the beginning of the modern era.

Here is one example among many: Antoine Du Verdier (d. 1602), a royal
chamberlain, teaches quite clearly in his *Diverses Leçons:* "Eden is evidently
the proper name of the place in which God at the beginning planted the
garden of delights. . . . This garden was watered by a fountain or stream which
as it left there divided into four great rivers." To those who would tend to
confuse the heavenly kingdom with paradise Du Verdier says:

> There is a great difference and dissimilarity between the heavenly king-
> dom and paradise. The heavenly kingdom is located above the firmament
> of heaven, while paradise is beneath the firmament on earth. . . . In addition,
> the pleasure of the heavenly kingdom comes from the vision of God and the
> eternal beatitude which we have there with the happy angels; the delights of
> paradise consist in agreeable and desirable trees and in that great and wonder-
> ful stream that waters them. Furthermore, the heavenly kingdom has not been

seen by any eye or heard by any ear.... But paradise was visible to the bodily eyes of Adam and Eve.

Unfortunately, "It [paradise] will remain empty of inhabitants."[3]

We find it difficult today to get an accurate idea of the place that the earthly paradise had in the concerns of the best minds of the sixteenth and seventeenth centuries, when it brought treasures of learning into play and at the same time inspired many great poetic works. A. Williams, in a study of the commentaries on the Pentateuch that were composed in England during the Renaissance, lists thirty-nine in Latin and six in English on the Book of Genesis alone, and thirteen on the entire Pentateuch; these numbers are in addition to commentaries on the entire Bible.[4] It has been estimated that from 1540 to 1700 the earthly paradise supplied the subject matter for at least 155 literary works written either in Latin or in the various languages of the European West.[5] The *Semaines* of Du Bartas (first edition, 1601), the *Adamus exul* of Hugo Grotius (also 1601), the *Adam banni* of Joost van den Vondel (1664), and the *Paradise Lost* of Milton (1667) are only the part most visible to us today of a very large iceberg. It becomes necessary, therefore, to select from the vast range of intellectual works that were produced at that period and devoted to a subject regarded as essential by Catholics and Protestants alike.

It was understandable that the attention of churchmen should be focused more than ever on the earthly paradise, since the sin of Adam and Eve was constantly seen in relation to the "freely given gifts" and idyllic situation that our first parents had enjoyed before sin caused them to lose them. Most of the Protestant Reformers (Zwingli was an exception) could have subscribed to the decrees of the Council of Trent on "original sin" and "justification" (fifth and sixth sessions). It is said there that as a result of his transgression the first man "at once lost...holiness and justice." He drew upon himself "the wrath and indignation of God and consequently death with which God had threatened him, and together with death captivity in the power of him who henceforth 'has the power of death,' i.e., the devil." On the other hand, the council says, in opposition to Luther and Calvin, that free will was not "extinguished" by original sin, but only "weakened and distorted."[6]

Because the idea of original sin was at this time central to Western culture,[7] it was logical that the earthly paradise should also have a central place, the two being theologically and historically inseparable. The first generation of Reformers could not avoid dealing with so essential a subject, nor did they try to do so; quite the contrary. Luther discusses it especially in his *Commentaries on the Book of Genesis* and Calvin in his *Commentary...on the First Book of Moses, Called Genesis*, which was published in Geneva in 1553.[8] By means of these commentaries the two men established a tradition within the Protestant world, if only through translations and adaptations of their works. The *Bishops' Bible* of 1568 contains a digest of Calvin's *Commentaries*, which were also translated into English in their entirety ten years later. As an obligatory theological subject during that period and as a privileged subject for the application of the learning of exegetes and Hebraists, the earthly paradise was discussed in sixteenth-century Protestant circles by the antitrinitarian Michael Servetus in his *Christianismi restitutio* (1553) and by Heinrich Bullinger, Zwingli's successor in Zurich, in his *Antiquissima fides et vera religio* (1544). Pietro Martire Vermigli, a Florentine who adopted the Reformed faith, published an *In Primum librum Mosis* (Zurich, 1569) that reached a relatively large readership. The same holds for his disciple, Zanchius (Girolamo Zanchi, d. 1590), another Italian who adopted the Reformed faith and took refuge in the Palatinate. His treatise, *De Operibus Dei intra sex diebus creationis* (1613), devoted no less that 864 folio columns to a commentary on the first chapter of Genesis. One of Zanchius's students was David Pareus (Wängler), a German Calvinist, whose *In Genesim commentarius*, published in 1609, was regarded as authoritative by Protestants throughout the seventeenth century.[9]

Joseph Duncan, who has made an exhaustive study of the sources of Milton's *Paradise Lost*, notes that Milton and many religious people of his time were very much influenced by the *Praelectiones in Genesim* (1582) of Franciscus Junius (Franz Du Jon), a Dutch Hebraist,[10] who was continually cited and lauded in the seventeenth century. Together with his father-in-law, Tremellius, a converted Jew, Junius had also published a Latin translation of the Bible (Frankfurt, 1579), the notes of which were often used by Protestant authors.

Among the theologians and exegetes of the French Reform of the seventeenth century who were especially interested in the earthly paradise and the text of Genesis that describes it, mention must be made of André Rivet (1572–1651), pastor at Thouars and deputy to five national synods, then professor at Leiden and Breda, and a zealous controversialist and rigorist. He devoted no less than 916 quarto pages to *Exercitationes* on Genesis (published in 1633). Samuel Bochart (1599–1667), another French Reformed theologian, a scholar of European stature, and a correspondent of Christina of Sweden,[11] likewise tackled, from the historical angle, the question of "the serpent tempter and the earthly paradise."[12] At the beginning of the following century interest in these matters was still alive among French Protestants, as is shown by the *Histoire du Vieux et du Nouveau Testament* of Jacques Basnage, which appeared at Amsterdam in 1705 and which devotes its opening pages to the "location" of the garden of Eden. In Switzerland, Giovanni

Diodati (1579–1649), a Genevan theologian born into a family of refugees from Lucca and a translator of the Bible into Italian, is of interest to us here because of his *Annotations pieuses et érudites sur la sainte Bible* (1644), which had an international readership. The work was translated into English three times during the seventeenth century. In 1639 Milton visited this famous Calvinist in Geneva.

It is perhaps in England that we can see most clearly the diversity and multiplicity of writings that took the earthly paradise as a matter of great importance. The first that I shall mention is Samuel Purchas's *Pilgrimage*, published in 1613. Purchas, a chaplain at Canterbury, provided Shakespeare with the inspiration for *The Tempest* and continued the task of publishing *The Principal Navigations*, the great work of the English geographer Hakluyt. The title of Purchas's book is *Pilgrimage throughout the World and All Religions . . . at All Times and in All Places*. The author inquires at length into the location of the earthly paradise. The second work to be mentioned is *A Treatise of Paradise* (1617) by a former Catholic, John Salkeld, who had become a rector in Somerset. His work may be regarded as the most complete ever produced in Great Britain on the garden of Eden. It is for this reason that I shall return to it a number of times in the pages that follow. The third and last book is *A Discourse of the Terrestrial Paradise* (1666) by Marmaduke Carver, rector of a parish in Yorkshire, who wrote his book to defend the historical truth of the story in Genesis and to determine "the most probable" location of the earthly paradise. The author tells us that the work had been written twenty-six years before its publication.

In addition to theological treatises there were the works of orientalists, travelers, and geographers. John Hopkinson, who taught Eastern languages for twenty-two years, composed a *Synopsis paradisi*, which was published in 1593, after his death; in it he attempts to prove that the garden of Eden was located in Mesopotamia. Walter Raleigh (d. 1618) was familiar with Hopkinson's *Synopsis* and refers to the author familiarly as "our Hopkinson." Raleigh's history of the world, which remained unfinished due to the author's beheading, begins with a description of the state of human beings before sin and a discussion of the location of the earthly paradise. The more technical treatise of Nathaniel Carpenter, *Geography Delineated Forth* (1625), is the first English work of theoretical geography. The author endeavors to reconcile Aristotle and Ptolemy with Mercator and Ortelius.

Geography also found a place in printed Bibles. The first Bible to contain a map dates from 1525. It accompanied a section of Luther's translation of the Old Testament that was printed in Zurich.[13] Among the subjects that subsequently found a place on maps was the earthly paradise. In fact, this had already appeared in a Bible printed at Cologne in 1483: here the creation of Eve is depicted in the middle of three concentric bands representing respectively the encircling ocean with its fishes, the firmament with the sun and the stars, and, finally, heaven with its population of saints. Calvin was, however, the first who decided that his commentary on Genesis should be accompanied by a map allowing the reader to locate the paradise said by Moses to be in the "land of Havilah": the Reformer places it east of Seleucia and Babylon. Even before the end of the sixteenth century Calvin's map appeared in a dozen or so printings of the Bible. This tradition was kept up for a long time, with the result that Protestant readers (Catholic Bibles had no map) had a supposedly accurate geographical representation enabling them to visualize the precise location in which the Creator had decided to place the earthly paradise.

The same emphasis on the earthly paradise can be seen in Catholics of the Renaissance and the classical age. Theological concerns, a better knowledge of Eastern languages than previous generations had had, and an increased curiosity about geography all combined to give specialists a better idea of the location of paradise and the time of its existence. On the Catholic side of the confessional dividing line there was likewise a long list of names worth mentioning. The important thing here is to call attention to the principal contributions, those that at the end of the development, that is, in the specialized works of the second half of the seventeenth century and the eighteenth, most often served as references. It should be kept in mind, however, that it was not always the lengthiest works that were most often cited. Some authors were given more attention because of their fame or because of the originality of their claims.

Enea Silvio Piccolomini (d. 1464) belongs in the first of these categories. He was a humanist who became pope with the name Pius II, and was the author of works of poetry, history, and geography; we can see him still in the scenes from his life that Pinturicchio painted in the library of the cathedral of Siena. His ambitiously titled *Historia rerum ubique gestarum,* published in 1477, devotes only a few paragraphs to the location of the earthly paradise. But it was still being reissued at the end of the seventeenth century.[14] Seventy-five years after Pius II and in a quite different style, but with the same interest in geography, Guillaume Postel, an orientalist who taught "foreign languages" (meaning Hebrew and Arabic) at the Royal College, created a stir when he located the earthly paradise at the North Pole or close to it.[15] Some years later, a doctor in Brabant named Jean Becan (better known as Goropius Becanus), a man well versed in Latin, Greek, and Hebrew, was endeavoring to prove, in his *Origenes antwerpianae* (1569), that Adam spoke Flemish in the earthly paradise.[16]

More classic in form are some works often mentioned by later writers.

First of all, there is the *Commentarii in quinque libros mosaicos* of Cardinal Cajetan, published in 1539 and containing 538 folio pages. This Dominican, who was general of his order and legate of Leo X in Germany in 1518, where his mission was to bring Luther back to the Roman confession, owed his international fame both to this mission, which failed, and to his commentary on the *Summa* of St. Thomas Aquinas.[17] Seventeenth-century specialists who wrote about the earthly paradise referred their readers quite frequently to the *Recognitio Veteris Testamenti ad hebraicam veritatem* (Venice, 1529) of Augustinus Steuchus Eugubinus, an Italian who was a bishop in Crete and a delegate to the Council of Trent.[18] Specialists also referred their readers to the *Commentaria in Moisi Pentateuchum*, published at Lisbon in 1556 by a Portuguese writer, Jerônimo Oleaster, who likewise took part in the Council of Trent. Eugubinus's work is 782 octavo pages in length, and Oleaster's contains 650 folio pages. Both men contributed to the decline of the medieval conviction that the Ganges and the Nile were two of the rivers that flowed out of paradise. In this they were joined especially by François Vatable, one of the six "royal readers" appointed by Francis I to what later became the Collège de France. Vatable published *Annotationes in Pentateuchum* (1545).[19]

The second half of the sixteenth century and the early decades of the seventeenth — the golden age of the Counter-Reformation — saw the multiplication of Catholic commentaries on Genesis, most of them from the pens of Jesuits, who were as prolific in this area as in others. Some of these Jesuits were: Benedicto Pererius (Pereira), a Spaniard whose four volumes of *Commentariorum et disputationum in Genesim,* published at Lyons in the 1590s, became the major reference work in this area; T. Malvenda, a Fleming, author of *De paradiso voluptatis* (1605); Cardinal Bellarmine, who wrote, as did others, on "the grace of the first man" and therefore also on the paradise in which God had placed him (1617–20);[20] Cornelius a Lapide, another Fleming, a Hebraist from Liège who composed learned *Commentaria in Pentateuchum Moysis* (1616, eleven hundred folio pages) that were printed eleven times before the appearance of Milton's *Paradise Lost;* finally, Francisco Suárez (d. 1617), the most prominent Jesuit author of his time, whose complete works occupy some thirty volumes. Suárez did not fail to take up questions about the earthly paradise in the chapters that he devoted to "the works of each of the six days of creation and the rest on the seventh."

Later in the seventeenth century and during the eighteenth, Jesuits kept returning to the subject of the earthly paradise. Thus we find a *Diatriba de quattuor fluviis et loco paradisi* (1635) by Nicholas Abram, a *Nouveau Traité sur la situation du paradis terrestre ou conformité de Pline avec Moïse, par rapport à la position des fleuves du paradis terrestre* (1716) by Jean Hardouin, and, in a fresh approach, geographical details on the garden of Eden in the *Histoire du peuple de Dieu* (1728) of Father Isaak Joseph Berruyer.

Increasingly, however, non-Jesuit writers turned their attention to sacred geography. Eugène Roger, a Recollect, composed *La Terre sainte* (1646), a work of popularization that claimed, after countless others before it, that the story of the earthly paradise "is to be taken and understood literally." Pierre Clément, a canon regular, published *Sainctes curiositez* on the same subject at Langres in 1651. Most importantly, Pierre-Daniel Huet, to whom La Fontaine had dedicated a "letter of praise," published a *Traité de la situation du paradis terrestre* (1691), just before being appointed bishop of Avranches. This work was long regarded as authoritative and was presented to the king by J.-B. Bossuet.[21] Some years later, Dom Calmet, a Benedictine, published a *Commentaire littéral sur tous les livres de l'Ancien et du Nouveau Testament* (1706), which endeavored to renew the question of the earthly paradise.

But, following Joseph Duncan,[22] I must here assign special importance to the work of a "Sicilian priest," Agostino Inveges, *Historia sacra paradisi terrestris et sanctissimi innocentiae status* (1649). The work does not seem to have been widely known, since it is not to be found either in Rome or in Paris (I have been able to read it thanks to a microfilm from Palermo). It is the Catholic counterpart of *A Treatise of Paradise* by the Anglican John Salkeld, which I mentioned earlier. Both books raise all possible and imaginable questions about the earthly paradise and its inhabitants and conscientiously make reference to the vast literature already in existence on the subject. Both books are therefore valuable guides through a dense forest.

Methods and Issues

According to Inveges, so many learned men had written about the earthly paradise that the number of books produced was really "infinite," so that "'paradise' might be called a labyrinth rather than a garden."[23] Why had so many efforts been made in the course of the ages to shed light on this story of our origins? Walter Raleigh and Anglican pastor Marmaduke Carver answered that "all of us have a deep-rooted desire to know the place where our first parents lived."[24] But the most usual answer, the one on which the majority of Catholics and Protestants agreed in the sixteenth and seventeenth centuries, was that this was a religious matter of major importance.

Suárez speaks very plainly: "Knowledge of the earthly paradise is important for faith and is needed when we have to inquire into the status of humanity before sin."[25] Further on, he adds, speaking this time of the location of the garden of Eden: "In my judgment, this question is not an in-

different matter but a matter of faith, or nearly so."[26] Walter Raleigh agrees
with Suárez: "You may object . . . that the curiosity which urges men to search
out diligently the location of paradise, as well as the knowledge they may
gain of it, are of little use or even simply useless. My answer is that there is
nothing in the scriptures that has not been written for our instruction."[27]

In a dissertation defended before the Protestant faculty of theology at
Jena in 1676 and devoted to "the location of Eden, Ophir, and Tarshish,"
Matthias Beck is of the opinion that God did not want to conceal the location of the garden of Eden from us, as he did the place of the tomb of
Moses. On the contrary, his plan was to make the earthly paradise known to
us "as a reminder of our disobedience. That is why he had Moses so carefully
and accurately describe and place before our eyes this garden that became a
place of misfortune through the lamentable sin of the human race."[28] The
same feeling and the same logic find expression in John Salkeld's *A Treatise
of Paradise*. As he explains it, it is only by considering "all the wonderful aspects of the place where we were before sin" that we can understand how so
good and merciful a God could inflict on humanity so lengthy and great a
punishment that will last to the end of time.[29]

Let me emphasize, then, the importance of the issue here, as understood
almost unanimously by Catholic and Protestant theologians in bygone days,
namely, that the enormity of the first sin and the magnitude of the punishment that followed it become intelligible and credible only when seen in
light of the idyllic situation that Adam and Eve initially enjoyed. A pessimistic anthropology and a particular conception of redemption flowed from
the commonly accepted image of the earthly paradise.

So important a question called for all possible care and for all the intellectual resources available. The Renaissance, which in this respect was imitated
by the classical age, utilized the learning of the age to shed as much light
as possible on the paradise that existed at the beginning. Its approach was
meant to be "multidisciplinary," in the sense of combining all the data that
the learning of the age could elicit from the better-known ancient languages,
especially Hebrew, from history, which was so exalted by humanist culture,
and from geography as revitalized by the voyages of exploration.

Thus the thousands upon thousands of pages devoted to the garden of
Eden for more than two hundred years were the product of inquiries that
were meant to be rigorously technical and that piled up citations, references,
and the most recently acquired knowledge in order to shed a definitive light
on the beginnings of humankind. Many commentators on Genesis could
have made their own the formulation of purpose enunciated by Cornelius a
Lapide, whose aim was "to bring out solidly, briefly, methodically, and clearly
the original and literal sense" of the sacred text.[30]

It is possible, then, to speak of the "rational" and "scientific" character of the many works that took the earthly paradise as an object of "historical" study. The works certainly had apologetic aims. But this "positive" theology also intended to make use of the most reliable exegetical methods and the most recent findings of geography and history. The text of Moses was certainly inspired, but the only valid approach to it was to recover its true meaning by a rigorous word by word analysis and by ascertaining with accuracy in what place and at what period Moses had written.

Thus it is significant that at the beginning of his history of the world Raleigh challenges those who had spoken of the earthly paradise "without consideration of geography, without regard for East and West, without taking into account where Moses was writing" and where he was standing when he pointed the way to the place of the garden of Eden, although he is "very detailed" on this point. Raleigh also criticizes those who deal with this question "without knowing Hebrew" or who, in their excessive self-confidence, "confuse one place with another."[31] In the same spirit, Marmaduke Carver tells his readers: "Without the help of sacred geography, the direct and literal meaning of the text (which is the basis of all correct interpretation) cannot be discovered at many points, nor can light be shed on history, nor can those questions be discussed which obviously arise almost spontaneously."[32] At the end of the seventeenth century Huet advises his readers that his method for determining the exact location of the earthly paradise will be a rigorous one: "Prepare yourselves for arid reading, tortuous research, and boring citations, and to suffer through some Greek and some Hebrew. It is not possible to shed light on so obscure a question as this without these aids."[33]

Paradoxical as it may seem to us, the surprisingly naive explanations that I shall be listing bore witness to a different spirit than that of the Middle Ages. The aim was to get rid of legends, to put an end to fanciful localizations, to establish accurately the chronology of the days of creation, and to determine with certainty the moment of the first sin. We smile today at these vast ambitions. In any case, the very vastness accounts for the exhausting work to which the best minds of the time subjected themselves in all seriousness.

First of all, in their concern for realism they most often vigorously rejected the allegorical interpretations of the earthly paradise that had been given by Philo, Origen, or Ephraem. For the men of the Renaissance the text of Genesis was a completely credible document that narrated a history that had really happened. In this respect the science of the humanists confirmed and strengthened the tradition of Isidore of Seville and St. Thomas Aquinas. There were indeed some seventeenth-century English "independents," some "blasphemers," who maintained the allegorical character of the Genesis story, but the science of the day, with all its concern for objectivity, asserted loudly and clearly and on a massive scale that the Pentateuch in its entirety was to be taken literally.

Luther says this in so many words: "Paradise he [Origen] takes to be heaven; the trees he takes to be angels; the rivers he takes to be wisdom. Such twaddle is unworthy of theologians, though for a mirthful poet they might perhaps be appropriate. Origen does not take into consideration that Moses is writing a history and, what is more, one that deals with matters long since past."[34] Calvin is no less categorical: "We entirely reject the allegories of Origen, and of others like him, which Satan, with the deepest subtlety, has endeavored to introduce into the Church, for the purpose of rendering the doctrine of Scripture ambiguous and destitute of all certainty and firmness."[35] Hopkinson, a Hebraist, took his turn in attacking Philo, who, urged on by an "evil genius," thought he could deny the "earthly" nature of paradise. But "the context makes it clear that paradise did exist on the earth."[36] Raleigh in his history cites these words of Hopkinson and adds: "I am very surprised that educated men [he is thinking especially of Philo and Origen] could have erred so stupidly and blindly."[37]

In order to demonstrate that the earthly paradise was "a real and corporeal place," Salkeld appeals to numerous authorities (St. Augustine, St. Basil, Epiphanius, Isidore of Seville, and others) and cites a homily of St. John Chrysostom in which the speaker says that "Moses has so clearly described paradise, its rivers, its trees, its fruits, and everything relating to it, that even the simple and the ignorant should not have their trust abused by the fantastic allegories and rambling daydreams which some offer as the only truth hidden beneath the description of paradise that is so concrete and full of imagery."[38] Carver in his turn complains that some "have emptied out the letter of the text and replaced it with a cabalistic and allegorical paradise of their own devising."[39] Finally, as a last citation from this list of Protestant writers, Jacques Basnage (d. 1723) advises his readers to "follow exactly" the description that Moses has given in his "history."[40]

The official Catholic position at this time was the very same. As evidence, here are statements of Suárez, a weighty authority on the Roman side: "The main question [regarding the garden of Eden] and almost the only one that is important to faith is whether paradise was really earthly, that is, planted on earth, and, consequently, whether everything said about it in Genesis is to be taken literally, as we hear it, or, on the contrary, is to be given a metaphysical and mystical meaning." Suárez recalls the errors of Philo and Origen, discusses opinions attributed to St. Ambrose, and then declares the official position: "It is Catholic teaching that the paradise which God planted at the beginning was an earthly place and that everything said about its creation is to understood in the proper and literal sense. This statement is a matter of faith and is proved by scripture."[41]

To the defenders of allegory Suárez opposes the Latin and Greek fathers, referring especially to St. Jerome and St. Thomas. When summing up the authorities on this question in the middle of the seventeenth century, the Sicilian scholar Inveges calls upon "Irenaeus, Tertullian, Epiphanius, Augustine, and Jerome." It is from their writings that the moderns — Sixtus of Siena, Pereira, Bellarmine, Malvenda — have drawn the arguments that confound the allegorists and show up "their obvious error," even their "heresy." "The justification" for this condemnation is that "Moses said that paradise was planted with trees, that it yielded fruits beautiful to the eye and sweet to the taste, that it was watered by rivers, and that Eve saw, touched, and tasted the fruit of knowledge. These words are not allegory but history."[42]

Gradual Abandonment of Medieval Beliefs

The careful study of Genesis led the scholars of the Renaissance and the classical age to jettison a number of naive medieval beliefs regarding the location of the earthy paradise. First of all, how could it have been set high in the air, close to the moon? The *Nuremberg Chronicles* (1492) devotes a chapter, at the beginning of the work, "to paradise and its four rivers." Also mentioned there — but without any position being taken on it — is the view, attributed especially to the Venerable Bede (but without any proof being offered), that located the garden of delights at an "inaccessible altitude," that is, in a "very elevated area of the ether." The waters that descended from that height made such a noise in striking the earth that people living near the cascade lost their hearing. In any case, the waters "give rise to four rivers," among them the Pishon, which is the Ganges, and the Gihon, which is the Nile.[43] This kind of talk was soon to be attacked as obscurantist by both Protestants and Catholics.

According to Calvin, "This garden was situated on the earth, not as some dream in the air."[44] Hopkinson and Raleigh are in full agreement. To those who placed the earthly paradise beyond reach, "on a very high mountain, within the orbit of the moon," Hopkinson replies by appealing to the calculations of Ptolemy. According to Ptolemy, the distance between earth and moon is 327,381 English miles. If the earthly paradise were located so high up in the heavens, the mountain on which it rested would require the entire surface of our planet for its base. In addition, it would hide the light of the sun from us.[45] Salkeld and Carver, among others, share the same view and find themselves, on this point, in the company of Pereira, Bellarmine, and Suárez.

Suárez explains at length that the view that locates the earthly paradise near the moon is not found either in the *Hexaemeron* of St. Basil or, as is often asserted, in Bede's commentary on Genesis. On the other hand, texts that can be given this interpretation may be found in John Damascene, in the *De paradiso* of St. Basil (which we know today is not from his pen), and in Rupert and Moses Bar Cephas. But how can anyone not see the difficulties that such teaching raises? So elevated a place would not have been "healthful or suited for human habitation both because of the closeness of the sun, the stars, and the igneous element, and because of the perpetual disturbance of the air due to the movement of the heavens."[46] By the middle of the seventeenth century Eugène Roger refers only with condescension to the ancient hypothesis that the earthly paradise was located high up in the heavens. He writes: "I shall not dwell on the frivolous opinion of those who located the earthly paradise in the concavity of the moon; there was no reason for calling it earthly when it was placed among the things of the heavens."[47]

Another solution to the problem of the geographical location of paradise, one known in the Middle Ages and repeated by some later writers, was rejected in the sixteenth and seventeenth centuries by the majority of commentators on Genesis. This was the opinion that identified the earthly paradise with the entire earth; it had its basis especially in chapter 2 of the *Annotationes in Genesim* of Hugh of Saint Victor.[48] Nonetheless, Joachim Vadian, a Reformed humanist, made it his own. He reminds his readers that in Genesis (1:28–29) God ordered the first human beings to "fill the earth," and he gave them "every plant yielding seed that is upon the face of all the earth." According to Vadian, this means that the whole earth was the garden meant for Adam and his posterity; the fountain (or river) of paradise was to be understood as meaning the ocean.[49]

Even more than Vadian, a Swiss, it was Goropius, a Fleming, who presented the age with "the most fully developed theory of the earth as paradise."[50] He says in his *Origines antwerpianae:* "Paradise, that is, the garden of delights, consisted of the entire earth, which was intended to feed human beings without fatigue on their part but, on the contrary, amid perpetual contentment. The fountain that watered the garden was the great ocean, source of the rivers that water the four parts of the world." In support of these claims, Goropius recalls the ancient descriptions of the Elysian Fields and the golden age. He goes on to show that Adam and Eve were not "expelled from a place but from a benign natural world" that supplied all their needs without their experiencing the hardship of labor. They changed not their place but their condition. "I do not see why I should not say that the entire earth was paradise before the divine curse." As for the statement that "God planted paradise *ab oriente,* this means that it was in this part of the world that man was created. In other words, God had to put man somewhere, but this does not imply that the entire earth was not a paradise."[51]

Like Goropius, Juan de Pineda, a Spanish Jesuit, defended the view that identified the earthly paradise with the entire earth. His supporting argument is one of common sense. If the original sin had not been committed, the innocent human race would nonetheless have multiplied. How could it have been housed in the narrow space of an enclosed garden? Would a distinction have been made between a privileged group living there and second-class folk who would visit it only to eat the fruit of the tree of life? In addition, how could those living two or three thousand leagues away have easily gone there to renew their supplies?[52]

The first answer that Pereira, Raleigh, and Suárez give to this kind of logic is to point to the text of Genesis: Adam was expelled from a garden, not from the entire earth, and the cherubim were placed at its entrance to bar humans from it. These authors then go on to argue in their turn that the earthly paradise must have had considerable dimensions, "at least those of a fairly large kingdom," in Suárez's estimation. The human race would easily have fitted into it, and this for two reasons: (1) when sin reigns, the elect are much less numerous than the reprobate; but in the reign of grace there would have been only the elect; therefore, their numbers would have been rather limited; and (2) after a certain time spent in the earthly paradise, these elect would have been regularly taken into the glory of heaven, thus leaving room for new generations. The Anglican Salkeld shares this view.[53] Thus the vast majority of specialists in the sixteenth and seventeenth centuries concluded that the earthly paradise was a "particular place." This formula occurs in the writings of, among others, Calvin, Steuchus Eugubinus, Oleaster, Raleigh, Suárez, and Diodati,[54] to give only a short list in which Protestants and Catholics are intermingled.

Finally, some medieval writers, especially Ephraem and Cosmas Indicopleustes, imagined the inhabitable world to be surrounded by the ocean, in the midst of which the earthly paradise was supposedly located. This geography was likewise rejected as unscientific in the sixteenth and seventeenth centuries. Pareus, a German Protestant, describes this location of paradise as a "utopia across the seas,"[55] and Raleigh calls it a "laughable opinion."[56] Pereira and Bellarmine explain why it is "implausible" and enjoys "no probability at all." "In our time," they note, "Spanish and Portuguese voyagers have crossed the entire ocean and circled the earth,"[57] but they have not found "that the land is surrounded by the ocean, nor that beyond the ocean there is some other land."[58] Furthermore, who can believe that this other land, "which would be much larger than ours, has remained empty and without human habitation from the beginning of the world until today?"[59] Recent geographical discoveries and common sense thus led to the rejection of this outdated doctrine.

In olden times, when people located the earthly paradise near the moon or on a continent separated from the inhabited world by an ocean, they could imagine that it still existed, inaccessible, no doubt, but preserved as it had been. We have seen that medieval cartographers did not fail to maintain the present existence of the earthly paradise somewhere in the depths of Asia. The Renaissance and the age that followed it discussed this question often and fiercely. One thing may surprise us, but is to be explained by the deep roots that beliefs acquire: many eminent minds maintained the traditional doctrine regarding the continued existence of the earthly paradise. Notable among them was Junius, a Protestant, who wrote:

> I am not impressed by the opinion of many that the earthly paradise had only a temporary existence and was destroyed after a few years, either after Adam's sin or after being submerged by the flood. Nowhere does Moses say anything such, nor is the opinion confirmed by any passage of sacred scripture. The continued existence of paradise seems more in keeping with the glory of God than does its disappearance, for it serves as proof of his wrath.[60]

But Junius is rather an exception among Protestant commentators on Genesis, and it is generally among Catholic writers that we find persisting the medieval conviction about the continued existence of paradise; indeed at this period such a view was described as a "papist error." Jesuits Malvenda, Bellarmine, and Suárez hold firmly to this ancient doctrine and claim, with Malvenda, that "the garden of delights did not perish in the waters of the flood but still exists in our time."[61] Bellarmine's position is revealing. After naming numerous Catholic writers according to whom no trace remains of the beauty and charm of the earthly paradise, he says: "For many reasons this view does not seem to me to have been proved, and first of all because it is new and contrary to the common thinking of the doctors, whether the Fathers of the Church or the Scholastics."[62]

Tradition thus weighs heavily on the reasoning of Suárez, who sets forth the pros and cons at length. "Serious writers," he acknowledges, think that the earthly paradise no longer exists, having been destroyed by the waters of the flood, which rose fifteen cubits above the highest mountains; in addition, no one has found it. But the contrary opinion seems to him to be "truer." Justin, Athanasius, Augustine, Jerome, and Isidore of Seville in ages past, and Bellarmine today hold that "paradise still exists in the form in which it was created, together with its delights and beauty." It is probable that Elijah and Enoch live there. Scripture says nothing of its destruction but, on the contrary, shows the divine intention of preserving it. Finally, if God had wanted to destroy it, why would he have waited for the flood? He could have destroyed it immediately after the fall or have removed the tree of life from it. And yet he assigns an angel to guard it. "According to the information given in the scriptures, then, the more credible view is that paradise still exists."[63]

Protestant writers were, of course, much freer in relation to tradition. On this question, Luther decides to stick to "historical facts." "This," he writes, "is something to which I carefully call attention, lest the unwary reader be led astray by the authority of the fathers, who give up the idea that this is history and look for allegories."[64] History bids us give up dreams of paradise and keep our feet on the ground:

> [The question of where Paradise is located] is an idle question about something no longer in existence. Moses is writing a history of the time before sin and the Deluge, but we are compelled to speak of conditions as they are after sin and after the Deluge.... For time and the curse which sins deserve destroy everything. Thus when the world was obliterated by the Deluge, together with its people and cattle, this famous garden was also obliterated and became lost.... Thus when we must discuss Paradise now, after the Flood, let us speak of it as a historical Paradise which once was and no longer exists.[65]

This clear-sightedness and this speech on method deserve to be emphasized. For Luther's will to renewal, in this area as in many others, was in strong contrast with the attachment of the age to traditions. It even led him to regard as being without any object the curiosity of those who seek at any cost to inquire into "something that does not exist after sin and the Deluge."[66]

Du Bartas adopts the same negative and abrasive view in his *Deuxième Semaine*. The poet there gives the following advice:

> Curious inquirer, ask not where
> God's own hands created that garden:
> whether on a mountain near the horns of Latona,
> or below the equator, or near Babylon,
> or in the shining East. Be humble and content
> to know that this park, whose king God made man,
> was a choice soil....
> Rather, if it pleases you to guess,
> presume that the flood, which drowned nature
> in revenge, did not spare the beauties of this place
> that first saw violence done to God's holy laws.
> Think that the flood swept away most of its plants,
> and killed the spirits of its most fragrant flowers.[67]

The conviction that the earthly paradise had been destroyed was almost universal among Protestant commentators on Genesis. Diodati, for example, warns that it is impossible to find the river of the garden of Eden, the river that divided into four branches. "Nor is this surprising, so much have things changed since then: first, because of the flood, and then because of earthquakes that have changed the course and names of rivers."[68] Salkeld, who collects and summarizes the most current opinions on this subject in his day and in his country, writes: "It seems most probable that the paradise in which Adam was created can no longer be discovered and that it was destroyed in the universal flood."[69]

Despite the authority of Malvenda, Bellarmine, and Suárez, Catholic commentators in increasing numbers agreed with their Protestant adversaries on this subject. As early as 1531, Steuchus Eugubinus, Italian bishop of a diocese in Crete, had said: "I think that the pleasant trees [of the garden of Eden] were swept away by the torrential waters and that the land [of paradise] itself was destroyed by the swift, eddying floods. Thus the place of delights was devastated. It disappeared from mortal eyes, so that after the flood no trace of it remained."[70] A half century later, Pereira, whom Protestants themselves cited with praise, took the same position: "If paradise has not been discovered and cannot be discovered, the most likely reason is that it was destroyed by the flood and that in the universal upsurge of waters that inundated the entire earth and covered its highest peaks, the beauties, charms, and amenities of paradise were completely destroyed and swept away."[71]

Cornelius a Lapide offers the same argument, though with perhaps a little more caution: "If we ask 'Do the pleasures of paradise still exist?' I answer: the place, yes; the pleasures, doubtful." He regards as "most probable" the view of those who think that paradise with its delights existed from the beginning up to the flood and was then "ruined, broken, and destroyed" by the waters that covered the earth "for a whole year."[72]

In the middle of the seventeenth century, in his summation of the debate on this subject, Inveges recalls Malvenda's view (the garden of delights still exists) and then says that "the majority of learned men reject it," while he himself judges it a view "hard" to accept.[73]

Thus was completed the break with a belief that had persisted for a millennium. At the end of the seventeenth century the most widely accepted view was that the earthly paradise had indeed existed as a "historical reality," but that it had been erased from the surface of the planet.

Inquiries into the Location of the Earthly Paradise (from the Sixteenth to the Eighteenth Century)

Abandonment of Fanciful Locations

Luther and Du Bartas warned, to no avail, that "we ask in vain today where and what that garden was."[1] The warning did not keep a good many "curious" persons from inquiring "where God's own hands had created that garden."[2] The majority of commentators on Genesis thought, like Calvin, that "since the eternal inheritance of man is in heaven, it is truly right that we should tend thither; yet we must fix our foot on earth long enough to enable us to consider the abode which God requires man to use for a time."[3]

Suárez spoke for many theologians and exegetes when he said that knowledge of the earthly paradise is "necessary" for us if we are to understand "all that the scriptures tell us of the condition of humanity before sin."[4] The passionate inquiry into the place of the garden of Eden was therefore legitimate and desirable. In addition, it was possible. For, as Raleigh wrote, "Although the garden itself cannot be found, inasmuch as the flood and other accidents of history reduced the land of Eden to the state of ordinary fields and pastures, the place nonetheless remains what it was, and its rivers are unchanged."[5]

Joseph Duncan's considered judgment is that in the sixteenth and seventeenth centuries "the location of paradise was given more consistent attention [by specialists] than any other question concerning it."[6] As the scholars of the time concentrated their attention on this subject, they were not satisfied simply to abandon the allegorical interpretations of Philo and Origen and the fanciful medieval localizations of paradise near the moon or beyond the encircling ocean. They also subjected to criticism other geographical hypotheses, whether ancient, revived, or new, that seemed to contradict either the letter of the sacred text or the new knowledge of the world that had resulted from the great discoveries.

We must therefore go back for a moment to the "equatorial" hypothesis. This hypothesis, put forward by Tertullian,[7] was recalled by St. Thomas Aquinas, who wrote in his *Summa theologica*, though he expressed himself with caution, that "we must hold that paradise was situated in a most temperate situation, whether on the equator or elsewhere."[8] St. Bonaventure and Durandus of Saint-Pourçain (d. 1334) are more categorical. The former says that in the earthly paradise "the heat was tempered by the purity of the air and the seasons were very similar because of the nearness of the equator."[9] In his view "paradise" was located in the East and near the equatorial line, a little to the south of it. Durandus in his commentary on the *Sentences* of Peter Lombard[10] and John of Genoa in the article "Paradisus" of his *Catholicon* (completed in 1288)[11] accept this same view, which was in harmony with the attraction that the warm regions of Asia — India or Ceylon — had for the Western imagination during the Middle Ages.

Roger Bacon (d. 1292) takes the opposite view, for while admitting that the equatorial zone is "temperate," he does not think that it is "very temperate." "Consequently, it is not certain that [the earthly] paradise must have been located there."[12] After some discussion and hesitation, Pierre d'Ailly in his *Ymago mundi* adopts Bacon's view and "deduces that below the equator the climate is not unqualifiedly temperate. It is therefore not obvious that the earthly paradise was placed there, since paradise must enjoy the most temperate conditions."[13]

The *Historia rerum ubique gestarum* of Pius II likewise casts "doubt" on the possibility of an equatorial habitat for human beings.[14] It is revealing, on the other hand, that Christopher Columbus, though a great reader and admirer of both Pierre d'Ailly and Pius II, should have disagreed with them on the point with which we are concerned here. Opposite the passage of Pius II to which I have just referred Columbus writes: "The contrary is proved for the south by the Portuguese and for the north by the English and the Swedes who sailed these parts of the world."[15] Further on, still annotating Pius II, Columbus returns to the subject in these words: "Eratosthenes says that the climate is very temperate below the equatorial line; Avicenna says the same.... The fortress of Mina, belonging to His Serene Highness the King of Portugal, is located directly upon the equatorial line. I have seen it."[16] According to Columbus, experience proved that the equatorial zone was habitable. This is why he believed that the Gulf of Paria was the way, barred perhaps but the way nonetheless, to the earthly paradise.

An imposing list could be compiled of sixteenth-century historians who were, if not convinced, at least impressed by the location that Christopher Columbus suggested.[17] Among them are to be found, in particular, Francisco López de Gomara (*Historia general de las Indias*, 1552),[18] Antonio de Herrera (*Historia general de los hechos de los Castellanos en las yslas y en tierre del Mar Oceano*, 1601–15),[19] and Father José de Acosta (*Histora natural y moral de las India*, 1590).[20]

Antonio de León Pinelo, son of a Portuguese Marrano, was more categorical in the great work that he composed in the years 1645–50 and in which he proved that the four rivers emerging from the earthly paradise were the Río de la Plata, the Amazon, the Orinoco, and the Magdalena. According to him, the earthly paradise was located in the heart of South America.[21] Pinelo's book was not printed until the twentieth century. It is likely that Simão de Vasconcelos did not know of it when he wrote his *Cronica da Companhia de Jesus* (1663), in which he too located the earthly paradise in South America and specifically in Brazil.

The question of an equatorial location of the earthly paradise was treated at length in Raleigh's *History of the World*. It was possible in times past (he thinks) to make a reasonable judgment that the regions below the equator were uninhabitable. But Tertullian and Avicenna, who expressed the opposite opinion, were correct. Instructed as we have been by the voyages of exploration, we know now that if a place exists anywhere that resembles the earthly paradise in its nature, beauty, and delights, that place must be sought in a region supposed formerly to be scorched and uninhabitable, that is, the region between the tropics or even close to the equatorial line. The heat of the day is there mitigated by the breezes, and the nights are cool. "I know of no other region of the world that has a better and more even temperature."[22]

A little later, Carpenter, the geographer, offers his own confirmation that Tertullian, Bonaventure, and Durandus of Saint-Pourçain were right when they disagreed with the ancients and said that the equatorial zone is "pleasant and makes a comfortable dwelling place. It is a fact that places on the equatorial line are not scorched by the sun as some used to think. Recent sailors have proved that, on the contrary, these places are most often very pleasant and fertile."[23]

When Suárez, a contemporary of Raleigh and Carpenter, tackles the question in his turn ("Was paradise on the equator?"), he agrees with them that "experience" (a word that is here rich with overtones of the modern age) has altered the facts of the problem: "Experience has shown that the regions of the torrid zone, thought uninhabitable by the ancients, are in fact made temperate by the abundant waters and frequent winds, and are very suited for habitation."[24] We shall see in a moment that, despite everything, not only Raleigh, Carpenter, and Suárez but also many scholars who commented on

Genesis at this same period located the now-vanished beautiful garden in the Near or Middle East. Nonetheless, in dealing with the question of the location of the earthly paradise we must face up to the historical fact of the revival of the "equatorial" hypothesis, which became then an "American" hypothesis (the reference being to the part of the Americas that had hot weather).

The recovery of credibility for an equatorial location in its new American version could only spur the search for fabled kingdoms (El Dorado, Ophir) in the interior of the New World. If the more serious commentators on Genesis in the sixteenth and seventeenth centuries rejected this attractive hypothesis that had been given new actuality by the voyages of discovery, the reason was that they had to deal with the letter of the sacred text, which placed the garden of Eden in the East and mentioned the Tigris and the Euphrates. Carpenter was therefore voicing the opinion of the experts when he wrote: "Paradise cannot have been located [on the equator], because the rivers of paradise that are mentioned in holy scripture have not been found there."[25]

On the other hand, there was a latecomer, Luis de Urreta, a Dominican, who at the beginning of the seventeenth century leaned toward an equatorial location of the earthly paradise, but in Africa. I have already mentioned his extravagant descriptions of the "great, distant kingdoms of Ethiopia and the monarchy of the emperor known as Prester John."[26] Because of the ancient geographical connection that collective belief had established between the kingdom of Prester John and the earthly paradise, Urreta was inclined to think that since the former was in Africa, the latter was also located there. He therefore thinks of Mount Amara as being an equatorial place worthy of containing the garden of Eden. He intends his statements on the subject to be circumspect, but they nonetheless suggest that this location is probable. He explains that in Ethiopic the word *amara* means "paradise." And in fact, he assures his readers, the mountain of this name is truly a *hortus deliciarum* that is separated by its altitude from the rest of the country. It is a place of happiness, a flowering garden, full of fruit trees and pleasant streams.

Urreta writes:

> I have no intention, no thought, of proving that this mountain is the earthly paradise created in the East on the third of the six days of creation, the place in which Adam and Eve were set and where humanity would have lived if Adam had not sinned. I am simply extolling the great privileges this mountain enjoys and showing that it possesses many characteristics which the holy doctors who treat of the earthly paradise attribute to the garden of delights in which our first parents were placed.

Recalling then the tradition that located the garden of Eden on the equator, Urreta observes that Mount Amara is located in that very latitude. Days and nights are of equal length; winter is never severe nor summer scorching. The temperature, which is moderate all year round, creates, "as it were, a perpetually joyous and flowering springtime." Thus all the traits of the earthly paradise are to be found on Mount Amara, where the trees yield fruit three times a year. When the sun moves toward the tropic of Capricorn, the fruits on south-facing branches ripen; when the sun moves toward the other tropic, it is the turn of the fruit on the northern branches; when the sun is at the equator, the fruit on the central branches reach maturity; thus nature never ceases producing fruit. "From this one may infer that we may well give the name 'paradise' to this mountain because of its fertility and delights."[27] This conclusion is followed, however, by a prudent question mark.

In the seventeenth century Urreta's book gave rise to discussion about Mount Amara, especially in England. Purchas in his *Pilgrims* devotes to this mountain a section that is at times a verbatim translation of Urreta. Purchas adds, and in this he is more categorical than Urreta, that "many have taken this place to be the paradise of our first parents."[28] Heyleyn, relying on Purchas, gives a description of Amara in his *Cosmographie* (1652), but refuses to identify it as the location of the earthly paradise.[29] Milton, who probably depends in turn on Heyleyn, gives Mount Amara a place in his *Paradise Lost*, but he locates the garden of Eden in Assyria. It is revealing, however, that he believed in the existence of a privileged place in the depths of Africa:

> Nor where Abyssin kings their issue guard,
> Mount Amara, though this by some supposed
> True Paradise under the Ethiop line
> By Nilus head, enclosed with shining rock,
> A whole day's journey high, but wide remote
> From this Assyrian garden, where the fiend
> Saw undelighted all delight, all kind
> Of living creatures new to sight and strange.
> (*Paradise Lost* 4.280–87)

After rejecting, perhaps regretfully, an equatorial location for the earthly paradise, Milton settled for the opinion of authoritative specialists of the day. In the end, the latter opted for the Near or Middle East, but were also persuaded that the earthly paradise in that location enjoyed conditions similar to those found now only in the equatorial regions. Thus they rejected with little discussion, and mentioned only for the record, the venturesome claim of Guillaume Postel, who had thought that humanity's original home could be located near the North Pole. Postel believed that the language of the Goths was the original human language and that the Scythians, who were hardened to cold, toil, and privations, had preserved, more than others, the physical characteristics of the inhabitants of the lost paradise.[30]

During the sixteenth and seventeenth centuries, there were, basically, three competing locations that won the allegiance of the best commentators on Genesis: Armenia, Mesopotamia, and the Holy Land. The commentators were almost unanimous in thinking that in Genesis the words *a principio,* "in the beginning," of the Vulgate should be replaced by *ab Oriente,* "in the East," and therefore that the text should read *plantavit Deus hortum ab Oriente* instead of *plantaverat autem Deus paradisum voluptatis a principio* (Gen 2:8).[31] This was the meaning that the Septuagint and the Greek fathers, among others, had given to the passage. Gregory of Nyssa had explained praying toward the East in light of this geography: "When we turn to the East, we do so because our original homeland, the paradise from which we fell, was in the East."[32] An earthly paradise in America or Africa was thus eliminated. The Renaissance and the classical age likewise abandoned (despite holdouts like Suárez)[33] the medieval identification of the Pishon with the Ganges and of the Gihon with the Nile, a view that made room for the hypothesis of an underground circulation of the waters that issued from the earthly paradise.

Armenia, Babylonia, or Palestine?

Armenia

Once these other sites were rejected, many writers wavered between Armenia and Mesopotamia, or at least refused to commit themselves to a more precise location within an area ranging from the foothills of the Caucasus Mountains to the Persian Gulf and even to Arabia Felix.[34] According to Pereira, "The regions to which the divine scriptures refer simply as 'eastern lands' are those around the Persian Gulf: Persia, Armenia, Arabia, Mesopotamia."[35] Cornelius a Lapide takes pretty much the same view: "It seems that [the earthly] paradise was in the direction of Mesopotamia and Armenia."[36]

On the other hand, Carver, in his *Discourse of the Terrestrial Paradise,* uses great stores of learning to show that the garden of Eden was located in Armenia. Piling up Hebrew, Greek, and Latin texts and relying on the geographical lore of the time, he manages ("with the help of God") to locate "the spring of the river of paradise."[37] The source of the Tigris is situated (he says) on the southern slopes of the Taurus Mountains. Initially a single river, it passed through the Eden that "the geographers call Sophene." It was within this region that the earthly paradise was set, where a nitrous lake mentioned by Pliny now exists.[38] The Tigris then divided into four streams, giving birth to the Euphrates, the Pishon, and the Gihon. To us, Carver's geography seems obviously fanciful, but the author feels a lively satisfaction when he sees that Ortelius, the great cartographer, locates the earthly paradise precisely here.[39]

At the beginning of the eighteenth century, Dom Calmet, a Benedictine exegete who exerted a considerable influence, inquired in his turn into the location of the "garden of delights." "There is," he writes, "perhaps no question about the scriptures that has given rise to a greater variety of views among the exegetes than the question of the location of the earthly paradise."[40] He tackles the problem in his turn, intending "to show that it was located in Armenia, between the sources of the Tigris, the Euphrates, the Phasis, and the Araxes. We suppose that Moses wrote Genesis while he was in Arabia Petraea and that it was in relation to that country that he described the location of the places of which he speaks."[41] The earthly paradise was in Armenia, but the land of Eden was larger and "included a part of Mesopotamia, Sophene, Adiabene [northern Assyria], and a part of Armenia and of Colchis."[42]

Mesopotamia

The Mesopotamian solution was adopted by some eminent minds in the sixteenth and seventeenth centuries, especially within Protestantism. Calvin opted for it and thus gave it wide acceptance. His reasoning can be taken as a model for the new "scientific" approach that was typical of the Renaissance in these matters. Having established that "the situation of Paradise lay between the rising of the sun and Judea," the reformer, unlike Luther, believed that "something more definite may be required concerning that region."[43] The problem was to identify the river that watered the garden and then divided into four streams. "No one disputes" that the Euphrates and the Tigris are two of the streams.[44] Now Strabo, "a diligent and attentive writer,"[45] showed that "at Babylon these two rivers unite: and then ... each is carried separately, in its own bed, into the Red Sea."[46]

I noted earlier that Calvin included a map in his commentary (Map 23). It shows a connection between the Tigris and the Euphrates north of Seleucia and Babylon, and then a complete joining of the two south of these two cities. This single river then divides again into two branches in the vicinity of the Persian Gulf. The lower Euphrates must have been the Gihon and the lower Tigris the Pishon. In order to be consistent with Genesis, Calvin is thereby led to locate the land of Cush (or Chus) to the west of the Gihon and the land of Havilah to the east of the Pishon.

Did Adam "live near Babylon and Seleucia or further north"? According to Calvin it makes little difference whether Adam "dwelt below the confluent stream towards Babylon and Seleucia, or in the higher part." "It is enough that he occupied a well-watered country."

> If there is anywhere under heaven a region pre-eminent in beauty, in the abundance of all kinds of fruit, in fertility, in delicacies, and in other gifts, that is the region which most writers celebrate. Wherefore, the eulogies with which Moses commends Paradise are such as properly belong to a tract of this description.... That the region of Eden was situated in those parts is probable.[47]

The reader will remember that the map accompanying Calvin's commentary was reproduced not only in the English translation of the commentary but also in the *Bishops' Bible,* so that it became very widely known.[48] But, like the commentary itself, the map raised a difficulty, since the complete joining of the Tigris and the Euphrates occurred south of the presumed location of the earthly paradise. For this reason a map included in the Dutch translation of Calvin's commentary kept the proper names in French but applied logic rather than geography to correct Calvin's map: here the Tigris and the Euphrates are linked only once, and the island that they formed on Calvin's map has disappeared (see Map 24).[49] We will not be surprised then to learn that while the *Annotations* on the Bible, which were composed by order of the Synod of Dordrecht (1619), acknowledge the mention of two "Edens" in the Bible, one in Syria, the other in Chaldea, they also agree with Calvin that the earthly paradise was located in the latter of the two.[50] This had become a quasi-official doctrine in Calvinist countries.

Junius, whom Protestants regarded as a great authority on this question, likewise distinguished two Edens, one in Syria near Damascus, the other in Chaldea. The second was the one that had to be regarded as the place of the earthly paradise. "All historians," he tells us, "agree that the soil of Babylonia, which is watered by the Tigris and the Euphrates, is the easiest to work and the most fertile not only in all of the East but in the entire world."[51] Hopkinson agreed and even claimed that the land of Eden did not include the whole of Babylonia but only its upper part, which some writers called Auranitis. An accompanying map in Hopkinson locates the garden of happiness on an island surrounded by the Tigris and the Pishon, the Gihon and the Euphrates being located farther west (Map 25).[52]

Raleigh, a great admirer of Hopkinson, reaches the same conclusion and

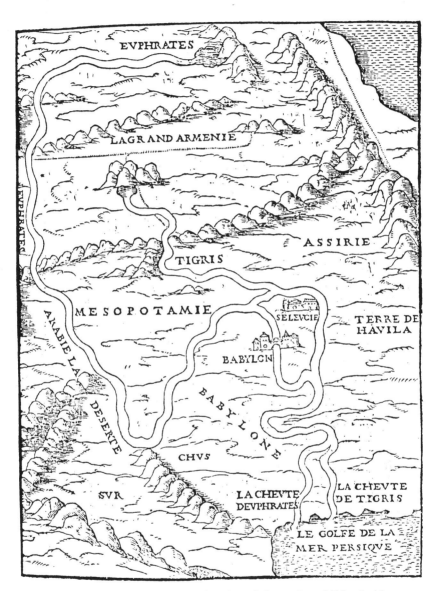

Map 23. Map showing Calvin's location of the garden of Eden in his
Commentaire . . . sur le premier livre de Moyse, dit Genèse (Geneva, 1556)

Earthly paradise

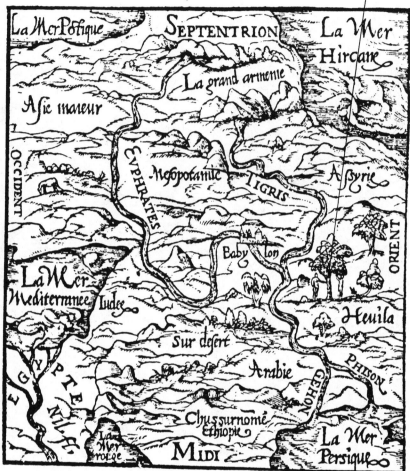

Map 24. Map in the Dutch translation of Calvin's Bible

confirms it with considerations of geography. Mesopotamia, he writes, enjoys the best climatic conditions, being 35° from the equator and 55° from the North Pole. It produces an abundance of excellent wines, fruits, oil, and various kinds of grain. There is no better proof of the excellence of the soil and the climate than the presence there of many date palms, which grow without human help. These are indeed to be found also in the East and West Indies, which are likewise favored with a perpetual spring and summer. On the other hand, the Indies are subjected "to dangerous thunder and lightning, terrible and frequent earthquakes, fierce diseases, and a multitude of

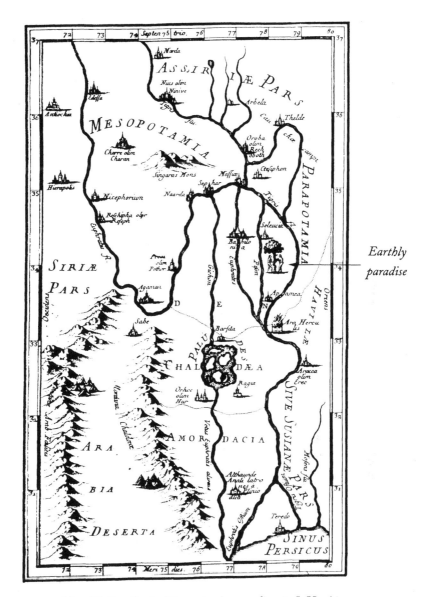

Earthly
paradise

Map 25. Paradise in Mesopotamia according to J. Hopkinson

beasts and poisonous worms, and other inconveniences." There is thus no comparison between Mesopotamia and the Indies.[53]

Peter Heyleyn, geographer and royal lampooner, devotes a chapter to "Assyria, Mesopotamia, and Chaldea" in his *Microcosmos: A Little Description of the Great World.* It provides him with an occasion for explaining the geography of the earthly paradise and knocking over with a flick of his finger the fanciful interpretations and localizations that had been current in the Middle Ages. The idea that the four rivers are allegories of the cardinal virtues cannot be defended. To place the earthly paradise within the orbit of the moon and to have the four rivers descend from there and circulate beneath the ocean is "such vain foppery that it does not deserve the honor of a refutation." The placement of paradise on the equator is inconsistent with the details given in sacred scripture. To claim that the earthly paradise occupied the entire earth is "absurd." Where would Adam and Eve have gone when they were driven from the garden? The Pishon cannot be the Ganges nor the Gihon the Nile, since both are too far distant from the regions mentioned by Moses.[54] In fact, the Gihon was the western branch of the Euphrates, and the Pishon the southern branch of the Tigris. The garden of Eden was therefore located in Mesopotamia.[55]

Pareus is of the same opinion, although he raises some questions. He cannot say whether the division of the river into four branches occurred "before the river entered paradise, inside paradise, or after exiting from paradise."[56] He regards it as certain, however, that the garden of Eden was located "either along the Euphrates or near this river."[57] For André Rivet, too, "The region of Eden is part of Babylonia and Babylonia is part of Mesopotamia."[58] Samuel Bochart (d. 1667), a nephew of Rivet and one of the most distinguished Hebraists in the Reformed Church of the seventeenth century, is quite blunt: "In short, I locate the earthly paradise in the same place in which Calvin puts it."[59] Diodati, for his part, thinks this location "probable." "I say 'probable,' because the great changes that have occurred in the world make it impossible to be certain." But, with this one reservation, it may be regarded as probable that Mesopotamia "was the orchard or garden of delights" of which Genesis speaks.[60]

A final name in this list, which is meant to show a range of scholars rather than to be complete, is Jacques Basnage, who has no doubts. He writes:

> [The earthly paradise] was located a little above ancient Nineveh, on the river of the Arabs. It is at that point that we can clearly see the four rivers named by Moses. We see the Euphrates and the Tigris which, after having joined together, divide into two broad streams which, after running along for some distance, empty into the Persian Gulf. Thus it can be said that in this area there is both one river and four rivers.[61]

When Moses wrote, he was in Arabia or Judea, and it was from there that he pointed out the earthly paradise, which was located in the east in relation to him.[62]

I said earlier that Milton too located the garden of Eden in Assyria.[63] This was also the view adopted by Grotius in his *Adamus exul.* The "argument," or summary, that precedes this tragedy says in so many words: "The scene is Eden, a region of Babylonia in which the garden was located on the banks of the Euphrates."[64] And in fact verses 1000–1005 describe "Adam beneath the leafy branches of a plane tree, his brow encircled by a wreath of green laurel, naked along with his affectionate spouse, seated on the bank of the river of Assyria. He is praising the wonders of the divine might in a melodious song that soars like a sacred bird."[65]

Catholic commentators rallied in increasing numbers to this geography of paradise. One of the first to do so was the Italian bishop Steuchus Eugubinus, whose work on the Old Testament appeared at Lyons in 1531. He clearly anticipated Calvin in locating the garden of Eden in Mesopotamia. He had several reasons for this "conviction." First of all, it is there that we find the four rivers said to flow out of paradise. Next, this land is very agreeable. Finally, the word "paradise" is Persian.[66] We must therefore believe that the starting point for the spread of the human race was Chaldea.[67]

The *Commentaria in Moisi Pentateuchum* of Hieronymus Oleaster (1556) took the same view. The author separated himself from the claims of medieval writers and wrote: "Although opinions differ [on the location of the earthly paradise] I think...that it was not far from Chaldea." Further on, he explains: "The probability is that it was located in Chaldea or close to it, because the Euphrates, one of the four rivers of paradise, flows through Chaldea."[68] In the course of his remarks Oleaster expresses serious doubts about the traditional identification of the Gihon and the Pishon with the Nile and the Ganges.[69]

When, in the mid–seventeenth century, Sicilian priest Agostino Inveges summed up the discussions of this subject (but without always distinguishing between those choosing Armenia and those choosing Chaldea), he ranked among the latter the Hebraist Vatable,[70] who was in the first group of appointees to the Royal College in 1530. After mentioning Steuchus Eugubinus, Oleaster, Pereira, Maldonatus, and others, Inveges observes that specialists opt for one of two main trustworthy opinions:

Some locate the garden [of Eden] in the eastern region of the world, that is, in some part of India. Others locate it east of Palestine, that is, in Mesopotamia. The first opinion is the older, the second is more favored by recent writers....If the reader wants my own view, I will say that the most probable opinion in my judgment is that [the earthly] paradise was planted east of Palestine, in Mesopotamia.[71]

If we keep these several views in mind, it will be clear that the *Traité de la situation du paradis terrestre*, which was published in 1691 by Bishop Pierre-Daniel Huet, former subtutor of the Dauphin and a member of the French Academy, brought nothing fundamentally new to the discussion. But when at the beginning of his book the author set before the reader the various opinions voiced down the ages on the location of the earthly paradise and gave a good-humored description of these, his aim was to provide a scientific solution that would sweep away all the whimsical interpretations and all the uncertainties:

> [The earthly paradise] has been located in the third heaven, in the fourth, in the heaven of the moon, on the moon itself, on a mountain close to the heaven of the moon, in the middle region of the air, outside the earth, on the earth, under the earth, and in a hidden place far removed from human knowledge. It has been placed under the Arctic pole.... Some have located it ... either on the banks of the Ganges or on the island of Ceylon, and have even derived the name "India" from the word "Eden." ... Others have located it in the Americas, others in Africa below the equator, others in the equinoctial East, others on the mountain of the moon, from which they believed the Nile to flow. Most have located it in Asia: some in Greater Armenia, others in Mesopotamia or Assyria or Persia or Babylonia or Arabia or Syria or Palestine. There have even been those who wished to honor our Europe and, in a move that strays into complete irrelevance, have located it in Hédin, a town in Artois, their reason being the similarity between the words "Hédin" and "Eden."[72]

Offering to guide the reader out of this labyrinth, Huet proposes his own location, which in the final analysis is close to the one proposed by Calvin, whom in fact Huet cites with praise in this context. "Of all those who have undertaken this study, none has come closer to the view I am proposing here than John Calvin in his *Commentary on Genesis*."[73]

In an effort to produce a work that would be both accurate and definitive, Huet intends to determine the "only" location that answers to Moses' description and to recover the true meaning of the biblical text; he will do so by bringing to bear all usable information. He shows, successively, that "Eden is the proper name of a place";[74] that Eden and paradise are "two different places ... (I mean: different as the whole differs from the part)";[75] that "paradise occupied the eastern end of the province of Eden";[76] and, finally, that "the greater part of the garden was on the eastern bank of the Tigris."[77] The land of Eden itself "occupied a good part of the large region which has since been named Babylonia."[78]

In fact, however, Huet does violence to the river system of present-day Iraq when he writes that "only through a lack of attention can one be mistaken" about what Moses wrote. It is quite obvious that "the four rivers into which the river of paradise divided were the upper Euphrates and upper Tigris, and, in the south, the two branches into which the single channel of the Tigris and the Euphrates divided again before emptying into the Persian Gulf."[79] Like Calvin, Huet invents this final separation into the Gihon to the west and the Pishon to the east; like Calvin, he locates the earthly paradise just upriver from the point of separation. A few days after Huet's *Traité* appeared, Bossuet wrote to him: "Your Grace, I arrived here Saturday evening, and the next morning I had the honor of presenting your book on the earthly paradise to the king. He certainly welcomed it and wanted me to explain the subject matter to him."[80] The *Traité* was quickly translated into Latin and English.

The Holy Land

Huet had hoped to put an end to the debate over the location of the garden of Eden. His hope was not fulfilled, for another solution had been put forward ever since the sixteenth century and had won some advocates: the solution that placed the earthly paradise in the Syria-Palestine area. This had already been the view of Michael Servetus who said in his *Christianismi restitutio:* "Eden was a pleasant spot in Syria.... The earthly paradise was located in the Promised Land." Admittedly, it has lost its privileges after the sin of Adam. But (he is here adopting a very medieval idea) Christ was born "in the middle of the inhabitable world." There is no other place in the world "as easy of access from all sides and toward which all the seas lead."[81] This solution to the problem was repeated in 1575 by Matthieu Beroalde (or Bérould), a Calvinist theologian and Hebraist who was a minister and professor in Geneva. In his view, the phrase "in Eden, in the east" referred to an area located in the eastern part of Canaan. He identified the area with Syria, although at the same time he shifted the course of the Tigris and Euphrates eastward and moved northward and eastward the boundaries usually set down for Syria.[82]

Pretty much the same sacred geography is to be found in the mid-seventeenth century in Isaac de La Peyrère, whose work on the "pre-Adamites" caused a scandal when it was published in the United Provinces in 1655. The revolutionary thesis of this Protestant, who was a native of Bordeaux, was that Adam was the father only of the Jewish people and not of the entire human race. This frontal attack on monogenism elicited strong opposition: some twenty refutations of his book appeared during the half-century following its publication. The author was arrested and forced to retract, and his work was burned by the executioner.[83] The important point in the present context is that by making Christ the counterpart of Adam on the basis of the Letter to the Hebrews, La Peyrère was able to locate the earthly paradise in the "Promised Land," the heart of which was the Jordan region.[84] At around the same time, two other Protestant writers, Heidegger, a Swiss, and Herbinus, a Silesian, pinpointed the location of the earthly paradise even more closely by placing it in Galilee. They also rediscovered an old medieval belief that Adam had been buried on Calvary.[85]

On the Catholic side, too, a number of writers, especially Jesuits, identified the earthly paradise with the "Promised Land." in 1635 Father Nicolas Abram, a member of the Society, published a commentary on the *Georgics* in which, like many others, he pondered "the four rivers and the location of paradise." He stated his own conviction that the Jordan satisfied "the conditions required for it to be the river of paradise." Its waters disappear into the bosom of the earth and then surface again as sources of other rivers (he is here reviving an ancient geographical idea). According to Abram, paradise comprised a territory that included the Sea of Tiberias, Sodom, and the Dead Sea. Even after the flood, but before the chastisement of Sodom, this region was "a very kindly one, very fertile, and very temperate, and it produced fruits in every season."[86]

Ten years after Nicolas Abram, Brother Eugène Roger, a Recollect, published a similar opinion. His *Terra saincte,* a work of popularization, asked a question that implied the expected answer:

> Is there any region on earth that has closer connections with the earthly paradise than the Holy Land or Land of Promise?... Is it not at the end of the Mediterranean Sea and enclosed by impassable mountains, namely, Mount Lebanon on the north, the mountains of Arabia to the east, and those of Idumea on the south? What climate is more temperate than this, which lies between the thirtieth and thirty-fourth degrees of latitude? Do not many learned persons maintain that Jerusalem is the highest place on earth?

As he develops his ideas, Roger explains that "the great inundation [the flood] changed the beds as well as the names of the rivers" and that "all are in agreement that it was in the field of Amacena that God created our father Adam, which field is near Hebron, seven leagues from Jerusalem." This leads to the question that should produce conviction in the reader: "Can we possibly say that the eternal Father would have denied his own Son this blessed land if it still possessed its original beauty? Of course not! We cannot make such a claim without insulting this fatherly love, which was incapable of refusing his Son the most important of regions for his birth."[87]

In the eighteenth century two French Jesuits likewise came out in favor of the Palestinian location. The better known of the two was Father Jean Hardouin, who was born in Quimper and died in Paris in 1729. A man who liked paradoxes, he claimed that Herod was an Athenian and that Jesus and his apostles preached in Latin. As far as the geography of Genesis is concerned, he had no trouble reconciling Moses and Pliny. He was a specialist in Pliny and in 1686 published a translation of the latter's *Natural History*, which was well received at the time.[88] It is in a work completed in 1716 and conceived as an answer to Huet that Hardouin says: "The river [of paradise] was the Jordan, and the place of delights was the entire region around the Sea of Tiberias."[89] Further on we read: "It seems to me a certain conclusion that this paradise was located in Galilee beside the Jordan, and in the place where the maps put Ennon, or at least in that neighborhood. . . . It lay on both banks of the Jordan."[90] "If we pay attention," Hardouin argues, "we will see that throughout the Pentateuch Moses' aim is to persuade the Israelites that God was calling them back and effecting their return to the ancient dwelling place of their first parents."[91]

Berruyer in his *Histoire du peuple de Dieu* (1728) reaches the same conclusions as Hardouin had in his *Traitez geographiques et historiques:* "The place of delights that was prepared for man on the third day of creation, three days before man himself was created, is certainly not to be looked for outside of Palestine, which until the time of the Messiah was intended as the inheritance and portion of the people of God."[92] According to Berruyer, sacred geography presented the following picture, prior to sin:

> In the northern part of Palestine an abundant spring poured out the best and finest waters in the world; these meandered through the neighboring plains and were enough to fertilize the land, after which they proceeded to form a great lake called the Lake of Gennesaret. . . . From here the waters flowed out through the countryside, forming the River Jordan. This beautiful river irrigated the entire land in its winding course and made up for rain, which did not fall until the flood. Its fertile and well regulated vapors turned the countryside on both banks — to the east as far as the Euphrates and to the west as far as the Mediterranean, which the Jews call the great sea — into the finest, healthiest, and most fruitful land in the world. For this reason it was given the name "Eden" or Land of Pleasure.[93]

On exiting from the Lake of Gennesaret, the river ran through the land for several leagues and then "entered the garden of delights which it irrigated with its waters."[94] "It was to these fortunate regions and to the beautiful garden at their center that the Lord God himself transported the first human being, immediately after his creation, so that he might cultivate and preserve it."[95]

In relation to the "scholarly" studies of the Protestant commentators on Genesis and of Pierre-Daniel Huet, the conclusions reached by Roger, Hardouin, and Berruyer may seem to be a throwback. Hardouin, in particular, with his unyielding attachment to the Vulgate, refuses to replace *a principio* with *ab oriente*. But, as we look back to it now, this Palestinian localization of paradise seems in the final analysis to be close to those that placed it in Armenia or in Babylon. In the eighteenth century people had abandoned the fantasies of the Middle Ages or the Renaissance, which had located paradise in the orbit of the moon or in the depths of Asia or even, as with Columbus, upstream from the Gulf of Paria. No one any longer identified the Pishon with the Ganges or the Gihon with the Nile. On the other hand, in the Christian churches it was only some fringe thinkers, especially among the Anglican dissidents ("members of the Family of Love, antinomians,... Quakers," and so on),[96] who interpreted the Genesis story of the garden of delights in a symbolic sense.

Some Related Questions

The question of the location of the earthly paradise necessarily led into the question of its dimensions. It is for this reason that Salkeld and Inveges each devote a chapter of their encyclopedic works to this awkward problem. The chapters are the third in Salkeld ("The Compasse and Greatnesse of Paradise") and the fourth in Inveges ("De Paradisi limitibus, seu paradisus quam late patuerit"). Both authors (who seem to have written in ignorance of one another) recall the different positions taken on this subject in the course of Christian history. According to Ephraem, as Salkeld reminds his readers, "Paradise was as large as the entire earth."[97] Inveges, for his part, cites a statement of St. Augustine: "Paradise was not a small area if so large a river watered it" (that is, large enough to give rise to four other rivers).[98] More generally, all the writers, including Vadian and Goropius as late as the sixteenth century, who made the earthly paradise coextensive with the earth itself, thereby answered the question of its dimensions. On the other hand, those who, especially from the sixteenth to the eighteenth century, proposed a particular location were unable to accept Luther's position that, although the garden of Eden was not coextensive with the entire earth, it was nonetheless "immense in its extent."[99]

The commentators were divided into two camps. On the one side there were those who, like Rivet, thought that the garden of Eden did not cover "a very large area (*non valde magna regio*)."[100] On the other side were those who agreed with Suárez that the garden must "have been the size of a fairly large kingdom (*saltem amplitudinem unius regni non parvi habuisse*)."[101] Salkeld does not conceal the trouble this question of spatial extent causes him: "It is a difficult question but not really necessary. But since a number of authors insist on it, I shall force myself to give some kind of answer, insofar at least as the principles of philosophy and theology and especially the great commentators on the holy scriptures have provided some solid basis for my discussion."[102]

The great difficulty was this: In a well-defined region of relatively small dimensions — Mesopotamia, for example — how could the whole of humanity have resided if Adam and Eve had not sinned? People (Salkeld claims) would have had more children than they do today ("because, as philosophy teaches, sin is no small impediment to generation").[103] In addition, they would have lived much longer. The earthly paradise would therefore have been too small for them. This Anglican rector's answer is that they would have remained there only "until the time of their transfer to a happier state," that is, to heaven.[104] Thus the garden of Eden would have regularly relieved itself of its excess inhabitants by sending them on to the kingdom of final blessedness.

Inveges, for his part, solves the problem of size in this way:

> Many arguments convince me that this garden of happiness had large and indeed very full dimensions. First of all, as Moses and John Damascene teach, it was God himself who planted this garden with his own hands. But all the works of God, especially those in the beginning, were great and in keeping with the magnificence of the divine Creator. Furthermore, as Augustine and Bar Cephas say with good reason, this garden could not have been a small one if there issued from it the Euphrates, the Ganges, the Tigris, and the Indus, which are the largest of all rivers. Finally, if the state of innocence had been maintained... either the whole of humanity or a large part of it would have lived there.[105]

On the other hand, Inveges refuses to make any more precise estimate of the size of the place and regards Suárez's formulation as quite reasonable ("at least the surface area of a good-sized kingdom").[106]

One question leads to another, and in the next chapter (his fifth) Inveges asks whether, given its vast size, the earthly paradise was located entirely on a plain or whether within its boundaries there were also mountains, hills, and valleys. As is his custom, he sets down the various opinions previously held on the subject. Tertullian, for example, placed the garden of Eden on a plain. But all the authors who have assigned large dimensions to the garden have logically concluded that the garden included mountains, hills, and valleys. Here again, Inveges sides with Suárez, whom he cites: "It is probable that within paradise the land was not uniformly the same and that on its very extensive surface some parts were higher than others and thus there were hills and fields. This kind of variety is a source of pleasure to the body as it is also of beauty and fruitfulness and therefore is not likely to have been lacking in this divine garden."[107] On the other hand, the commentators, including Inveges, could assign to the garden only such variations in altitude as were to be found in the regions in which they located paradise: Armenia, Babylonia, or Judea.

Chapter 9

Fine Points of Chronology

When Was the Earthly Paradise Created?

To the question, Where was the earthly paradise located? the commentators on Genesis added a series of other questions having to do with the precise moment in time when it was created and with the chronology of the decisive events that took place there down to the expulsion of our first parents. But was it worth spending time on such difficult problems?

André Rivet did not think so. He wrote somewhat humorously in his *Exercitationes CXC in Genesim:*

> Some of the schoolmen are full of inquisitive questions on this subject: How many hours, days, or years did the first parents spend in paradise? Jewish doctors had previously sweated over such subjects, and many among the ancient cabalists thought that Adam could not have been condemned [by God] before twenty years had passed since his creation. Some calculate several years, others forty days, some a single day, some only six hours, others a little more, and some eight days. But all of them rely on shaky conjectures in which they indulge without convincing themselves or others. They must finally admit that no precise and definitive answer is possible in this area. For such an answer cannot be concluded from the divine scriptures nor inferred with certainty from the sacred writers nor be conjectured on the basis of probable arguments. Pereira and others on his side [the Catholics] say that this question is more than difficult for pilgrims such as we are.... Mersenne rightly warns us that we can say nothing about this matter unless we receive a divine revelation.[1]

The warnings of Rivet, Pereira, and Marin Mersenne did not prevent many commentators from trying, Genesis in hand, to penetrate the mystery of the first age of the world and of the first steps of humankind. With Inveges' general survey as guide, the reader can see the variety of chronological questions raised down the ages with regard to the earthly paradise and the stay of Adam and Eve in it. The following questions in particular were asked:

- "In what month, on what day, and at what hour did God plant the garden?"[2]

- "In what month, on what day, and at what hour did God form the body of Adam?"[3]

- "On what day and at what hour... did God lead Adam from the place where he was created into paradise?"[4]

- "Where and when was Adam given knowledge of [the commandments]: 'Eat of all the trees in paradise,' and 'But do not eat of the tree of knowledge'?"[5]

- "On what day, at what hour, and how were [the animals] brought before Adam?"[6]

- "On what day, at what hour, and in what place did Adam give names to the animals?"[7]

- "At what hour, where, and how did Adam begin to sleep? How many hours did he sleep?"[8]

- "On what day, at what hour, and where did God create the body of Eve?"[9]

- "At what hour, where, and by whom was Eve brought to Adam for their marriage?"[10]

- "How many hours, days, months, or years did Adam and Eve live together in paradise?"[11]

- "At what hour did they eat the deadly meal?"[12]

- "At what hour were Adam and Eve expelled from paradise?"[13]

What answers were given, especially in the sixteenth and seventeenth centuries, to these questions that had behind them fifteen centuries of thought about the earthly paradise?

It was generally accepted that the garden of delights had been "planted" before the creation of Adam, for whom it was to be, in the words of Moses Bar Cephas, "like a bed prepared by God for the spouse."[14] But differences arose when it came to a more precise dating of the event. According to such authors as Gregory of Nazianzus, John Damascene, Isidore of Seville, Rabanus Maurus, and Bede, the event took place in March, at the spring equinox, when the trees are covered with leaves and nature dons its most beautiful finery. According to others, it took place in July; that is why in Noah's time the year began in July. According to still others (Pereira joins them despite the prudence on which he ordinarily prides himself),[15] it took place at the autumn equinox. It is, after all, in autumn that the trees yield their fruits, and Adam and Eve had to eat of these. Anglican archbishop James Ussher even pinpoints October 25 as the date of the creation of the world and of the earthly paradise.[16]

Inveges opts for the first of these opinions, which was also the most widely accepted: "I think that God made the paradise at the same time as he made the earth, in the spring and in March, because Christ became incarnate and suffered in the spring and in March. Adam's enslavement [to sin] and the redemption by Christ should have taken place at the same season."[17] The symmetry thus supposed to exist between the history of Adam and the history of Jesus played an important role in the reconstruction of the calendar of Eden.

Is it possible to gain a more detailed knowledge of the calendar of creation? Granting that the earthly paradise came into being at the same time as the earth, that is, on the third day, and granting (this was the most widely accepted view) that these events took place in March, several hypotheses can be envisaged, depending on the date assigned to the beginning of creation within this month. Inveges, adopting "the common opinion of the most recent authors," thinks that Adam was created on March 25, the day on which Mary conceived Jesus, and therefore that the earthly paradise was established on March 22.[18]

But at what hour of the day? The question arose because scholars disagreed on the times of the day at which God produced the different parts of his creation. Thus the Protestant theologian Beroalde thought that the heavens and the earth had been formed in the middle of the night.[19] Steuchus Eugubinus placed their creation around six in the morning and believed that the heavens and the earth reached their full form during a half-day of darkness, until the light came into being around six in the evening. It is then that germination would have taken place and therefore also the growth of the plants in the earthly paradise.[20] Inveges prefers, once again, to agree with Suárez[21] and to place the creation of the garden of delights "in the spring, on March 22, a Tuesday, at the beginning of the first hour of the day, . . . at the moment of sunrise."[22]

The Use of the Time between the Creation of Adam and the Creation of Eve

Next comes the question: At what moment are we to place the creation of Adam? A general persuasion of the specialists was that man was created after all other animate and inanimate beings had been created. That is the sequence that emerges from Genesis. Furthermore, Pereira explains, logic requires that the "more perfect" come after the less perfect.[23] But is it possible to go beyond this general statement?

The learned try to do so but disagree on the date of the creation of Adam,

depending on whether they place the first week of the world's existence in
the autumn or in July or in March. Thus Anglican archbishop James Ussher,
who enjoyed a high reputation in his country in the seventeenth century and
who insists on the month of October, gives October 28 as the date of the
creation first of Adam and then of Eve.[24] Inveges, on the contrary, notes
that the most widely held opinion is that this creation took place in March
and more precisely on March 25 (and not March 23, as the Venerable Bede
had claimed).[25]

Finally, as to the very hour when the first man was formed "there is a great
debate" among the learned. Suárez thinks that the hour "is completely unknown to us." Nevertheless, he regards the following sequence as "probable":
the appearance of the animals on the sixth day around sunrise; the appearance of man on the same day when the sun had already risen, that is, one or
two hours after the creation of the brute animals.[26] Inveges, for his part, considers "the most probable" hypothesis to be that the creation of Adam took
place "at dawn" on March 25, that is, at the moment when the Holy Spirit
formed the body of Christ in the womb of the Virgin. Thus the tradition of
the church assigns the first Angelus of the day to the hour of dawn.[27]

In Gen 2:8 it is written: "The Lord God planted a garden in Eden, in the
east; and there he put the man whom he had formed." Taking this statement
quite literally, the commentators of the past concluded that Adam was created outside the earthly paradise and then led into it by God. Salkeld, among
others, explained as follows why God acted in this way: it was "in order that
man might be better able to understand the divine goodness and generosity
toward him and realize that this place [the garden of blessings] was given to
him as an unmerited gift rather than something owing to his nature."[28]

Theology and chronology then gave rise to a new question: When did
God bring Adam into the garden of Eden? "We are left uncertain," says
Suárez, because "the answer has not been revealed."[29] In the past, some writers, for example, Anastasius the Sinaite (d. after 700), were of the opinion
that forty days passed between the creation of the first man and his entrance
into the earthly paradise. Anastasius placed the former on March 25 and
the latter on May 2, the feast of the Finding of the Cross. But Suárez, despite the prudence we saw him showing a moment ago, thinks that Adam
"was placed in paradise immediately after his creation."[30] Inveges is much
closer to Suárez than to Anastasius, but he thinks that Suárez's "immediately" goes too far and, while admitting that the hour of Adam's transfer to
the garden is "completely unknown" to us, he thinks it "probable" that it took
place "a few hours" — doubtless two hours — after the formation of the first
man. The transfer would thus have been effected around nine or ten in the
morning.[31] What did Adam do during the period before this transfer? He

probably spent his time adoring God and "philosophizing about the beauty, variety, and harmony of the world" that he was just discovering.[32]

The question, When was Adam given the two commands: "Eat of all the trees," "but do not eat of the tree of knowledge"? caused a great deal of ink to flow and divided the specialists into two camps. One group joined St. John Chrysostom, St. Ambrose, St. Augustine, St. Thomas Aquinas, and Francisco Suárez in thinking that these two commands were made known to Adam alone before the creation of Eve and then communicated to the latter by her husband. The other group, including, in particular, Cajetan and Pereira, thought that, on the contrary, the two commands were promulgated after the creation of Eve and made known separately and personally to each member of the first human pair. Inveges, for his part, inclines to the first hypothesis and calculates that the revelation of these two commandments was given to Adam while he walked among the sacred groves of paradise, that is, around eleven in the morning.[33]

A further question: When did the episode take place that is described in Gen 2:19–20, which shows God bringing the beasts of the field and the birds of the air to Adam in order that he might give each species its name? But there is a prior question: Are we to think that God brought the entire animal world into Adam's presence in the earthly paradise? According to Pereira, those brought to him did not include the fishes, since the garden of Eden was not located beside the sea, nor "animals born of rotting matter." Furthermore (says Pereira) only one male and one female of each noble species were presented to Adam. "For if all the beasts of the earth had entered paradise and if all the birds of the air had flown into it, the spectacle would have been one of horror rather than delight. Consider also that a great throng of animals and birds would have crushed and disfigured the beauty of paradise."[34]

Once this difficulty has been surmounted, it is easy to tackle the chronological problem proper, although, says Inveges, "the investigation is difficult."[35] Following Suárez, he calculates (as we saw) that the animals must have been created at sunrise and man himself one or two hours later. Therefore the animals would have been brought into the earthly paradise between seven in the morning and midday, and their naming would have gone on until around two in the afternoon. This period was long enough, on the one hand, for the angels, acting like shepherds, to lead the land animals and the birds into paradise and, on the other hand, for Adam to "philosophize" about their nature and, after some thought, "to invent so many names."[36]

"It may be piously thought that," having accomplished this task, "Adam called the most beautiful animals and the most charming birds to him and caressed them, in order to show both his dominion over them and his pleasure in them. In obedience to his voice, the animals and birds approached him and expressed their gentleness and joy by singing, flying, and moving their ears and tails."[37] A spectacle worthy of a Walt Disney animated film!

From the Creation of Eve to the Expulsion from the Earthly Paradise

The sleep of Adam, the creation of Eve, and the marriage of our first parents were obviously important moments in the calendar described by Genesis. Inveges explains that after "the lengthy process of naming" the animals, which must have taken three or four hours of intense thought, Adam was wearied and quickly fell into a deep sleep.[38]

But what kind of sleep was this? According to Cajetan, it was not a real, natural sleep but rather "allegorical and metaphorical."[39] But important authorities — Pereira, Suárez, Cornelius a Lapide, and others — think that it was both "natural and supernatural."[40] "Despite the silence of the scholars," it may be accepted that this sleep occurred in the same place in the garden where Adam had given the animals their names.

At what hour on Friday did the first man begin to sleep? And how long did he sleep? In view of the necessary chronological symmetry between this first Friday and Good Friday, Inveges thinks it "probable" that sleep descended on Adam around three o'clock or, in any case, before four, that is, at the time of day when Christ died. The same kind of reasoning leads this author to think that the sleep was short: approximately the time between the death of Jesus and the blow of the lance that pierced his side.[41] In addition, it is not conceivable that the marriage of Adam and Eve was celebrated in the evening, at sunset. It must have taken place in broad daylight while the sun was shining. This leads Inveges to suppose that Adam slept only from three to four in the afternoon. This left two hours of full daylight in which the marriage might be celebrated and Adam might instruct his wife regarding the commandments he had received from God and the revelations given to him while he slept. Finally, this chronology would allow him to enjoy the delights of paradise with her, in friendship and for a reasonable period.

This reconstruction of the calendar of creation places the creation of Eve between three and four in the afternoon on the first Friday. This date and hour were, however, objects of debate down the ages. St. Thomas Aquinas, for example, has Eve born after the seventh day.[42] But at the end of the Renaissance, Luis de Molina,[43] Pereira,[44] and Suárez,[45] among others, opted for Friday, which was certainly a very crowded day but which had to be accepted nonetheless, because on Saturday God rested. Inveges here emphasizes once again the importance of the fourth afternoon hour: it was the time when

Christ's side was pierced and when, as symmetry required, the side of Adam was likewise opened.[46]

All this requires that the creation of Eve be followed by her marriage to Adam; scholars had never disagreed as to the fact that the two events took place on the same day. According to Suárez, "As soon as Eve was formed, she was presented to Adam and joined with him in marriage."[47] The reason for this haste is a matter of analogy and had already been explained by St. Augustine.[48] The blood and water that flowed from the pierced side of Jesus represent the marriage of Christ with the church, as well as the sacraments flowing from this union. If then, as we will recall, the lance blow occurred around four in the afternoon, the marriage of Adam and Eve must have taken place at the same time of day.[49] As for the place of the marriage, there is every reason to suppose that it was celebrated "in the fragrant, luxuriant shade of the trees of life and knowledge, at an elevated spot in the center of the garden whence the fountain of paradise flowed."[50]

Two very important and interconnected questions now arise: How long did Adam and Eve remain in the earthly paradise? When did original sin take place? Over the centuries the first of these questions received many and varied answers, which Inveges sorts into three main categories according to whether the respondents allowed the first parents a stay of a few hours, a few days, or several years in the garden of delights.[51] Our Sicilian priest speaks of the "turbulent crowd of scholars" who have studied this problem, and the "disagreement" of their opinions. It is therefore very difficult, in his view, to reach certitude on the point.[52] In the same way, Salkeld, who devotes a chapter of his *A Treatise of Paradise* to the question, acknowledges that there can be legitimate caution in dealing with "a matter so full of doubt and uncertainty."[53] John Swan, whose *Speculum mundi* (1635) enjoyed a real popular success (the Bodleian has copies of four seventeenth-century printings), likewise leaves it to the reader to choose "the opinion that pleases him best" on this point, since all the different views can offer good arguments.[54]

In the seventeenth century, specialists hardly shared any longer the once widespread belief that Adam and Eve sinned on the day they were created. Malvenda was by his time an exception in this respect.[55] "The common view" among recent authors, says Inveges, is that our first parents lived "for several days" in the earthly paradise. This view was based especially on the argument of Moses Bar Cephas, who thought it unlikely that so many events could have taken place in a single day: the creation of Adam, his entrance into the garden, his learning of the divine commandments, the naming of the animals, the formation of Eve, the temptation, the fall, and the expulsion.[56] Suárez thinks that at least a day and a half were required for all these important events.[57] Inveges, for his part, prefers Pereira's opinion when he

calculates that Adam and Eve lived for a week in the blessed garden.[58] Inveges indeed says, like others, that it is "rash" to try to count the number of
days, months, or years that Adam and Eve spent in the earthly paradise, but
he nonetheless says that the eight-day hypothesis is the one "that pleases us
most."[59] The Anglican Salkeld reaches the same conclusion: "I like to think
that [our first parents] stayed only eight days in paradise. That was enough
for them to have a real experience of this happy state."[60] Anglican John
Swan, however, places the first sin on the fourteenth day after the creation
of Adam.[61]

While there was disagreement about the time spent in the garden, there
was broader agreement about the day of the week that saw the fatal sin committed. Suárez is pretty much isolated here, when he figures that one should
not assign too many events to the day of Adam's creation, and he therefore
places the original sin on the following day.[62] The most widespread view in
the sixteenth and seventeenth centuries was that the sin was committed on
a Friday.

Such is the explanation given by Salkeld, who is here the heir to a lengthy
tradition. What he says, in substance, is that just as our Savior was conceived
and died on a Friday, so the first sin was also committed on a Friday.

> By a special providence of almighty God, the sin of Adam, as well as his
> creation and his redemption,... took place on the same day [of the week].
> Although there is no convincing argument for this nor any decisive proof
> based on the sacred text, it cannot be denied that there is a correspondence
> and rational suitability in having the evil and the remedy appointed for the
> same day by God, who from all eternity, foresees the end and the means.[63]

Inveges disagrees with Suárez and opts for Friday, because "all the Fathers
said that Adam stretched out his hand to the tree of knowledge on the same
day, that is, Friday, on which Christ was nailed to the cross."[64] These were
the two most "memorable" Fridays in history, with the Friday of sin being
April 1 and Adam having been created on March 25.

Still to be determined is the very hour of the "deadly eating." Inveges, our
faithful guide, recalls the common belief handed down through the centuries
from St. Augustine and St. Jerome to Suárez. People have always believed
that Adam sinned at the hour when Jesus was to be nailed to the cross, and
therefore around midday. To this may be added the fact that according to
the story in Genesis, Eve was the first to pluck the fruit and that after the
sin the two guilty parties heard the voice of God as he walked in the garden
"in the breeze of the day," that is, according to the general belief, at the
time when the breeze is felt after the heat of midday. Here, then, is Inveges'
reconstruction: Eve sinned around eleven in the morning; then she persuaded

her husband to eat of the fruit in his turn; Adam agreed around midday; and God walked in the garden in the afternoon but before evening,[65] that is, around three o'clock. Adam and Eve would thus have spent three hours "in anxiety, fear, and sadness,"[66] as they awaited the divine judgment.

Turning, finally, to the expulsion from the earthly paradise, Inveges tells us that "many historical circumstances must be carefully examined, and first of all the question of the hour at which the expulsion took place."[67] Moses Bar Cephas, followed by many commentators, had claimed that the expulsion took place at the moment of the day corresponding to that in which Jesus brought the soul of the good thief into paradise;[68] clearly, the symmetry between the first and second Adams is still decisive. Inveges, however, inclines to a more detailed and "more probable" chronology. If (he says, reminding us of what he had said previously) the condemnation took place around three in the afternoon, we may think that the whole process lasted about an hour. "This period of time seems long enough for the questioning of the guilty parties, the pronouncing of the sentence, and the unfolding of the entire judgment. We may therefore think that Jesus was taken down from the cross around four o'clock and that around the same hour Adam made his way down from the heights of Paradise."[69]

It is now possible, for the sake of greater clarity, to summarize in tabular form all the chronological details given in Inveges' work. The table seems to me indicative of the meticulousness with which the commentators on Genesis in the sixteenth and seventeenth centuries studied the sacred text, as they brought their learning to bear in an effort to shed light on a sacred text that they regarded as "historical":

CHRONOLOGY OF THE STAY OF ADAM AND EVE IN THE EARTHLY
PARADISE ACCORDING TO AGOSTINO INVEGES (1649)

Friday, March 25, the sixth day of creation:

— At dawn, the creation of Adam in the land of Eden.

— Around nine o'clock, entrance into the earthly paradise.

— From nine to eleven, Adam walks about within the woods of paradise. The Almighty gives him two commands: "Take care of the garden, and keep it."

— Around eleven o'clock, Adam reaches the middle of the garden and receives two further commands: "Eat of all the fruits," "but do not touch those from the tree of the knowledge of good and evil."

— From twelve noon to about three in the afternoon, the animals are brought to Adam, who "names" them.

— From three to four, Adam sleeps and Eve is created.

— Around four, the marriage of Adam and Eve, followed by a week of happiness.

Friday, April 1:

— Around ten in the morning, Satan begins the tempting of Eve.

— Around eleven, "He wins his wretched victory over her."

— Around noon, Adam in turn sins.

— Around three, the two sinners are called to judgment. They are condemned.

— Around four, expulsion from the earthly paradise. The garden is closed off and an angel is set to guard it.[70]

In England, scholars were far from unanimous agreement that Adam was created on March 25. One of the best English Hebraists of the time, John Lightfoot (1602–75), opted for September 18, with the creation of Adam taking place at nine in the morning.[71] John Swan, for his part, chose April 23 as the date of Adam's creation.[72] On the Continent, however, scholars thought it reasonable to make March 25 the date both of the creation of the first man and of the announcement of redemption.

Not all the writers of the Renaissance and the classic age who dealt with the earthly paradise went into such precise chronological detail as Inveges did. But the latter's passion for the problems of time and place in the first week of humanity's existence can be better understood if we locate it in a broader context and link it with the widely shared desire to determine in a precise way the year of the creation of the world. We should not be surprised at this desire. We share it today when we try to calculate the precise moment of the big bang. On the other hand, the conceptual means available for getting back to the origins of the universe were obviously not the same as those available to us today.

For most of the contemporaries of Kepler and Galileo it was in the Bible that light on this difficult and fascinating question was to be sought. As Anglican theologian Hugh Broughton said in 1594: "Anyone who denies that the course of time down to its consummation is clearly set down in the Bible, as is the year of salvation in which Our Lord died, is also capable of denying that the sun is shining."[73] In an excellent study on which I am drawing heavily here, C. A. Patrides rightly observes that "Renaissance computations of chronology were among the most typical [intellectual] products" of the Renaissance and of a great part of the seventeenth century.[74] We ought not be surprised, then, to see one Girolamo Vecchietti, a religious who died in prison, reckoning that 1,442,801 days passed between the creation of the first Adam and the birth of the second.[75]

The Renaissance, which revived the study of Hebrew, most often preferred the Hebrew text of the Old Testament to the Greek Septuagint translation (which was begun in the third century B.C.); this was true especially but not exclusively in Protestant countries. The Hebrew Bible dates the creation of the world in 3760 B.C. (a date that is still the basis of the Jewish calendar), while the Septuagint dates it earlier, in 5200 B.C.

In addition to the initial choice of either the Hebrew or the Greek text there were other factors that, when combined (but thereby also complicating the problem), led to further, more specific reckonings. One of these factors was the divisions of history that were currently accepted at that time. One such periodization, attributed to Elijah, divided history into three parts: two thousand years from the creation to the promulgation of the Law, two thousand from the Law to the Messiah, and two thousand from the Messiah to the end of the world. Another division, accepted by St. Augustine, Isidore of Seville, and the Venerable Bede, divided time into six periods: from Adam to Noah and then, successively, to Abraham, David, the Babylonian Captivity, the birth of Jesus, and the final judgment. Furthermore, in dealing with such subjects as this, writers often cited Ps 90(89):4 and the Second Letter of Peter (3:8), both of which said that in the sight of God "a thousand years are as a day." Finally, the Hebrew Bible dates the flood in the year 1656 from the creation, while the Septuagint dates it in the year 2242 or 2262 from the creation.

The commentators on Genesis and the many writers of the sixteenth and seventeenth centuries who took an interest in chronology all tried their hand at suggesting a date for the first day of the world's existence; in doing so they took into account the various options and factors that I have just described. C. A. Patrides, in the article I am using here, draws up an admittedly incomplete list of 107 sixteenth- and seventeenth-century writers who proposed a date for the year of the creation of the universe. The readers of the time were thus faced with a choice among forty-three dates ranging from 3928 B.C. back to 4102 B.C.[76] I think the reader here will find it of interest if I select from Patrides' list some important names and the dates they chose:

3928 B.C. Beroalde, Hebraist John Lightfoot, and German Calvinist David Pareus.

3947   Protestant scholar Joseph Justus Scaliger, author of an *Opus de emendatione temporum* (1583), which is a treatise on chronology.

3950   Girolamo Vecchietti and Friedrich Spanheim, a theologian from the Palatinate (d. 1649).

3951   Scholar Cornelius a Lapide, of Liège.

3954   Johannes Sleidan, seventeenth-century German Protestant historian.

3955   Spanish Jesuit Maldonato.

3960   Hugh Broughton.

3963   Sixteenth-century German Protestant mathematician and historian Car-
            ion (d. 1538), author of the *Chronicle* that was rewritten by Philipp
            Melanchthon.

3967   English theologian William Perkins.

3974   Heinrich Bullinger, Zwingli's successor in Zurich.

3980   French Reformed theologian Lambert Daneau.

3983   French humanist Charles de Bovelles (1470–1553?), a disciple of
            Lefèvre d'Étaples, and French Jesuit theologian Denis Petau (d. 1652),
            whose works on chronology inspired Bossuet's *Discours sur l'histoire
            universelle.*

3984   Bellarmine.[77]

3992   Kepler.

3996   Belgian physician and chemist Jan Baptista van Helmont (d. 1644).

4000   Luther, Suárez, and Louis Cappel, a Reformed theologian and Hebraist
            from Sedan.

4004   Anglican archbishop James Ussher.

4022   Spanish Jesuit Benedicto Pereira.

4051   French humanist and poet Jean de Sponde (d. 1595), who converted
            from the Reform to Catholicism.

This poll of the exegetical and eschatological literature enables us to
understand the chief value that John Napier (d. 1617), a Scottish theologian and mathematician, saw in logarithms, of which he was the discoverer:
they would facilitate calculations of the "number of the Beast," to which the
Apocalypse refers, and of the date of the end of the world.[78] For at this
period of history there was a close connection between studies dealing with
the first week of creation and calculations of the day on which the world
would end.

Chapter 10

"As Soon as the Man Opened His Eyes, He Knew Himself to Be Happy..."

In the *Mistere du Viel Testament* (end of the fifteenth century) we see God taking Adam's hand and showing him the earthly paradise. To the astonished first man the Creator says:

> Adam, we have prepared for you
> this place made by divine power,
> where you will have the happiness
> of every noble delight.
> Here you will make your dwelling
> in this beautiful earthly paradise
> where you will have glory and pleasure
> on all sides, right and left.[1]

Further on, after the creation of Eve, God tells our first parents:

> You will have under your control
> all without exception of the fishes
> that make their dwelling in the sea;
> then also under your obedience
> you will have the beasts
> that move on earth
> by our divine power.
> For your pleasure you will have the birds
> that fly, free and agile.
> In short, all rule will be yours
> over beasts, fishes, and reptiles.
> Then to sustain your life
> you can use all these fruits,
> except for the tree of life.[2]

Like the authors of the mystery plays, the commentators on Genesis wrote inexhaustibly about the advantages, gifts, and privileges that Adam and Eve enjoyed in the garden of Eden. They also asked what the conditions were under which the descendants of Adam and Eve would have lived if original sin had not spoiled everything. Under the pens of these writers the earthly paradise becomes a utopian place whose loss evokes the most melancholy regrets; it also becomes an occasion for describing an extraordinary, though unreal, past.

The Perfection of Being

Taking up anew some questions that had long been asked, both Salkeld and Inveges, who surely did not know one another, inquire into the age and stature of Adam.[3] The Sicilian priest refuses even to consider the "ravings of some rabbis" who claimed that our first parents were created as infants and that only later on did they learn of the prohibition relative to the tree of knowledge. In Christian countries thinkers had long since followed St. Augustine's position on this point. According to the bishop of Hippo, since Adam was not born of parents but was formed out of the earth, God created him a fully developed man.[4] At the end of the Renaissance, Bellarmine, Pereira, and Suárez, all Catholics, adopted this viewpoint; Bellarmine added that our first parents were created at an age and with a constitution that would enable them to beget children, for they were ordered to people the earth.[5] Salkeld, an Anglican, shares this belief,[6] while in Milton's *Paradise Lost* Adam and Eve likewise come into existence as adults.

A twofold tradition, Christian and pagan, led to this assurance. Genesis says that God created man in his own likeness. But God, by definition, can have neither beginning nor end, but exists from all eternity in the fullness of his being. In human terms, he has always been an adult. Meanwhile, the Greeks and Romans described Athena (Minerva) as having been born fully armed (and therefore an adult) from the brain of her divine father. Whence this statement of Cicero, which L. B. Alberti cited in the fifteenth century: "Nothing is simultaneously born and complete." It is not necessary, in order to be complete, to have passed through the stages of human birth and childhood. Adam was complete because it was as an adult that he came from the hands of God.[7]

But at what age were persons adults in the earthly paradise? Neither Augustine nor Bellarmine had risked giving a precise age. Suárez, on the other hand, following an opinion voiced by St. Jerome,[8] suggested that Adam was created at the same age that Jesus was at the moment of his resurrection; therefore, between thirty and forty and, to be more precise, at around thirty-four.[9] But was this not to forget that in the state of innocence the "dimensions" of life would not have been the same as they are today? Life would have been much longer. Pereira therefore suggests that Adam was fifty at the moment of his creation.[10] Cajetan thinks that he was of "an age to have the full use of reason,"[11] and was therefore perhaps seventy. Suárez asks, somewhat ironically: Why not a hundred? The cautious Salkeld is of the opinion that "God created our first parents with a perfect stature and a perfect age: either, as many claim, between thirty and forty, or, as others think, around fifty."[12]

But what does "perfect stature" mean? Were Adam and Eve giants? According to Moses Bar Cephas, a number of writers suggested this scenario: when our first parents were driven from paradise, they would have crossed the sea; their heads must therefore have risen above the water or even have touched the clouds. But "this," says Moses, "is ridiculous."[13] Suárez thinks that Adam had the height required by the perfection of human nature.[14] Inveges, on the other hand, cites some commentators who made him six feet (1.95 m) tall, because, they thought, this was Christ's height and will be our height at the resurrection.[15] On this question Salkeld shows good sense: it is improbable (he says) that our first parents were giants; Adam must have been "the greatest of human beings, not in quantity but in quality; not in bodily dimensions but in beauty of body and soul; not in height but in dignity, prerogatives, and other distinctive bodily and spiritual traits. Otherwise he would have been more like a monster than a human being in relation to us." He must have been gifted with "the most beautiful stature" and the "best proportions" any human being has ever had or will ever have, "except only for our Savior."[16]

The perfection of Adam was matched by that of Eve, except that hers was adapted to the characteristics of her sex. Inveges therefore devotes a chapter to "the age, stature, beauty, holiness, and privileges" of the first woman. One thing is certain: Eve was as beautiful as Adam was handsome. But since a woman reaches marriageable age sooner than a man, we may suppose that God created her ten years younger than her husband. Assuming, then, the figures given above for Adam, Eve would have been "fifty according to Cajetan, forty according to Pereira, and twenty-four according to Suárez." Given this difference, it is permissible to think that Eve lived another ten years after the death of Adam.[17]

Similar reasoning leads Inveges to calculate the height of the first woman, taking it as axiomatic that the female body is smaller than the male. He rejects the opinion that our first parents were giants and thinks reasonable Suárez's view that Eve was a foot or a half-foot shorter than her husband.[18] In all likelihood, God made her the same height as the Virgin Mary, just as Adam had the same measurements as Christ.

There was a twofold tradition, attested from St. Irenaeus[19] through St. Bernard,[20] that "the body of Eve was created in the image and likeness" of the body of the future Mother of God. A key passage on this subject was written by a Byzantine, St. Nicephorus (d. 829), who at one time was patriarch of Constantinople. Inveges repeats word for word Nicephorus's description of the Virgin and from it infers a picture of the first woman:

> Eve was of medium or slightly more than medium height. Her face was neither round nor angular but elongated, though not noticeably so; her complexion was rosy, her hair blond, her eyebrows arched and rather dark, her eyes keen, with pupils that were on the golden side and almost the color of the olive (*pupillis sub flavis, et tamquam olee colore*), her nose well formed, her lips like a flower and filled with sweet speech. Her hands and fingers were slender. In every respect Eve appeared dignified and earnest, like the future Mother of God.[21]

This portrait, which combines decorum and desire, has the merit, among others, of showing us an ideal of female beauty that was widely shared by artists, especially in the fifteenth- and sixteenth-century West. The proportions assigned to Adam and Eve may be seen as, by and large, close to the canons set down in learned works such as the *De architectura* of Vitruvius, the *Della pittura* of L. B. Alberti (1540), the *De divina proportione* of Luca Pacioli (1509), the *De harmonia mundi totius* of Francesco Giorgi (1509), the *Traité des proportions du corps humain* of Dürer (1528), and others.[22]

This does not mean, of course, that all depictions of Adam and Eve show the former as twenty or twenty-five centimeters (7.8 or 9.75 in.) taller than the latter. In the polyptych painted by Hans Memling (around 1480), now in Vienne,[23] and in the well-known panels by Dürer (1507), now shown in the Prado and in the Uffizi (Florence), our first parents are of almost the same height. On the other hand, another of Dürer's works, a copperplate engraving (1504),[24] shows Adam as taller than his companion. This latter option, which was in fact the most common, was also taken by Michelangelo for the ceiling of the Sistine Chapel (1508–12) and by Lukas Cranach in his picture *Original Sin* (1533).[25]

Furthermore, if we examine the paintings, miniatures, and stained-glass windows devoted either to Eve or to the Virgin Mary, especially during the Renaissance, we see that as a general rule both have blond or light auburn hair (Milton too gives Eve "golden tresses")[26] and that the artists have followed the rules of which Inveges will remind his readers in the next century, by giving both the mother of the human race and the mother of Christ arched eyebrows, a well-shaped nose, regular features, flowerlike lips, and slender hands. The Virgins painted by Raphael are the best examples of an iconography that combined aesthetics with religion in representing the ideal woman. In the seventeenth century it was clear to Anglican rector Salkeld and most of the theologians that Eve too had been created in the image of God, despite St. Paul's statement that the man "is the image and reflection of God, but woman is the reflection of man" (1 Cor 11:7). Of all human beings the one who most resembled God is obviously Mary.[27]

In the earthly paradise, before sin, Adam and Eve were immortal and protected against all diseases. Luther explains: "Adam was so created that if anything troublesome to his nature had happened, he would have a protection against it in the tree of life, which preserved his powers and perfect health at all times."[28] If our first parents had remained "in the state of innocence," their children "would have not needed their mother's milk for so long a time. Perhaps they would have stood on their feet immediately, as we see in the case of chicks, and would have sought their food without any effort on the part of their parents."[29] "It is certain that man was created for an immortal and spiritual life, to which he would have been carried off or translated [without dying] after living in Eden and on the rest of the earth without inconvenience as long as he wished."[30] The same belief is expressed by John Swan in his *Speculum mundi* (Cambridge, 1635): "If the man had not sinned, death would not have come upon him; his body and soul would have been translated from earth to heaven, as the Fathers of old maintained."[31] If Adam lived 950 years despite his sin, the reason is perhaps that he retained some traces of his first state.

But the adjective "immortal" as applied to man before the fall calls for some explanation, and David Pareus, of the Reformed tradition, endeavors to supply it. His explanation comes down to this: God alone is, in the strict sense of the words, incorruptible and immortal. The angels are also incorruptible and immortal; they are so by God's will. So too the "new heavens" and the "new earth" will become such by the command of the Almighty. He is able to give what is mortal the gift of immortality. When Adam enjoyed the state of innocence, "He was not incapable of dying but did have the power not to die"; this power would have become an impossibility of dying at the moment of his entrance into the kingdom of heaven.[32]

Like most of the Protestant theologians, Inveges takes it as a principle that Adam was both "immortal" and "impassible," that is, incapable of suffering; this was the accepted view of the body of specialists at that time. Suárez tells his readers that this is "an article of faith." But, given bodies made up of "opposing and dissimilar humors," how could our first parents have escaped death and not experienced suffering? Inveges acknowledges that "this is not easy to explain," and he settles finally for explaining the various solutions offered. Would Adam and Eve have been translated to heaven before sickness could have settled in their bodies? That was Duns Scotus's opinion. Would they have received from God a "gift" that would have been inserted in their bodies and have preserved these from any breakdown? St. Augustine, St. John Chrysostom, and many others opted for this solution. In any case, our first parents would have been both mortal and immortal.

Suárez distinguishes three "immortalities." There is a "natural" immortality that belongs to the angels and the "incorruptible" heavens. There is, second, a "glorious" immortality, which is that of the blessed. There is a third that is simply "halfway between," and this is what innocent humanity had. It did not definitively exclude the corruption caused by the humors and the possibility of dying, but these two tragic outcomes were prevented by the beneficent action of the fruits of paradise and especially by the fruit of the tree of life. Thus "natural death" had no hold on Adam and Eve. Meanwhile, violent death was averted from them by the special protection of God. Such was Suárez's argument.[33]

It is obvious that prior to the fall work done in the garden of paradise was not wearying. Human beings certainly worked there (since idleness is an evil), but only for their own greater pleasure. On this point Luther says:

> If Adam had remained in the state of innocence, he would have tilled the earth...not only without inconvenience but, as it were, in play and with the greatest delight....It is appropriate here also to point out that man was created not for leisure but for work, even in the state of innocence. Therefore the idle sort of life, such as that of monks and nuns, deserves to be condemned.[34]

In this passage Luther combines the two condemnations of laziness that were issued respectively by even the oldest Christian moral theology and by business circles in the Renaissance,[35] and he uses these to justify his hostility to monastic life. But the key point for us here is the statement that prior to original sin work was one way of being happy. How could it have been otherwise since, says Calvin, the soil had not yet been "accursed" nor "reduced from its native beauty to a state of wretched defilement" and had not yet put on its present "garb of mourning."[36] "No corner of the earth was then barren, nor was there even any that was not exceedingly rich and fertile."[37]

Protestant writing on this subject continued the thinking of Luther and Calvin. In Salkeld's *A Treatise of Paradise* we read:

> God in his goodness placed Adam in paradise *ut operaretur et custodiret illum*, "in order that he might work it and keep it." By his work he could keep paradise, and the latter in turn, thanks to Adam's work, could keep him from idleness and sin. For idleness is the usual cause of sin, and the poet is correct when he says that work blunts the arrows of Cupid and the other darts of the demon.

Will someone object that work was not in keeping with the blessedness of paradise, which comprised tranquility, rest, and happiness? "I answer that work was a necessary consequence of this happy state, inasmuch as it did not entail fatigue or difficulty but was rather a source of pleasure ... a recreation, and a joy to the will and spirit."[38] Salkeld here refers to book 8, chapter 8, of St. Augustine's *The Literal Meaning of Genesis*.

The exaltation of work in the form it supposedly took before the fall achieves a rare pedagogical power in 1632 under the pen of Bishop Joseph Hall, a moderate Calvinist whom Laud persecuted:

> Consider! Man's storehouse [the earthly paradise] was also his workshop. Work was his pleasure. Paradise not only gratified his senses but also exercised his hands. If happiness had consisted in doing nothing, man would have remained unemployed. But all the delights [offered to him] would not have made him happy had his life been one of idleness. As a result, we see that as soon as he has been created, he is put to work. No greatness, no perfection is compatible with crossed arms. Man had to work because he was happy. How much more should we, too, work in order that we may some day be happy [in heaven].

"In the beginning work was not a necessity nor was it accompanied by difficulty or fatigue. The more cheerfully we give ourselves to our occupation, the closer we draw to paradise."[39] What a striking and very Puritan defense of an activism based, paradoxically, on a description of man's time in paradise!

Milton made this theme his own, except that he admits into the garden of Eden the reality of fatigue following upon work, although it is a fatigue that allowed the worker better to appreciate the sweetness of rest. Otherwise, he is completely in agreement with Hall in condemning idleness, a state unknown to man and woman before sin:

> They sat them down; and after no more toil
> Of their sweet gardening labor than sufficed
> To commend cool Zephyr, and made ease
> More easy, wholesome thirst and appetite
> More grateful, to their supper fruits they fell,
> Nectarine fruits which the compliant boughs
> Yielded them, sidelong as they sat recline
> On the soft downy bank damasked with flowers.[40]

Further on, Adam says:

> Other creatures all day long
> Rove idle, unemployed, and less need rest;
> Man hath his daily work of body or mind
> Appointed, which declares his dignity,
> And the regard of Heaven on all his ways;

> While other animals unactive range,
> And of their doings God takes no account.
> To-morrow ere fresh morning streak the east
> With first approach of light, we must be risen,
> And at our pleasant labor.[41]

According to Milton, then, Adam and Eve were up and about before dawn. No question of them lying in in the morning, even in the earthly paradise.

Catholic writing on work in the earthly paradise is of course very much like that of the Reformers, and is based, like the latter, on Genesis and St. Augustine. Catholics too condemn idleness; their originality consists perhaps in a special insistence on the high value of agriculture. In his *Origines antwerpianae*, Goropius, a physician and etymologist, asks: "If the entire earth [prior to sin] served only [man's] happiness, why did God place man there [in the earthly paradise] to work and keep it, since these tasks are the source not of pleasure but of fatigue and trouble?" The answer is twofold: on the one hand, Aristotle was correct when he wrote that all real pleasure is connected with the exercise of virtue, which is incompatible with idleness; on the other hand, "Before man's sin, the working and keeping of the garden was necessarily a source of pleasure."[42]

In the poetic vein, Tasso says in his *Il mondo creato* that God "set man as guardian of this happy and pleasant garden, in order that he might work. He did not create him for a life of idleness and uselessness."[43] Suárez expresses a thought widely shared by commentators on Genesis when he writes, invoking St. Thomas Aquinas:[44]

[In the earthly paradise] work was not fatiguing nor was it a punishment, but rather an easy occupation, a pleasant bodily exercise.... Furthermore, it was not needed in order to procure one's sustenance, as it is today, but was a means of perfecting nature, making it fruitful, and exploring it, as St. Thomas says, by experimenting with the forces at work in the soil and with seeds and plants.[45]

But, to be more specific, in what did Adam's "agricultural" work in the earthly paradise consist? According to St. Augustine and many generations after him, the work consisted in sowing, taking cuttings, transplanting shrubs, making grafts, and, more generally, all the tasks that cultivation of various kinds requires.[46] But Bar Cephas sees things differently: Adam, he thinks, had neither to sow nor to prune nor to tire himself out using heavy tools. His function was to create level areas and clear paths and avenues that allowed him to walk in the paradisal woods.[47] According to Malvenda, the role of the first man in the garden of Eden was to adorn the garden with great care and watch to see that nothing disfigured its beauty.[48]

Despite these disagreements on details, all the Catholic commentators of that age, like those of the Reformation churches, were convinced that agricultural work in paradise was "not difficult" but a "source of pleasure" (*non laboriosa, sed delitiosa*), in a phrase of St. Augustine that was repeated countless times after him.[49] This was all the less surprising since people had long been convinced, with Cicero, that "nothing is more kingly than the study of agriculture." It is Pereira who cites these words from the *De senectute*.[50]

For the sake of completeness, Inveges raises an unexpected question at the end of his chapter on the command given to Adam about "cultivating" the earthly paradise: Was the command of God about the cultivation of the earthly paradise given to Adam alone or to both of our first parents? The Sicilian priest notes that the text of Moses is not clear on this point and that both interpretations are possible. Therefore he does not take sides.[51]

Poets and commentators on Genesis wrote inexhaustibly about the idyllic conditions that prevailed in the biblical golden age. Du Bartas bids his reader not be surprised

> If I tell you that with face ever serene
> All-embracing heaven looked down on this plain,
> That hollow rocks distilled sweet honey,
> That nourishing milk flowed through the fields,
> That even rue had the same odor as the roses,
> That every plot of land yielded everything in every season
> And on the same branches countless different fruits
> Flourished constantly, not too ripe and not too green,
> That the tartest fruit and bitterest herb
> Were as sweet as sugar from Madeira,
> And the myrobolans with their potent beneficence
> Gave much better nourishment to their healthy bodies....
> Music held sway there, and on the bank
> A sweet music always accompanied the voice.[52]

John Swan, in his *Speculum mundi*, tells us that we are "pygmies" by comparison with the "cedars" that our first parents were before their sin. They knew no bodily sickness or infirmities. The air was "gentle and pure." Fruits were much more nourishing than after the flood.[53] Joseph Hall waxes almost lyrical on the subject: the first man (he says) had no experience of sickness and no reason for discontent. No ailment afflicted his veins, arteries, and muscles. God had made him both actor and spectator, for he had the earth for his use and the heavens for his contemplation. Around him all was beauty, power, and harmony. In the universe that encircled him there was nothing that did not stir wonder. At that time, man "had no need of a savior. His enjoyment of God filled him with happiness. The sweetness he experienced in contemplation of a creation still new and the glory of its creator delighted him to the point of leaving no time or reason for complaint.... He had the perfection of being.... As soon as he opened his eyes, he knew himself to be happy."[54]

Powers and Knowledge of Adam and Eve

One of the sources of the happiness of Adam and Eve in the earthly paradise was that they had complete control of nature and received the docile obedience of all the animals. Genesis 1:26 has the Creator say: "Let them [humankind] have dominion over the fish of the sea, and over the birds of the air, and over the cattle, and over all the wild animals of the earth." From this, says Suárez, it follows "necessarily that even the wild animals, which we now fear may kill or injure us, were then submissive and obedient to man."[55] St. Augustine had long since said that before sin Adam and Eve could not be afraid or suffer or die. Nothing could attack either their bodies or their souls.[56]

But what concrete form did this obedience of the animals take? We should note in passing how questions arose, each out of the preceding, once the biblical story of creation was taken literally. Cajetan shows some originality when he tells his readers that control of nature is a power given to human beings after as well as before sin, since it is still up to them to tame, capture, and kill animals.[57] But St. Augustine had thought that God in his providence had arranged things so that the dangerous animals would set aside their aggressiveness in dealing with man and would do him no harm (he is speaking, of course, of the state of innocence).[58] This was the generally accepted opinion. According to St. Thomas Aquinas, God saw to it that the animals would be afraid of man and would respect him as their lord and master.[59] Pereira, for his part, thinks that before sin man had enough insight and wisdom for a complete knowledge of the nature and inclinations of the animals; consequently he knew how to make them obey him. Furthermore, as need required (*quantum opus erat*), God could, through the agency of the angels, easily make obedient any animals who had difficulty in obeying Adam's commands.[60]

Suárez in turn explains that even today animals have a kind of "natural prudence" (consider bees) and can even acquire a real familiarity with humans, as we see with horses. We may therefore think that before sin God had endowed them with a tendency — at that time instinctive — to obey and respect man. It is true, indeed, that even in the state of sin we retain the ability to control. But we should reflect that before sin Adam and Eve did not eat meat, nor did they have any need of wool or skins for clothing, and they had no need of animal motive power. Why, then, should the animals have had any aggressive designs against our first parents, who made use of them only "for honorable intellectual recreation or to gain knowledge (*usum scientiae*) or for raising their minds to God"?[61]

It is worth pointing out once again, in connection with the obedience of the animals, how like each other Catholic and Protestants were in their commentaries on Genesis. Salkeld speaks out strongly on the subject we have just been examining:

> Nothing shows more clearly the excellence of man, especially in the state of innocence, than the power and dominion he had over all creatures; these, being at his service, were always ready to obey his commands. The lion was not fearsome [as it is today], nor the elephant terrifying, nor the tiger ferocious, nor the eagle predatory, nor the whale monstrous. Everything was subject to the authority of man, just as he himself was subject to his Lord and Creator.[62]

In the setting of paradise, the logic of a creation not yet disordered would have required the inferior naturally to obey the superior. All flesh would have feared man, who would have had dominion over the beasts and birds of prey.

The naming of the animals by Adam was clear proof of the authority God had given him over all the animals. Joseph Hall writes that "man received his name from God, and the animals received theirs from man."[63] Poets and artists on both sides of the confessional barrier did not fail to describe the happy age in which human beings and animals lived side by side in harmony. In the earthly paradise, Tasso says, "Man lived safely and happily as master and lord of the animals which land and sea produced. All were constrained to obey him. Under his gentle authority many of them learned to serve him gladly and in happy peace."[64] Milton had written even more lyrically when he described the handsome couple that Adam and Eve made, and added, with Isaiah in mind, that

> About them frisking played
> All beasts of the earth, since wild, and of all chase
> In wood or wilderness, forest or den;
> Sporting the lion ramped, and in his paw
> Dandled the kid; bears, tigers, ounces, pards,
> Gamboled before them; the unwieldy elephant
> To make them mirth used all his might, and wreathed
> His lithe proboscis.[65]

Think of all the artists down the centuries who have delighted to describe this scene! Adam and Eve did not have command only of the animals; all of nature obeyed them. Salkeld explains that this obedience reflected the logic of a creation not yet disordered by sin. Had there been no sin,

> all creatures would have remained subject to human beings, who themselves would have obeyed God alone. For all the inferior creatures are subject to their superiors by reason of their nature and of the order, perfection, and decree of God: the imperfect to the more perfect, matter to form, corporeal to spiritual, accident to substance, elements to compounds. Thus even the heavens, stars, and planets were for man. He alone was for God and was subject only to him for so long he did not break this sacred chain and order by which all things were placed in his power and were connected with God through him.[66]

The question of the occupations of Adam and Eve in the earthly paradise was broken down into a great variety of further questions. One, for example, was whether our first parents worshiped God, offered sacrifices, and sang psalms. Suárez acknowledges his own lack of certainty on this point. "For, just as no affirmative answer can be given in view of the short time they spent [in Eden], so there is no sufficient proof to justify a denial. The scriptures do not say, but it does not follow that they did not do so."[67]

But if the original sin had not been committed, would a nonsinful humanity have had temples, altars, and priests? Following St. Thomas, Suárez is inclined to say yes, because "the natural law" orders human beings to offer sacrifices to God. But how would priests have been chosen? Probably by selecting them from among the eldest sons, since primogeniture bestows the maximum dignity. What rites would these priests have celebrated during these ceremonies? Suárez has no answer, but he regards it as certain that the offerers would have sacrificed naked, after the manner of "glorified" bodies.[68]

Back to Adam and Eve in the earthly paradise. Whether or not they offered sacrifices to God, it is obvious that in addition to their agricultural occupations, they "engaged with pleasure in divine contemplation and meditated on the joys of the heavenly homeland"; the words are those of Inveges and closely resemble those of Moses Bar Cephas, according to whom our innocent first parents lived "in intimacy with God."[69] This intimacy necessarily gave rise to a wisdom and knowledge far beyond ours. Adam and Eve were endowed with qualities far superior to ours. Luther writes:

> If Adam had remained in innocence...we would have had no need for paper, ink, pens, and that endless multitude of books which we require today, although we do not attain a thousandth part of that wisdom which Adam had in paradise....If they [Adam and Eve] had not fallen into sin, Adam would have transmitted this single command [namely, "You may freely eat of every tree of the garden, but of the tree of the knowledge of good and evil you

shall not eat"] later on to all his descendants. From it would have come the best theologians, the most learned lawyers, and the most expert physicians.[70]

In addition to the grace, holiness, and faith that our first parents received from God, what knowledge of nature did they have? This question, too, theologians debated in the past; Suárez sums up current thinking at the beginning of the seventeenth century:

> Adam had complete natural knowledge.... His knowledge did not embrace the whole heavens nor all the power of the stars, nor did it give him knowledge of contingent futures that depend on free will. On the other hand, it enabled him to foresee contingent futures that result from the concurrence of numerous natural non-free causes. He did not know the entire past but only so much of the past as is revealed by the present. In addition, his knowledge extended to all species actually created: birds, fishes, wild animals, trees, herbs, flowers.

He did not, of course, receive a revelation of everything "creatable" or of the individuals making up each species, or, unlike Christ, of the secret thoughts of others. But, relying on the approval of St. Augustine and St. Thomas, Suárez says: "So great was the natural, innate knowledge of Adam and Eve before sin that they could not be mistaken nor deceived, that is, they could not mistake the false for the true and vice versa, unless they chose to do so. For ignorance and error are a punishment for sin." In short, their knowledge and their wisdom far surpassed those of the best-educated and wisest among their successors, including Solomon.[71]

On the Protestant side, Salkeld does not see things any differently. "It is the common opinion of the Fathers and other theologians that Adam had a very perfect infused knowledge of all natural objects."[72] For proof he refers to Ecclus 17:3–11, which says: "The Lord...granted them authority over everything on the earth. He endowed them with strength like his own, and made them in his own image. He put the fear of them in all living beings, and gave them dominion over beasts and birds." Salkeld goes on to say that because Adam had complete knowledge of the natures of lesser beings, he was able to name them in light of their characteristic traits.[73]

Later on, Solomon was certainly "the wisest of human beings." The Book of Wisdom puts some astonishing claims on his lips: the Lord "gave me unerring knowledge of what exists, to know the structure of the world and the activity of the elements; the beginning and end and middle of times, the alternation of the solstices and the changes of the seasons, the cycles of the year and the constellations of the stars, the natures of animals and the tempers of wild animals,... the varieties of plants and the virtues of roots" (7:17–20). But what is true of Solomon was even truer of Adam. "Beyond any possible doubt, he [Adam] was the wisest of all human beings except for our Savior, the author of his wisdom and all wisdom" (wisdom here including forms of knowledge and prudence).[74]

A new question, which to us is no less surprising than the preceding ones: How did God communicate his precepts to Adam and Eve — by intelligible speech or by an interior revelation? St. Augustine opted for the first answer: "We are led [by Scripture] rather to assume that God spoke to man in Paradise as He spoke later to the patriarchs, such as Abraham and Moses, namely, under some corporeal form,"[75] that is, by using language. But what language? St. Augustine, again, and then, following him, Pereira and other Catholic commentators at the end of the sixteenth century and the beginning of the seventeenth, answered that the "idiom" that our first parents understood and used was Hebrew, the primitive language of the human race and the mother of all others.[76]

On the Protestant side, writers were for a long time of the same persuasion. Hebrew, they thought, was shot through with revelation; logically, therefore, the text of the Bible had reached all generations without the slightest alteration.[77] Joseph Justus Scaliger (d. 1609) claimed that "the oldest of all languages is the one in which the sacred books were written."[78] Later, Johannes Buxtorf II endeavored to show that since the human race is descended from a single man, Hebrew was the only language spoken by human beings until the confusion of tongues at Babel. It is thus the sacred language because God is its author.[79]

The school of Saumur subsequently modified this overly categorical claim. Louis Cappel in his *Critica sacra* (1650) suggested a modification of the special status of Hebrew, by moving its origin back to the beginning of time and making it the source of all languages.[80] Bochart, a first-rate Arabist, then suggested that Hebrew be compared with the other Eastern languages. But despite this innovative methodology he maintained the old genealogy of languages and continued to derive all of them from Hebrew.[81] Not until the end of the seventeenth century and the works of Jean Le Clerc, an editor of Erasmus, do we find a scholarly challenge to the priority of Hebrew. And yet even in the article of the *Encyclopédie* on language Hebrew is still regarded as the mother language of the human race.

There were some original — which is to say, marginal — minds who claimed that another language than Hebrew was spoken in the earthly paradise. One of these was Goropius, who undertook to prove that Adam and Eve spoke Flemish. His argument was as follows: according to the Bible (see Gen 10:5), Magog, grandson of Noah and son of Japheth, migrated "to the islands of the Gentiles." At the beginning of the eighteenth century, Leibniz praised Goropius, "a learned physician" of Antwerp, who was "not too far wrong in claiming that the Germanic language, which he calls Cimbrian, gives as many, and even more, evidences of being primitive, as Hebrew does."[82] According to Goropius, the German shores of the North Sea marked the terminus of the migration of Magog and his kinsfolk.[83] But in the seventeenth century, some Swedish scholars, especially Georg Stiernhielm (d. 1672) and Olaus Rudebeck (d. 1702), contended that this migration was in the direction of Sweden and brought there the first of all human languages. It follows that Adam and Eve spoke Swedish.

The question of the language spoken in paradise seemed sufficiently debatable at this period that another Swede, Andreas Kempe, devoted to it a work written in German and entitled *Die schwedische Standarte erhöhet* (The Swedish banner raised high [1683]).[84] In this book we see some Swedish pastors gathered around a table and tankards of beer and discussing the language spoken in the earthly paradise. One of them suggests Hebrew. But the author's own spokesman explains and proves that in the earthly paradise God spoke Swedish to our first parents. The latter, on the other hand, spoke Danish. As for the serpent... he spoke French, "a language that brings the whole body into play, so that it can deceive even the wisest."

Kempe has evidently ceased to be serious at this point. The fact remains that the question of the language spoken in the earthly paradise continued to receive the attention of many distinguished minds, including Richard Simon (1678).[85]

Marriage and Society in the Earthly Paradise

In his commentary on Genesis, Luther describes the wonderful conditions of life in the earthly paradise and asserts the following in particular:

> He [man] would have eaten; he would have drunk; and the conversion of food in his body would have taken place, but not in such a disgusting manner as now. Moreover, this tree of life would have preserved perpetual youth. Man would never have experienced the inconveniences of old age; his forehead would never have developed wrinkles, and his feet, hands, and any other part of his body would not have become weaker or more inactive. Thanks to this fruit, man's powers for procreation and for all tasks would have remained unimpaired until finally he would have been translated from the physical life to the spiritual....
>
> Man still has feet, eyes, and ears the way each part was created in Paradise, but after sin these very members have been most wretchedly corrupted and misshapen. Before sin Adam had the clearest eyes, the most delicate and delightful odor, and a body very well suited and obedient for procreation....

There would have been the innocent and pure love of sex for sex. Procreation would have taken place without any depravity, as an act of obedience. Mothers would have given birth without pain. Infants would not have been brought up in such a wretched manner and with such great toil....

There still remains in nature the longing of the male for the female, likewise the fruit of procreation; but these are combined with the awful hideousness of lust and the frightful pain of birth. Shame, ignominy, and embarrassment arise even among married people when they wish to enjoy their legitimate intercourse. So universal is the most oppressive evil of original sin! The creation indeed is good, and the blessing is good; but through sin they are so corrupt that married people cannot make use of them without shame.[86]

In this passage Luther is summarizing in a striking way the conception that Christianity had long had of the paradisal life in the garden of Eden. He is also answering a question that had long stirred the curiosity of theologians: If Adam and Eve had not sinned, how would they have had children? Would they have made love? And, if original sin had not intervened, how would the human race have subsequently multiplied?

To this set of questions a further one was added: Did Adam and Eve have carnal relations before sin? Inveges' answer: "All the Fathers regard it as certain that before their sin Adam and Eve were virgins.... This view is shared by St. John Chrysostom, St. Jerome, and St. Augustine." "It was after the loss of paradise," Chrysostom says, "that the use of sex began. For before their disobedience Adam and Eve lived an angelic life, and there was no question of the pleasures of Venus."[87] This reference to the "angelic life" merits emphasis. For the belief was long held in the church that God had created the human race so that it might occupy the place in heaven left empty by the fallen angels; this initial supposition gave rise to an entire disincarnate anthropology.[88]

But St. Thomas Aquinas, Pereira, and Suárez added some interesting points and nuances to this view of the virginity of Adam and Eve while still in their state of innocence. They distinguished between virginal integrity (for Eve), the absence of lustful desire, and the deliberate will to abstain from sexual union.[89] According to Suárez, our first parents, while in the garden of Eden, had the intention of engaging in sexual union in order to obey the Creator's order to "increase and multiply," but they preserved "materially" a virginity that they lost only after their disobedience. Inveges adopts this distinction and concludes from it: "Adam and Eve probably slept in separate places in the holy garden as in different beds, without kisses, without embraces, without amorous words either during the day or at night." This was not abnormal, since they did not experience the disturbance caused by desire.[90] John Swan, an Anglican, adds a further argument: "It can be accepted

that Adam sinned before knowing his wife. Otherwise Cain would have
been conceived without sin.... But it is unthinkable that Cain was conceived
without sin."[91]

This kind of theological reasoning did not convince everyone. Milton
would have robbed his *Paradise Lost* of one of its most beautiful passages
if he had removed the pure and tender love-making of Adam and Eve in
the garden of Eden:

> So passed they naked on, nor shunned the sight
> Of God or angel, for they thought no ill;
> So hand in hand they passed, the loveliest pair
> That ever since in love's embraces met.
> ...[B]y a fresh fountain side
> They sat them down....
> ...[T]o their supper fruits they fell....
> Nor gentle purpose, nor endearing smiles
> wanted, nor youthful dalliance, as beseems
> Fair couple linked in happy nuptial league,
> Alone as they.[92]

Leaving aside the special case of Adam and Eve, the commentators on
Genesis could not avoid the more general question: If the original sin had
not been committed, in what way would men and women have experienced
love and begotten children? There was complete agreement on two points:
in the paradisal state nudity would have been without shame and childbirth
without pain. Nonetheless, the fear of sexuality and the "angelic anthropology" of the time led many theologians to assertions that we find surprising.
St. John Chrysostom, St. Gregory of Nyssa, St. Augustine (at least in his
Contra Manichaeos, for his thinking evolved), St. John Damascene, and others
thought that in a paradisal situation the multiplication of human beings
would have been effected not by sexual union but by divine creation, since
humanity would have been in an angelic state. St. John Damascene explains:
"The words 'increase and multiply' did not mean that the propagation [of
the species] was to be effected through the embrace of love. For God could
accomplish the propagation in another manner."[93] St. Augustine had already
said in his *De religione* that in the state of innocence, in which human beings
were not multiplied through the union of the man and his companion, there
would have been neither marriages nor consanguinities nor kinships, since all
of these affinities are the result of sin and not of nature.[94]

St. Augustine's views on this question did indeed change and develop in
the course of his career, but he always maintained, as did many theologians
after him, that there is a strong taint of guilt in sexuality as we experience it
after original sin. In the *City of God* he wrote:

When mankind was in such a state of ease and plenty, blest with such felicity, let us never imagine that it was impossible for the seed of children to be sown without the morbid condition of lust. Instead, the sexual organs would have been brought into activity by the same bidding of the will as controlled the other organs. Then, without feeling the allurement of passion goading him on, the husband would have relaxed on his wife's bosom in tranquillity of mind and with no impairment of his body's integrity. Moreover, although we cannot prove this in experience, it does not therefore follow that we should not believe that when those parts of the body were not activated by the turbulent heat of passion but brought into service by deliberate use of the power when the need arose, the male seed could have been dispatched into the womb, with no loss of the wife's integrity, just as the menstrual flux can now be produced from the womb of a virgin without loss of maidenhead. For the seed could be injected through the same passage by which the flux is ejected.[95]

In the twelfth century Alexander of Hales, a Scholastic, goes beyond (the early) Augustine and asserts that in the state of innocence coitus and procreation would have taken place without the breaking of the hymen. Copulation would have been effected by the mere contact of the sexual organs of man and woman, the former's member being brought to "the closed door of female vulva." The male seed ejected outside of the female vagina would then have been carried into the womb by a special action of God (speciali Dei providentia).[96]

In fact, however, St. Augustine eventually corrected the opinions just recalled here and said that sinless humanity would have been multiplied through natural generation.[97] The vast majority of theologians, from St. Thomas Aquinas to Suárez, followed him on this point. A passage of St. Bonaventure was often cited in this context. Bonaventure distinguishes three aspects of the sexual act:

the opening of the female door, the passion which is the price paid for sin, and the shameful pleasure. The first is in conformity with nature; the second is a punishment; the third is a corruption in the form of a vice, half-way between punishment and sin. If man had known woman in the state of innocence, the door would indeed have opened, but there would have been no punishment in the form of passion and no unbefitting pleasure. For then the generative power would not have been corrupted or contaminated, and the members (which the generative power sets in motion) would have obeyed reason, says St. Augustine, as do mouth, hands, and tongue. Just as hands and mouth open and close without the presence of passion and shameful pleasure, so would it have been with the [sexual] members. Then it would have been no more disgusting to speak of them than of other members. Now, however, it is shameful to speak of what is repugnant to nature. But this act causes people to blush by reason of the ugliness inherent in it.[98]

This position of St. Bonaventure, which is like that of St. Thomas, was subsequently the one most widely adopted by commentators on Genesis and by Suárez in particular. These writers also concluded that there would have been sexual pleasure in the act of love (St. Thomas even thinks it would have been greater than after sin),[99] but it would have been completely under control. Suárez writes: "The sexual organs would have been roused not by a natural and involuntary change in the degree of heat, but by reason and will." The "pleasure" would therefore have been "restrained and measured by reason."[100] Drawing conclusions from this great debate, Inveges thinks that in the earthly paradise, had there been no sin, Adam and Eve would have expressed their mutual love by "honorable embraces, kisses, chaste touches, and words filled with a holy affection."[101] Furthermore, we must think that

> marital coitus would not have been as frequent in paradise as it is now in the state of corrupted nature, where it takes place very often. For now this unrestrained copulation is the result of a raging, disordered concupiscence. In paradise, on the contrary, it would have taken place as well defined moments (*statuto tempore*), that is, for the sake of reproduction.[102]

This is a typically Augustinian statement.[103]

It is worth taking a moment to emphasize, once again, the similarity between Catholic and Protestant thinking on this subject as on others. Salkeld expresses a view very widely held in the Reformed world when he says, in words that Suárez might have written:

> As long as the higher human powers obeyed God, so long would the lower powers have obeyed man. As long as sin had not warped the will, there could have been nothing filthy or abominable about natural activities. Just as our eyes and other senses are still subject to our wills, so too the other lower powers, which today rebel against us, would have remained docile to the higher power. All deformities and disorders would have been excluded. Conformity [to the will] and order would have remained unbroken. The sense appetites would have obeyed reason, reason would have obeyed the spirit, and the spirit would have obeyed God. Just as no disorder in nature can come from the author of nature, so in the normal course of events no disorder could have arisen in natural activities. Consequently, in the state of nature there would have been human generation as we now have it: I mean as far as the substance of the act is concerned, but not in the kind of enjoyment or in the predominance of violent pleasure.[104]

Was woman equal to man in the conditions that prevailed in paradise? Inveges answers: "The holiness and gifts of Eve were almost the same as those of Adam."[105] But Adam enjoyed the protection both of an archangel, since he, Adam, had a "public" responsibility as head of the future human race, and of an angel in his "private" conduct. Eve was aided only by a "private" angel.[106] Salkeld for his part discusses at greater length the quality of man and woman before sin, and returns to the question several times. He finds himself placed in a quandary by the famous passage in the First Letter to the Corinthians: "He [a man] is the image and glory of God, but woman is the glory of man. Indeed, man was not made from woman, but woman from man" (11:1–16, at vv. 7–8). For Gen 1:27 says the opposite: "God created humankind in his image, in the image of God he created them; male and female he created them."

Salkeld extricates himself from this difficulty with the help of St. Augustine[107] and by distinguishing two senses of the word "image." If we take the word to include only "natural endowments," we will conclude that the man is "the head of the woman." But if we bring in "supernatural gifts," such as an immortal soul, grace, free will, and so on, we will be convinced that man and woman were and are equals before God and even that "some women [are] adorned with these privileges and supernatural gifts in a higher degree than men and are therefore more like God." The Virgin Mary is proof of this claim.[108]

But this answer does not entirely resolve the problem of Eve's status in relation to Adam in their paradisal setting. Was woman submissive to man before sin, or is this submission a consequence of sin? Here is Salkeld's answer, which represents the current view of the theologians of his time:

> There are two kinds of submission of woman to man: one is voluntary, the other involuntary; one springs from nature, the other from sin; one is difficult, the other pleasant; the latter is strengthened by grace, the former is contrary to nature. The one is therefore in no way incompatible with the state of innocence, while the other is a punishment for original sin.
>
> Certainly, if Eve had not sinned and disobeyed the divine command by eating of the forbidden fruit, her nature would nevertheless have required submission to her husband, because she was a weaker vessel; I am speaking, however, of a submission that is voluntary and not coerced, natural and not imposed, and therefore free and exempt from the movements of rejection which today even the best descendants of Eve feel toward their husbands.[109]

This theologically grounded anthropology makes possible a correct understanding of the passage in *Paradise Lost* in which Milton, basing himself implicitly on St. Paul and Genesis ("He [your husband] shall rule over you"), strongly emphasizes the superiority of Adam over Eve, even before sin:

> ...though both
> Not equal, as their sex not equal seemed;
> For contemplation he and valor formed,
> For softness she and sweet attentive grace;
> He for God only, she for God in him.

> His fair large front and eye sublime declared
> Absolute rule; and hyacinthine locks
> Round from his parted forelock manly hung
> Clustering, but not beneath his shoulders broad:
> She as a veil down to the slender waist
> Her unadorned golden tresses wore
> Disheveled, but in wanton ringlets waved
> As the vine curls her tendrils, which implied
> Subjection, but required with gentle sway,
> And by her yielded, by him best received,
> Yielded with coy submission, modest pride.[110]

We today see this as a fine example of machismo hidden by ideology and emerging even more strongly, a little further on in the poem, in Eve's answer to her husband when he asks her to help him in pruning the plants in the garden and taking care of the flowers:

> O thou for whom
> And from whom I was formed flesh of thy flesh,
> And without whom am to no end, my guide
> And head, what thou hast said is just and right....
> Pre-eminent by so much odds, while thou
> Like consort to thyself canst nowhere find.[111]

If humanity had remained in a state of innocence and had continued its paradisal way of life, children would have caused no concern and would have experienced no pain. St. Augustine even taught that children, who obviously have to be born quite small "because of the capacity of the womb," would have immediately after birth been brought by God to the completeness of adult age.[112] St. Thomas Aquinas and Suárez corrected Augustine on this point: in their opinion, in the state of innocence human children would have experienced, as we do, childhood, adolescence, and young adulthood. They would have needed a mother's milk. They would have grown to full adulthood. But at that point they would have escaped old age and decay. They would have been spared white hair, wrinkled face, shaking limbs, hoarse voice, and viscous spittle.[113]

Inveges, following the logic at work in this overall view of the state of innocence, adds that childbirth would have been painless and would even have brought a "certain refreshment of the soul"; that the baby, emerging streaked with blood, would have been immediately washed and cleaned by the very flow of the liquid from the womb; and that the newborn child would not have cried, whimpered, or shivered. On the contrary, it would have been happy; it would have "roared laughing and would have exulted at being born immortal." Obviously, it would not have needed either diapers or swaddling clothes. In addition, we may think, with Suárez, that mothers would have breast-fed their children until at least the age of twelve.[114]

In St. Augustine's view, just as a child would have become an adult immediately after birth, so it would have almost instantaneously acquired the use of reason and a vast store of knowledge.[115] But most of the specialists once again distanced themselves from the bishop of Hippo on this point. Hugh of St. Victor, St. Thomas Aquinas, St. Bonaventure, and Suárez, among others, thought that even in the state of innocence young humans would not have had the use of reason "from conception," but would have acquired it gradually. On the other hand, they would not have experienced "movements and appetites contrary to reason." Knowledge, too, would have been acquired gradually, but all would have enjoyed, from the very beginning, an "infused prudence."[116] Here is Inveges' summary:

> In the state of fallen nature, human beings pass through infancy, childhood, and adolescence, all of which they traverse in wretchedness, in tears, sadness, fear, and suffering. For infancy is marked by bitterness and tears, while childhood and adolescence are spent under strict paternal discipline and the mother's rod, and all three ages are full of fears and sufferings. In the state of integral nature, on the other hand, mothers would have fed at their breasts infants who would not have whimpered or wept; parents and teachers would have reared and instructed children and adolescents who would have had no experience of fear and suffering. All activities would have been constantly filled with joy.[117]

This "vale of tears" is the converse of the garden of Eden, and this point-by-point contrast was long considered to be obvious.

New questions follow from the ones we have seen: In the society of paradise would there have been superiors and subjects, emperors, kings, and princes, and other people who obeyed these? According to St. Augustine, in the state of innocence cities and realms would have had no need of kings, archons, or consuls, or any of the marks of respect that nowadays are the trappings of authority. The only dominion human beings would have exercised would have been over the fishes, birds, and wild animals.[118] But here again St. Thomas Aquinas, Pereira, and Suárez dissociate themselves from the author of the *City of God;* their reasoning on this point runs parallel to that of Salkeld, which we saw above, on the question of man and woman.[119]

There are (say these three writers) two kinds of authority. One is natural and elicits a free and joyful obedience; the other is a result of sin and entails coercion. In a paradisal society the first of these two kinds of authority would have been exercised, amid peace, gentleness, and freedom, with the help of "laws that gave guidance and were not penal." Inveges, who once against serves as our guide, asks next whether in that blessed land governments would have been hereditary. His answer is that they would have been elected. Sinless humanity would certainly have been governed by a monarchy. Aristotle recommends such a system, and the Catholic Church is shepherded by a single pontiff.[120] But this monarchy would have been elective.

I must introduce a parenthesis here on the subject of the original thinking that appeared in fifteenth-century Spain on the subject of the nobility. In his *Nobiliario vero*, published in 1492, Fernando de Mexia argued thus: God created our first parents as "nobles." But while Abel preserved this nobility, Cain lost it. Original sin has left us our free will that enables us to gain merits or demerits, to draw closer to or distance ourselves from our likeness to the Creator, who is the Noble par excellence. Thus, since the beginning of the world, "The wicked have departed from their initial nobility...and have become full of darkness and without lineage, drawing ever closer to the wickedness and darkness of sin and evil habits and abandoning themselves to evil activities and shameful habits."[121] How surprising to find Genesis supplying a defense of the nobility!

St. Augustine, St. Gregory the Great, St. Thomas Aquinas, Pereira, and Suárez all agree that a paradisal society would have had no need of servants. Being a servant is indeed not the same as being a slave, but it does imply a certain dominion of one human being over another; it is therefore a consequence of sin.[122] Finally, the leaders of the community in Eden would not have lived in palaces or worn crowns or carried scepters, nor would they have been surrounded by a court. Their style of life would have been simple and without any pomp, like that of superiors in religious orders. All the present adornments of power are the result of original sin.[123]

But what about the possession of personal property and real estate in the paradisal society? A long Christian tradition dating back to St. Ambrose and to St. John Chrysostom[124] asserted that this society did not acknowledge any private property in land, animals, or trees, nor would it have done so, had it continued in existence; and that the fruits of the earth would have belonged to all in common. At the beginning of the seventeenth century, however, Suárez thought it necessary to qualify these claims in two ways. We must, he says, distinguish between personal possessions and real estate. In the state of innocence, some division of the former would have been necessary, since the person who, for example, gathered the fruits of a tree would thereby have acquired a special right to them, and it would have been unjust to take them from him. This private property would have extended to trees and animals, but not to gold, riches, and clothing. In fact, there would have been no need of clothing. When we turn to real estate, some correction is again necessary, since a complete lack of division of real property would have harmed a person who did not have a field at his disposal in which to sow, and a piece of land on which to build. "But these things can be regarded as practically nothing and they do not unqualifiedly contradict the essential possession of goods in common in the state of innocence."[125] Whence the communist dreams of all the people who down the centuries have tried to restore the earthly paradise.

Chapter 11

The Disappearance of the Enchanted Garden

If we jump abruptly from 1667, the year Milton published his *Paradise Lost*, to 1779, when G.-L. Buffon published his *Époques de la nature*, we can gauge the profound change in the way in which leading intellectuals of the later period thought and spoke of the garden of Eden and the opening chapters of Genesis. One writer has remarked, with good reason, that the century following the publication of Milton's masterpiece saw a sharp decrease in works both of literature and exegesis that dealt with Adam and Eve and the earthly paradise.[1] It is therefore chiefly for the record, because it appeared so belatedly, that I mention the French adaptation of *Paradise Lost* that a poetess of Rouen, Mme Dubocage, published in 1760.

The salient point to be noted about the age of the Enlightenment, as far as my subject here is concerned, is the progressive challenge to the "historical" content and veracity of the beginning of Genesis. Several different approaches, which ultimately converged, led to this outcome, but they were slow in gaining possession of men's minds. Thus it is revealing that P. Bayle's *Dictionnaire historique et critique* (1696–97), which was intended not only as a collection of foolish historical errors of the day but also as a work of positive criticism, uses fully traditional language in speaking of Adam and Eve. The article "Adam" has this to say:

> Adam, stem and father of the entire human race, was created directly by God on the sixth day of creation. When God had formed his body from the dust of the earth, he then breathed the breath of life into his nostrils, that is, he gave him life and made of him the composite which we call a human being and which comprises an organized body and a rational soul. The same God who had made Adam placed him in a beautiful garden and then brought the animals to him so that he might give them their names. He then cast Adam into a deep sleep and took from him a rib out of which he formed a woman.... There was in the garden a tree of which God forbade him to eat under penalty of death. But the woman, enticed by a serpent, did not refrain

from eating of it and persuaded Adam likewise to eat of it. At that moment they realized that they were naked and they made coverings for themselves by sewing fig leaves together. God then pronounced the penalty with which he meant to punish their sin; he expelled them from the garden and made them garments of skins.[2]

Bayle's intention, throughout this article, is to confine himself closely to "what we know for certain" about this subject. He therefore rejects "a great many things said about Adam that are either false or quite uncertain." But he considers it "probable" that Adam "possessed infused knowledge when he came from the hand of his creator" and that he was very handsome. In the article "Abel" he voices the further opinion that the first sin took place shortly after the nuptial blessing and that Eve "was tempted and seduced almost immediately after she was formed."[3] Thus Bayle does not question the "historical" character of the first chapters of Genesis.

The same holds for *The Reasonableness of Christianity as Delivered in the Scriptures*, which John Locke published anonymously in 1695. The work does indeed challenge traditional Christianity inasmuch as the latter would have "all Adam's posterity doomed to eternal infinite punishment, for the transgression of Adam, whom millions had never heard of, and no one had authorized to act for him, or be his representative."[4] But Locke does not doubt that "the state of paradise was a state of immortality, of life without end, which he [Adam] lost that very day that he ate" the forbidden fruit.[5] He also writes: "The earthly paradise was a place of happiness as well as of immortality; in that fortunate abode there was neither fatigue nor tears to wipe away."[6]

The best that can be said about the article "Adam" in the *Encyclopédie* is that its aim is to be circumspect and even conservative. It does indeed observe that "Adam" means human beings generally. It rejects the creation of Eve from Adam's side, clears away the "fables" about the beauty and stature of the first man, and refuses to assess the extent of his "infused knowledge" or to attribute to him the invention of the Hebrew alphabet. But in its essentials the article repeats Bayle's article, although more briefly, and shows a conformity to traditional theology. In it we read the following:

The entire history of Adam is to be seen in Genesis, chapters 1–4: how he was formed of mud and placed in the earthly paradise, and appointed head and king of the earth and of the animals, which were created for his use; and what his initial innocence and original justice were; by what disobedience he fell from that state and what punishments he drew down upon himself and his posterity. We have to hark back to those two states of happiness and wretchedness, weakness and greatness, in order to understand how human beings, even in their present state, are such strange composites of vices and virtues, so enthusiastically swept on to the supreme good, so often drawn to evil and subject to so many troubles which unaided reason can see are punishments for a crime committed long ago. Even the pagans glimpsed hints of this truth, and it is at bottom the basis for their metempsychosis, as it is the only key to the entire Christian system.

As a result, the article "Earthly Paradise" in the *Encyclopédie* is likewise entirely classical. It presents it as certain that Adam and Eve were placed in Eden after their creation. "They dwelt there as long as they were in the state of innocence, and they were expelled from it as soon as they disobeyed God by eating of the forbidden fruit." Then comes a discussion of the different locations of paradise that had been proposed down the ages and especially those of Hopkinson, Huet, Bochart, and Father Calmet; the opinion of the author of the article is that it was probably located in Asia.

In light of all this, it is outside the dictionaries and encyclopedias, even though written with the intention of being critical, that we must look for the intellectual journeys that caused doubt to be cast on the garden of Eden.

The Questions Raised by Fossils

The growing attention paid to fossils provided one of the roundabout ways in which minds gradually turned away from the "historical" description of the earthly paradise that is contained in Genesis. For in some "novels of the flood," which were inspired by the study of fossils and of which I shall speak shortly, attention was drawn away from original sin and its immediate punishment to the cataclysmic flood. Furthermore, a closer study of fossils led to the conclusion that the true age of the earth was not to be harmonized with the biblical chronology.

Leonardo da Vinci had already cast doubt on the theory that stones containing figures came into existence on hilltops under the influence of the stars. Then Girolamo Fracastoro, in 1517, explained fossils as the remains of animals that had once lived.[7] Most importantly, Bernard Palissy, who had brought numerous fossils from his native Saintonge and from the Ardennes, became convinced that fossiliferous strata were the result of sedimentation at the bottom of the seas. He therefore rejected the theory of Jerome Cardan, a mathematician, according to whom these "badges of creation" were a result of the flood; but this latter idea was to have a long life.[8]

In the seventeenth and especially the eighteenth century a growing curiosity drew attention to fossils. In 1669, Niels Stensen, a Danish scholar living in Italy and better known as Steno, published a little work entitled *Prodromus de solido intra solidum naturaliter contento.* The "solid naturally contained in a solid" is a fossil. Steno was the first to have realized that the upper strata must have been deposited after the lower. He was thus the discoverer of stratigraphy. But he attempted to integrate the vertical distribution of strata with the flood.[9] In 1708, Nicholas Lange, a scholar of Lucerne, published his *Histoire des fossiles,* which was embellished by 163 plates. In 1718, Antoine de Jussieu called attention to the plant fossils of the Saint Chamond region; all were foreign to the region and were the ancestors of plants in the East and West Indies. R.-A. Réaumur drew the attention of scientists to the shell deposits of Touraine, enormous masses of shells used there as fertilizer; he concluded that "at one time, and for a long period, the lands now most densely inhabited formed the bed of the sea."[10] Observe, in passing, the words "for a long period," which were in obvious disagreement with the classical idea of a violent but brief flood. In 1729 the *Lettres philosophiques* of Louis Bourguet, a Protestant settled in Zurich, stressed the fact that fossils are found everywhere.[11]

When in 1746 Voltaire derided the views of paleontologists on fossils and interpreted these last as fish tossed from Roman tables or shells brought back from Syria by pilgrims, he had not yet caught up with the science of his day.[12] He withdrew his jest when he published the first edition of his *Philosophical Dictionary* in 1764. In the article "Inundation" we read: "The beds, or layers, of shells which have been discovered several miles from the sea are incontrovertible evidence of the gradual deposit of these maritime products on terrain that was once the shore of the ocean."[13]

The increased interest in the possible consequences of the flood led to the composition of what may be called "novels of the flood," some at least of which deserve mention. The first in order of time was Thomas Burnet's *Telluris theoria sacra* (1691), of which Buffon wrote: "It is a well-written novel and a book that may be read for entertainment but it is not to be consulted for instruction."[14] According to Burnet, the earth had been smooth and flat before the flood, having been originally made up of a chaotic mixture of fluid materials that were covered by an external crust. But the flood, a punishment that sinful humanity had earned for itself, covered the earth in its entirety, as Genesis says. The cause of the catastrophe was in part torrential rains, in part the rupturing of the surface crust and the consequent unleashing of the waters in the abysses beneath the crust. In a moment, the land collapsed and fell in pieces into this abyss; this was the origin of the mountains. The eventual drying out left the soil in the twisted and uneven condition in which we find it today. Thus, for Burnet, the flood was a major event and an unparalleled revolution in the history of the earth.[15]

In 1695, another English geologist, John Woodward, published his *Essay towards a Natural History of the Earth;* this was later translated into Latin and then into French. He had realized that in England and elsewhere the ground is made up of strata piled one on another, many of them containing fossils, which are found on mountaintops as well as in deep pits. But, in order to make these observations harmonize with Genesis, Woodward imagined that the water of the flood entirely dissolved the earth's crust. This dissolved matter made its way into shells and filled them. The shells thus gave their own form to this intrusive matter and served as moulds for it.[16] Buffon acknowledged the accuracy of Woodward's geological observations but wrote humorously of his "system," which gave the waters of the flood "both the power to act as a universal solvent and the ability to preserve the shells, which alone were not dissolved, even though marble and rocks were."[17]

The most characteristic of the "novels of the flood," however, was that of William Whiston, who was both mathematician and geologist and succeeded Newton at Cambridge. In 1696 he published *A New Theory of the Earth from Its Original to the Consummation of All Things*. The subtitle deserves mention: *Wherein the Creation of the World in Six Days, the Universal Deluge and the General Conflagration, as Laid Down in the Holy Scriptures, Are Shown to Be Perfectly Agreeable to Reason and Philosophy*.[18] According to Whiston, on November 18, 2349 B.C., a comet passed close to the earth, which remained for two days in the vaporous tail of this heavenly body. The result was extraordinary rains. In addition, due to the attraction exerted by the comet, the liquids contained in the great abyss in the interior of the earth broke through the earth's crust and spread over the surface of the globe.

The three "theories" or "histories" of the earth that I have just recalled were presented as scientific justifications of Genesis and did not call into question (quite the contrary!) the idea that the flood was a punishment of sinful humanity. But they also tended to maintain that paradisal conditions persisted down to the time of the flood, although each of the three offered various qualifications. Burnet, for example, explained the longevity of antediluvian human beings by the then prevailing climate, which was the same all year round: no cold or burning heat, but a "perpetual mildness of the heavens," as on certain islands even today.[19] According to Woodward, too, it took the flood "to destroy and change the state in which the entire earth existed at that time, when, it seems, it was arranged in a manner befitting the state of innocence."[20] We may think, therefore, that before the great catastrophe "no wheeled vehicle was used; it was invented only later on. The soil needed very little or no cultivation." After the "universal rain" "the amount of matter providing vegetation was greatly reduced. For before the Flood there had been a great deal of it on the surface of the earth, and it was of very high quality; as a result, the earth was extremely fertile."[21]

Whiston, too, believed that before the flood the land had been much more densely populated and much more fertile than it is today. Human beings and animals lived ten times longer because of the great warmth issuing from the central core. Before the flood the axis of the poles was perpendicular to the ecliptic. There were, therefore, no seasons, and antediluvian peoples, even in our latitudes, enjoyed a perpetual springtime. The earth was so fruitful that they did not have to eat meat. On the other hand, the warmth, while beneficial, also produced passions, violent actions, and crimes, which had to be punished. God then sent the avenging comet, which caused the opening of "the floodgates of heaven," of which Genesis speaks.[22]

These "novels of the flood" certainly shifted the great punishment of the human race from the time of Adam and Eve to the time of the flood. Furthermore, they placed a new emphasis on second causes. But in any case they intended to hold fast to Genesis, although now with the aid of science. Buffon, on the contrary, in his "Théorie de la terre" (1749), criticizes Whiston in the light of methodological considerations that Galileo would not have repudiated:

> Whenever we are so rash as to try to give reasons from physics for theological truths, whenever we allow ourselves to interpret the divine text of the sacred books according to purely human opinions, and whenever we try to give reasons for the decisions of the Most High and the execution of his decrees, we inevitably fall into the darkness and chaos into which the author of this system — though it has been received with great applause — has fallen. He questions neither the fact of the flood nor the authenticity of the sacred books; but, being much less concerned with these than with physics and astronomy, he has taken passages of scripture as reports of physical events and results of astronomical observations. And he has mingled the divine knowledge with our human sciences in so strange a way that the result is the most extraordinary thing I have ever seen: the system [of Whiston] which I have just presented.[23]

Not everything in the "Théorie de la terre" (the "Second Discours" of Buffon's *Histoire naturelle*, 1749) is in the same very modern vein. Buffon was convinced of "the unity of the period of creation" and refused to believe that "the shellfish and other animals living in the seas, whose remains are found buried on land, existed first, and long before man and the land animals. Even independently of the testimony of the sacred books, do we not have reason to believe that all the species of animals and plants are just about equally old?"[24]

On the other hand, Buffon disagrees with the authors of the "novels of the flood" and minimizes the importance of the flood. He regards it as a "miracle" intended to punish humanity, but one "that did not in any way alter the earth," which still remained capable of "being cultivated" and "producing vines and fruits," contrary to what happens when flood waters carrying mud and refuse make the soil unfit for cultivation for several centuries in some places.[25] "It does not seem possible that the waters of the flood could have caused the upheaval of the lands on the earth's surface to such a great depth [as Whiston claims] in the short time that this universal inundation lasted."[26] Above all, when locating the flood in the context of universal history, Buffon does not hesitate to write: "The changes which have taken place in the terrestrial globe in the course of two or three thousand years are inconsiderable by comparison with the revolutions that must have occurred in the period immediately following on creation."[27] Thus the flood was only an episode and did not radically affect the history of the earth. The story of the flood in Genesis is thus relativized: it is the story of a "miracle." Buffon deliberately uses this term: that which is not explainable by the laws of physics.

But Voltaire does not miss the chance to wax humorous over the word "miracle." In his *Philosophical Dictionary* he writes:

> In the history of the deluge everything is miraculous: it is miraculous that forty days of rain should inundate the four quarters of the earth and that the water should rise fifteen cubits above all the highest mountains; miraculous that there should be cataracts, gates, openings in the heavens; miraculous that all the animals from every part of the world should betake themselves to the ark; miraculous that Noah should find enough to feed them for ten months; miraculous that the ark should be able to accommodate all these animals with their provisions; miraculous that most of them should not have died; miraculous that they should have found something to eat when they left the ark.[28]

Henceforth the credibility of the first chapters of Genesis as a "historical" account was openly challenged: the earthly paradise and the flood were no longer things beyond question. Benoît de Maillet, former French consul in Egypt, had clearly said as much in a work that appeared in 1749 but was probably written at the beginning of the century: *Telliamed ou Entretiens d'un philosophe indien avec un missionaire français.* In this oddly titled book, the author describes as an "untenable opinion" the doctrine that uses the flood to explain the presence of fossils. On the other hand, it must be "agreed that there was a time when the sea covered the highest mountains of our planet; that it covered them for a number or years or centuries sufficiently great that it could mould and form them within its bosom." Furthermore, "It is necessary to abandon the story of creation as we read it in Genesis."[29] The word "day" is used there in an "improper" and "metaphorical" sense.[30]

Sacred Scripture and Reason

An entire line of critics, English in particular and active especially from 1640 to 1660, had anticipated Voltaire's abrasive sarcasm in regard to the opening chapters of Genesis. Then, in 1693, a book entitled *The Oracles of Reason* was published in London by Charles Blount, a deist who wanted to show that religion and reason are not opposed to each other. His argument was that human beings are endowed with reason and therefore have the right and duty to use reason even in interpreting the sacred scriptures. Blount therefore thanked Burnet for having used science to shed light on Genesis. In the name of reason Blount also rejected the doctrine of original sin: a "pill" that "had never gotten past his Adam's apple." For no one (he claimed) can reasonably believe that wars, scourges, and sicknesses should be imputed to Adam without distinguishing between "natural sin" and "sin against the law." "Natural sin" is simply the weakness and imperfection of our nature; and the native weakness of human beings is their main natural calamity.[31]

In the eighteenth century other nonconformists speak in the same vein: David Whitby, who regards the doctrine of original sin as "excessively cruel"; Mathew Tindal, who ridicules the conversation between Eve and the serpent and thinks the enormous punishment supposedly inflicted on our first parents to be incompatible with the divine nature; John Taylor, who finds no basis for the doctrine of original sin either in scripture or in reason.[32]

Among the writings of Conyers Middleton, a deist and violent antipapist who died in 1750, there is an *Essay on the Allegorical and Literal Interpretations of the Creation and Fall of Man*. In it we read the following, among other things: "It would be wearisome to cite the strange variety of inventions people have thought up just on [the earthly] paradise. The main argument against the reality of paradise is the ignorance of all generations about its location."[33] If it was guarded by one of the cherubim brandishing a fiery sword, that is proof that it still exists somewhere. Adam himself must have made his dwelling not far from it. How is it, then, that no one has ever been able to say where it is located? Middleton, who maintains that Moses derived all his knowledge from the Egyptians, goes on to say that "the Mosaic account of the fall" displays "principles and ideas which Moses had absorbed as a young man in the Egyptian schools."[34]

The challenge to the historical value of Genesis is also found in the writings of Lord Bolingbroke (d. 1751), a restless individual who had a tortuous political career and was a friend of Swift, Pope, and Voltaire. In his essay *On the Study and Use of History* he endeavors to show that the author or authors of the Pentateuch were not trying to write a universal history, but simply to tell the Jewish people about their origins and to justify their claim to the land of Canaan.[35]

This was a laicized answer to de La Peyrère's thesis regarding the "preadamites," a thesis I must briefly recall for the reader. In his book *Praeadamitae*, Isaac de La Peyrère (1594–1676), a Huguenot, had offered a hypothesis that was daring for its time: Adam was not the first human being, but only the ancestor of the chosen people; before Adam there had been preadamites. As soon as the work appeared, it elicited the hostility of both Catholics and Protestants. Its author was arrested in Belgium by order of the archbishop of Malines, and his book was condemned by the Parliament in Paris. La Peyrère retracted and abjured Protestantism.

Bolingbroke went beyond La Peyrère and dealt satirically with the history and geography of the first ages of the world as based on Genesis:

> The creation of the first man is described by some [commentators] as though they themselves were preadamites and had witnessed this creation. They speak of his beauty as if they had seen it, of his giant stature as if they had measured it, and of his prodigious knowledge as if they had conversed with him. They have a record of the entire conversation between the serpent and the mother of the human race, who condemned her children even before giving birth to them.[36]

Bolingbroke's conclusion is that the sacred and profane authors provide us with no material that would enable us to establish the chronology and history of the first ages of the world.[37]

Six years after Bolingbroke's death, David Hume published *The Natural History of Religion*, which expresses views directly contrary to the developmental history usually deduced from Genesis. Contrasting "historical facts" with "speculative opinions,"[38] he completely jettisons the accepted idea of a first couple living in intimate closeness with the one true God on a paradisal earth. In his view, "a barbarous, necessitous animal (such as a man is on the first origin of society)"[39] was quite obviously a polytheist. "The farther we mount up into antiquity, the more do we find mankind plunged into polytheism. No marks, no symptoms of any more perfect religion. The most ancient records of the human race still present us with that system as the popular and established creed."[40]

The abandonment of the belief in an original paradisal situation underlies this statement:

> We may as reasonably imagine, that men inhabited palaces before huts and cottages, or studied geometry before agriculture; as assert that the Deity appeared to them a pure spirit, omniscient, omnipotent, and omnipresent, before he was apprehended to be a powerful, though limited being, with human pas-

sions and appetites, limbs and organs. The mind rises gradually, from inferior to superior.[41]

This argument from absurdity eliminates both the garden of Eden and original sin. Hume is a typical man of the Enlightenment when he also writes: "It appears to me, that, if we consider the improvement of human society from rude beginnings to a state of greater perfection, polytheism or idolatry was, and necessarily must have been, the first and most ancient religion of mankind."[42]

Birth of Evolutionism

When the new conception of time was expanded, it had two simultaneous results: the overthrow of the "fixist" thesis — still cherished by Linnaeus at the heart of the eighteenth century — of a creation in six days of plants and animals, all completely distinct from one another right from the outset; and an emphasis on the long labor of nature down the ages. The first evolutionist descriptions date from the eighteenth century. Concordant observations (some by Linnaeus himself) made by different scientists brought new species to light, identified "zoophytes" intermediate between insects and plants, and in 1776 led Duchesne, the horticulturist who was director of the experimental garden at Versailles, to write concerning a new strain of strawberry plants: "The genealogical order is the only one that nature makes known, the only one that fully satisfies the mind; any other is arbitrary and empty of ideas."[43]

Researchers were on their way to the new idea of the variability of species, an idea obviously incompatible with the rigid creationist schema that had long been derived from a literally interpreted Book of Genesis. The idea of continuity in the work of nature could quite readily be integrated into a spiritualist and hierarchized vision of the universe; Leibniz had in fact incorporated it into his system of universal harmony. But the idea nonetheless became increasingly an element in a materialist conception of reality, as we see especially in Julien La Mettrie, author of *L'Homme machine* (1748).

In his *Dissertation* of 1746, in which he wrote sarcastically of fossils, Voltaire was still a convinced "fixist." He wrote: "Nothing in the plant and animal worlds has changed; all the species have remained the same, without any variation. It would be odd indeed if the grain of millet were to keep its nature forever unchanged, while the globe in its entirety changed its nature."[44] But as early as 1722 Bernard Fontenelle had maintained the contrary and had challenged the idea of a rigid compartmentalization: "If we look at things from a methodological viewpoint, everything in nature advances by degrees and nuances."[45] It was in Fontenelle's wake that Buffon wrote, a quarter-century later: "The more we increase the number of divisions in nature's productions, the closer we come to the truth, for in nature only individuals really exist, while genera, orders, and classes exist only in our imagination."[46]

In similar fashion, Charles Bonnet did not hesitate to move beyond the classical distinction of the three kingdoms and, in his reflections on the "zoophytes," to see in these "the link joining the plant kingdom to the animal kingdom." In his view, this is a proof of the continuity in nature and in the "ladder of beings," which in turn leads our minds to "the infinite Wisdom that has formed and combined the different elements of the world." Thus he regards it as certain that "the more [our knowledge] increases, the more gradations and degree we will discover."[47] Hence this other statement of Bourguet in his *Contemplation de la nature:* "There are no leaps in nature; everywhere there are gradations and shadings. If there were a gap between any two beings, why should there be a passage from the one to the other?"[48] Bourguet had no inkling of mutations.

Shortly after the discovery of the "zoophytes," another naturalist, F. Boissier de Sauvages, inquired into the possible existence of "lithophytes," which would establish a link between the plant and mineral kingdoms. He reaches the conclusion that "if we study nature even a little, we will come across one or other of its products of which we cannot say to which of the three kingdoms it belongs; there are situations in which the boundaries of the mineral and plant kingdoms are blurred in some respects, as shades of difference disappear into one another."[49]

This new light shed on the continuity to be found in the great work of nature led to a reassessment — downward — of the primacy of the human being among all created things. Buffon writes on this subject: "The first truth that emerges from this examination of nature is a humbling one for human beings: namely, that they must place themselves in the class of animals."[50] Buffon did not himself draw a materialist conclusion from this statement of fact. But La Mettrie, and others with him, did not fail to do so. In any case the Adam and Eve of the earthly paradise were disappearing from view.

In 1761, philosopher Jean-Baptiste Robinet (1735–1820), who had his run-ins with Voltaire, had remarked that a perpetual springtime would be monotonous and insipid.[51] Some years later — in 1768 — he published a work with a remarkably modern title: *Considérations philosophiques de la gradation des formes de l'être, ou les Essais de la Nature qui apprend à faire l'homme* (Philosophical remarks on gradation in the forms of being, or nature's experiments as it learned to produce the human being). In it we read: "In the immensely varied succession of animals lower than man I see Nature in labor, advancing gropingly toward this being that crowns her work. . . . Nature unceasingly perfects her work, adding faculties to faculties and organs to organs," as she forms species, these "lasting monuments to her step-by-step advance."[52] Some of Robinet's ideas strike us today as naive; for example, according to him nature had conceived a prototype in the light of which it then sought to produce man in a series of attempts. Thus it fashioned stones in the form of hearts, kidneys, and skulls, then sea lions with two breasts, and so on. Having gotten under way in this direction, Robinet saw in the orangutan "an intermediate species filling the gap between ape and man," since it "resembles man more than it does any other animal."[53] The fact remains, however, that Robinet was one of those who launched minds on the journey of evolutionism.

During the Enlightenment period and especially during the second half of the century there occurred a convergence of opinions and observations that was to lead to a genuine cultural revolution. Today we see M. de Maupertuis, a mathematician who also enjoyed experimenting with hybridization, as one of the founders of evolutionism and one of the forerunners of contemporary mutationism. He anticipated Charles Darwin when he wrote:

> May we not say that since, in the fortuitous combination of nature's productions, only those possessing certain types of fitness could survive, it is not surprising this fitness should be found in all naturally existing species? We might say that chance produced a countless multitude of individuals, but that only a small number were so constituted that the parts of the animal were able to satisfy its needs, while in another, infinitely greater number there was neither aptitude nor orders; all of the latter perished.

This text was published in 1756.[54]

Another precursor of evolutionism was Michel Adamson (1727–1806), whose major work, Les Familles des plantes, was published in 1763. In it, using language that Lamarck would take over almost word for word forty-four years later, he had this to say about classes, genera, and species: no one has been able to "prove that these exist in nature," for in nature there are only "individuals following one upon another and, as it were, basing themselves one upon another by means of variations."[55] Adamson realized that many fossil shells belonged to ancient species that have today disappeared, and with remarkable sensitivity he distinguished, better than anyone else in his time, between the individual variations that we today call somatic, and hereditary variations or mutations.[56]

Around 1800, a number of voices were again heard emphasizing the continuity and evolution of the world of organisms. P. Cabanis, a physician, stated: "At this time physicians seem to be on the eve of determining at least a part of the changes that occur in matter as it passes from the inorganic state to that of plant organisms, and from the incomplete life of a tree or plant to the life of the more perfect animals."[57] Here he is already formulating what would later be called the theory of "acquired characteristics," and is saying that new ways of existing perpetuate themselves or reproduce themselves, even in the absence of the causes on which they depend. When E. de Lacépède, a student of Buffon and later a professor at the Museum, speaks of the duration of species, he concludes: "What is said of genus, order, and class must be said of species as well: it is at bottom only an abstraction formed by the mind." Let our study of the past reveal to us "the successive modifications of organic, living, ensouled, and sensible matter."[58]

Erasmus Darwin, grandfather of Charles, was both botanist and poet; he was also a deist and the author of religious hymns. Without reaching the concept of natural selection, he did observe "the analogies between the anatomies of all warm-blooded animals" and was led thereby to think that all these animals must have had a common point of departure that determined their structure.[59] Finally, Jean-Baptiste Lamarck, another student of Buffon and a botanist turned zoologist, likewise insisted, first in his *Discours d'ouverture* to the Museum (1800) and then in his *Système des animaux sans vertèbres* (1810), on "the finely shaded gradations" that are shown by the organization of living beings and that "give a glimpse of the progress of nature."[60] He observed a basic tendency of living matter to complexification and improvement, shed light on the process of adaptive transformations, and formulated the law of the inheritance of acquired characteristics.

Like Erasmus Darwin and unlike Cabanis, Lamarck was a deist. He saw no way in which chance could explain the order and progression that are inherent in life. Life displays an immanent finality. "Nothing exists except by the will of the sublime Author of all things; had not his infinite power been able to create an order of things in which existence was successively given to all that we see?"[61] The fact was, however, that the evolutionary conception that was gradually being formulated broke with the account in Genesis when this was taken literally. It abandoned the hitherto accepted idea of creation as producing clear-cut categories: "birds, great sea serpents, . . . cattle, tiny creatures, wild animals with their varied species," and so on, and it reduced to a pious fancy the touching scene in which Adam "gave names to all cattle, and to the birds of the air, and to every animal of the field." A page had been turned in the history of Christian civilization.

When we recall all the efforts by first-rate minds in the sixteenth and seventeenth centuries to calculate the age of the earth as accurately as possible and to establish its birth between 4051 and 3928 B.C., we can gauge the revolutionary character of the evolutionism now arising and the new role given to sheer length of time in the history of the world. In 1800 Lacépède gave a good description of the new scientific spirit when he urged his readers to question "nature in the name of time." This study of the past, he claimed, would reveal to us "the successive modifications of organic, living, ensouled, and sensible matter."[62] Not for nothing had Lacépède been a student of Buffon, and we must here recall the decisive contribution of the latter to the undermining of the chronology drawn from Genesis.

Buffon refused to "mix bad physics with the purity of the holy book,"[63] and he excluded the biblical flood from the general geological history of the planet. In his "Second Discours," published in 1749, he urged that explanations appealing to catastrophes be replaced by the study of nature's slow transformations. He wrote: "Causes whose effects are rare, violent, and sudden should not affect us; they are not part of the ordinary course of nature. But effects that occur every day, movements that are successive and renewed without interruption, operations that are constant and always repeated — these are the causes and reasons that concern us."[64] For the Sieur de Montbard, the history of the earth was infinitely longer than the history of humanity — the thing that played havoc was the application of biblical chronology to the history of nature:

> We can judge only imperfectly when it comes to the succession of revolutions in nature. . . . We lack both experience and time; we fail to reflect that the time which is lacking to us is not lacking to nature; we want to relate past centuries and the ages to come to the brief moment of our existence, without taking into account that this brief moment of human life, however much we extend it in the form of history, is only a point in the total duration, a single event in the history of God's doings.[65]

The first three volumes of the *Histoire naturelle* enjoyed success and in 1749–50 were given laudatory reviews by the Jesuits in their monthly review, *Mémoires de Trévoux*. But *Nouvelles ecclésiastiques*, the semiunderground but regularly published organ of the Jansenist party, would have its readers "realize the poison" being distilled by Buffon, a "Pyrrhonian."[66] The author was accused of considering man to be simply an animal and of contradicting Genesis. The Faculty of Theology had the documents seized. D'Argenson could then write: "Mr. Buffon's . . . head is spinning from the distress which the success of his book has caused him. The devout are furious and want to have it burned by the executioner. In fact, he contradicts Genesis at every point."[67]

In order to avoid a condemnation, Buffon agreed to write a clarification in which he said that he believed "very firmly all that [scripture] says about the creation, both as to the order [of events] in time and to the circumstances in which the events took place" and that he had presented his theories "as a purely philosophical hypothesis."[68] For almost thirty years beginning in 1753, this retraction appeared in further printings of the *Histoire naturelle*. With the aid of this safe-conduct Buffon was able to republish the offending texts without changing a word in them.

In 1749 Buffon had assumed that the sun had been struck a glancing blow by a comet and had released a "torrent" of liquified matter that had then divided into rapidly rotating spheres.[69] In 1778, in his *Les Époques de la nature*, he refined his theory of the earth and showed that the entire geological history of our planet can be explained in terms of its gradual cooling.[70] At this point he could not avoid the question of the earth's age, which he had dodged in 1749. As the result of careful calculations he estimated that 74,832 years had passed between the formation of the earth and the point at which it reached its present temperature.[71] Life would then have appeared 35,983 years after the formation of the earth.

Jacques Roger, in his outstanding biography of Buffon, has shown that the Sieur de Montbard was not satisfied with these figures, but repeated his calculations, using different hypotheses and reaching higher and higher assessments: seven or eight hundred thousand years, or even more.[72] The manuscripts of *Les Époques de la nature* show the traces of these uncertainties. But, Jacques Roger asks, why this timidity, since "seventy-five thousand years were as scandalous as ten million"?[73] The reason seems to have been that Buffon did not want to offend against the intellectual habits of his contemporaries and plunge them "into the dark abyss of time." At any rate, the manuscript edited by Jacques Roger has this piece of advice from Buffon to himself: "Although it is very true that the more we stretch time out, the closer we will come to the truth and reality of the use which nature makes of time, yet the expanse of time must be shortened as far as possible in order to adapt ourselves to the limited power of our understanding."[74]

Present-day science makes the earth to be about four billion years old. We are obviously very far removed from even the highest of Buffon's estimates. The fact remains, however, that he scaled a barrier that until then had blocked the scientific study of the past of our planet; that barrier was a literal reading of the first chapters of Genesis when the latter was taken to be a "historical" work. As he had been thirty years earlier, so again in 1779, after the publication of *Les Époques de la nature*, Buffon was exposed to the attacks of some defenders of religion. It was indeed more difficult to challenge him now than it had been in 1749. He had become a famous person, had always spoken respectfully of the Creator, and had not had a hand in the *Encyclopédie*. Nevertheless, the theologians of the Sorbonne certified that "his general principles for the way scripture is to be understood" were unacceptable and that his "different epochs...had no relation to the different days of creation, either in the temporal sequence or in the circumstances surrounding the events."[75] Once again, Buffon signed a retraction that he promised to publish at the beginning of his next volume. This time, he did not keep his promise. But the Faculty of Theology published it in 1780 in a Latin pamphlet about the whole affair, which ended there. The age of Galileo was past.

When he felt death approaching in 1788, Buffon was anxious to receive the sacraments of the church. Was he motivated simply by respect for the established order? There is no way of answering the question. But he probably expressed his deepest conviction when he wrote in *Les Époques de la nature:* "The more deeply I have penetrated to the heart of nature, the more I have admired and profoundly respected its Author; a blind respect would, however, be superstition, whereas true religion supposes an enlightened respect."[76] We must "depart from this holy tradition...when the letter kills, that is, when it seems directly opposed to sound reason and to the truth about the facts of nature."[77] The age of the earth, whose longevity scientists were now beginning to measure, was a factor in henceforth relegating to the realm of legend a primitive, almost divine humanity set in a magical garden.

The "State of Nature" according to Rousseau and Kant

Consequently, the idyllic picture of the "state of nature" that Rousseau paints seems to us today a step backward by comparison with the scientific research of his day, insofar as he retains a belief in a golden age. His *Discourse on the Origin of Inequality* (1755) certainly does not claim to find "King Adam"[78] back there. He does strip man in his "natural state" of all "supernatural gifts" and all "artificial faculties." He describes him as an animal "weaker" than some and "less agile" than others, "but, taking him all round, the most advantageously organized of any. I see him satisfying his hunger at the first oak, and slaking his thirst at the first brook; finding his bed at the foot of the tree which afforded him a repast." This primitive human race lived happily amid a bountiful nature:

> While the earth was left to its natural fertility and covered with immense forests, whose trees were never mutilated by the axe, it would present on every side both sustenance and shelter for every species of animal. Men, dispersed up and down among the rest, would observe and imitate their industry, and thus attain even to the instinct of the beasts, with the advantage that, whereas every species of brutes was confined to one particular instinct, man,

who perhaps has not any one peculiar to himself, would appropriate them all. . . .

Accustomed from their infancy to the inclemencies of the weather and the rigour of the seasons . . . men would acquire a robust and almost unalterable constitution. . . .

In old age, when men are less active and perspire little, the need for food diminishes with the ability to provide it. As the savage state also protects them from gout and rheumatism, and old age is, of all ills, that which human aid can least alleviate, they cease to be, without others perceiving that they are no more, and almost without perceiving it themselves.[79]

Such, according to Rousseau, was the natural state before "one man began to stand in need of the help of another." The help requested from others led to dependence, labor, inequality, and enslavement. All the knowledge and all the progress amassed by the human species have not been able to replace the happy condition it enjoyed when in its "primitive state." Happiness is for us something in the past. The golden age existed, but it disappeared when "vast forests became smiling fields, which man had to water with the sweat of his brow, and where slavery and misery were soon seen to germinate and grow up with the crops."[80]

No less profound, but in a different way, is the viewpoint expressed by Immanuel Kant in 1785 in his essay *Conjectural Beginning of Human History*,[81] in which the philosopher of Königsberg undertakes a new reading of Genesis that will reconcile the traditional conception of original sin with confidence in progress; in so doing, he separates himself from Rousseau. Kant takes as his point of departure human beings of adult age, living as a couple in "a place secure, . . . blessed with a perpetually mild climate, hence a garden, as it were." What happened before the coming of human beings seems beyond our ken, and Kant prefers to say nothing about it. These human beings are already able to stand, speak, and think. But they are still "novices," obeying, like the animals, "the voice of God," that is, instinct. But their rational powers are beginning to awaken, and they want to extend their knowledge beyond the limits set by instinct. The result is the birth of concupiscence. The plucking of fruit that seemed pleasant when it was in fact harmful may well have been the first attempt at exercising "a free choice." Human beings were in effect discovering that they could choose their manner of life for themselves. But this entailed risks and dangers, since this soon repeated choice gave birth to anxiety and restlessness.

By thus opening himself to an infinity of objects, in choosing among which he had no way of taking his bearings, man cast himself forth "from the womb of nature" and "from the safe and harmless state" of childhood: a state that was "a garden, as it were, which looked after his needs without any trouble on his part." He was henceforth torn between, on the one hand, "the wish for a paradise, the creation of his imagination, where he would dream or while away his existence in quiet inactivity and permanent peace" and, on the other, the stimuli of "restless reason...irresistibly impelling him to develop the faculties implanted within him" and that "would not permit him to return to that crude and simple state from which it had driven him to begin with." Man's departure from the earthly paradise was "nothing but the transition from an uncultured, merely animal condition to the state of humanity."

This being the case, the question of whether humanity gained or lost by this change does not arise. For the "destiny" of our species "consists in nothing less than progress toward perfection," which is made possible by the use of reason and by the "conflict with animality." It is, of course, true that this struggle has been and is accompanied by evils and even vices "such as had been wholly alien to the state of ignorance and innocence." To use the language of the Bible: the history of nature was begun by the Good, since it is the work of God. On the other hand, the history of freedom began with evil, since it is the work of human beings. Fall and punishment did indeed occur, but no one should shift to Adam either the "original sin" or the responsibility for his own sins. For "under like circumstances he [each of us] would act exactly like his first parents, that is, abuse reason in the very first use of reason, the advice of nature to the contrary notwithstanding." However — and here Kant distances himself from the Augustinian pessimism that had long enveloped Western Christianity — despite individual mishaps, the use of reason was a "gain" for the human species, which has "perfection" as its natural end. Consequently, the course of human affairs "considered as a whole...is not a decline from good to evil, but rather, a gradual development from the worse to the better; and nature itself has given the vocation to everyone to contribute as much to this progress as may be within his power." Let us not regret original sin; it was a *felix culpa* that was also necessary.

Let us, however, reject the "empty yearning" for the "golden age, an image so highly praised by poets. In that age we are to be rid of all those imagined needs which voluptuousness now imposes on us. There is to be contentment with the mere satisfaction of natural needs, universal human equality and perpetual peace: in a word, unalloyed enjoyment of a carefree life, dreamt away idly, or trifled away in childish play." Even supposing that humanity could return to that primitive state, it could not persist in it. Furthermore, it is not disposed to return to it despite our daydreams that "are stimulated by stories such as Robinson Crusoe and reports of visitors to the South Sea Islands." Reason and nature urge the human race to build a future worthy of it. It is ahead of us that the sun is shining.

Another Reading of a Myth

In the Christian Europe of the Middle Ages the most widespread belief about the earthly paradise was that it still existed on our earth. It was, of course, inaccessible, girt with fire, and guarded by swordbearing cherubim, but it had not disappeared. Mapmakers had no hesitation about locating it in a far distant corner of the East. Travelers tried to get close to it, and the explorers of the Renaissance thought they had reached areas that retained some aspects, traces, and privileges of the wonderful garden of Eden.

Following the impulse given by the two religious reformations, commentators tackled the first chapters of Genesis with new energy, only to reach a distressing conclusion: the earthly paradise had disappeared. The flood had swallowed it up. On the other hand, the scientists of the time, in their thirst for knowledge, made use of all the information at their disposal in an attempt to pinpoint as accurately as possible the place in which God had put the first human couple before the fall. These scholars abandoned any location in the distant East for a closer site, their preference being for Mesopotamia or sometimes Armenia or the Holy Land.

But in the eighteenth century a new factor had to be taken into account. The study of fossils proved that the earth was not a mere six thousand years old. The conclusion was soon reached that human history too was far longer than people had thought; that humanity had gradually emerged from the animal world; that in its beginnings it could not have possessed all the "preternatural" gifts with which theologians had obligingly endowed it in their learned works. From this moment on the "garden of delights" vanished. At best, it continued to exist only in the works of Rousseau and Kant in the form of the sheltering nature that had mothered the first human beings, who still followed their instincts. It was becoming ever clearer that the earthly paradise was only a symbol, even though official pastoral practice endeavored for a long time yet to hide this obvious fact behind a literal reading of the Genesis story.

There was a close theological link between the earthly paradise and original sin. The two were interdependent. The more attractive one made that winterless orchard and the more one assigned our first parents gifts, privileges, and knowledge far superior to ours, the more one was led to maximize the scope of the first sin. They lived amid a generous and smiling nature; God had heaped blessings upon them, and they had everything they needed for their happiness. And yet they freely committed an act of disobedience that had incalculable consequences, and they repaid their creator with an ingratitude that deserved the greatest punishments. Their punishment was suffering and death, to which St. Augustine added hell, of whose existence the writers of Genesis were ignorant. Due to the sin of Adam and Eve, the human race became "a condemned mass" in which all shared the guilt of the first sin. Only the Savior's sacrifice would deliver a minority of the elect from the condemnation that all had earned. The tragic theology of Western Christendom can be explained only by an exaggerated view of the beauties of the garden of Eden and the unparalleled advantages that God had granted to our first parents.

But our age is now compelled to agree with Teilhard de Chardin that there is "not the least trace on the horizon, not the smallest scar, to mark the ruins of a golden age or our cutting off from a better world."[1] Furthermore, according to the Gospels, Jesus often spoke of "the sin of the world," but never of "original sin." Judaism likewise assigned little importance to "original sin," its whole attention and hope being focused on the "covenant," which Christ later confirmed and extended to the whole of the human race on Holy Thursday evening.

The question arises, then: Was it not possible to give a different Christian reading of the first chapters of Genesis? We know today that it is possible. The exegetes, who have tools that our forebears did not have, distinguish in chapters 1–3 of Genesis two different accounts of the origin of things. The first account (1:1–2:4a) speaks of a creation in six days, while the second (2:4b–3:24) tells the story of Adam and Eve. The account of creation in six days may be dated to the fifth and fourth centuries B.C., while the story of Adam and Eve was composed during the ninth to the sixth centuries. The latter text retains traces of very ancient Sumerian and Assyrian ideas. The former, on the other hand, is given to us as an essay in understanding the universe, which is composed of elements that appeared in a certain order. Original sin is not mentioned in this account! Furthermore, the Psalms often emphasize personal sins, while in the Second Book of Maccabees this formula occurs twice: "We are suffering because of our own sins" (7:32, 18),[2] but there is nothing in these sources about the sin of our first parents.

Long before the modern age, a less dramatic reading of the story of Adam and Eve was given, especially by St. Theophilus of Antioch and St. Irenaeus, two bishops who wrote at the end of the second century. Admittedly, both took the Genesis account of the earthly paradise and the first sin to be "historical," but they did not assign "preternatural" gifts and privileges to Adam and Eve. According to these two writers, God had given them only a "means of advancement" (the words are those of Theophilus), that is, of "maturing and becoming perfect."[3] Most importantly, these two bishops were convinced that our first parents were like children. Theophilus wrote:

> The tree of knowledge itself was good, and its fruit was good. For it was not the tree, as some think, but the disobedience which had death in it. For there was nothing else in the fruit than only knowledge; but knowledge is good when one uses it discreetly. But Adam, being yet an infant in age, was on this account unable as yet to receive knowledge worthily. For now, also, when a child is born it is not at once able to eat bread, but is nourished first with milk, and then, with increment of years, it advances to solid food.[4]

Had Irenaeus read Theophilus? In any case, he shares the latter's belief that Adam and Eve were like children. He writes: "[In the beginning] man was quite little, for he was a child and had to grow in order to reach the adult state.... He did not yet have a fully developed power of judgment."[5] Another, even more explicit passage that is very close to Theophilus in its formulations, is the following:

> Inasmuch as they [created things] are not uncreated, for this very reason do they come short of the perfect. Because, as these things are of later date, so are they infantile; so are they unaccustomed to, and inexperienced in, perfect discipline. For as it is certainly in the power of a mother to give strong food to her infant [but she does not do so], as the child is as yet unable to receive more substantial nourishment; so also it was possible for God Himself to have made man perfect from the first, but man could not yet receive this [perfection], being as yet an infant.[6]

This statement from book 4 of the *Adversus haereses* is completed a little further on by another that is in harmony with it: it was "through want of care, no doubt, but still wickedly [on the part of another], [that man] became involved in disobedience."[7] In contemporary language we might say that according to Theophilus and Irenaeus, Adam and Eve were in too much of a hurry. They were children, but they wanted to possess knowledge that they could not grasp until they had grown up.

Following the logic of this conception of things, Irenaeus assigns the main responsibility for the first sin to the tempter. Consequently, God "turned the enmity by which [the devil] had designed to make [man] the enemy of God, against the author of it."[8] In contrast, he took "pity on man." As we can see, in Irenaeus's explanation there is no trace of "the condemned mass" or of a universal condemnation to hell that sinful humanity had supposedly deserved. Theophilus and Irenaeus both think that God banished human beings from paradise in order that they might make atonement, and that he allowed death in order that sin "might not be immortal." Theophilus writes: "God showed great kindness to man in this, that He did not suffer him to remain in sin for ever; but, as it were, by a kind of punishment, cast him out of Paradise, in order that, having by punishment expiated, within an appointed time, the sin, and having been disciplined, he should afterwards be restored."[9] Irenaeus is even more explicit:

> Wherefore also He drove him out of Paradise, and removed him far from the tree of life, not because He envied him, as some venture to assert, but because He pitied him [and did not desire] that he should continue a sinner for ever, nor that the sin which surrounded him should be immortal, and evil interminable and irremediable. But He set a bound to his [state of sin], by interposing death, and thus causing sin to cease, putting an end to it by the dissolution of the flesh, which should take place in the earth, so that man, ceasing at length to live to sin, and dying to it, might begin to live to God.[10]

Theophilus and Irenaeus do not look back with melancholy to the lost paradise. On the contrary, they are much more sensitive to the dynamics that will some day lead human beings of good will to "the vision of God" that "brings incorruptibility."[11] For after the first sin the human race received a "new call." Theophilus writes: "For as man, disobeying drew death upon himself, so, obeying the will of God, he who desires is able to procure for himself life everlasting . . . and, obtaining the resurrection, can inherit incorruption."[12]

According to Irenaeus, not only in the time of Adam and Eve but even at the time of the Savior's coming, humanity was still in a state of infancy:

> Thus it was that He who was the perfect bread of the Father offered Himself to us as milk because we were infants. He did this when He appeared as a man, that we, being nourished, as it were, from the breast of His flesh, and having, by such a course of milk-nourishment, become accustomed to eat and drink of the Word of God, may be able also to contain in ourselves the Bread of immortality, which is the Spirit of the Father.[13]

Let us therefore not try to take short cuts; let us be "human beings first of all," so that we may become "God later on."[14] "For it was necessary, at first, that nature should be exhibited; then, after that, that what was mortal should be conquered and swallowed up by immortality."[15] Irenaeus says again: "How, then, shall he be a God who has not as yet been made a man? Or how shall he be perfect who was but lately created? How, again, can he be immortal who in his mortal nature did not obey his Maker? For it must be that thou, at the outset, should hold the rank of a man, and then afterwards partake of the glory of God."[16]

The scholar who provides the introduction to the *Three Books to Autolycus* in the Sources Chrétiennes series bids the reader see in this work "a faithful echo of the doctrine taught and passed on by the Church around the year 180."[17] The same remark can be made of the writings of St. Irenaeus, another bishop and Christian apologist. But these two concordant voices take us far from the pessimistic anthropology that originated with St. Augustine and was based on the terrible sin committed by a perfect couple in a magical garden. Theophilus and Irenaeus do not, of course, deny the garden of Eden or the fact that the disobedience of Adam and Eve resulted in suffering and death. But they do not see the beginning of human history as marked by the anger of a God who punishes and, in particular, a God who, were it not for the redemption, would have condemned humanity to hell. They give the first sin its proper proportions as one committed by "children." They are convinced that the human race, after incurring guilt at the beginning, received a "new call" and that, thanks to the coming of the Lord and his salutary help, it is on the way to incorruptibility and divinization.

My reason for setting forth the viewpoint of these two bishops at the end of this book on the earthly paradise is that in the West the myth of the garden of Eden, "understood as an historical, eyewitness report,"[18] had become a dogma giving rise to a gloomy image of humanity and of God. Furthermore, while there is no possible way of reconciling, on the one hand, what science tells us about the origin of the human race and, on the other, the earthly paradise of our holy cards and the position given to our first parents by Western theology, it is indeed possible to harmonize the viewpoint of Theophilus and Irenaeus with the results of modern science. In this harmonization the emphasis is on the trajectory followed by the human race from its infancy to our time. This trajectory has certainly not been "sinless." Quite the contrary! But science and the only Christian theology that is acceptable today agree with Theophilus and Irenaeus in not assigning an excessive guilt to the stammering human race that first came on the scene.

It is not a bad thing, is it, that the disappearance of the earthly paradise also meant the disappearance of the repulsive image of a vengeful God?

Abbreviations

ACW	Ancient Christian Writers
ANF	The Ante-Nicene Fathers
CSCO	Corpus scriptorum christianorum orientalium
CSEL	Corpus scriptorum ecclesiasticorum latinorum
DACL	*Dictionnaire d'archéologie chrétienne et de liturgie*
DBS	*Dictionnaire de la Bible: Supplément*
DTC	*Dictionnaire de théologie catholique*
PG	Patrologia graeca
PL	Patrologia latina
SC	Sources chrétiennes

Notes

Introduction

1. M. Reeves, *The Influence of Prophecy in the Later Middle Ages: A Study in Joachimism* (Oxford: Clarendon Press, 1969) 504.
2. H. Michaux, *Connaissance par les gouffres* (reprint, Paris: Gallimard, 1978) 9.
3. T. Zeldin, *Le Bonheur* (Paris: Fayard, 1988) 328.

Chapter 1: The Mingling of Traditions

1. For bibliographical leads I refer the reader to the article "Paradise" in *DBS* 6:1177–1220; *Catholicisme* 10:621–32; and M. Eliade, ed., *Encyclopedia of Religion* 11:184–89.
2. H. Limet, "Dilmun et la mythologie sumérienne des pays lointains," in Fr. Jouan and B. Deforge, eds., *Peuples et pays mythiques* (Paris: Les Belles Lettres, 1988) 9–21.
3. The close connections between Dilmun and the earthly paradise of the Bible that were claimed by S. N. Kramer in his *History Begins at Sumer* (New York: Doubleday, 1959), chap. 19, now seem exaggerated.
4. On this question there are two fundamental works: A. B. Giamatti, *The Earthly Paradise and the Renaissance Epic* (Princeton, N.J.: Princeton University Press, 1966), esp. 15–48; and J. E. Duncan, *Milton's Earthly Paradise: A Historical Study of Eden* (Minneapolis: University of Minnesota Press, 1972), esp. 19–38. These two works are indebted in their turn to E. R. Curtius, *European Literature and the Latin Middle Ages,* trans. W. R. Trask (New York: Bollingen, 1953).
5. Hesiod, *Works and Days,* vv. 111–21, trans. H. G. Evelyn-White, in *Hesiod, the Homeric Hymns and Homerica* (Loeb Library; New York: G. P. Putnam's Sons, 1929) 11.
6. Ibid., vv. 170–75 (p. 15).
7. Plato, *The Statesman* 272A, trans. H. N. Fowler and W. R. M. Lamb (Loeb Library; New York: G. P. Putnam's Son, 1925) 59.
8. Virgil, *Eclogues* 4.5–10, 18–46.
9. Ovid, *Metamorphoses* 1.90–112, trans. F. J. Miller, in *Ovid: Metamorphoses* (Loeb Library; New York: G. P. Putnam's Sons, 1928) 1:9, 11.
10. Homer, *Odyssey* 4.563–68, trans. A. T. Murray, in *Homer: Odyssey* (Loeb Library; Cambridge, Mass.: Harvard University Press, 1966) 1:149.
11. Pindar, *Olympian Odes* 2.78–84, trans. J. Sandys, in *Pindar: Odes* (Loeb Library; New York: G. P. Putnam's Sons, 1930) 25.

12. Virgil, *Aeneid* 6.637–75, trans. J. W. Mackail, *The Aeneid of Virgil* (London: Macmillan, 1953) 137–38.

13. Homer, *Odyssey* 7.110–33 (Murray, 1:241).

14. Hesiod, *Theogony*, vv. 215–17 (Evelyn-White, *Hesiod*, 95).

15. Horace, *Epodes* 16.43–62, trans. C. B. Bennett, in *Horace: The Odes and Epodes* (Loeb Library; Cambridge, Mass.: Harvard University Press, 1934) 405, 407.

16. See Diodorus Siculus, *The Library of History*, trans. C. H. Oldfather (Loeb Library, 12 vols.; New York: G. P. Putnam's Sons, 1933) 2:65–81.

17. I adopt here the very useful division given in Giamatti, *Earthly Paradise*, 34–48.

18. *Hymn to Demeter*, vv. 5–10 (Evelyn-White, *Hesiod*, 289).

19. Theocritus, *Idylls* 7.134–46, trans. C. S. Calverley, in M. Hadas, ed., *The Greek Poets* (New York: Modern Library, 1953) 334.

20. Pseudo-Justin, *Cohortatio ad Graecos* (PG 6:294).

21. Tertullian, *Apologeticum* 47 (PL 1:517).

22. Clement of Alexandria, *Stromata* (SC 30:126).

23. Ibid., 30:91

24. Lactantius, *Divinae Institutiones* 5 (SC 30:126)

25. Giamatti, *Earthly Paradise*, 30–31.

26. Basil of Caesarea, *Hexaemeron* (SC 26bis); M. Thibaut de Maisières, *Les Poèmes inspirés du début de la Genèse à l'époque de la Renaissance* (Louvain, 1931) 18–29.

27. Pseudo-Basil, in *Appendix operum s. Basilii magni* (PG 30:63–66).

28. Ephraem, *Hymnes sur le Paradis* 10 (SC 137:139); for preceding citations, SC 137:47, 48, 135, and 137.

29. Ibid. (p. 181).

30. *Minor Latin Poets* (Cambridge, Mass.: Harvard University Press, 1954) 650–65. See Giamatti, *Earthly Paradise*, 69–70; Duncan, *Milton's Earthly Paradise*, 60–61.

31. Appendixes *De variis Marcionis haeresibus* (PL 2:1094–95); Giamatti, *Earthly Paradise*, 70–71.

32. Prudentius, *Cathemerinon* 3.101–10 (PL 59:803–4) and 2.113–24 (PL 59:826–27).

33. Claudius Marius Victor, *Alethia* (CSEL 5; Vienna, 1898) 372–75.

34. Sidonius Apollinaris, *Panegyric on Anthemius* (PL 58:640).

35. Avitus, *Poematum de mosaicae historiae gestibus libri quinque* (PL 59:327–28). See H. R. Patch, *The Other World according to Descriptions in Medieval Literature* (Cambridge, Mass.: Harvard University Press, 1950) 140; Giamatti, *Earthly Paradise*, 73–74; Duncan, *Milton's Earthly Paradise*, 64–65.

36. Dracontius, *Carmen de Deo* (PL 60:704f.).

37. Ibid., 704.

38. Isidore of Seville, *Etymologiae* 14.6.8 (PL 82:514).

39. See Giamatti, *Earthly Paradise*, 79–80; A. Graf, *Miti, legende e superstizioni del Medio Evo* (reprint, Bologne, 1980) 1:209–17.

40. Walter Raleigh, *The History of the World*, in *Works* (Oxford, 1829) 2:74. [Translated from the author's French. — Tr.]

41. Philo, *De plantatione* 9 (36), in *The Works of Philo*, trans. C. D. Yonge (reprint, Peabody, Mass.: Hendrickson, 1993) 194.

42. Ibid., 8 (32) (p. 193).

43. Origen, *On First Principles* 4.3, trans. G. W. Butterworth (London: SPCK, 1936; New York: Harper Torchbooks, 1966) 288.

44. See above, p. 13.

45. Ephraem, *Hymnes sur le paradis* (SC 137:36, 125).

46. Ibid., 146.

47. Gregory of Nyssa, *De beatitudinibus* (PG 44:1212).

48. Gregory of Nyssa, *De creatione* (PG 44:196B).

49. Theophilus of Antioch, *The Three Books to Autolycus* 2.24, trans. B. P. Pratten, M. Dods, and T. Smith (ANF 3; Edinburgh: T. & T. Clark, 1875) 90.

50. Irenaeus, *Adv. haer.* 5.5, trans. A. Roberts and W. H. Rambaut (ANF 5 and 9; 2 vols.; Edinburgh: T. & T. Clark, 1871 and 1874) 2:66.

51. Hippolytus, *Fragmenta in Hexameron* (PG 10:583, 586). This citation and the preceding are taken from J. Daniélou, "Terre et paradis chez les Pères de l'Église," *Eranos Jahrbuch* 22 (1953) 443.

52. Epiphanius, *Panarion* 2.1.36 (PG 41:1148C), cited in Daniélou, "Terre et paradis," 444.

53. Theodore of Mopsuestia, *Fragmenta alia in Genesim* (PG 66:638).

54. John Damascene, *The Orthodox Faith* 2.11. "On Paradise," in John Damascene, *Writings*, trans. F. H. Chase, Jr. (Fathers of the Church 37; New York: Fathers of the Church, 1958) 230.

55. Moses Bar Cephas, *De paradiso* (PG 111:583–602). See C. R. Beasley, *The Dawn of Modern Geography* (London, 1887) 333; Patch, *Other World,* 147; Duncan, *Milton's Earthly Paradise,* 50–51.

56. Ambrose, *De paradiso* (PL 14:276).

57. Lactantius, *Divinae institutiones* 2 (SC 337:175).

58. Augustine, *The Literal Meaning of Genesis* 8.1.1, trans. J. H. Taylor (ACW 41–42; New York: Newman, 1982) 2:32.

59. Ibid., 8.2.5 (Taylor 2:35, 36).

60. On this subject see also Augustine, *De civitate Dei* 13.

61. *The Literal Meaning of Genesis* 8.1.3; 8.5.10; 8.7.13; 8.7.13–14 (Taylor 2:33, 41, 43, 43–44).

62. See J. Fontaine, *Isidore de Seville et la culture classique dans l'Espagne wisigothique* (Paris: Études Augustiniennes, 1959). See also *Histoire des saints et de la sainteté chrétienne* (10 vols.; Paris: Livre de Paris, 1986–87) 4:194, 195.

63. Isidore of Seville, *De ordine creaturarum* 1.10.7–11 (PL 83:939–40).

64. See J. Le Goff, *La Civilisation au Moyen Âge* (Paris: Arthaud, 1964) 577.

65. Rabanus Maurus, *De universo libri XXII* 12.2 (PL 111:334).

66. Honorius of Autun, *Elucidarium* 1.18 (PL 172:1117). See also his *De imagine mundi* 1 (PL 172:121–25).

67. Herrad of Landsberg (or Hottenburg), *Hortus deliciarum* (2 vols.; Leiden: Brill, 1979) 2:36.

68. Peter Lombard, *Sententiarum libri IV* (PL 192:686).

69. In this passage St. Thomas (next note) is citing St. Augustine, *De civitate Dei* 13.21.

70. Thomas Aquinas, *Summa theologica* 1, 102, 1, in St. Thomas Aquinas,

Summa theologica, trans. by Dominicans of the English Province (3 vols.; New York: Benziger, [1920] 1946) 1:499.

71. Ibid., art. 1, ad 4 (1:500).

72. Ibid., art. 2, ad 3 (1:501).

73. Vincent of Beauvais, *Speculum historiale* 56; edition used: *Speculum maius* (Douai, 1623) 4:22.

Chapter 2: Paradise as a Place of Waiting

1. A. Dupont-Sommer and M. Philolenko, eds., *La Bible: Écrits intertestamentaires* (Paris: Gallimard, 1987) lxxix.

2. See C. Kappler, ed., *Apocalypses et voyages dans l'au-delà* (Paris: Cerf, 1987) 187, 202–3.

3. Translated in J. H. Charlesworth, ed., *The Old Testament Pseudepigrapha* (2 vols.; New York: Doubleday, 1983, 1985) 1:5–89; citations are from 1:24, 28. See especially the various articles of P. Grelot that are listed in the bibliography for the article "Paradise," *DBS* 6:1220.

4. Charlesworth, *Old Testament Pseudepigrapha,* 1:653–79; citations from 657.

5. Dupont-Sommer and Philolenko, *La Bible,* 1395–96. And see J. Le Goff, *The Birth of Purgatory,* trans. A. Goldhammer (Chicago: University of Chicago Press, 1984) 31–33.

6. Charlesworth, *Old Testament Pseudepigrapha,* 1:517–59; citations from 539–40.

7. Le Goff, *Birth of Purgatory,* 32–33.

8. Ambrose, *De bono mortis* (PL 14:560). See also Ambrose, *In Lucam* (PL 15:1653).

9. Eusebius of Caesarea, *Praeparatio evangelica* (PL 21:535).

10. Cited in Il. de Vuippens, *Le Paradis terrestre au troisième ciel* (Paris, 1925) 10.

11. *Apocalypse of Peter* (Ethiopic text) 16, in W. Schneemelcher, ed., *New Testament Apocrypha* (Louisville: Westminster/John Knox Press, 1991–92) 2:634–35. In French: F. Amiot, *Le Bible apocryphe: Évangiles apocryphes* (Paris: Fayard, 1952) 291–94.

12. Kappler, *Apocalypses,* 237–40.

13. Ibid., 254–58.

14. *Apocalypse of Paul* 12, 14, 21, in Schneemelcher, *New Testament Apocrypha* 2:719–20, 721, 725. In French: Amiot, *Évangiles,* 306. See Kappler, *Apocalypses,* 258.

15. On the *Passio Perpetuae* see Le Goff, *Birth of Purgatory,* 49–51, with bibliography (in nn. 68–74, pp. 381–82).

16. *The Martyrdom of Saints Perpetua and Felicitas* 12–13, in H. Musurillo, ed. and trans., *The Acts of the Christian Martyrs* (Oxford: Clarendon Press, 1972) 119–23.

17. Tertullian, *De anima* (PL 2:744). See J. Daniélou, "Terre et paradis chez les Pères de l'Église," *Eranos Jahrbuch* 22 (1953) 448.

18. See de Vuippens, *Le Paradis terrestre,* 20–21; "Paradis," *DACL* 13:1582.

19. "Paradis," *DBS* 6:1214.

20. This citation and the following are from de Vuippens, *Le Paradis ter-*

restre, 15–16, and "Paradis," *DACL* 13:1580. See Athanasius, *Expositio fidei* 1 (PG 25:201f.).

21. Gregory of Nyssa, *Oratio in baptismum Christi* (PG 46:600); *Oratio in Christi resurrectionem* 1 (PG 46:617); *Oratio II in XL martyres* (PG 46:772).

22. John Chrysostom, *De cruce et latrone* (PG 49:401).

23. Proclus, *Oratio in Parasceve* (PG 65:784).

24. John Damascene, *Homiliae* 3 (PG 96:620).

25. Theophylact, *In s. Lucam* (PG 123:1104).

26. Leo the Great, *Sermones* 66 (PL 54:367).

27. Ibid., 73 (PL 54:396).

28. See "Paradis," *DACL* 13:1593–1601.

29. On this subject see the remarks of Daniélou, "Terre et paradis," 447.

30. Basil, *Homilia in Ps. 33* (PG 33:377).

31. Augustine, *Enarrationes in Psalmos* 36 (PL 36:361); *Enchiridion* 63; *The Literal Meaning of Genesis* 8.4 (Taylor 2:38–30) (see chap. 1, n. 58, above).

32. Augustine, *Confessiones* 9.3.6.

33. Jerome, *Ep.* 22 (PL 22:405); *Contra Joan.* (PL 23:381).

34. "Paradis," *DBS* 6:1219.

35. As previously, the citations are drawn mainly from de Vuippens, *Le paradis terrestre*, 21–25.

36. J. D. Mansi, *Sacrorum conciliorum nova et amplissima collectio* (31 vols.; Paris, 1759–89) 1:669f.

37. Irenaeus, *Adv. haer.* 5.5, trans. A. Roberts and W. H. Rambaut (ANF 5 and 9; 2 vols.; Edinburgh: T. & T. Clark, 1871 and 1874) 2:140.

38. Clement of Alexandria, *Quis dives salvetur?* (PG 9:652).

39. Origen, *On First Principles* 152–53.

40. See above, p. 16.

41. *On First Principles*. [Translated from the author's French. —Tr.]

42. Inscription published with commentary in "Paradis," *DACL* 13:1599–1600.

43. Athanasius, *Expositio fidei, De incarnatione*, and *Ep. heortast.* 5.3 (PG 26:201, 989, 1380); Johannes Aloysius Mingarelli, *De Didymo commentarius* (PG 39:180); *De Trinitate* 1.16 (PG 39:337); Epiphanius, *Adv. haer.* 64.47, 69 (PG 41:1148, 1192); Gregory of Nyssa, *Oratio II in XL Mart., Oratio in funere Pulcheriae*, and *Oratio in baptismum Christi* (PG 46:772, 869, 600); John Chrysostom, *De cruce et latrone*, hom. 1.2 (PG 49:401); *Sermo VII in Genesim* 5 (PG 54:614).

44. See Graffin in Patrologia Syriaca 1 (Paris, 1884) 402.

45. Ephraem, *Hymnes sur le paradis* (SC 137:36, 37, 47, 66, 77, 87, 92).

46. Theodoret of Cyr, *Dialogus I* (PG 83:72).

47. Cassiodorus, *De anima* and *In Ps. CI* (PL 70:1301, 713, 180).

48. Isidore of Seville, *De ordine creaturarum* (PL 83:927, 928, 940).

49. The Venerable Bede, *Homiliae* 4 and 22 (PL 94:30, 96).

50. "Paradis," *DACL* 13:1581.

51. Daniélou, "Terre et paradis," 448.

52. Thomas Aquinas, *In IV Sent.*, dist. 45, qu. 1, a. 2 (Paris: Vivès, 1888) 790.

53. "Limbes," *DTC* 9:760–72.

54. Cassiodorus, *Expositio in Ps. XXIV* (PL 70:180).

55. Cited in "Défunts," *DACL* 4/1:444; translation in L. Deiss, *The Springtime of the Liturgy: Liturgical Texts of the First Four Centuries*, trans. M. J. O'Connell (Collegeville, Minn.: Liturgical Press, 1979) 208. On the funeral liturgies see J. Ntedika, *L'Évocation de l'au-delà dans la prière pour les morts: Étude de patristique et de liturgies latines: IVe–VIIIe siècle* (Louvain: Nauwelaerts, 1971), esp. chap. 5, pp. 227f.

56. *Liturgia Ignatii Antiocheni* (PG 5:976). This and the following citations from liturgies are from de Vuippens, *Le paradis terrestre* 26–28; "Paradis," *DACL* 13:1582–83; and "Ciel," *DTC* 2:2500–2503.

57. *Liturgia Clementis Romani* (PG 2:613).

58. *Liturgia Basilii Caesariensis*, in E. Renaudot, *Liturgiarum orientalium collectio* (Paris, 1715) 1:18.

59. Ibid., 2:249.

60. *Sacramentarium Gelasianum*, no. 91 (PL 74:1232–33).

61. *Sacramentarium Gregorii Magni* (PL 78:28).

62. *Liturgia Gallicana* (PL 72:539, 568); see J. Mabillon, *Musaeum Italicum* (Paris, 1687) 1:280, 281.

63. *Liturgia Mozarabica* (PL 86:982); see M. Férotin, ed., *Le Liber ordinum en usage dans l'Église wisigothique et mozarabe d'Espagne du Ve au XIe siècle* (Monumenta Ecclesiae liturgica 5; Paris, 1904) 111.

64. P. Ariès, *The Hour of Our Death*, trans. H. Weaver (New York: Knopf, 1981) 25–26, and Le Goff, *Birth of Purgatory*, 46–48.

65. Ariès, *Hour of Our Death*, 24. See J. Bonnet, *Artémis d'Éphèse et la légende des Sept Dormants* (Paris: Geuthner, 1977).

66. Jacob of Voragine, *The Golden Legend*, cited in Ariès, *Hour of Our Death*, 24. See also Gregory of Tours, *Les Livres des Miracles et autres opuscules* (Paris: Librairie de la Société d'histoire de France, 1964) 121–23.

67. Ariès, *Hour of Our Death*, 23–24.

68. M. Vovelle, *La Mort et l'Occident de 1300 à nos jours* (Paris: Gallimard, 1983) 63.

69. Ibid.

70. Le Goff, *Birth of Purgatory*, 186–89. The text was published by M. Inguanez in *Miscellanea Cassinese* 11 (1932) 83–103.

71. Cl. Carozzi, "Structure et fonction de la vision de Tnugdal," in A. Vauchez, ed., *Faire croire* (Rome: École Française de Rome, 1981) 223–34; Le Goff, *Birth of Purgatory*, 190–93. Text: A. Wagner, ed., *Visio Tnugdali* (Erlangen, 1982). See also H. Spilling, *Die Visio Tnugdali* (Munich, 1975).

72. In Wagner, *Visio Tnugdali*, 32.

73. Le Goff, *Birth of Purgatory*, 193–201, with bibliography. For the *Purgatorium sancti Patricii* see especially the edition of E. Mall in *Romanische Forschungen* 6 (1891) 139–97.

74. Under the title *L'Espurgatoire Saint Patriz*.

75. Gervase of Tilbury, *Otia imperialia*, ed. Leibniz (Scriptores rerum brunsvicensium; Hanover, 1707) 897, cited in Le Goff, *Birth of Purgatory*, 203.

76. Le Goff, *Birth of Purgatory*, 204.

77. Vovelle, *La Mort*, 64. See M. Dykmans, *Les Sermons de Jean XXII sur la vision béatifique* (Rome: Gregorian University, 1973) 93, 145.

Chapter 3: The Earthly Paradise and Medieval Geography

1. *Jubilees* 8, in J. H. Charlesworth, ed., *The Old Testament Pseudepigrapha* (2 vols.; New York: Doubleday, 1982 and 1985) 2:72–73.

2. Josephus, *The Antiquities of the Jews* 1.1 (38–39), in *The Works of Josephus*, trans. W. Whiston (reprint, Peabody, Mass.: Hendrickson, 1987) 29–30.

3. See above, pp. 16–16.

4. Ephraem, *Hymnes sur le paradis* (SC 137:36–37).

5. Ephraem, *In Genesim commentarii* (CSCO 72; Louvain, 1955) 21.

6. Philostorgius, *Historia ecclesiastica* (PG 65:491–95), according to the summary given by Photius. On Philostorgius see Pauly-Wissowa, *Realencyclopädie* 93:191–92.

7. K. Kitamura, "Cosmas Indicopleustès et la figure de la terre," in A. Desreumaux and Fr. Schmidt, eds., *Moïse géographe: Recherches sur les représentations juives et chrétiennes de l'espace* (Paris: Vrin, 1988) 79–98. See also the article by Lettrone, "Des opinions cosmosgraphiques des Pères de l'Église," *La Revue des deux mondes* 1 (1834) 606–33.

8. John Damascene, *The Orthodox Faith* 2.11, "On Paradise," in St. John of Damascus, *Writings,* trans. F. H. Chase, Jr. (Fathers of the Church 37; New York: Fathers of the Church, 1958) 230.

9. Ibid., 9 (p. 61).

10. Moses Bar Cephas, *Commentaria de paradiso*, esp. 1.7–9 (PG 57:491–94); H. R. Patch, *The Other World according to Descriptions in Medieval Literature* (Cambridge, Mass.: Harvard University Press, 1950) 147; J. E. Duncan, *Milton's Earthly Paradise: A Historical Study of Eden* (Minneapolis: University of Minnesota Press, 1972), 50.

11. Isidore of Seville, *Differentiae* (PL 83:75).

12. Isidore of Seville, *Etymologiae* (PL 82:496).

13. The Venerable Bede, *Hexaemeron* (PL 91:43–44).

14. Rabanus Maurus, *De universo libri XXII* 12.3 (De paradiso) (PL 111:334).

15. Honorius of Autun, *De imagine mundi* (PL 172:123). See also his *Elucidarium* (PL 172:1117). A medieval Italian translation of the *Imago mundi* has been published by Fr. Chiovaro, *L'Ymagine del mondo* (Naples: Loffredo, 1977).

16. Peter Lombard, *Sententiarum libri quattuor* (PL 82:496).

17. I refer the reader to a thesis entitled "La vision et la représentation dans les milieux intellectuels du XIIᵉ siècle," presently being written by Danielle Lecoq under the direction of G. Duby, and to an article by the same writer, "Le Paradis au commencement du monde," published in a special number of the *Revue de la Bibliothèque nationale* (June 1992).

18. For all that follows see Patch, *Other World*, 148–51; Gervase of Tilbury, *Otia imperialia*, 911 (see chap. 2, n. 75, above).

19. Hugh of St. Victor, *De situ terrarum* (PL 177:209–10).

20. PL 178:775, no. 8.

21. F. Zarncke, "Der Priester Johannes," *Abhandlungen der sächsisch.-kön: Gesellschaft der Wissenschaften, Phil.-hist. Klasse* 8 (Leipzig, 1883) 123.

22. Bernard Silvestris, *De mundi universitate*, ed. Barach and Wrobel, 24–25.

23. See A. Hilka, in L. P. G. Peckham and M. S. La Du, eds., *The "Prise*

de Defur" and the *"Voyage au Paradis Terrestre"* (Elliott Monographs 35; Princeton, N.J.: Princeton University Press, 1935) xxxiii–lii and 73–90; G. Cary, *The Medieval Alexander* (Cambridge: Cambridge University Press, 1956) 19, 20, 151, 373. 374.

24. Peckham and La Du, *Prise de Defur,* xlii.

25. Ibid., 1.

26. Ibid., 78, 79.

27. *Huon de Bordeaux* in F. Guessard and C. Grandmaison, eds., *Les Anciens Poètes de France* (1860) 5:165ff.

28. Thomas Aquinas, *Summa theologica,* trans. Dominican Fathers, 1:500–501 (see chap. 1, n. 70, above).

29. Bonaventure, *Commentaria in quatuor libros Sententiarum,* in *Opera omnia* (Florence: Quarachi, 1938) 2:66.

30. Vincent of Beauvais, *Speculum majus,* 24.

31. Joinville, *The Life of St. Louis,* pt. 2, chap. 6, in Joinville and Villehardouin, *Chronicles of the Crusades,* trans. M. R. B. Shaw (Baltimore: Penguin, 1963) 211–12, cited in Jacques Le Goff, *La Civilisation de l'Occident médiéval* (Paris: Arthaud, 1964) 177.

32. On this subject see the bibliography in Patch, *Other World,* 152–53. And see A. B. Giamatti, *Earthly Paradise and the Renaissance Epic* (Princeton, N.J.: Princeton University Press, 1966), 79–82; Duncan, *Milton's Earthly Paradise,* 83–84.

33. Gautier of Metz, *Le Miroir du monde* (Geneva, 1517) 2.2. The poem is also titled *L'Image du monde.*

34. Brunetto Latini, *Li Livres dou trésor* (Paris: Collection des inédits de l'histoire de France, 1863) 161.

35. Dante, *Purgatorio,* canto 28, in *The Divine Comedy of Dante Alighieri,* trans. A. Mandelbaum (paperback ed.; New York: Bantam, 1984) 259–65.

36. Fazio degli Uberti, *Il Dittamondo* (Milan, 1826) 35.

37. Federico Frezzi, *Il Quadriregio,* ed. E. Filippini (Scrittori d'Italia 65), bk. 2, chap. 13 (pp. 158–62).

38. See G. H. T. Kimble, *Geography in the Middle Ages* (London: Methuen, 1938) 24; J. de Hesse, *Itinerarius* (Deventer, 1504) fol. 5.

39. G. de Marignolli, *Relatio,* in *Sinica Francsicana* (Florence, 1929) 1:352. See also 1:531–34.

40. See the recent work of C. Deluz, *Le Livre de Jehan de Mandeville: Une "Géographie" au XIVe siècle* (Louvain: Publications of the University of Louvain-la-Neuve, 1990), esp. 3–8.

41. *The Travels of Sir John Mandeville,* trans. C. W. R. D. Moseley (New York: Penguin, 1983) 47.

42. Ibid., 183.

43. Ibid., 184–85.

44. See *Mandeville's Travels,* texts and translation by Malcolm Letts (London: Hakluyt Society, 1953) 2:336f.

45. B. Penrose, *Travel and Discovery in the Renaissance* (Cambridge, Mass.: Harvard University Press, 1952) 16.

46. R. Higden, *Polychronicon* (London, 1965) 1.10 (pp. 66–70). [Translated from the author's French. —Tr.]

47. Ibid. (p. 74).

48. Ibid. (p. 74–76).

49. *Orto do esposo*, ed. B. Maier (2 vols.; Rio de Janeiro, 1956). See S. Buarque de Holanda, *Visão do paraíso* (São Paulo: Companhia editora nacional, 1969) 172–73. This book, which I shall be using frequently, is fundamental for the subject of this chapter.

50. *Orto do esposo*, 1:14–15.

51. Pierre d'Ailly, *Ymago mundi*, 55, ed. Buron (Paris: Maisonneuve, 1930) 2:460–61.

52. "Narrative of the Third Voyage," in *The Four Voyages of Christopher Columbus*, trans. J. M. Cohen (New York: Penguin, 1969) 220–22.

53. See Christopher Columbus, *Oeuvres*, trans. and annot. A. Cioranescu (Paris: Gallimard, 1961) 20.

54. Bartolomé de Las Casas, *Historia de las Indias*, in *Obras* (Biblioteca de autores españoles; Madrid: Atlas, 1957) 1:379.

55. Buarque de Holanda, *Visão*, xxiii–xxiv.

56. Kimble, *Geography*, 31.

57. M. F. de Barros et Sousa, vicomte de Santarem, *Essai sur l'histoire de la cosmographie et de la cartographie* (3 vols. + *Atlas*; Paris, 1842) 2:16 and *Atlas*, plate 3.

58. Ibid., *Atlas*, plate 4.

59. Ibid., *Atlas*, plate 11, and E. F. Jomart, *Les Monuments de la géographie* (Paris, 1854). See J. Lelewel, *Géographie du Moyen Âge* (4 vols. in 2; Brussels, 1854–57) 4:115–17.

60. Santarem, *Essai*, 2:197, 224, and *Atlas*, plate 13, 4.

61. Ibid., *Atlas*, plate 7, 3.

62. P. Gautier Dalché, *La "Descriptio mappe mundi" de Hugues de Saint-Victor* (Paris: Études augustiniennes, 1988) 88 and plate 1.

63. Santarem, *Essai*, 2:241, and *Atlas*, plate 14. This map of the world is found at the beginning of a manuscript, dated 1410, of the *Imago mundi*.

64. J. B. Harley and D. Woodward, *The History of Geography* (Chicago: University of Chicago Press, 1987) 1:291; the map is reproduced in Jomart, *Monuments*, plate 14. See the two articles of R. Lindemann and A. Wolf in M. Pelletier, ed., *Géographie du monde au Moyen Âge et à la Renaissance* (Paris: Comité des Travaux historiques et scientifiques, 1989) 45–68. On the Ebstorf map see A. Wolf, *Neues zur Ebstorfer Weltkarte in dem Benediktinerinnenkloster Ebstorf im Mittelalter* (Hildesheim, 1988); English text in Pelletier, *Géographie*, 51–68.

65. See F. Plaut, "Where Is Paradise? The Mapping of a Myth," *The Map Collector* 24 (1984) 2. See Jomart, *Monuments*; Santarem, *Essai*, 2:292; Lelewel, *Géographie*, 4:141–43.

66. Lelewel, *Géographie*, 4:145–61; Santarem, *Essai*, 3:32.

67. Plaut, "Where Is Paradise?" 3.

68. Santarem, *Essai*, 3:314, and *Atlas*, plate 22.

69. Ibid., 3:247–301, and *Atlas*, plate 35.

70. Ibid., 3:381–82, and *Atlas*, plate 38; Lelewel, *Géographie*, 2:85–89.

71. Lelewel, *Géographie*, 2:89–96. See Kimble, *Geography*, 194–96.

72. A. E. Nordenskiöld, *Facsimile-Atlas in the Early History of Geography* (New York: Dover, 1973) 51.

73. Ibid., 3.

74. R. W. Shirley, *The Mapping of the World: Early Printed World Maps, 1472–1700* (London: Holland Press, 1972) 115.

75. W. G. L. Randles, *De la terre au globe terrestre: Une mutation épistémologique* (Paris: A. Colin, 1980), esp. 20–28. See F. Lestringant, *André Thévet, Cosmographe du Levant* (Geneva: Droz, 1985).

76. Santarem, *Atlas,* plate 44.

77. Lelewel, *Géographie,* 2:135–39.

Chapter 4: The Kingdom of Prester John

1. I shall be relying at several points on J. Richard, "L'Extrême-Orient légendaire au Moyen Âge: Roi David et Prêtre Jean," *Annales d'Ethiopie* 2 (1957) 225–42, and on L. Hambis, "La Légende de Prêtre Jean," *La Tour Saint Jacques* 8 (Jan.–Feb. 1957) 31–46; both articles have abundant bibliography. However, a recent publication has completely renewed the entire approach to the subject. I am referring to J. Pirenne, *La Légende du Prêtre Jean* (Strasbourg: Presses Universitaires de Strasbourg, 1992). This work of a prematurely deceased scholar is supported by a bibliography, several titles from which I shall be using in the following pages. I thank my colleagues at Strasbourg for providing me with this basic study of the subject.

2. The Nestorian Christians had accepted the heresy of Nestorius (fifth century), who denied that the two natures, divine and human, were united in the one person of Jesus and accepted only a "conjunction" of the human nature with the divine person. After the condemnation of Nestorius (431) his followers spread throughout Asia.

3. The fundamental study of this letter and of the entire documentation concerning Prester John is F. Zarncke, "Der Priester Johannes," *Abhandlungen der sächsisch.-kön: Gesellschaft der Wissenschaften, Phil.-hist. Klasse* 7 (1879) 829–1030; 8 (1883) 1–186. Here see 7:837–43.

4. Ibid., 7:843–47.

5. Ibid., 7:847–50. Otto von Freising, *Chronicon* 7.33, in *Monumenta Germaniae Historica* 20:266. See also Richard, "L'Extrême-Orient légendaire," 232.

6. Pirenne, *La Légende du Prêtre Jean,* 31–46.

7. Ibid., 25.

8. Ibid., 32.

9. Ibid., 36.

10. Ibid., 19, 45–46.

11. Ibid., 49.

12. V. Slessarev, *Prester John: The Letter and the Legend* (Minneapolis: University of Minnesota Press, 1959).

13. E. Ullendort and C. F. Beckingham, *The Hebrew Letters of Prester John* (Oxford: Oxford University Press, 1982).

14. Pirenne, *La Légende du Prêtre Jean,* 65.

15. Ibid., 66.

16. Ibid., 81.

17. Ibid., 86.

18. Zarncke, "Der Priester Johannes," 7:909–24.

19. Cited in Pirenne, *La Légende du Prêtre Jean*, 45, from J. de Saint-Genois, "Sur des lettres inédites de Jacques de Vitry," *Mémoires de l'Académie royale de Belgique* 23 (Brussels, 1849) 42–43.

20. Ibid.

21. Joinville, *Life of Saint Louis*, 283–85 (chap. 3, n. 31, above).

22. Vincent of Beauvais, *Speculum historiale* (Venice, 1591) 449, citing Giovanni del Piano Carpino.

23. Thomas of Cantimpré, *De Apibus* (Douai, 1605) 526–27.

24. Willem of Rubruck, *Voyage dans l'empire mongol*, trans. with commentary by C. and R. Kappler (Paris: Payot, 1985) 123–24.

25. *The Travels of Marco Polo*, trans. R. Latham (New York: Penguin, 1958) 93–96.

26. Ibid., 105–6.

27. Odoricus of Pordenone, *Les Voyages en Asie du bienheureux frère Odoric de Pordenone*, in *Recueil de voyages et documents pour servir à l'histoire de la géographie*, ed. H. Cordier (Paris, 1891) 10:433.

28. Hambis, "La Légende," 36; Richard, "L'Extrême-Orient légendaire," 236. See N. Egami, "Olon-Sume et la découverte de l'Église catholique romaine de Jean de Montecorvin," *Journal Asiatique* 240 (1952) 155ff.; J. Dauvillier, "Les Provinces chaldéennes de l'extérieur au Moyen Âge," in *Mélanges offerts au P. F. Cavallera* (Toulouse, 1948) 230–316.

29. Zarncke, "Der Priester Johannes," 8:117–19; Richard, "L'Extrême-Orient légendaire," 236. The *De gestis trium regum* was published by C. Horstmann in his *The Three Kings of Cologne: An Early Translation of the Historia trium regum by John of Hildesheim* (Early English Text Society 85; London, 1886); see chaps. 44 and 45.

30. The *Nouvelles de la terre de Prestre Jehan* is in P. d'Alcripe, *Nouvelles fabriques des excellents traits de vérité, suivies des Nouvelles de la terre du Prestre Jehan* (Paris, 1853) 207–8. There is an extract from this work in J.-P. Albert, "Le légendaire médiéval des aromates," in *Le Corps humain, nature, culture, surnaturel* (110ème congrès des Sociétés savantes; Montpellier, 1985) 40–41.

31. I shall be summarizing here the most important passages from chaps. 30–32 of *The Travels of Sir John Mandeville* (see chap. 3, n. 41, above). See also C. Deluz, *Le Livre de Jehan de Mandeville: Une "Géographie" au XIVᵉ siècle* (Louvain: Publications of the University of Louvain-la-Neuve, 1990) 182–86.

32. *The Travels of Sir John Mandeville*, 167–71, 182.

33. Ibid., 178.

34. Ibid., 179–80.

35. Ibid., 171–72.

36. Odoricus of Pordenone, *Les Voyages en Asie*, 474. See C. Kappler, *Monstres, démons et merveilles à la fin du Moyen Âge* (Paris: Payot, 1980) 88, 308.

37. *The Travels of Marco Polo*, 70–73.

38. Ibid., 70.

39. *Les Mille et une nuits*, "Cinquième voyage de Sindbad" (Paris: Garnier-Flammarion, 1965) 1:268–69.

40. Ibid., 3:79.

41. See especially Suras 56 (vv. 27–30), 61 (v. 12), 69 (vv. 22–23), 76 (v. 14), 78 (vv. 31–32).

42. Jordan of Séverac, *Mirabilia,* ed. Coquebert de Monbret, in *Recueil de voyages et mémoires* 4 (1824) 50–51.

43. *The Travels of Sir John Mandeville,* 65.

44. *The Travels of Marco Polo,* 299.

45. Ibid., 125–26.

46. Kappler, *Monstres,* 82.

47. *Les Mille et une nuits,* "Histoire des amours de Camaralzaman," 2:156.

48. *The Travels of Sir John Mandeville,* 183.

49. Ibid., 173–74. [The last two passages cited are translated from the author's French. —Tr.]

50. Odoricus of Pordenone, *Les Voyages en Asie,* 490.

51. On this story see Kappler, *Monstres,* 102–4.

52. *The Travels of Marco Polo,* 85.

53. This "information" given in the twelfth century is passed on, but with reservations ("si tamen verum est quod dicitur"), by Hugh of St. Victor; see P. Gautier Dalché, *La "Descriptio mappe mundi" de Hugues de Saint-Victor* (Paris: Études augustiniennes, 1988) 141. I thank Michel Mollat de Jourdain for calling my attention to this book.

54. *The Travels of Sir John Mandeville,* 183.

55. Pierre d'Ailly, *Ymago mundi,* ed. Buron (Paris: Maisonneuve, 1930) 2:260.

56. *Secret de l'histoire naturelle,* Paris, B.N., MS fr. 22971, fol. 60v.

57. Dalché, *La "Descriptio mappe mundi,"* 11.

58. Ibid., 82, 83.

59. See Richard, "L'Extrême-Orient légendaire," 228, 229.

60. Ibid., 236. See Santarem, *Essai,* 3:195 (see chap. 3, n. 57, above).

61. J. Lelewel, *Géographie du Moyen Âge* (4 vols. in 2; Brussels, 1854–57) 3:169.

62. Ibid., 228.

63. Vincent of Beauvais, *Speculum historiale,* bk. 31, chaps. 4f., fols. 448–49.

64. G. de Santisteban, *Libro del Infante Don Pedro de Portugal,* text and commentary by Fr. M. Rogers (Lisbon, 1962); Eng. trans. by Rogers, *The Travels of the Infante Dom Pedro of Portugal* (Cambridge, Mass.: Harvard University Press, 1961).

65. I have been summarizing chaps. 11–19 of Dom Pedro's travels according to Rogers's English translation (pp. 134–50). [Translated from the author's French. —Tr.]

66. On this whole matter I once again refer the reader to Hambis, "La Légende," 36–38, and to Richard, "L'Extrême-Orient légendaire," 236–42.

67. Jordan of Séverac, *Mirabilia,* 55–56.

68. *Itineraria Symonis Symeonis,* ed. J. Nasmith (Cambridge, 1778) 36.

69. In *Sinica Franciscana,* ed. van de Wyngaert (1929) 1:532.

70. Lelewel, *Géographie,* 2:52.

71. Santarem, *Atlas,* plate 37.

72. *Il Mappemondo di Fra Mauro,* ed. Tullia Gasparrini Le Portace (Rome: Istituto Poligrafico dello Stato, 1954), map 10.

73. Lelewel, *Géographie,* 2:102; Santarem, *Atlas,* plate 37, and *Essai,* 3:281–96.

74. Lelewel, *Géographie,* 2:109–110; E. F. Jomart, *Les Monuments de la géographie* (Paris, 1854) plate 16; Santarem, *Atlas,* plate 60.

75. B. Penrose, *Travel and Discovery in the Renaissance* (Cambridge, Mass.: Harvard University Press, 1952) 27, 138–41, 284.

76. F. Álvarez, *Narrative of the Portuguese Embassy to Abyssinia during the Years 1520–1527*, Eng. trans. by Lord Stanley of Alderley (London: Hakluyt Society, 1881).

77. See J. E. Duncan, *Milton's Earthly Paradise: A Historical Study of Eden* (Minneapolis: University of Minnesota Press, 1972), 196–98.

78. Mercator, *Atlas* (1636; reprint, Amsterdam, 1968) 2:431. See Jomart, *Monuments*, facsimile plate 31.

Chapter 5: Other Dreamlands

1. G. de Marignolli, *Relatio*, in *Sinica franciscana* (Florence, 1929) 1:532–33.

2. Jordan of Séverac, *Mirabilia*, 1:50–51 (chap. 4, n. 42, above).

3. *The Travels of Sir John Mandeville*, trans. C. W. R. D. Moseley (New York: Penguin, 1983) 167.

4. C. Kappler, *Monstres, démons et merveilles à la fin du Moyen Âge* (Paris: Payot, 1980) 35.

5. Ibid., 36.

6. French translations in J. Lelewel, *Géographie du Moyen Âge* (4 vols. in 2; Brussels, 1854–57) 2:58. The detail about the two growth seasons is already to be found in the *Etymologiae* (14.6) of Isidore of Seville, where it refers to "Taprobana," a name that in the Middle Ages refers sometimes to Ceylon, sometimes to Sumatra.

7. See above, pp. 6–10.

8. Isidore, *Etymologiae* (PL 82/2:514).

9. Gervase of Tilbury, *Otia imperialia*, 2, chap. 11 (pp. 10–11).

10. See Barthélemy l'Anglais, *Le Grand Propriétaire de toutes choses* (Paris, 1556) 65, chap. 62, fol. 128.

11. Pierre d'Ailly, *Ymago mundi*, ed. Buron (Paris: Maisonneuve, 1930) 2:389–90.

12. Geoffrey of Monmouth, *The "Historia regum Britanniae,"* 11.2, ed. Action Griscom (London, 1929) 501.

13. Geoffrey of Monmouth, *The "Vita Merlini,"* ed. J. J. Parry (Urbana: University of Illinois Press, 1925) 82f.

14. H. R. Patch, *The Other World according to Descriptions in Medieval Literature* (Cambridge, Mass.: Harvard University Press, 1950) 284–87.

15. See, above, p. 56.

16. P. Gautier Dalché, *La "Descriptio mappe mundi" de Hugues de Saint-Victor* (Paris: Études augustiniennes, 1988) 82 and 135.

17. Lelewel, *Géographie*, 3:161; E. F. Jomart, *Les Monuments de la géographie* (Paris, 1854) plate 14; Santarem, *Essai*, 2:127–53 (see chap. 3, n. 57, above).

18. Lelewel, *Géographie*, 3:145f.; Santarem, *Essai*, 3:60–82.

19. Jomart, *Monuments*, plate 10; Lelewel, *Géographie*, 2:49.

20. Translated in Lelewel, *Géographie*, 2:49.

21. Ibid., 2:66–67.

22. M. de la Roncière and M. Mollat du Jourdin, *Portulans du XIIIᵉ siècle* (Paris, 1984), map 19 (Graciozo Benincasa, 1467).

23. *The Anglo-Norman Voyage of St. Brendan by Benedeit*, ed. E. G. R. Waters (Oxford, 1928) 90; cited in Buarque de Holanda, *Visão do Paraíso* (São Paulo: Companhia editora nacional, 1969) 66, 167. See also R. Hennig, *Terrae Incognitae* (4 vols.; Leiden, 1936–38) 4:318–27, and *Journal de bord de saint Brendam à la recherche du paradis* (n.d.) 203–8; also T. Severin, *The Brendan Voyage* (New York: Isis, 1978).

24. Buarque de Holanda, *Visão do Paraíso*, 167.

25. Santarem, *Essai*, 2:43; Lelewel, *Géographie*, 3:160–61.

26. On this point Buarque de Holanda, *Visão do Paraíso*, 167 (n. 49), corrects V. W. Babcock, *Legendary Islands of the Atlantic* (New York, 1922) 48, who gave 1570 as the date of the last appearance of St. Brendan's island.

27. Buarque de Holanda, *Visão do Paraíso*, 178; M. Martins, *Estudos de Literatura Medieval* (Braga, 1956) 23.

28. Hennig, *Terrae Incognitae*, 4:326; Buarque de Holanda, *Visão do Paraíso*, 168.

29. The map of Angelino Dalorto: see Buarque de Holanda, *Visão do Paraíso*, 168.

30. Ibid.

31. Ibid., 178; E. Carus-Wilson, *Medieval Merchant Ventures* (London, 1954) 97.

32. Buarque de Holanda, *Visão do Paraíso*, 168.

33. B. Penrose, *Travel and Discovery in the Renaissance* (Cambridge, Mass.: Harvard University Press, 1952) 13.

34. Ibid., 149–52.

35. Santarem, *Atlas*, plate 12.

36. Ibid., plate 38.

37. Reproductions in R. W. Shirley, *The Mapping of the World: Early Printed World Maps, 1472–1700* (London: Holland Press, 1972) xiii, xxi, and 15.

38. Columbus, *Oeuvres*, trans. and annot. by A. Cioranescu (Paris: Gallimard, 1951) 305.

39. J. T. Medina, *El Veneciano S. Caboto al servicio de España* (2 vols.; Paris, 1882; Santiago de Chile, 1908).

40. Penrose, *Travel*, 112–19.

41. See A. Métraux, "Les Messies de l'Amérique du Sud," *Archives de sociologie des religions* 4 (1957) 109.

42. On the Monomotapa see again Penrose, *Travel*, 133–38, and W. G. L. Randles, *L'Empire du Monomotapa di XIe au XIXe siècle* (Paris, 1975).

43. See the work by various authors, *Archéologie* (Paris, 1986) 98–101.

44. "Digest of Columbus's Log-Book" for Friday, October 19, 1492, in *The Four Voyages of Christopher Columbus*, trans. J. M. Cohen (New York: Penguin, 1969) 68.

45. Ibid.

46. S. Arnoldsson, *Los Monumentos históricos de América* (Madrid: Spanish-American Institute of Göteborg, 1956) 10; Buarque de Holanda, *Visão do Paraíso*, 179.

47. H. Vignaud, *Améric Vespuce* (Paris, 1917) 410.

48. Ibid., 309.

49. Pietro Martire d'Anghiera, *De Orbe Novo* (1st complete ed.; Alcalà, 1531), bk. 10, decade 3, chap. 9, in *Recueil de voyages et de documents* (Paris, 1907) 21:325.

50. F. Hernández, *Antigüedades de la Nueva España* (Mexico City, 1945), cited in Buarque de Holanda, *Visão do Paraíso*, 180.

51. R. Hakluyt, *The Principal Navigations, Voyages, Traffiques and Discoveries of the English Nation* (London, 1927) 5:174. The first edition of this work appeared in 1589, the second (much expanded) in 1598–1600. [Translated from the author's French. —Tr.]

52. Walter Raleigh, *The History of the World*, 89 (see chap. 1, n. 40, above).

53. Vicente de Salvador, *Historia do Brasil*, completed in 1627 but published only in the twentieth century by the University of São Paulo (n.d.), 23f.; Buarque de Holanda, *Visão do Paraíso*, 283.

54. Cited without a reference in Buarque de Holanda, *Visão do Paraíso*, xxi.

55. A. de L. Pinelo, *El Paraíso en el Nuevo Mundo*, written in 1650–55 and published, in two volumes, only in 1942; here see 2:373f.; Buarque de Holanda, *Visão do Paraíso*, xxii, 135, and 230–31.

56. D. do Rosario, *Frutas do Brasil* (Lisbon, 1702) 20f.; Buarque de Holanda, *Visão do Paraíso*, 234–43.

57. Buarque de Holanda, *Visão do Paraíso*, 233.

58. Ibid., 68.

59. Ibid., 207–9.

60. Ibid., 208.

61. For all that follows see ibid., 239–42.

62. E. Faral, *La Légende arthurienne* (Paris, 1929) 3:234.

63. Pierre d'Ailly, *Ymago mundi*, 2:393.

64. Vignaud, *Améric Vespuce*, 411 (letter to Lorenzo dei Medici, 1502).

65. Ibid., 308.

66. Ibid., 13–15.

67. A. Pigafetta, *Relation du premier voyage autour du monde par Magellan* (Paris: Club des Librairies de France, 1956) 152–53.

68. Jean de Léry, *Histoire d'un voyage faict en la terre antarctique* (Geneva: Droz, 1975), chap. 8, p. 95.

69. B. de Las Casas, *Colección de tratados, 1552–53* (Buenos Aires, 1924) 7–8, cited in L. Hanke, *Bartolomé de Las Casas: An Interpretation of His Life and Writings* (The Hague, 1951) 11.

70. Jean de Léry, *Histoire d'un voyage*, 95.

71. Montaigne, *The Complete Essays of Montaigne*, trans. D. M. Frame (Stanford, Calif.: Stanford University Press, 1958) 153.

72. C. L. Sanford, *The Quest for Paradise* (Urbana: University of Illinois Press, 1961) 111. [Translated from the author's French. —Tr.]

73. Ibid., 83–85.

74. Ibid.

75. I will deal with this matter in the next volume of this series.

Chapter 6: Nostalgia

1. J. Delumeau, *La Civilisation de la Renaissance* (2nd ed.; Paris, Arthaud, 1973) 347f. (pocketbook ed.: Paris: Flammarion, 1984) 310f.; and idem, *Le Péché*

et la peur (Paris: Fayard, 1983), 189–210; Eng. trans.: *Sin and Fear: The Emergence of a Western Guilt Culture 13th-1th Centuries,* trans. E. Nicholson (New York: St. Martin's Press, 1991).

2. See H. Levin, *The Myth of the Golden Age in the Renaissance* (Urbana: Indiana University Press, 1969) 26, 39, and 112. For Elizabeth, see F. Laroque, *Shakespeare et la fête* (Paris: PUF, 1988) 77.

3. G. de Lorris and J. de Meun, *Le Roman de la rose,* vv. 8355–454, trans. H. W. Robbins, *The Romance of the Rose* (New York: Dutton, 1962), sec. 41, pp. 169–70.

4. C. Salutati, *Epistolario,* ed. Fr. Novati (Rome, 1891–1911) 1:270–71; cited in A. Tenenti, *Il senso della morte e l'amore della vita nel Rinascimento* (Turin: Einaudi, 1957) 64.

5. Sebastian Brant, *La Nef des fous,* trans. M. Horst (Strasbourg: Nuée Bleue, 1977) 64.

6. Erasmus, *The Praise of Folly,* trans. H. H. Hudson (Princeton, N.J.: Princeton University Press, 1969) 44.

7. Marot, *Oeuvres complètes* (Paris: Garnier, 1951) 438–49.

8. French translation: A. de Guevara, *L'Horloge des princes* (Paris, 1550), fol. 92; cited in Levin, *Myth of the Golden Age,* 30.

9. Cervantes, *Don Quixote,* pt. 1, chap. 11, in Miguel de Cervantes, *The History of Don Quixote de la Mancha,* trans. J. Ormsby (Chicago: Encyclopedia Britannica, 1952) 27.

10. Lope de Vega, *La Vega del Parnaso* (Madrid, 1637), "El siglo de Oro," fol. 3. See Levin, *Myth of the Golden Age,* 143–44.

11. "Avertissement déclaratif" by B. Aneau in the French translation of More's work: *La République d'Utopie* (Lyons, 1559) 3. See J. Céard, "République de Platon et pensée politique," in *Platon et Aristote à la Renaissance* (16ème Colloque international de Tours; Paris: Vrin, 1976) 180.

12. Thomas More, *Utopia,* in *Complete Works of St. Thomas More,* ed. and trans. E. Surtz and J. H. Hexter (New Haven: Yale University Press, 1965) 4:113, 115, 121.

13. For discussion of this subject I refer the reader to my *Civilisation de la Renaissance,* 359–65 (Flammarion pocketbook ed., 318–33).

14. Ronsard, *Oeuvres complètes,* ed. P. Laumonnier (Paris, 1914–19) 5:160.

15. Ibid., 5:161.

16. Rabanus Maurus, *Operum Pars I* (PL 107:479). See H. Comito, *Sacred Spaces and the Image of Paradise* (New Brunswick, N.J.: Rutgers University Press, 1978), esp. 25–50.

17. Herrad of Landsberg (or Hottenburg), *Hortus deliciarum* (2 vols.; London: Brill, 1979) 1:38.

18. Cited in P. Riché, *Petite Vie de Saint Bernard* (Paris: Desclée de Brouwer, 1989) 32–33.

19. See R. King, *Les Paradis terrestres* (Paris: Albin Michel, 1980) 76–79; T. Comito, in *Histoire des jardins,* ed. M. Mosser and G. Teyssot (Paris: Flammarion, 1990) 33.

20. Comito, in *Histoire des jardins,* 37.

21. See the French translation: *Rational ou Manuel des divins offices* (Paris, 1848) 59.

22. Cited in G. Cohen, *Histoire de la mise en scène dans le théâtre religieux français du Moyen Âge* (Paris: Champion, 1951) 91.

23. Painting in the Staedelsches Kunstinstitut, Frankfurt. See F. Russell et al., *Dürer and His Age* (New York: Time-Life, 1967). See also J. Wirth, *L'Image médiévale: Naissance et développements (VIᵉ-XVᵉ s.)* (Paris: Klinksieck, 1989) 294–95.

24. See *Adam et Eve* (Collection: L'Art et ses Grands Thèmes, ed. L. Mazenod; Paris, 1967) 39–42.

25. I thank Mme Danièle Alexandre-Bidon for drawing my attention to this document.

26. Formula of Albert the Great, *Opera omnia* (Paris: Vivès, 1898) 36:707. For this reference and for what follows see M. Levi d'Ancona, *The Garden of the Renaissance: Botanical Symbolism in Italian Painting* (Florence: Olschki, 1977) 176–78.

27. Jerome, *Adv. Jovinianum* (PL 23:254).

28. See L. Hautecoeur, *Les Jardins des dieux et des hommes* (Paris: Hachette, 1959) 81.

29. I thank the president and board of the Academy of Verona for calling my attention to this fresco.

30. Adam of Perseigne, *Mariale* (PL 211:707).

31. On these developments see Levi d'Ancona, *Garden of the Renaissance*, passim, and the catalogue *Flore en Italie*, published for the exhibition "Flore en Italie" in the Museum of the Petit Palais (of Avignon) in 1991. Preface by M. Laclotte, passim.

32. Levi d'Ancona, *Garden of the Renaissance*, 365.

33. Ibid., 332.

34. *Flore en Italie*, 68. On the religious meaning of flowers see O. Speer, "Les Jardins du paradis: Les plantes dans les tableaux des primitifs du paradis du musée d'Unterlinden," *Annuaire de la Société d'histoire et d'archéologie de Colmar* 29 (1980–81) 27–46. See Ambrose, *Hexaemeron* (PL 17:175).

35. See Comito, in *Histoire des jardins*, 33–34.

36. Erasmus, *The Godly Feast*, in *The Colloquies of Erasmus*, trans. C. R. Thompson (Chicago: University of Chicago Press, 1965) 46–78.

37. I am using the edition by K. Cameron (Geneva: Droz, 1988).

38. B. Palissy, *La Recepte veritable* (Geneva: Droz, 1988), 126. See A. M. Lecoq, "Le Jardin de la Sagesse de B. Palissy," in *Histoire des jardins*, 65–75.

39. Palissy, *La Recepte veritable*, 128.

40. Ibid., 160.

41. Ibid., 186.

42. Ibid., 196.

43. Ibid., 153.

44. Ibid., 128, 144, 149, etc.

45. A. Labbé, *L'Architecture des palais et des jardins dans les chansons de geste* (Paris-Geneva: Champion-Slatkine, 1987) 377, with bibliography.

46. This *Livre de l'échelle de Mahomet* was known in the West through at least three manuscripts of the thirteenth and fourteenth centuries; see M. Brossard, "Verg-

ers et jardins dans l'univers médiéval," *Sénéfiance* ("Cuerma," University of Provence) 28 (1990) 55–61.

47. Labbé, *L'Architecture*, 315–17.

48. See especially M. Charageat, "Le Parc d'Hesdin, création monumentale du XIIIe siècle, ses origines arabes," *Bulletin de la Société d'histoire de l'art français* (1950) 94–106.

49. *Le Roman de Thèbes*, ed. C. Raynaud de Lage (Paris: Champion, 1966–67), vv. 2173–74; cited in M.-F. Notz, "*Hortus conclusus:* Réflexions sur le rôle symbolique de la clôture dans le description romanesque du jardin," *Mélanges de littérature... offerts à J. Lods* (Paris: E. N. S., 1978) 461.

50. *Floire et Blancheflor*, ed. M. Pelan (Paris: Publications de l'Université de Strasbourg, 1937), vv. 1746–71, cited in Notz, "*Hortus conclusus*," 461.

51. Chrétien de Troyes, *Romans* (Paris: Champion, 1970) 193, vv. 6332–33.

52. P. Trannoye, "Le Jardin d'amour dans le *De Amore* d'A. Le Chapelain," *Sénéfiance* 28 (1990) 375–86.

53. *Roman de la Rose*, vv. 129–520, trans. Robbins, sec. 2, p. 11.

54. Ibid., v. 590, trans. Robbins, sec. 3, p. 13.

55. J. Froissart, *Le Joli Buisson de jonece* (Paris-Geneva: Droz, 1975) 94, vv. 1377–78.

56. Cited in G. Polizzi, "Sens plastique: Le spectacle des merveilles dans le *Livre du Cueur d'amour espris*," *Sénéfiance* 25 (1988) 206.

57. Francesco Colonna, *L'Hypnérotomachie ou Songe de Poliphile* (Paris: Club Français du Livre, 1963), 106r-106v. On the link between the orchard in the *Roman de la Rose* and the garden of Cytherea see G. Polizzi, "Le Devenir du jardin médiéval: Du verger de la Rose à Cythère," *Sénéfiance* 28 (1990) 267–88.

58. Colonna, *L'Hypnérotomachie*, 110.

59. On this subject see King, *Les Paradis terrestres*, 87–155, and *Histoire des jardins*, 21–105.

60. Comito, in *Histoire des jardins*, 37.

61. Ibid., 36.

62. L. Puppi, in *Histoire des jardins*, 43.

63. Ibid., 52.

64. Cited in K. Thomas, *Man and the Natural World* (New York: Pantheon, 1983) 236. A painting by the school of Tintoretto shows the "Labyrinth of Love" in the park at Hampton Court; reproduced in *Histoire des jardins*, 81.

65. Puppi, in *Histoire des jardins*, 146.

66. Montaigne, *Oeuvres* (Paris: Pléïade, 1962) 1193–94.

67. In addition to his article, "*Naturalia* et *curiosa* dans les jardins du XVIe siècle," *Histoire des jardins* (with bibliography on p. 63), L. Zangheri has also published *Pratolino: Il Giardino delle meraviglie* (2d ed.; Florence, 1987).

68. L. Zangheri, in *Histoire des jardins*, 55.

69. L.-T. Tomasi, in *Histoire des jardins*, 77.

70. Puppi, in *Histoire des jardins*, 50.

71. Partially cited in Thomas, *Man and the Natural World*, 236. Full text: J. Shirley, *The Dramatic Works and Poems* (6 vols.; London, 1833) 6:453. I thank my friend André Rannou for having provided me with the full text of this poem and for having explained its meaning to me.

72. This reading is proposed by Br. Adorni, in *Histoire des jardins*, 89.

73. I refer the reader here to the very interesting catalogue, *Her aarts Paradijs: Dierenvoorstellingen in de Nederlanden van de 16de en 17de eeuw* (Antwerp, 1982).

74. Drawing by Solimena. I thank Mme. Danièle Alexandre-Bidon for drawing my attention to this work and providing me with photographs of it.

75. Colonna, *Hypnérotomachia*, 107–15.

76. Thomas, *Man and the Natural World*, 224.

77. Ibid.

78. Ibid., 226.

79. Ibid.

80. Pierre-Joseph Buchoz, *Le Jardin d'Éden* (2 vols.; Paris, 1783–85, with two hundred plates).

81. Since I have already dealt with this question several times in earlier books, I refer the reader to my *Civilisation de la Renaissance*, 350–51 (Flammarion ed., 313–14); idem, *La Mort des pays de Cocagne* (Paris: Publications de la Sorbonne, 1976); and idem, *Le péché et la peur*, esp. 143–52.

82. Rijksmuseum, Amsterdam, item no. 1452–A2.

83. I have repeated here the description I gave in my *Civilisation de la Renaissance*, only in the Arthaud ed., 356, with plate 122.

84. The information on Pietro Martire d'Anghiera and Fernández de Oviedo is from V. Murga Saenz, *Juan Ponce de León* (Rio Piedras: University of Puetro Rico Press, 1972) 118–20: P. Martire (decade 2, bk. 10, chap. 2); Oviedo (bk. 16, chap. 2). See also L. Olschki, "Ponce de León's Fountain of Youth: A History of a Geographical Myth," *Hispanic-American Review* 21 (1941) 361–85.

85. On Hieronymus Bosch see especially W. Fraenger, *Le Royaume millénaire de J. Bosch* (Paris: Denoël, 1966), and C. de Tolnay, *Hieronymus Bosch* (London: Methuen, 1966).

86. A. de La Salle, *Le Paradis de la reine Sibylle*, trans. F. Mora-Lebrun (Paris: Stock, 1983) 94.

87. O. de Saint-Gelais, *Le Séjour d'Honneur*, ed. J. Alston James (Chapel Hill: University of North Carolina Press, 1977). See P. Chiron, "Les Représentations du paradis dans la littérature entre 1450 et 1563" (Ph.D. thesis, University of Paris, 1990–91) 52–60.

88. Edmund Spenser, *The Poetical Works*, ed. J. C. Smith and E. de Selincourt (New York: Oxford University Press, 1912) 477.

Chapter 7: The New Learning and the Earthly Paradise

1. Met de Bles's painting (ca. 1520) is in the Mauruitshuis, The Hague. Rubens's painting is in the same museum (Rubens painted Adam and Eve; Jan Brueghel painted the animals and the trees).

2. See E. Gondinet-Wallstein and E. Rousset, *Une Rose pour la création* (Paris: Mame, 1987) 74–75.

3. A. Du Verdier, *Diverses Leçons* (Lyons, 1580) 16–20.

4. A. Williams, *The Common Exposition: An Account of the Commentaries on Genesis* (Chapel Hill: University of North Carolina Press, 1948) 3–19.

5. K. Kirkconnell, *Celestial Cycle* (reprint, New York: Gordian Press, 1979) 541–639.

6. Decrees of the Council of Trent on original sin (session 5) and justification (session 6), translated in *The Christian Faith in the Doctrinal Documents of the Catholic Church*, ed. J. Neuner and J. Dupuis (Staten Island, N.Y.: Alba House, 1982), nos. 508, 1925 (pp. 137–38, 555).

7. I refer the reader to my *Le Péché et la peur* (Paris: Fayard, 1983) 273–89.

8. Luther, *Lectures on Genesis*, in *Luther's Works*, ed. J. Pelikan, vol. 1 (St. Louis: Concordia, 1958); Calvin, *Commentaries on the Book of Genesis*, in *Calvin's Commentaries*, trans. J. King, vol. 1 (Grand Rapids: Eerdmans, 1948).

9. See F. Laplanche, *L'Écriture, le sacré et l'histoire: Érudits et politiques protestants devant la Bible en France au XVIIᵉ siècle* (Holland University Press, 1986; in France: Lille: Publications Universitaires), esp. 70. The complete works of Zanchius were published in Geneva in 1613.

10. J. E. Duncan, *Milton's Earthly Paradise: A Historical Study of Eden* (Minneapolis: University of Minnesota Press, 1972), esp. 93, 96, 134, and 206.

11. On Bochart see Laplanche, *L'Écriture*, esp. 250–54.

12. In his *Opera omnia* (3 vols.; Leiden, 1692) 1:833–34. See also the preface by Saint-Morin, ibid., 9–28.

13. On the maps included in (Protestant) Bibles see C. Delano-Smith, "Maps in Bibles in the Sixteenth Century," *The Map Collector* 29 (Dec. 1984) 2–16, and especially C. Delano-Smith and E. Morley Ingram, *Maps in Bibles, 1500–1600: An Illustrated Catalogue* (Geneva: Droz, 1991), esp. xxi–xxxix.

14. Enea Silvio Piccolomini, *Historia rerum ubique gestarum* (ed. of Helmstedt, 1699) 7, 10, and 75–80 (on Armenia).

15. G. Postel, *Cosmographicae disciplinae compendium* (Basel, 1561) 25.

16. J. Goropius, *Origines antwerpianae* (Antwerp, 1569) 5:539.

17. Cajetan, *Commentarii in quinque libros mosaicos* (Paris ed., 1539).

18. Edition used: Lyons, 1531; see esp. 83–101.

19. Edition used: Lisbon, 1556; see esp. 58–60.

20. Bellarmine, *Opera omnia* (1916) 4. *De gratia primi hominis*, chap. 51.

21. Bossuet, *Correspondence* (Paris: Hachette, 1920) 4:355.

22. Duncan, *Milton's Earthly Paradise*, esp. 210–15.

23. A. Inveges, *Historia sacra paradisi terrestris et sanctissimi innocentiae status* (Palermo, 1649), "Lectori."

24. M. Carver, *A Discourse of the Terrestrial Paradise* (London, 1666), "To the Reader" [Translated from the author's French. —Tr.]; Raleigh, *History of the World*, 78 (see chap. 1, n. 40, above).

25. Suárez, *Opera omnia* (Paris: Vivès, 1856) 3; *De hominis creatione*, 198.

26. Ibid., 202.

27. Raleigh, *History of the World*, 75.

28. M. F. Beck, *Schediasma hagiographicum de locis Eden, Ophir atque Tarsis* (Jena, 1676), chap. 1, in *Thèses d'Iéna* (Paris: Faculty of Theology) 4:251.

29. J. Salkeld, *A Treatise of Paradise* (London, 1617) 19–20. [Translated from the author's French. —Tr.]

30. Cornelius a Lapide, "Proemium et Encomium S. Scripturae," in his *Commentaria in Pentateuchum Mosis* (Antwerp, 1671) 13–15.

31. Raleigh, *History of the World*, 74.

32. Carver, *A Discourse*, "To the Reader."

33. Pierre-Daniel Huet, *Traité de la situation du paradise terrestre* (1691; ed. of 1701) 3–4. See, on Huet's work, J.-R. Massimi, "Montrer et démontrer," in *Moïse géographe*, ed. A. Desreumaux and F. Schmidt (Paris: Vrin, 1988) 203–25.

34. Luther, *Lectures*, 90.

35. Calvin, *Commentaries*, 114.

36. J. Hopkinson, *Synopsis paradisi* (edition used: Lyons, 1598) 9. [Translated from the author's French. —Tr.]

37. Raleigh, *History of the World*, 67.

38. Salkeld, *A Treatise*, 8.

39. Carver, *A Discourse*, "To the Reader."

40. J. Basnage, *Histoire du Vieux et Nouveau Testament* (Amsterdam, 1705) 6.

41. Suárez, *Opera omnia*, 3:198–99.

42. Inveges, *Historia sacra*, 12.

43. Schedel, *Chroniques de Nuremberg* (n.p., n.d.), in Réserve, B.N., fol. 9.

44. Calvin, *Commentaries*, 114.

45. Hopkinson, *Synopsis paradisi*, 9.

46. Suárez, *Opera omnia*, 3:206.

47. Roger, *La Terre sainte*, 7.

48. B. Pereira, *Cummentariorum et disputationum in Genesim*...(edition used: Mainz, 1912) 3, fol. 97, and Suárez, *Opera omnia*, 3:301, are in effect going back to Hugh of St. Victor when they expound this view.

49. Vadian, *Epitome trium terrae partium, Asiae, Africae et Europae* (Zurich, 1534) 183–87.

50. Duncan, *Milton's Earthly Paradise*, 200.

51. Goropius, *Origines antwerpianae*, 481–82.

52. J. de Pineda, *Los Treynta libros de la monarchia ecclesiastica o historia universal del mundo* (Salamanca, 1558) 1:16–17; Duncan, *Milton's Earthly Paradise*, 200–201.

53. Suárez, *Opera omnia*, 3:202–4; Salkeld, *A Treatise*, 26.

54. Calvin, *Commentaries*, 114; A. Steuchus Eugubinus, *Recognitio Veteris Testamenti ad hebraicam veritatem* (Lyons, 1531) 83–84; J. Oleaster, *Commentaria in Moïsis Pentateuchum* (Lisbon, 1556) 58; Raleigh, *History of the World*, 66–67; G. Diodati, *Annotations upon all the Books of the Old and New Testament* (London, 1657), chap. 2, v. 8 (no pagination).

55. D. Pareus, *In Genesim Mosis commentarius* (Geneva, 1614) 316.

56. Raleigh, *History of the World*, 77.

57. Pereira, *Commentariorum*, f. 98.

58. Bellarmine, *Opera omnia*, 4:50.

59. Pereira, *Commentariorum*, f. 98.

60. F. Junius, *Protoktisia seu Creationis*...*historia* (Heidelberg, 1589) 107.

61. T. Malvenda, *De Paradiso voluptatis* (Rome, 1605), chap. 8, p. 179.

62. Bellarmine, *Opera omnia*, 4:51.

63. Suárez, *Opera omnia*, 3:209–10.

64. Luther, *Lectures*, 93.

65. Ibid., 88.

66. Ibid., 90.

67. Du Bartas, *Le Deuxième Semaine (1er jour: Éden)* (Rouen, 1608), v. 125f.
68. Diodati, *Annotations,* chap. 2. [Translated from the author's French. —Tr.]
69. Salkeld, *A Treatise,* 39.
70. Steuchus Eugubinus, *Recognitio,* 98.
71. Pereira, *Commentariorum,* fol. 101.
72. Cornelius a Lapide, *Commentaria,* 85.
73. Inveges, *Historia sacra,* 93.

Chapter 8: Inquiries into the Location of the Earthly Paradise

1. Luther, *Lectures on Genesis,* in *Luther's Works,* ed. J. Pelikan (St. Louis: Concordia, 1958) 1:89.
2. Du Bartas, *La Deuxième Semaine,* 5, vv. 125–26 (see chap. 7, n. 67, above).
3. Calvin, *Commentaries on the Book of Genesis,* in *Calvin's Commentaries,* trans. J. King (Grand Rapids: Eerdmans, 1948) 1:114–15.
4. Suárez, *Opera omnia,* 3:198 (see chap. 7, n. 25, above).
5. Raleigh, *History of the World,* 78–79 (see chap. 1, n. 40, above).
6. J. E. Duncan, *Milton's Earthly Paradise: A Historical Study of Eden* (Minneapolis: University of Minnesota Press, 1972), 99.
7. Tertullian, *Apologeticum,* 47 (PL 1:520), and *Adv. Marcionem* (PL 2:288).
8. Thomas Aquinas, *Summa theologica* 1, 102, 2 ad 4, in *Summa theologica,* trans. by Dominicans of the English Province (3 vols.; New York: Benziger, [1920] 1946) 1:501.
9. Bonaventure, *Commentaria in quatuor libros sententiarum = Opera omnia,* 2:408.
10. Durand de Saint-Pourçain, *In Sententias theologicas Petri Lombardi commentariorum libri quatuor* (Lyons, 1586) 361.
11. Pierre d'Ailly, *Ymago mundi,* ed. Buron (Paris: Maisonneuve, 1930) 3:647.
12. Cited in ibid. See R. Bacon, *Opus majus* (ed. of 1733) 83.
13. Pierre d'Ailly, *Ymago mundi,* 3:648.
14. Piccolomini, *Historia,* 10.
15. Cited in Pierre d'Ailly, *Ymago mundi,* 3:742.
16. Cited in ibid., 3:745.
17. See Antonio de León Pinelo, *El Paraíso en el Nuevo Mundo,* written between 1650 and 1665, published in 2 vols. in 1943 (Lima: Imprenta Tomes Aguirre); see Buarque de Holanda, *Visão do Paraíso* (São Paulo: Companhia editora nacional, 1969) 138.
18. F. López de Gomara, *Historia general de las Indias* (2 vols.; Barcelona, 1954) 1:150–51.
19. A. Herrera y Tordesilas, *Historia general de los hechos de los Castellanos en las yslas y en tierra del Mar oceano (1499–1552)* (12 vols.; Madrid, 1933–53), decade 1, bk. 3, chap. 12 (p. 281).
20. J. de Acosta, *Historia natural y moral de las Indias* (1st ed.: Seville, 1590; 1st French ed.: 1598; ed. O'Gorman: Mexico City, 1962), bk. 2, chap. 14 (pp. 84–85).
21. De León Pinelo, *El Paraíso,* 3–45. See J. L. Phelan, *The Millennial Kingdom of the Franciscans in the New World* (Berkeley: University of California Press, 1956) 69.

22. Raleigh, *History of the World*, 87–88.

23. N. Carpenter, *Geography* (1625; reprint, 1976), 211–12. [Translated from the author's French. —Tr.]

24. Suárez, *Opera omnia*, 3:208–9.

25. Carpenter, *Geography*, 212.

26. See above, p. 89.

27. L. de Urreta, *Historia eclesiastica, politica, natural y moral de los grandes y remotos regnos de la Etiopia, monarchia del emperador llamado presté Juan de las Indias* (Valencia, 1610) 96–100.

28. Purchas, *His Pilgrims* (5 vols.; London, 1625), pt. 2, p. 1064. [Translated from the author's French. —Tr.]

29. P. Heyleyn, *Cosmographie in Foure Books* (1st ed.: 1652; edition used: London, 1677) 4:53.

30. G. Postel, *Cosmographiae disciplinae compendium* (Basel, 1561) 25.

31. See, for example, the discussion of the subject in Suárez, *Opera omnia*, 3:208, although he maintains both meanings simultaneously; and Cornelius a Lapide, *Commentaria*, 82–83 (see chap. 7, n. 30, above).

32. Gregory of Nyssa, *De oratione dominica* (PG 44:1184); see M. Alexandre, *Le commencement*, 248–49.

33. Suárez, *Opera omnia*, 3:207.

34. This (unusual) location in Arabia Felix was proposed by a Protestant, M. Beck, in his *Schediasma hagiographicum de locis Eden, Ophir, atque Tarsis* (Jena, 1676) 258.

35. Pereira, *Commentariorum*, fols. 95–96.

36. Cornelius a Lapide, *Commentaria*, 84.

37. Carver, *A Discourse*, 52 (see chap. 7, n. 24, above).

38. Ibid., 135.

39. Ibid., 151; see A. Ortelius, *Theatrum Orbis terrarum* (London, 1606; reprint, Amsterdam, 1968), 2d table, fol. J.

40. Dom Calmet, *Commentaire littéral sur tous les livres de l'Ancien et du Nouveau Testament* (Paris, 1706) 49.

41. Ibid., 50.

42. Ibid., 53.

43. Calvin, *Commentaries*, 115.

44. Ibid., 118.

45. Ibid., 121. See Strabo, *Geographia*, ed. A. Tardieu (Paris, 1873) 2:446.

46. Calvin, *Commentaries*, 121–22.

47. Ibid., 122.

48. See above, p. 142.

49. C. Delano-Smith, "Maps in Bibles in the Sixteenth Century," *The Map Collector* 29 (Dec. 1984) 9–11.

50. *The Dutch Annotations upon the Whole Bible*, trans. Rh. Hoak (London, 1657), sig. B3; see Duncan, *Milton's Earthly Paradise*, 210 and 309.

51. Junius, *Protoktisia*, 99–100 (see chap. 7, n. 60, above).

52. Hopkinson, *Synopsis*, 17–18 (see chap. 7, n. 36, above).

53. Raleigh, *History of the World*, 127.

54. P. Heyleyn, *Microcosmos: A Little Description of the Great World* (1621; edition used: Oxford, 1636) 610–12. [Translated from the author's French. —Tr.]

55. Ibid., 629 and 668. Same geography in A. Ross, *The First Book of Questions upon Genesis Containing Questions upon the Sixe First Chapters* (London, 1620) 40–44.

56. Pareus, *In Genesim*, 324 (see chap. 7, n. 55, above).

57. Ibid., 329–34.

58. A. Rivet, *Exercitationes CXC in Genesim* (Lyons, 1633) 247.

59. S. Bochart, *Opera omnia* (Leiden, 1692) 1:833. On Bochart see Laplanche, *L'Écriture*, 252–56 (see chap. 7, n. 9, above).

60. Diodati, *Annotations*, chap. 2, v. 8 (see chap. 7, n. 54, above).

61. Basnage, *Histoire*, 7 (see chap. 7, n. 40, above).

62. Ibid.

63. See above, p. 146.

64. Grotius, *Adamus exul* (Assen, 1970) 33.

65. Ibid., 107.

66. Steuchus Eugubinus, *Recognitio*, 85 (see chap. 7, n. 54, above).

67. Ibid., 88.

68. Oleaster, *Commentaria in Moïsis Pentateuchum*, 58 (see chap. 7, n. 54, above).

69. Ibid., 60.

70. F. Vatable, *Biblia Sacra: In Genesim* (ed. of Salamanca, 1584) 31.

71. Inveges, *Historia sacra*, 14–15 (see chap. 7, n. 23, above). See also Salkeld, *A Treatise*, 16 (see chap. 7, n. 29, above).

72. Huet, *Traité*, 4–6. See Massimi, "Montrer et démontrer," 203–26 (for both works see chap. 7, n. 33, above).

73. Huet, *Traité*, 21.

74. Ibid., 30.

75. Ibid., 63.

76. Ibid., 66.

77. Ibid., 67.

78. Ibid., 35.

79. Ibid., 70–71.

80. Bossuet, *Correspondence* (Paris: Hachette, 1920) 4:355.

81. M. Servet, *Christianismi restitutio* (Vienne [Dauphiné], 1553) 373–74.

82. M. Beroalde, *Chronicum, scripturae sacrae auctoritate constitutum* (Geneva, 1575) 80–87. See Duncan, *Milton's Earthly Paradise*, 209–10 and plate 7.

83. Duncan, *Milton's Earthly Paradise*, 110.

84. I. de la Peyrère, *Praeadamitae sive exercitatio super... versibus epistolae D. Pauli ad Romanos* (1665), esp. 116–28. The author thinks of the "Promised Land," taken in a broad sense, as extending from Egypt to the Euphrates.

85. J. Heidegger, *Historia sacra patriarchum* (Amsterdam, 1667) 1:142–43; J. Herbinus, *Dissertationes de admirandis mundi cataractis* (Amsterdam, 1678) 147–51. See Duncan, *Milton's Earthly Paradise*, 211–12.

86. N. Abram, *Diatriba de quatuor fluviis et loco paradisi* (Rouen, 1635) 64–65.

87. E. Roger, *La Terra saincte* (Paris, 1646) 7–10.

88. Massimi, "Montrer et démontrer," 224.

89. J. Hardouin, *Traitez geographiques et historiques pour faciliter l'intelligence de l'Ecriture sainte* (ed. of The Hague, 1730) 1:43.

90. Ibid., 1:56.

91. Ibid., 1:69.

92. J. Berruyer, *Histoire du peuple de Dieu* (Paris, 1728) 1:18.

93. Ibid., 1:19.

94. Ibid., 1:20.

95. Ibid., 1:21.

96. See the scornful list in Carver, *A Discourse*, "To the Reader"; C. Hill, *Antichrist in Seventeenth-Century England* (London, 1971), goes into this question at length (passim).

97. Salkeld, *A Treatise*, 23–24

98. Inveges, *Historia sacra*, 15; Augustine, *In Genesim ad litteram* (PL 34:381).

99. Luther, *Lectures*, 100.

100. Rivet, *Exercitationes*, 246.

101. Suárez, *Opera omnia*, 3:203.

102. Salkeld, *A Treatise*, 23.

103. Ibid., 25.

104. Ibid., 33.

105. Inveges, *Historia sacra*, 16–17.

106. Ibid., 17.

107. Ibid., 18; Suárez, *Opera omnia*, 3:207.

Chapter 9: Fine Points of Chronology

1. Rivet, *Exercitationes*, 206 (see chap. 8, n. 58, above).

2. Inveges, *Historia sacra*, 7–11 (see chap. 7, n. 23, above).

3. Ibid., 83–86.

4. Ibid., 112–16.

5. Ibid., 124–27.

6. Ibid., 132–36.

7. Ibid., 136–38.

8. Ibid., 140–43.

9. Ibid., 145–48.

10. Ibid., 154–56.

11. Ibid., 158–63.

12. Ibid., 261.

13. Ibid., 158–89.

14. Moses Bar Cephas, *Liber de paradiso* (PG 111:490–91).

15. Pereira, *Commentariorum*, nn. 117–18, fol. 41 (see chap. 7, n. 48, above).

16. J. Ussher, *Annales veteris testamenti* (London, 1650) 1.

17. Inveges, *Historia sacra*, 8.

18. Ibid., 9.

19. This statement of Beroalde is in a *Chronologia, hoc est supputatio temporum*, which was published at Basel in 1577, at the same time as a reprinting of the *Chronologia* of Mercator, who gives the entire work its name; see bk. 2, chap. 3, p. 131.

20. Steuchus Eugubinus, *Recognitio,* 51 (see chap. 7, n. 54, above).

21. Suárez, *Opera omnia,* 3:208 (see chap. 7, n. 25, above).

22. Inveges, *Historia sacra,* 11.

23. Pereira, *Commentariorum,* fol. 116.

24. Ussher, *Annales,* 1.

25. Inveges, *Historia sacra,* 84.

26. Suárez, *Opera omnia,* 3:368.

27. Inveges, *Historia sacra,* 85–86.

28. Salkeld, *A Treatise,* 142 (see chap. 7, n. 29, above).

29. Suárez, *Opera omnia,* 3:368–69.

30. Ibid., 3:192.

31. Inveges, *Historia sacra,* 126.

32. Ibid., 125–26.

33. Ibid., 126.

34. Pereira, *Commentariorum,* fol. 176.

35. Inveges, *Historia sacra,* 133.

36. Ibid., 134–37.

37. Ibid., 136.

38. Ibid., 141.

39. Cajetan, *Opera* (Paris, 1539), fols. 23–35.

40. Suárez, *Opera omnia,* 3:182; Pereira, *Commentariorum,* fol. 177; Cornelius a Lapide, *Commentaria,* 69 (see chap. 7, n. 30, above).

41. Inveges, *Historia sacra,* 142.

42. Thomas Aquinas, *Summa theologica* 1, 73, 2.

43. L. Molina, *Commentaria in primam D. Thomae partem,* "De opere sex diereum" (Lyons, 1662), disp. 22 (pp. 691–92).

44. Pereira, *Commentariorum,* fols. 156, 158.

45. Suárez, *Opera omnia,*, 3:180.

46. Inveges, *Historia sacra,* 147.

47. Suárez, *Opera omnia,* 3:369, 183.

48. Augustine, *Opera* 10, *Appendicis pars 3a: Sententiae ex Augustino delibatae,* no. 329 (PL 45:1888).

49. Inveges, *Historia sacra,*, 155.

50. Ibid.

51. Ibid., 158–59.

52. Ibid., 162–63.

53. Salkeld, *A Treatise,* 228.

54. J. Swan, *Speculum mundi or A Glasse Representing the Face of the World* (3d ed.; London, 1665) 456. [Translated from the author's French. —Tr.]

55. T. Malvenda, *De Paradiso voluptatis* (Rome, 1605), chap. 75, pp. 241–45.

56. Moses Bar Cephas, *De paradiso,* 580.

57. Suárez, *Opera omnia,* 3:372.

58. Pereira, *Commentariorum,* f. 238.

59. Inveges, *Historia sacra,* 163.

60. Salkeld, *A Treatise,* 228.

61. Swan, *Speculum mundi,* 456.

62. Suárez, *Opera omnia,* 3:372.

63. Salkeld, *A Treatise*, 227–28.

64. Inveges, *Historia sacra*, 236.

65. Ibid., 261–62.

66. Ibid., 270.

67. Ibid., 285.

68. Moses Bar Cephas, *De paradiso*, 579.

69. Inveges, *Historia sacra*, 285–86.

70. Ibid., 289–99.

71. J. Lightfoot, *Works* (London, 1684) 1:692. See C. A. Patrides, "Renaissance Estimates of the Year of Creation," *The Huntington Library Quarterly* 26 (1962–63) 319. In the pages that follow I shall make extensive use of this very thought-provoking article.

72. J. Swan, *Calamus mensurans* (London, 1653) 1:35–346; Patrides, "Renaissance Estimates," 319.

73. H. Broughton, *A Selder Olam, That Is: Order of the World* (London, 1954) 1; cited in Patrides, "Renaissance Estimates," 315. [Translated from the author's French. —Tr.]

74. Patrides, "Renaissance Estimates," 319.

75. G. Vecchietti, "Tabulae majores," in *De Anno primitivo ab exordio mundi* (Augsburg, 1621); Patrides, "Renaissance Estimates," 319.

76. Patrides, "Renaissance Estimates," 316–18.

77. I have added Bellarmine to Patrides' list on the basis of Malvenda, *De Antichristo* (ed. of Lyons, 1647) 1:106.

78. C. Hill, *Antichrist in Seventeenth-Century England* (London, 1971) 25.

Chapter 10: "As Soon as the Man Opened His Eyes..."

1. *Le Mistere du Viel Testament*, ed. J. de Rotschild (Paris, 1878) 1:31.

2. Ibid., 1:35.

3. Salkeld, *A Treatise*, 133–35 (see chap. 7, n. 29, above); Inveges, *Historia sacra*, 90–92 (see chap. 7, n. 23, above).

4. Augustine, *In Genesim ad litteram* 6.23.

5. Bellarmine, *Opera* (Paris: Vivès, 1873), 5: *De amissione gratiae*, bk. 3, chap. 4 (p. 308).

6. Salkeld, *A Treatise*, 134.

7. See G. Majorino, *Adam "New Born and Perfect": The Renaissance Promise of Eternity* (Urbana: Indiana University Press, 1987) 3–4, 10–13. L. B. Alberti, "Della Pittura," in his *Opere volgari*, ed. C. Grayson (Bari, 1860–73).

8. Jerome, *Ep. 108 ad Eustochium* (PL 22:902).

9. Suárez, *Opera omnia*, 3:186 (see chap. 7, n. 25, above).

10. Pereira, *Commentariorum*, fol. 138 (see chap. 7, n. 48, above).

11. Cajetan, *Commentarii in quinque Mosaicos Libros: Genesis I* (Paris, 1539) 20.

12. Salkeld, *A Treatise*, 134.

13. Moses Bar Cephas, *De paradiso* 14 (PG 111:498).

14. Suárez, *Opera omnia*, 3:187.

15. Inveges, *Historia sacra*, 91 (see chap. 7, n. 23, above).

16. Salkeld, *A Treatise*, 134–35.

17. Inveges, *Historia sacra*, 151–52.
18. Ibid., 152.
19. Irenaeus, *Adv. haer.* 5, trans. A. Rousseau (Paris: Cerf, 1984) 626.
20. Bernard, *Sermones* (PL 183:429).
21. Inveges, *Historia sacra*, 153.
22. See A. Chastel, *Le Mythe de la Renaissance, 1420–1520* (Geneva: Skira, 1969) 137–43.
23. In the Kunsthistoriches Museum.
24. In the Fogg Museum of Art, Cambridge, Mass. On the iconography of the first couple see J.-D. Rey and A. Mazure, *Adam et Eve* (Paris: Mazenod, 1967).
25. In the Landesmuseum, Gotha.
26. Milton, *Paradise Lost*, 4.305.
27. Salkeld, *A Treatise*, 103–6.
28. Luther, *Lectures on Genesis*, in *Luther's Works*, ed. J. Pelikan (St. Louis: Concordia, 1958) 1:93.
29. Ibid., 102.
30. Ibid., 104.
31. J. Swan, *Speculum mundi or a Glasse Representing the Face of the World* (Cambridge, 1635; edition used: London, 1665) 460. [Translated from the author's French. —Tr.]
32. D. Pareus, *In Genesim Mosis commentarius* (Geneva, 1614) 202–3.
33. Suárez, *Opera omnia*, 3:271–72.
34. Luther, *Lectures*, 102–3.
35. See J. Delumeau, *Le Péché et la peur* (Paris: Fayard, 1983) 255–65.
36. John Calvin, *Commentaries on the Book of Genesis*, in *Calvin's Commentaries*, trans. J. King (Grand Rapids: Eerdmans, 1948) 1:119.
37. Ibid., 116.
38. Salkeld, *A Treatise*, 143–45.
39. J. Hall, *Works* (1863) 1:15 ("The creation of man"). [Translated from the author's French. —Tr.]
40. Milton, *Paradise Lost*, 4.327–34.
41. Ibid., 4.616–25.
42. Goropius, *Origines antwerpianae*, 497 (see chap. 7, n. 16, above).
43. T. Tasso, *Opere*, ed. B. Maier (Milan: Rizzoli, 1964) 4:810–14 (p. 313).
44. Thomas Aquinas, *Summa theologica* 1, 102, 3.
45. Suárez, *Opera omnia*, 3:230.
46. Augustine, *The Literal Meaning of Genesis* 8.8.16 (Taylor 2:45) (see chap. 1, n. 58, above).
47. Moses Bar Cephas, *De paradiso* 28 (PG 111:530).
48. Malvenda, *De paradiso* (1605) 65 (pp. 202–6).
49. Augustine, *The Literal Meaning of Genesis* 8.8.15 (Taylor 2:45).
50. Pereira, *Commentariorum*, bk. 4, fol. 146.
51. Inveges, *Historia sacra*, 122.
52. Du Bartas, *Le Deuxième Semaine: L'enfance du monde, 1er jour: Éden* (ed. Chouet; 1593). Rue has a very strong odor; the plant is toxic in large doses. Myrobolans are fruits from India.
53. Swan, *Speculum mundi*, 457–58.

54. Hall, *Works*, 1:10–14.
55. Suárez, *Opera omnia*, 3:280.
56. Augustine, *De civitate Dei* 14.10.
57. Cajetan, *Commentarii*, 23.
58. Augustine, *The Literal Meaning of Genesis* 3.15.24 (Taylor 1:91).
59. Thomas Aquinas, *Summa theologica* 1, 96, 1.
60. Pereira, *Commentariorum*, bk. 4, fol. 175.
61. Suárez, *Opera omnia*, 3:407–8.
62. Salkeld, *A Treatise*, 122.
63. Hall, *Works*, 1:10.
64. T. Tasso, *Il Mondo creato*, vv. 862–67 (p. 315).
65. Milton, *Paradise Lost*, 1.340–47.
66. Salkeld, *A Treatise*, 123–24.
67. Suárez, *Opera omnia*, 23. *Commentaria ac disputationes in tertiam partem D. Thomae*, disp. 73, sec. 8, p. 622.
68. Ibid., n. 5, p. 622. Inveges, *Historia sacra*, 166–69, 217–19.
69. Inveges, *Historia sacra*, 168; Moses Bar Cephas, *De paradiso* (PG 111:525).
70. Luther, *Lectures*, 105.
71. Suárez, *Opera omnia*, 3:232.
72. Salkeld, *A Treatise*, 185.
73. Ibid., 186.
74. Ibid., 189.
75. Augustine, *The Literal Meaning of Genesis* 8.18.37 (Taylor 2:59).
76. Augustine, *De civitate Dei* 18.39; Pereira, *Commentariorum*, bk. 4, fol. 176.
77. On this question see the extensive work of Laplanche, *L'Écriture*, esp. 81, 93, 245–54, 593, 594 (see chap. 7, n. 9, above).
78. J. J. Scaliger, *Opuscula varia antehac non edita* (Paris, 1610) 439.
79. J. Buxtorf II, *Dissertationes philologico-theologicae*, vol. 1: *De linguae hebreae origine, antiquitate et sanctitate* (Basel, 1645).
80. I. Cappel, *Critica sacra* (Paris, 1650), bk. 6, chap. 10.
81. S. Bochart, *Opera omnia* (Leiden, 1692) 1:799ff.
82. Leibniz, *Nouveaux essais sur l'entendement humain* (1704), in *Oeuvres philosophiques*, ed. Janet (Paris, 1900) 1:238f., cited in M. Olender, *Les Langues du paradis* (Paris: Gallimard, 1989) 12–13.
83. Goropius, *Origines antwerpianae*, 534–39.
84. See C. C. Elert, "Andreas Kempe (1622–1689) and the Language Spoken in Paradise," *Historiographica linguistica* 5, no. 3 (1989) 221–26.
85. R. Simon, *Histoire critique du Vieux Testament* (Rotterdam, 1685) 85. See Olender, *Les Langues*, 16.
86. Luther, *Lectures*, 92, 100, 104, 104–5.
87. Inveges, *Historia sacra*, 157; John Chrysostom, *Homiliae* 15.4 (PG 53:123).
88. Following Robert Bultot, I have developed this theme in *Le Péché et la peur*, 205–50.
89. Thomas Aquinas, *Summa theologica* 2-2, 151, 1; Pereira, *Commentariorum*, bk. 4, fol. 176.
90. Inveges, *Historia sacra*, 166.
91. Swan, *Speculum mundi*, 454.

92. Milton, *Paradise Lost,* 4.318–40.

93. See the preceding note.

94. Augustine, *De vera religione* 46.88.

95. Augustine, *City of God* 14.26, trans. H. Bettenson, *St. Augustine: City of God* (New York: Penguin, 1972) 591.

96. Alexander of Hales, *Summa theologica* (Venice, 1575) 2.89.1, fol. 184v.

97. Augustine, *The Literal Meaning of Genesis* 9.6.10 (Taylor 2:76).

98. Bonaventure, *Opera omnia* 2 (Quaracchi, 1875), 2, dist. 20, q. 1, dubia 2; and Augustine, *City of God* 14.26.

99. Thomas Aquinas, *In libros Sententiarum* (Paris: Vivès, 1873), 2, dist. 20, q. 1, art. 2.

100. Suárez, *Opera omnia,* 3:386.

101. Inveges, *Historia sacra,* 180.

102. Ibid., 181.

103. Augustine, *The Literal Meaning of Genesis* 9.3.5–7 (Taylor 2:73–74).

104. Salkeld, *A Treatise,* 180–81.

105. Inveges, *Historia sacra,* 153.

106. Ibid., 154.

107. Augustine, *De Trinitate* 12.7.

108. Salkeld, *A Treatise,* 105–6.

109. Ibid., 130–31.

110. Milton, *Paradise Lost,* 4.295–310.

111. Ibid., 4.441–47.

112. Augustine, *De peccatorum meritis et remissione* 37–38 (PL 44:149–56).

113. Thomas Aquinas, *Summa theologica* 1, 99, 1, ad 1; Suárez, *Opera omnia,* 3:403.

114. Inveges, *Historia sacra,* 88.

115. Augustine, *De peccatorum meritis et remissione* 36–37 (PL 44:148–49).

116. Hugh de St. Victor, *De sacramentis* (PL 176:278–79); Thomas Aquinas, *Summa theologica* 1, 101, 2.

117. Inveges, *Historia sacra,* 190.

118. Augustine, *De civitate Dei* 19.15.

119. Thomas Aquinas, *Summa theologica* 1, 96, 4; Pereira, *Commentariorum,* lib. IV, f. 132; Suárez, *Opera omnia,* 3:415–16.

120. Inveges, *Historia sacra,* 194. The reference is to Aristotle, *Pol.,* 3.7, 14.

121. F. de Mexia, *Nobiliario vero* (Seville, 1492). The passage was made known to me by Adeline Rucquoi, who has my profound gratitude.

122. Augustine, *De civitate Dei* 19.15; Gregory the Great, *Moralia* 21.15 n. 689 (PL 76:203); Thomas Aquinas, *Summa theologica* 1, 96, 4; Pereira, *Commentariorum,* fol. 132; Suárez, *Opera omnia,* 3:415–16.

123. Pereira, *Commentariorum,* bk. 4, fol. 132; Suárez, *Opera omnia,* 3:415–16.

124. Inveges, *Historia sacra,* 195–96; Ambrose, *Expositio evangelii secundum Lucam* 122 (PL 15:1730); John Chrysostom, *De beato phylogonio* 6 (PG 48:749–50).

125. Suárez, *Opera omnia,* 3:418.

Chapter 11: The Disappearance of the Enchanted Garden

1. J. E. Duncan, *Milton's Earthly Paradise: A Historical Study of Eden* (Minneapolis: University of Minnesota Press, 1972), 269.

2. P. Bayle, "Adam," *Dictionnaire historique et critique* (edition used: Paris, 1820) 1:197–207.

3. Ibid., "Abel," 1:45.

4. J. Locke, *The Reasonableness of Christianity as Delivered in the Scriptures*, ed. and abridged by I. T. Ramsey (Stanford, Calif.: Stanford University Press, 1958) 25. See B. Cottret, *Le Christ des Lumières* (Paris: Cerf, 1990) 39–65.

5. Locke, *Reasonableness of Christianity*, 26.

6. Ibid. [Translated from the author's French. —Tr.]

7. On this whole topic see E. Guyenot, *Les sciences de la vie au XVII᷊ et XVIII᷊ siècles: L'idée d'évolution* (reprint, Paris: A. Michel, 1957) 349–53.

8. B. Palissy, *Discours admirables "des pierres,"* in *Oeuvres complètes* (Paris: Librairie Scientifique et Technique A. Blanchard, 1961) 273.

9. Guyenot, *Les sciences*, 344; J. Roger, *Buffon* (Paris: Fayard, 1989) 138–39.

10. *Mémoires de l'Académie royale des sciences*, in *Histoire de l'Académie* (for 1720, published in 1722) 400–16. See also pp. 5–9 (unsigned article).

11. L. Bourguet, *Lettres philosophiques sur la formation des sels, des cristaux et la génération et le mécanisme organique des plantes et des animaux* (Amsterdam, 1729).

12. Voltaire, *La défense de mon oncle*, in *Oeuvres* (ed. Moland) 26 (=vol. 5 of *Mélanges*) (Paris, 1879) 408.

13. Voltaire, "Inundation," *Philosophical Dictionary*, trans. P. Gay (2 vols.; New York: Basic Books, 1962) 1:327.

14. Buffon, *Histoire naturelle*, "Second Discours," in *Oeuvres complètes* (15 vols.; Paris, 1749–63) 1:182.

15. On T. Burnet, see Guyenot, *Les sciences*, 345–46; J. Ehrard, *L'Idée de nature en France à l'aube des Lumières* (Paris: Flammarion, 1970) 1:200; Roger, *Buffon*, 138.

16. On J. Woodward, see Guyenot, *Les sciences*, 347; Ehrard, *L'Idée de nature*, 1:20; Roger, *Buffon*, 139–40.

17. Buffon, *Histoire naturelle*, "Second Discours," 1:186.

18. W. Whiston, *A New Theory of the Earth...* (London, 1696). [Passages cited translated from the author's French. — Tr.]

19. Burnet, *Telluris historia sacra*, 163–81.

20. J. Woodward, *Géographie physique ou Essay sur l'histoire naturelle de la terre*, trans. from English by M. Boguez (Paris, 1735) 51.

21. Ibid.

22. Whiston, *A New Theory*, esp. 178–79.

23. Buffon, *Histoire naturelle*, "Second Discours," 1:220.

24. Ibid., 1:196.

25. Ibid., 1:201.

26. Ibid., 1:79.

27. Ibid., 1:77.

28. Voltaire, "Inundation," *Philosophical Dictionary*, 1:327–28.

29. B. de Maillet, *Le Telliamed* (Basel, 1749) xlvii.

30. Ibid., liii.

31. C. Blount, *The Oracles of Reason* (London, 1693), preface. [Translated from the author's French. —Tr.]

32. D. Whitby, *Six Discourses* (Worcester, Mass., 1801); M. Tindal, *Christianity as Old as the Creation* (London, 1731); J. Taylor, *The Scripture: Doctrine of Original Sin Proposed to Free and Candid Examination* (2d ed.; London, 1741). See Duncan, *Milton's Earthly Paradise*, 278–79.

33. C. Middleton, *Miscellaneous Works* (London, 1752) 2:127. [Translated from the author's French. —Tr.]

34. Ibid., 2:151.

35. H. Bolingbroke, *Works*, ed. H. G. Bohn (4 vols.; London, 1962ff.) 2:209. [Translated from the author's French. —Tr.]

36. Ibid., 2:207.

37. Ibid., 2:211.

38. D. Hume, *The Natural History of Religion*, ed. H. E. Root (Stanford, Calif.: Stanford University Press, 1957) 25.

39. Ibid.

40. Ibid., 23.

41. Ibid., 24.

42. Ibid., 23.

43. Cited in Guyenot, *Les Sciences,* 377. Duchesne (fils), *Histoire naturelle des fraisiers* (Paris, 1766).

44. Voltaire, *Dissertation envoyée… à l'Académie de Bologne,* in *Oeuvres* (ed. Moland) 22:228.

45. Cited in Ehrard, *L'Idée de nature,* 1:194. I am making extensive use of this work in my exposition here.

46. Buffon, *Histoire naturelle,* 38.

47. C. Bonnet, *Traité d'insectologie, ou observations sur les pucerons* (Paris, 1745) xxvii–xxxi.

48. C. Bourguet, *Contemplation de la nature,* in *Oeuvres* (Neuchâtel, 1781) 7:52.

49. F. Boissier de Sauvages, "Mémoire contenant des observations de lithologie, pour servir à l'histoire do Languedoc et à la théorie de la terre," *Mémoires de l'Académie royale des sciences* (1746) 749–51.

50. Buffon, *Histoire naturelle,* 12.

51. J.-B. Robinet, *De la nature: Petit extrait d'un gros livre* (Geneva, 1761) 49.

52. Idem, *Considérations philosophiques…* (Paris, 1768) 3.

53. Ibid., 151.

54. M. de Maupertuis, *Essai de cosmologie,* in *Oeuvres* (Lyons, 1756) 1:11.

55. M. Adamson, *Les Familles des plantes* (Paris, 1763) 105, 164.

56. Guyenot, *Les Sciences,* 377–78.

57. P. Cabanis, *Rapports du physique et du moral,* in *Oeuvres philosophiques* (Paris: PUF, 1956) 518.

58. E. de Lacépède, *Discours sur la durée des espèces,* which begins vol. 2 of his *Histoire naturelle des poissons* (Paris, 1800) 24.

59. E. Darwin, *Zoonomia* (French ed.; Ghent, 1810) 2:282.

60. J.-B. Lamarck, *Système des animaux sans vertébres, précédé du "Discours d'ouverture"* (Paris, 1801), "Avertissement," 6.

61. Ibid., "Discours d'ouverture," 16.

62. Lacépède, "Discours sur la durée des espèces," 2:24.

63. Buffon, *Histoire naturelle,* "Preuves," 203.

64. Ibid., "Second Discours," 99.

65. Ibid., "Conclusion," 612.

66. Roger, *Buffon,* 248–54.

67. Ibid., 252.

68. Ibid., 254.

69. Buffon, *Histoire naturelle,* 22.

70. Buffon, *Les Époques de la nature* (1778), critical ed. by J. Roger (Paris: Éditions du Museum) 17.

71. Ibid., 41, and *Supplément à l'histoire naturelle* 2 (1775) 362–499.

72. Roger, *Buffon,* 540.

73. Ibid., 541.

74. Buffon, *Les Époques de la nature,* "Première Époque," manuscript ed. by J. Roger, 40.

75. Roger, *Buffon,* 555. See J. Stengers, "Buffon et la Sorbonne," *Études sur le XVIIIe siècle* (Brussels: Université de Bruxelles, 1974) 109–24.

76. Buffon, *Les Époques de la nature,* "Premier Discours," 18.

77. Ibid., 22.

78. An expression of Rousseau in *The Social Contract,* bk. 1, chap. 2, trans. G. D. H. Cole (New York: Dutton, 1950) 6.

79. J.-J. Rousseau, *A Discourse on the Origin of Inequality,* trans. Cole, 199–200, 200–1, 203–4.

80. Ibid., 244.

81. I. Kant, *Conjectural Beginning of Human History* (1785), trans. E. Fackelheim, in Immanuel Kant, *On History,* ed. L. W. Beck (Indianapolis: Bobbs-Merrill, 1963) 53–68.

Conclusion

1. P. Teilhard de Chardin, "Note on Some Possible Historical Representations of Original Sin," in *Christianity and Evolution,* trans. R. Hague (New York: Harcourt Brace Jovanovich, 1969) 47.

2. On the question of original sin I suggest that the reader refer to M. Neusch, *Le Mal* (Paris: Centurion, 1990), esp. 44–51. See also P. Ricoeur, "Le Péché originel," in his *Le Conflit des interprétations* (Paris: Seuil, 1969) 265ff.; A.-M. Dubarle, *The Biblical Doctrine of Original Sin,* trans. E. M. Stewart (New York, 1964); G. Martelet, *Libre réponse à un scandale* (Paris: Cerf, 1986); P. Gibert, *Bible, mythes et récits du commencement* (Paris: Seuil, 1986).

3. Theophilus of Antioch, *The Three Books to Autolycus* 2.22, trans. B. P. Pratten, M. Dods, and T. Smith (ANF 3; Edinburgh: T. & T. Clark, 1875) 90.

4. Ibid., 2.24 (pp. 90–91).

5. Irenaeus, *Demonstratio praedicationis apostolicae* 12, cited in H. Lassiat, *Pour une théologie de l'homme: Création, liberté, incorruptibilité. Insertion du thème anthropologique de la jeune tradition romaine dans l'oeuvre d'Irénée de Lyon* (reprint, 2 vols.; Lille, 1972) 2:465.

6. Irenaeus, *Adv. haer.* 4.38.1, in *The Works of Irenaeus*, trans. A. Roberts and W. H. Rambaut (ANF 5 and 9; 2 vols.; Edinburgh: T. & T. Clark, 1871, 1874) 2:42.

7. Ibid., 4.40.3 (2:50).

8. Ibid.

9. Theophilus, *The Three Books* 2.26 (pp. 91–91).

10. Irenaeus, *Adv. haer.* 3.23.6, cited in Lassiat, *Pour une théologie de l'homme*, 2:507–8.

11. *Adv. haer.* 4.

12. Theophilus, *The Three Books* 2.27 (pp. 92–93).

13. Irenaeus, *Adv. haer.* 4.38.1 (2:42).

14. See ibid., 4.38.3 (2:44).

15. Ibid., 4.38.4 (2:45).

16. Ibid., 4.39.2 (2:46).

17. G. Bardy, in *Trois livres à Autolycus* (Paris: Cerf, 1965) 7.

18. K. Rahner, *Foundations of Christian Faith: An Introduction to the Idea of Christianity*, trans. W. V. Dych (New York: Seabury, 1978) 114.

Index of Names of Persons

University of Illinois Press
1325 South Oak Street
Champaign, IL 61820-6903
www.press.uillinois.edu